The One and the Three

The One
and the Three

*Nature, Person and Triadic Monarchy
in the Greek and Irish Patristic Tradition*

Chrysostom Koutloumousianos

James Clarke & Co

James Clarke & Co
P.O. Box 60
Cambridge
CB1 2NT
United Kingdom

www.jamesclarke.co
publishing@jamesclarke.co

ISBN: 978 0 227 17514 9

British Library Cataloguing in Publication Data
A record is available from the British Library

First Published by James Clarke & Co, 2015

Contents

Part II
Subjectivity and Catholicity: The Monastic Paradigm

Foreword

Over most of the last century, Orthodox reflection on ecclesiology has revolved around what has been called 'Eucharistic ecclesiology'. The origins of this are not difficult to divine: the theologians of the Russian diaspora, rudely expelled from the territory that had been 'Holy Russia', were forced by circumstances to reconsider what was meant by the Church. For nearly a millennium and a half, the Church had been conceived on an analogy with human imperial structures, initially the Roman Empire, and then analogously with the Russian Empire and the Orthodox nations that emerged from the fragmentation of the Ottoman Empire. Reaching back behind the conversion of Constantine, the Russian theologians in Paris, notably Fr Nikolai Afanasiev, rethought an ecclesiology focused on the Eucharistic community, presided over by the bishop, which they found in the letters of St Ignatius of Antioch. Such an ecclesiology has been widely influential outside Orthodox circles: it profoundly informed the ecclesiology of the Second Vatican Council and lies behind much ecumenical ecclesiological reflection found, for instance, in the reports of the World Council of Churches.

In Orthodox circles, a widely influential proponent of Eucharistic ecclesiology, inspired by, though critical of, the ideas of Fr Afanasiev, is Professor John Zizioulas, Metropolitan of Pergamon. With Zizioulas, the foundations of Eucharistic ecclesiology are extended from the pre-Nicene theology of St Ignatius to the Trinitarian theology of the Cappadocian Fathers, who, it is alleged by Zizioulas, developed a profound notion of the person, that lies at the heart of both their understanding of the mystery of the Trinity and of Zizioulas' own development of Eucharistic ecclesiology. Zizioulas' ideas have been received with a mixture of enthusiastic agreement and critical questioning, and debate has revolved around interpretation of passages from the Cappadocian Fathers, a debate that has become increasingly narrow and sterile. Zizioulas' linking of Eucharistic ecclesiology with his Trinitarian personalism has led to what one might call 'episcopocentrism' (or even episcopomonism), with ecclesial structures of authority focused on the bishop as guarantor

of ecclesial unity. More recently still, this episcopocentrism has led to
an appreciation of the notion of primacy in Orthodox theology, which
has provoked alarm in some quarters.

Fr Chrysostom shares much of the alarm of those who see
episcopomonism as distorting ecclesial experience. His book is,
however, far more than a tract for the times. In this book, the fruit
of long and considered meditation, Fr Chrysostom explores the
motives behind recourse to personalist ontology, and revisits the
theology of the Cappadocian Fathers from whom Metropolitan
John draws his personalism. He draws attention to the dangers of
the polarisation between person and nature, taken for granted by
Zizioulas' personalist ontology, a polarisation that distorts the
balance between person and communion he finds in the Fathers
and, even more dangerously, with its negative assessment of nature,
seems to call in question the Christian doctrine of creation, according
to which God created nature that was 'exceedingly good'. There is,
however, much more to this book. In an earlier work in two volumes
(*God of Mysteries: The Theology of the Celts in the Light of the Greek East*
(2008) and *Lovers of the Kingdom: The Encounter of Celtic and Byzantine
Monasticism* (2009), available, alas, only in Greek), Fr Chrysostom had
explored parallels between Celtic and Byzantine monastic theology,
finding in both cases a theology founded on ascetic experience and
markedly Trinitarian in its concerns. He draws on this extensively
in the central part of the book, in a way that draws attention to
the common fund of ecclesial experience of the mysteries of the
Trinity and the incarnation to be found in the Byzantine East and
the Celtic West. In contrast to the one-sidedness that all too easily
characterises Eucharistic ecclesiology and personalist ontology, we
find an embracing of contrasts that is deeply enriching. Pages on
the complementarity of eremiticism and communal monasticism in
the monastic traditions highlight the balance found in Cappadocian
theology (and Dionysius the Areopagite and St Maximus) between
the monad and the triad in their understanding of the Triune God. A
theology of obedience that flows all too easily from episcopocentric
Eucharist ecclesiology is balanced by an emphasis on mutuality,
personal responsibility and spiritual freedom. A failure of much
Eucharistic ecclesiology has been an inability to accommodate
the rich ascetic theology that marks both the Celtic and Byzantine
traditions: this is counterbalanced by Fr Chrysostom's reflections in
this book.

Furthermore, Fr Chrysostom's reflections are marked by a humane
appreciation of the breadth of human experience: he draws on poets
as well as theologians; he embraces the richness of human experience
of the created order that is such a marked feature of the ascetics,

both Celtic and Byzantine, for all the apparent harshness of much of their ascetic practice. It is a book that transcends the pastoral concern for the dangerous consequences, as he sees it, of the academic and institutional bias of much Eucharistic ecclesiology, and becomes a profound meditation on the riches of the ascetic and theological tradition shared by East and West in the first millennium.

Andrew Louth
Professor Emeritus of Patristic and Byzantine Studies

Prologue

'Because God looked upon me, I had and have to look towards God,' says Kierkegaard. God reveals Himself to man within a personal relationship; or, rather, this *I–Thou* relationship originates in the very act of creation. At the same time God reveals Himself as a Three-Personed Absolute. And He 'enthrals' the human heart, drawing it to Himself, suggesting, as it were, the divine 'mode of existence' to His creature: God is simultaneously one and three – three Persons, yet only one I – and so is humanity.

The way we approach God has a radical impact on the way we see the world and the human being. The trinitarian mystery stands before us like a mirror in which the most secret and sacred purposes of creation are reflected. Accordingly, the way we approach and understand the Trinity determines fundamental perceptions of humanity and the Church, and affects the *modus vivendi* of both individuals and society.

Early Christian theology was the domain in which the notion of person was for the first time fervently discussed in a trinitarian setting. As for the human person, concrete individuality and its dignity lie at the centre of Christian teaching: it stands in uniqueness and in communion, according to 'a more excellent way' (1 Cor. 12:31). But human cultures and civilisations would not so easily accept Christian infiltration. Collectivism, as well as its verso, namely radical individualism, disregarded and crushed the person, threatening both unity and particularity. Then, personalism, in its various philosophical and theological strains, developed throughout the nineteenth century as a reaction to those depersonalising attitudes, underscoring personhood as the ultimate principle of all reality, and emphasising its relational dimension.

Our culture is coloured by the same two apparent extremes: impersonalisation and egocentricity. The dialectic of the 'internal'–'external' relationship, which characterises the language of modernity, often finds expression in the severance of the part from the whole and, consequently, the opposition between the individual and society.

Within this context, certain pioneering theologians who have followed and expanded assumptions of philosophy have, with a view to meeting the existential demands of modern man, built up a personalist thought based on a specific understanding of divine personhood: everything comes from a person, and that person within the Trinity is the person of the Father. This view is supposedly ratified by patristic triadological teaching, particularly the teaching on the 'monarchy of the Father'. In the forefront of this trend, Professor John Zizioulas, Metropolitan of Pergamon, attributes everything to the person of the Father: the cause of the Trinity is the person of the Father; love is identified with the Father; God's immortality, indeed His very essence, derives from the person of the Father. The ontological 'principle' or 'cause' of being is not seen as either essence or nature but invertedly as that which makes up the person. On these grounds the person was detached from nature, aggrandising the imbalance between the two. A transcendental perception of the former makes the latter a bleak necessity.

But the most challenging part of the story is the application of the above thesis in the fields of ecclesiology and anthropology. This 'monarchy' of the person of the Father, accommodated in the 'Eucharistic ecclesiology', invests the 'first' in the Church (either local or universal) with supreme authority, and in the long run becomes the fulcrum for totalitarian patterns and behaviours. Its anthropological corollary is that the esoteric and creative dimension of man, which springs from the spiritual capacity of the 'inner man', tends to be eclipsed by structure and relations; furthermore, that 'inner man' goes unacknowledged because of fear and distrust of what is seen to be either esotericism or the influence of modern psychology. John Zizioulas is neither the sole nor the first theologian to espouse a personalist understanding of the Trinity. The reason that this study focuses on him is that he is credited with bringing the Greek patristic tradition into contemporary discourse on personhood.

How far can this interpretation, together with its ecclesiological implications, find justification in patristic writings? That was the point of departure for this venture into the thought and experience of the Fathers of the Church. This work pursues a thorough understanding of the patristic notion of person and essence, and traces its ecclesiological and anthropological implications, with special reference to the monastic paradigm.

In the process, the study provides a full account of how the early Greek Fathers, as well as the theologians of the pre-Norman Irish tradition, conceived, used and interpreted the theological term 'monarchy', and explores their references to inter-trinitarian relations, simultaneously tracing any repercussions of triadological doctrine on anthropology, Church structure and spiritual life. It then proceeds to consider and assess the multiform substantiation of the above doctrine in the philosophy and life of the monastic world of the Greek East and the Irish West. Sources examined from the Eastern tradition include the Cappadocian Fathers, St Athanasius of Alexandria, St Cyril of Alexandria, St John Chrysostom, St Dionysius the Areopagite, St Maximus the Confessor, St John of Damascus, the ascetic works of Asia Minor; and from the Irish tradition, St Columbanus, Ériugena, anonymous theological treatises, early lives of saints and ascetic writings.

Irish Christianity is included for two reasons: the first is that monasticism plays a prominent role in the perception of spiritual life and the formation of ecclesiastical conscience; the second is the astounding affinity between the two traditions. The Irish Church was a vigorous and growing local Church, which combined its distinct spiritual identity with the consciousness of belonging to a catholic tradition. Strongly influenced by St Cassian and the Eastern monastic spirit and theology, it seems to cleave more to the Greek Fathers on issues regarding the doctrine of grace, original sin, trinitarian perceptions and the interpretation of theophanic events. One does not mean to say that what appears in the Irish mind is entirely absent from Latin Christendom. Still, elements that are to be found in strands of the Western tradition appear to shape the special character of early Christian Ireland. Having devoted considerable research in a previous study to the correlations between the spiritual insights of the Greek and the early Irish Fathers, now I summon the latter to make their own contribution to the overall picture. Such an alignment of two geographically remote traditions seems to create a second strand in the study, in which the identity of spiritual life as being based upon trinitarian faith is clearly exemplified.

Although I do not espouse either the stereotype of collective 'Celticity' or an undifferentiated view all over the Greek-speaking East, I do see an identity of mind, vision and experience within each tradition, an identity not to be separated in parallel streams or conflicting powers. In both worlds, varying expressions of truth (owing their robustness to a multitude of vivid individuals) do not really indicate varying 'truths' in a climate of disagreement. If there are cases of divergence among the Fathers, they are to be understood at the level of 'signifiers' and in the framework of the quest for the measure in religious doctrine and life, not as expressions of a different understanding of the transcendental realities or of a desire to penetrate God's mystery.

Certain questions emerge from studying the foregoing themes in historical context: Is there any precedence given to either the individual or the corporate body? To what degree and in what way is the individual incorporated in the totality/catholicity? In what way and by which means does the totality live and how is it expressed in the individual as understood as person? What is the relation and interaction between the 'inner' and the 'outer' in the human person? The objective of the study is the exposition of the intertwining of personhood and catholicity in the thought and life of the Church (especially among monastics) at that early period, a relationship that is a fundamental necessity for man and the malfunction of which would seem to lie at the core of contemporary social and existential anxiety.

Part I provides, in the first chapter, a survey of the quest for a personalistic ontology made by contemporary Orthodox theologians, focusing on their peculiar interpretation of the patristic notion of the 'monarchy' of the Father in trinitarian theology. Such interpretation has led in recent times to a specific ecclesiological vision that accords a supremacy of power to the person of the bishop in the ecclesial community.

The second chapter traces the theological notion of 'monarchy' in the writings of the Greek and the Irish Fathers. In particular, we delve into some key patristic concepts that form the background to the trinitarian understanding of these theologians, namely: the conception of trinitarian doctrine as the Aristotelian mean; the incomprehensibility of the mode of existence; the basic distinction between theology and economy and the patristic interpretation of the 'submission' of Christ to the Father; the understanding of identity and otherness, or nature and hypostasis, within God and in the human being; the concept of *perichoresis* (interpenetration) of the Divine Persons with regard to the essential unity of Divine Being; and the importance of essence/nature and co-essentiality for the integrity of hypostases.

Part II explores the substantiation of patristic trinitarian doctrine in the philosophy and life of the monastic world of the Greek East and the Irish West and raises the question of the relation of subjectivity and catholicity within the Church as a model of the Trinity. In this framework, I elucidate topics such as the place of the individual in society, the esoteric dimension of the self, the relationship and dialectic of impersonal institutions and personal charisma, and specific monastic virtues as ways to the fulfilment of authentic personhood. A conclusion summarises the findings of the study concerning these contemporary personalistic interpretations of the Trinity, the unique intertwining of personhood and catholicity in the thought and life of the early Church, and the relevance of the patristic theological and anthropological message today.

In the field of theology, one has the impression of moving along a circumference or a spiral without an end, for there is no end in following the infinite. This is why the epilogue of this book has the title "Last Prologue", a title to be found in the Martyrology of Oengus.

The more one delves into God's revelation, the more one realises that one but glimpses through a mirror and needs to shun the sirens of confidence and, instead, participate in the awe of the Fathers as they look from the heights of divine words and figures at the mystery of the uncreated. At the same time, one feels that what is granted from above is the reassuring experience of God's encircling presence, instructing every humble heart and mind, and also the need to remain more humble and more open, in other words, more true and positive towards one another's mind, heart and experience; and, most of all, to listen to those from the past who entered the cloud of unknowing in their lives and became witnesses to transcendental realities. Their work beckons us on a wonderful journey through carved reliefs of a humble art that pictures the Uncontainable.

My intention was not to help to recover the past, nor to seize upon some useful ideas from the writings of the Fathers, but, as far as possible, to grasp their 'soul', imprinted as it is in their discourse, incarnate in history and even transcending time. I cherish the view, unreservedly taken up by the Fathers themselves, that the whole truth was revealed and received – as far as human beings can contain – at Pentecost, and has been ever present and ever active since then, even though the same content has varied across time in terms of linguistic sophistication or idiosyncrasy. This is why it is possible to perceive a high degree of spiritual homogeneity among the Fathers actually having the same vision of God and not simply trying to interpret the Nicene formula, not because the theology of the past has to be the norm merely on account of its antiquity, but because holiness – that is, union/affinity with God, considered as the utmost criterion for a right theological pronouncement – makes those persons eligible to give an account of the truth, even in diverse contours; in their journey into God they progress within the same light, using its beams to construct their own colourful language, methods and imagery. The saints, St Maximus states, 'forerunners' of the same mysteries, can stand in the place of each other. This, I think, justifies my effort toward a synthetic account of their theology.

Clearly, understanding the Fathers and saints involves more than an accurate explication of what they say or an analysis of what has been objectified – knowledge is more of a loving affection and enduring introspection in the light of Divinity, a goal which demands an ascetic effort to identify spiritually with and apprentice oneself to them. And this is what I have attempted in this study, not so as to refute a thesis, but, by breathing with the Fathers' breath, to juxtapose a modern school of theological thought with patristic theology and anthropology as a point of departure for approaching the meaning and experience of unity and otherness within the Triadic Monad and the cosmos.

This work was completed, thanks to a Visiting Fellowship at the Hellenic Institute of Royal Holloway, University of London. I am indebted to its diligent Director, Dr Charalambos Dendrinos, for his ardent support, wholehearted encouragement and brotherly trust, which I hope I have not betrayed. My profound thanks go to the Revd Andrew Louth, Professor Emeritus of Patristic and Byzantine Studies, Durham University. Fr Andrew not only read various versions of the manuscript, offering his judicious remarks, but also guided me on risky paths. I also extend my deep gratitude to Dr John Carey for his most instructive comments on the Irish material, and Dr Norman Russell for his valuable suggestions. My warmest thanks are due to Denise Harvey for her editorial suggestions and overall generous help. Last but not least, I am indebted to a circle of friends in England for their support: the family of Theo and Louisa Hadjipavlou, Fr Aimilianos Papadakis, and Anthony Smith for his comments on language and style. Finally, it was a privilege and pleasure to co-operate with Adrian Brink and the team of the Lutterworth Press. Needless to say, nothing would have been done without the blessing and 'shield' of my spiritual father, Archimandrite Christodoulos, abbot of Koutloumous Monastery.

Abbreviations

BC	J. Zizioulas (1993), *Being as Communion: Studies in Personhood and the Church*. Crestwood, New York
CC	*Corpus Christianorum*
CO	J. Zizioulas (2006), *Communion and Otherness*. London
ECW	J. Zizioulas (2011), *The Eucharistic Communion and the World*. Bloomsbury
GNO	*Gregorii Nysseni Opera*
HVSH	W. Heist (1965), *Vitae Sanctorum Hiberniae*
ILH	*Irish Liber Hymnorum* (1898), London.
ILit	C. Plummer (1925), *Irish Litanies*. London
OM	J. Zizioulas (2010), *The One and the Many: Studies on God, Man, the Church, and the World Today.* California
PG	*Patrologia Graeca*, ed. J.P. Migne
PL	*Patrologia Latina*, ed. J.P. Migne
PO	*Patrologia Orientalis*
SC	*Sources Chrétiennes*. Paris: Éditions du Cerf
SCO	*Sancti Columbani Opera* (1997), Dublin
SHM	*Scriptores Hiberniae Minores* (1973–1974), Turnhout
ThPal	*Thesaurus Palaeohibernicus: A Collection Old-Irish Glosses Scholia Prose and Verse* (1987), Dublin

Part I

Approaching the Trinitarian Monad

I carved the beloved name
In the shade of the aged olive tree
In the roaring of the lifelong sea.

Odysseus Elytis

God, my God, and God, triple oneness.

Gregory of Nazianzus

ONE:
The Quest for a Personalistic Ontology

1. Transcending the tragedy

Man walks along weeping, and no one can say why. The integrity of the human being, its deliverance from fragmentation, denial, annihilation and all forms of death, has been an innate demand, a perennial call to a 'blissful seat'[1] in a world that turns and changes. The human person, no matter whether or in what way it has been conceived and defined,[2] lies at the heart of the human struggle through the dramatic flow of the streams of history. Truly, over the ages, the concrete human subject – the living person with a proper name – has often been buried and lost in a vast glimmering desert of structures and ideologies and vague '-isms', creations of a fragmented vision utterly discredited. This, in turn, has led to polarisation and antagonism between the individual and society, between the unique particular and the undifferentiated whole, the personal and the impersonal. The consequence of this has been the creation of mirror images: both individualism and collectivism 'signal the loss of the person, the disappearance of the one into the many and the many into the one' and the person, in the syncretism of our times, remains 'most fervently celebrated and most ardently denounced',[3] enhanced and evaporated in the post-modern 'irony which plays not on negation but on empty positivity'.[4]

This theme takes as a point of departure a dilemma that strikes at the very core of being. It was first raised by Heraclitus and Parmenides, who posed clearly and reflected remarkably upon the ontological question: What has priority, the one or the many? Unity or diversity? Since this is primarily applicable to the being of God, the Supreme Being, philosophy enters in a fertile manner into the field of theology. And since God reveals and, in some way, presents His own 'mode of existence' to human beings as a model to imitate, the way one conceives and approaches God determines one's own perception of oneself and, consequently, theology affects society's *modus vivendi*.

In the last five decades, theologians and religious thinkers have been wholeheartedly committed to establishing and safeguarding the reality of the person on a personalistic ontology of the Deity. Personal ontology has become an assertion of the metaphysics of particularity.[5] Moreover, following the thread that runs through modern philosophical thought from Kant to Heidegger, and after inheriting the dialectical scheme in construing reality, the same thinkers have built upon the severance of the individual, understood as 'person', from the common and supposedly static essential nature. On theological and anthropological levels, total precedence has been afforded to the notion of the person, as a distinct category, over essence or substance.[6] Furthermore, this precedence has been narrated as the alternative presented by the Greek East to the 'essentialism' ascribed to the Latin West.[7]

'No, the ground of God's ontological freedom lies not in His nature, but in His personal existence,' asserts one of the more influential contemporary Orthodox theologians, John Zizioulas.[8] Similarly, since *person* transcends nature, the notion of the image of God 'cannot relate to nature . . . but to personhood'.[9] The identification of God's being with a *person*, whose will abolishes the necessity of its essence, carries profound existential significance, for it liberates the human being from the 'necessity' of existence, which is the ultimate challenge to the freedom of the person. Nature, signifying the common substrate, represents the impersonal element or, worse, a blind force opposing the realisation of the authentic person. Indeed, should one accept that God's freedom lies in His 'nature', the created human being cannot be expected to receive authentic personhood. If personhood is to achieve otherness, it must be freed from nature.[10] Personhood, as absolute freedom, is incommensurable with existence, let alone created existence, in which nature has priority over the person; for nature 'subjugates' the person within its homogeneous prescriptions. The vain pursuit of freedom is a tragic and intrinsic feature of humanity, a feature stemming from the very condition of being created. It follows that the ancestral and ongoing Fall is inherent in the human being or, more specifically, in the 'biological' hypostasis.[11]

This biological hypostasis is associated with the notion of the *individual*, which is to be distinguished from and opposed to the notion of *person*. The *individual* – a natural category – denotes the isolated entity, the autonomous, monolithic, singular self, the post-lapsarian self, an 'island' determined by its own boundaries and equated with the 'essential' being. On the other hand, *person* means a 'being in relationship', a being that breaks through the natural boundaries in a movement of communion. This is 'the hypostasis of ecclesial existence', not determined by nature, but born from above.[12]

On closer inspection, these positions reflect the absolute divisions, existential oppositions and antithetical schemes that are used to decipher the intricate fabric of creation, life, history and culture.

2. *The monarchy of the Father*

St Gregory Nazianzen witnesses the paradox of the personal encounter with the Trinity when he confesses that he conceives the One in the splendour of the Three, contemplating each One as the whole, and the Three together as one torch.[13] The mind is invited to be filled with the perception of the Trinity, for, as another representative of the same tradition states, such perception is the Kingdom of God.[14] Trinitarian doctrine lifts the mind to dizzying heights; it appears, at least to Western reasoning, as a logical antinomy – a dynamic dialectic – that calls for an unfolding of its secret layers.

The fact that the one and undivided Divine Being *is* three distinctive hypostatic Realities provides a firm basis for the validation of the essential content of the person. The fact that these persons are One points to a common essence, by virtue of which they constitute the being of God. Yet, how are we to understand this unity if not monadically? Does it suffice to anchor the oneness in the perfect empathy of the distinct persons, thus presenting a social model?[15] According to John Zizioulas, who strives for the justification of the person, 'if otherness is to be ontologically primary, the one in God has to be a person and not substance, for substance is a monistic category by definition.'[16] This personalistic ontology, as opposed to essentialism, is allegedly ratified by the emphasis on the monarchy of the Father that figures in the Greek Patristic literature.

John Zizioulas is the theologian *par excellence* who has been engaged in a prolific outworking of this notion with a view to meeting contemporary existential questions and tensions head on. For him, 'unless the ontological ἀρχή [principle] in God is placed clearly and unequivocally in a Person – and who else but the Father could be such a person in the Trinity? – substance becomes the obvious candidate for such an ontological ἀρχή.'[17] Thus, the teaching of the monarchy in God is understood and used within the conceptual system of antithetical schemes; namely that the unequivocal aim of the Greek Fathers was to stress and undergird the precedence of the person over a common substance; a precedence that determines a new ontology. In this way, from the anthropological point of view, the priority of the particular over the whole, the many over the one, the difference over the identity, would also be sustained.

According to this view, the person of the Father in the Triune Deity is the ultimate ontological principle, ground or, more precisely, cause of the divine being itself. The personal existence of the Father not only generates the other divine Persons, but constitutes His very substance, the common divine nature. On similar lines, every attribute of God, say love, freedom, or immortality, derives from the person of the Father in juxtaposition with the common essential ground.[18] The word 'one' referring to God in the first clause of the Nicene Creed is deemed an intentional addition to the early Western 'limited' version, which confesses simply *'deum patrem'*. In contrast, in the Eastern Creed, and according to Greek patristic thought and biblical language, the 'one' God is identified with the Person of the Father, thus providing a final answer to the question of divine unity, without recourse to the category of essence/substance that subjects freedom to necessity.[19]

Zizioulas admits that in St Gregory Nazianzen one encounters the two senses of *monarchia*: as unity of rule, 'or what we may call the "moral" sense' and as personal origination, 'which can be described as the ontological sense'. It seems strange that beyond the sense of personal derivation, the unity has to be illustrated in moral terms, as if it were lacking any ontological basis. It is at this point that we find a biased gap between person and substance. The Father 'as a person, and not as substance', formulates what God is.[20] Thus, the persons' common essence receives a derivative value. The creed of Nicaea-Constantinople (AD 381) supposedly promotes this new ontology by striking out the word *'ousia'* from the Nicene Creed, yielding that the Son was born *simply* 'from the Father'.[21]

This thesis is a logical outflow of the premise that has deep roots in philosophical discussion: *ousia* (essence) is equated with necessity, whereas the person represents freedom from necessity. The unequivocal connection of essence with freedom, made by St Athanasius, supposedly falls short of being an accurate response to the Arian contrivance.[22] Instead, St Gregory Nazianzen and St Maximus the Confessor are recruited by Zizioulas in support of his assumption, as the former rejects the Platonic automatic 'overflowing' of essence and the latter refers to the element of love in the generating movement of the Father.[23] The modern theologian seems confined in this bipolarity of exclusive and evident opposites inherited from the Western tradition: essence, associated with blind necessity, *versus* person as ontological freedom and love.

Thus, love becomes a personal rather than an essential property. The person of God the Father is the absolute Willing One, the ultimate ontological category, the initiator of the otherness of other persons and of divine freedom itself. This assumption has immense and far-reaching consequences. Given that such interpretation includes a kind of subordination of the Son to the Father – albeit without degrading the Son's ontological status – it is most likely that the oppressive and totalitarian element, which the personalist strives to avert, would eventually enter the scene in a more subtle way.[24]

3. Drawing implications for the many

We are images of God – of the trinitarian prototype. As St Porphyrios says, 'the three persons of the Holy Trinity constitute the eternal Church . . . the uncreated Church' and, since 'the love of God created us in his image and likeness',[25] theology is transferred into ecclesiology and the matrix of human relations. Yet, danger always lurks insofar as human conceptual images, societal or ecclesial, are projected on to God's mystery.

What do we learn from the immanent Trinity? 'Freedom from nature and dependence on the person is a lesson learnt from divine causality.'[26] This is how the personalist unravels the implications of his trinitarian concept for anthropology. Moreover, personal otherness, being dictated by the one, cannot but be 'a-symmetrical'.[27] The other, who bestows us otherness, is 'ontologically prior' to us. Thus, we are directed to the field of ecclesiology, where the asymmetrical character of personhood implies hierarchical structures grounded in ontology. Since the person can exist only in communion, and communion can never exist without the one, the concept of hierarchy is inherent in the idea of a personhood.[28] Strangely enough, it is such hierarchy that 'brings forth . . . equality of nature'.[29] The ministry and, in the first instance, the bishop, reflect and image God the Father to the rest of the members. The bishop is 'the one in whom the "many" united would become "one", being brought back to him who had made them'. He comprises the unity of the Church, and it is in his person and in his role that all divisions are transcended. Such relational primacy is to be seen even in God's being.[30]

Undoubtedly, the conviction about the ontological priority of the person has served as the theoretical basis for an ecclesiological vision that accords a supremacy of power to the person of the bishop in the ecclesial community, notwithstanding the rhetoric of service. For, if a bishop is to be placed *ex officio* on the seat of God the Father, the assumption above, by giving particular emphasis to the role of a hierarchical 'primus', paves the way for excessive exaltation and cloaks him with dominating authority, even if his status is described in relational terms. Within this interpretative framework, it has been argued in an exaggerated manner that the denial of a primacy among bishops cannot but be a heresy. The belief that common faith and worship are the locus of unity is considered no less false, since these are 'impersonal factors', whereas the cause of unity is always a person and not an 'idea'.[31] This is commensurate with the triadological thesis: the explanation of the Divine Being lies 'in a free person', the 'One of the Many'. On this view, caution has been drawn: is not this precedence, although presented as emerging 'freely from the communion of love', in great peril of rendering the communion of love an empty demand degenerating into ideology with regard to the relationship between bishop and congregation?[32] Therefore, may not the 'homogeneity' of the essence be substituted by the despotism of the one, even though the one is conditioned by the many?

No less significant is the anthropological corollary. The Person of the Father is the ultimate ontological principle that causes the being and secures the otherness of the other Persons, while keeping for Himself the monarchy in a non-reciprocal manner.[33] Therefore, in anthropological terms, personhood is something that comes from outside, as an addition to the natural concrete being, the outcome of an external will. While this idea may be speculated upon with reference to the relationship between the creature and the Creator, what significance does it acquire when woven into the fabric of human relationships? The concrete person is in danger of losing any internal dimension, any substantial inherent character, insofar as it receives its being and identity exclusively from the 'willing' and 'loving' Other, whose love is not a common essential fund but a personal property. Not surprisingly, when treated in the wrong manner, personhood is dissolved. After all, personhood is not ascribed to any individual who remains within the confines of nature.[34]

Working towards recapturing the patristic threads, one is bound to ask: Does this 'monarchical' logic actually stem from a coherent reading of the theology of the Cappadocians and the Greek Fathers in general? This question – raised also in the recent past – does not touch solely upon a historical issue; rather, it opens or blocks paths towards the charismatic experience of the saints. To this venture we now turn, seeking to come closer to the patristic trinitarian mind and draw out its impact – factual and potential – on anthropology and ecclesiology. At the same time one should never lose sight of the fact that according to the methodology of the Fathers, approaching the divine mystery is not a matter of speculation, nor a product of a historical evolutionary process, but rather a personal initiation in the event of Pentecost, attained by cleansing the divine image within.

Two:
Monarchy and Trinity in the Greek and Irish Fathers

1. The 'middle point'

In this chapter, we shall delve into some key concepts that are the background to the trinitarian understanding of the Greek and the Irish Fathers. Among them is the idea of trinitarian doctrine as the Aristotelian 'mean'.[1]

The Greeks were haunted by the idea of measure or moderation. What was considered by classical Greeks as the means to attain virtue in personal and social life then became the cardinal concern for medieval Greeks in the wide spectrum of religious life. This measure was defined by Aristotle as the mean, the 'middle point' between two extremes: meagreness and surplus, or deficiency and excess. Indeed, virtue receives its status from its very nature and not through addition or subtraction. It is rather the extremes that suffer a deviation from that 'royal road'; they drift away from the ingredients of truth, namely symmetry, proportion and harmony. That is why in the final analysis μεσότης indicates not distance but quality; it was equated not literally with a 'middle point', a kind of third alternative or simply moderation, but with truth itself,[2] which lies beyond juxtaposition but which can also be seen from two opposite points of view. It is remarkable that the definition and framing of the truth revealed by God and experienced by the community was given in the aforementioned Aristotelian terms. Far from being considered simply a figure of speech or a rhetorical device, μεσότης, for the Greek Fathers, is an essential part of life. This principle is no less evident in the Irish Christian mentality, where virtue as the middle point between extremes became the prescriptive rule of authentic spiritual life: standing between 'the poor and the excessive', virtue 'ever recalls us from every superfluity on either side', and for this reason, it is associated with 'the light of discretion that illumines the true worshippers'.[3]

In the world of late antiquity the Christians cultivated the consciousness of their faith being the mean between two extremes: the first was the rigid monotheism represented at that time by Judaism; the second was the chaotic polytheism of the ancient religious systems. In the first case, God was perceived as a dominating single personal figure establishing exclusive contracts/covenants; in the second, the whole being was imagined as a patchwork of worldly and transcendental entities in harmonious co-operation or fierce rivalry. As Gregory of Nyssa says, 'The truth passes in the mean between these two conceptions, destroying each heresy, and yet accepting what is useful to it from each . . . of the Jewish conception, let the unity of the nature stand; and of the Hellenistic, only the distinction as to persons; the remedy . . . being thus applied on either side.'[4]

According to Aristotle, while there is one way of going right, there are many ways of going wrong. Thus, mainstream orthodoxy, in the face of insidious internal threats, applied the principle of the 'mean' also in defining itself in relation to the notorious archetypal heresies of the Eastern world, namely Arianism and Sabellianism. The former divided God into unequal parts; the latter denied any kind of distinction within the Godhead. Each was the by-product of a speculative penetration of skilful minds into the depths of the divine mystery at the expense of paying poor homage to the living marrow of the mystery, which presented an antinomy. Pseudo-Athanasius associates Sabellianism with Judaism as advocating a stringent monotheism, and regards Arianism as espousing Greek heathenism. Here, polytheism is overtly matched to 'monarchy', representing the two extremes, each lying far beyond the 'mean' of true faith.[5]

The term 'monarchy' as an attribute of the Judaic perception of God is also used by Gregory Nazianzen. He insists that the Godhead is neither diffused beyond the three, shaping 'a mob' of entities, 'nor is it bounded by a smaller compass than these' for the sake of 'monarchia'. 'For the evil on either side is the same, though found in contrary directions,' that is, in the defect of the absolute One or in the excess of the unequal and factious multitude. Equidistant from both was the 'middle and royal road'.[6]

The 'rich' conception of Deity transcends this polarisation, attaining the 'extreme' of right and perfection; yet at the same time it embraces a kind of synthesis of what is the right and genuine part of the two diametrical opposites. This synthesis furnishes the crucial antinomy of the Christian Mystery, according to which God is simultaneously 'monadic' and 'triadic'. Undoubtedly, for the Christian Fathers, this faith was the product not of a philosophising mind, but of the common experience of God's revelation.

2. The unfathomable mode of existence

The mind is shown to be outwitted in its total effort to understand the trinitarian mystery. How far can we unfold the hidden layers of the *divine being*? To what extent can our intellects fathom the mystery of the Godhead, as revealed in the salvific economy? From the point of view of gnosiology, the Greek Fathers stand at the mean between two extremes: agnosticism and the rational grasp of God's essence and persons. They unanimously adopted an apophatic approach, which has stood as a stumbling block for many venturing minds ever since. This approach is shared by their Western brothers in the insular world.

According to the Cappadocian Fathers, the infinite and boundless Being cannot be named or defined by words; it escapes all conception of time and nature, as is evident from the appearance of God to the baffled Moses.[7] What we can confess is what has been disclosed to us by God Himself, and this is the existence of the three distinct personal realities within the Godhead, characterised as *hypostases* or *persons* with no separation or confusion. The Cappadocians, with a view to presenting the divine reality in ontological terms, proceeded to what proved to be an innovatory contribution to philosophy: the distinction between essence (*ousia*) and *hypostasis*, and the equation of the latter with the notion of 'person'.[8] That meant, in the first place, that there can be otherness within one essence, in other words, co-essential identities;[9] in the second place, hypostasis directly implied relationship. Last but not least, the term 'person' acquired an essential aspect, for it ceased to be merely a persona or 'role'.

Here, one is tempted to override apophatic theology so as to scrutinise with a certain optimism and confidence the interpersonal communion within the triune God. What does it mean to say that God is Father, Son and Spirit without ceasing to be one God? A possible answer is the identification of the person with the being itself. The being of God Himself is identified with the person. The person *constitutes* being, it is the 'principle' or 'cause'. And this is the person of the Father, 'who makes the one divine substance to be . . . the one God'.[10]

But does this contemplation of the mystery of the Trinity imply knowledge of the Persons themselves? At the same time as this 'knotty'[11] Trinity is revealed to us, equally it is concealed. Being infinite, it is intangible to rational faculties, and, as Gregory Nazianzen insists, the internal 'order' of the hypostases and their relations within the divine being is known only to itself.[12] General doctrinal statements are articulated to set forth a logic of relationship,[13] but there is no evidence at all in patristic writings that the divine hypostases are offered for further investigation beyond the confession of their revealed unique and incommunicable personal properties.

Confronting the deviating effects of unduly inquisitive minds and their desire to possess a logical grasp of the mystery, the whole lineage of Greek theologians warn against scrutinising the 'mode of existence' of the divine Persons, for such an 'audacity' would bring about the same result as that of using any natural capacity to excess: the human voice can surpass its fixed limits only to lose its power altogether, and human sight is lost by gazing directly into the sun.[14] There is something of the divine nature that is held in the treasuries beyond, and something that stays and dances within the human being, to be loved and revered by the created person.[15] Indeed, Gregory confesses, the Trinity itself may reserve for the saints, that is for purified hearts, some shadowy knowledge of the internal relation of the divine Persons. That knowledge is to perceive the one, undivided and identical divine nature in the revealed hypostatic attributes.[16] But, the divine Persons retain for themselves the exclusive knowledge of each other's mode of being, a knowledge that is not of the same order as human knowledge. Thus, biblical references to the Holy Spirit signify its natural affinity with the other divine Persons, while at the same time 'Its mode of existence is kept unutterable'.[17] Although the Fathers do confess the 'unoriginate', 'begotten', and 'proceeding' Divinity, namely the Father, Son and Holy Spirit, they refrain from giving any ontological account of a divine Person and its mode of existence. The unfathomable *tropos hyparxeos*, the 'how' of the Persons, is the 'ungeneracy' of the Father, the 'generation' of the Son, and the 'spiration' or 'procession' of the Spirit – terms that merely assert the Persons' origin or lack of origin.[18] Hence, 'one does not find in pro-Nicenes extended attempts to develop an ontology of divine personhood.'[19]

Therefore, if God 'has a simple, unknowable and inaccessible existence',[20] if 'that which is above essence will also be above knowledge',[21] are we justified in saying that the very being of the Persons *is* communion or the absolute freedom of being other, which, in turn, is one and the same with *eros* and *agape,* identified, in the final analysis, with the hypostasis of the Father?[22] By contrast, all the Fathers make clear that the Persons as well as their mode of existence, being uncreated, remain behind the borders of cognition and language. Far beyond human understanding, ineffable and inconceivable are both the communion and the distinctiveness of the divine hypostases. The trinitarian 'being, together with the mode, the nature and the quality of its being, is altogether inaccessible to creatures'.[23]

Even 'the great mystery of the incarnation remains an eternal mystery . . . even what is revealed still remains entirely hidden and is by no means known as it really is.'[24] This is elaborated upon by St Maximus the Confessor, who wrestles with the Christological matters of his time. Maximus sheds light on St Paul's statement that 'he has but a partial knowledge of the divine Logos' by saying that 'the Logos is known from His energies only to a limited degree, while knowledge of Him *as He is in essence and hypostasis* is altogether inaccessible to all angels and men alike.'[25] Within this frame of mind, the orthodox stance is to confess a state of 'harmless ignorance'. As St Nilus of Ancyra said in the sixth century, the 'darkness' where God was (Exodus 20:21) indicates the 'incomprehensible and inscrutable' of God; it hides what lies inside and impedes the 'curious ventures' of human intellect.[26] Notwithstanding the patristic use of philosophy for the formation of the faith in a classical milieu, the ancient Fathers shared the conviction that the revelation of the divine Persons in history does not really justify a prying into the immanent Trinity. To some degree, God's activity is incomprehensible and its minute knowledge is concealed from creatures. For, His essential 'surroundings' are infinite; and there is no end to His splendour, His glory, His holiness, as is proclaimed by prophecy.[27] Having said that, the patristic message is unequivocal and uncompromising: man is called to become – and can become – in a very real manner, partaker of the uncreated divine nature (2 Peter 1:4), something which will be addressed in due course.

Let us now turn to the western parallel, manifested in the Irish monasticism of the pre-Norman era. It has been argued that the Irish theologians developed a more acute sense of trinitarian doctrine than that expressed by the religious minds of Latin Europe.[28] Be that as it may, it is clear that Irish piety expresses itself in a trinitarian perspective, and the opening and closing apostrophe to the divine Persons is a distinctive ancient Celtic formula in poetry.[29] No less evident is that in their worship of the triune God and in their manner of speaking of God, the Irish also share the Greek apophaticism. There is an absolute ontological gap between the created and the uncreated and, because of this gap, God's being always remains a transcendental and unapproachable awesome mystery. The 'Celtic' God of the mysteries is ineffable, incomprehensible, beyond all, immeasurable, boundless, intangible: 'who can trace His existence at all, what is He, who is He, or how does He exist?' asks St Columbanus, and this is reiterated by Ériugena.[30] God is summoned in a variety of names expressing His energies, but is not gathered up by discourse, since He is above all these names.[31] Since His absolute transcendence refers not only to His nature, but also to the mode of His being, not only to the essence but also to the Persons, 'pious silence knows better and more than impious garrulity'.[32] By the same token, apophaticism characterises the appropriate stance of mind before the trinitarian distinction. God remains the mysterious paradox of three Persons and one being, Three in One and One in Three.[33] It is noticeable that even in the fullest self-revelation of the triune God in history through the incarnation, the

Son remains 'He whom nobody knows save the Father only'. Nobody can narrate or scrutinise His magnitude and altitude and obscure mysteries; He remains 'God unutterable in the unity of the Trinity'.[34] For He is not unity or trinity of such a kind as can be conceived by any created nature.[35]

The question is raised as to whether this apophatic approach leads in the long run to a kind of 'defunctionalisation' of the divine Persons, rendering the trinitarian doctrine irrelevant for us. Well, apophaticism is not the gloomy obscurity of an unidentified bewildering presence; rather it is gnosis as contemplation. Abiding by a clear distinction between the immanent and the economic Trinity – that is, God in Himself and God in relation to His creation – but also recognising the direct connection between them, since God reveals His true self, the Greek as well as the Irish Fathers maintained a clear vision of what is knowable and what lies beyond human grasp in the very revelatory act of God. The economy shows the immanent Trinity, since everything in creation and history is acted out *ex patre per filium in spiritu sancto*.[36] Explaining this in the insightful terms of St Basil, *ex* denotes the 'original cause'; *per* signifies the 'creative cause'; *in* connotes the 'perfecting cause'.[37] Thus, the experience of the multiform divine presence and activity – what we call theophanic experience – not only introduces the distinction of the Persons and of their unique status and their distinctive forms of activity, but also communicates their common indivisible will and energy, operating one and the same work.[38] That is why Mary, in her conception, became '*Trinitatis thalamus*'.[39] This is also stated by the best representative of the Irish tradition in Carolingian Europe. For John Scottus Ériugena, the extrinsic activities of the Trinity are common, yet each of the three Persons has a particular role in the shared trinitarian operation.[40] Still, Ériugena was the scion of a rich insular trinitarian tradition. St Patrick himself in his dramatic autobiography recounted time and again the distinct role of the divine Persons in their common interventions in his life.[41] Such union and distinction is equally witnessed in the apophatic context of 'mystical' prayer, where the supplicant co-operates with the unutterable energetic presence of the Spirit – addressing the Father and leading to the new creation, which is Christ. This internal dialog is 'not a simple communication between an individual and a divine monad, but rather a movement of divine reflexivity, a sort of answering of God to God in and through the one who prays' (Rom. 8:15-21, 26-27).[42]

In conclusion, we may recall the words of the Areopagite: 'those fully initiated into our theological tradition assert … that the indivisible Trinity holds within a shared undifferentiated unity its supra-essential subsistence, … its ineffability, its many names, its unknowability' as well as 'the abiding and foundation of the divine persons who are the source of oneness', and they are grounded 'in an unconfused and unmixed way'.[43] 'There is distinction in unity and there is unity in distinction,' the same Father remarks, summarising the earlier tradition, and this is what is 'revealed by Scripture'.[44] This balance between the unity and distinction within the Godhead is another facet of the patristic *mean*. But of 'what is beyond, let the Trinity have knowledge'.[45]

3. The semantic value of 'monarchy' in trinitarian theology

i. Aition and the source of unity

The ancient Fathers would not dispense with the fact that 'right belief' (the literal meaning of the word 'orthodoxy') stood as a 'middle point' between polar opposites. They realised that on the one hand they had to protect trinitarian doctrine from a modalistic interpretation – the core of the Sabellian heresy – by emphasising the reality and integrity of the Persons. Thus, they invented the image of 'three suns' or 'three torches'. On the other hand, they had to explain to the philosophical mind how real distinctions can avoid the charge of tritheism or the endorsement of ontological grades within the Divinity. Indeed, 'shaping our attention to the union of the irreducible persons in the simple and unitary Godhead' was their most profound concern.[46]

The patristic intention to safeguard unity in diversity and diversity in unity was assisted by the Nicene linguistic device which we now call 'X from X' language: The Son is 'Light from Light' and 'God from God'. This brings forward what came to be accepted as a typical theological feature of the Greek Fathers, namely, the 'monarchy' of the Father, a notion introduced quite early in patristic literature. The Father is the 'source', the 'principle' (ἀρχή) and the 'cause' (αἴτιον) in the Trinity.[47]

Now, X from X, or the notion of cause, has recently been interpreted in strictly personalistic contours, and this is often exhibited as the achievement of the Cappadocians. Accordingly, the vindication of the monarchy of the person has been suggested as the reason for the determinative decision of the second Ecumenical Council (AD 381) to substitute the credal phrase 'from the Father' for the initial Nicene clause 'from the essence of the Father', with reference to the Son's generation,[48] as if the Fathers of Nicaea wished to disjoin the person of the Father from His essence.

According to the above interpretative thread, Western theology, in order to face the Arian challenge, erred by dissociating the word 'God' from that of 'Father' and by attaching 'one' to God only, making of divine essence a notion prior to that of the Father, and assigning to the essence the role of expressing divine unity. The East instead preferred to solve the problem 'in a way that was faithful to the biblical equation of God with the Father'.[49] For the Cappadocians the ground of unity remains the Father. Gregory Nazianzen puts the matter clearly: 'The three have one nature . . . the union being the Father [ἕνωσις δέ, ὁ Πατήρ], out of whom and towards whom the subsequent persons are reckoned.'[50]

In accord with the above reasoning, it is the person of the Father as 'principle' and 'cause' who gives being, identity and freedom to the other Persons; He is the giver of ontological otherness in the Trinity. In order to justify or elucidate the oxymoron of the bestowal of ontological freedom, Zizioulas is forced to introduce concepts implying temporal priority within the Trinity. Thus, the Father's 'freedom in bringing them forth into being does not impose itself upon them, since they are not already there, and their own freedom does not require that their consent be asked, since they are not established as entities before their relationship with the Father'.[51] Moving within the structure that emerges from the relations of origin, and, moreover, considering the person of the Father as the ultimate ontological category, the personalist advocates a one-way traffic from the Father to Son and Spirit, implying a vague idea of subordination. The Trinity is a 'movement' initiated by a person.[52] Indeed, there is a significant detail missing in this articulation. In the mystery of generation and procession of the other Persons there is no spatial or temporal interval: the Father is not senior to the Son, says Patrick. Their existence 'is synchronous, sundered by no distance of time', 'without time or distinction in glory or separation'.[53] It has been rightly argued that if 'to cause and to be caused . . . cannot be conceived in a "successive" way, this means that "cause" and "causation" are ultimate and reciprocal presuppositions of one another'.[54]

But the radical personalist is starting from an uncompromising premise. For him the fact that causation takes place 'on the hypostatic or personal level and not on that of *ousia* implies *freedom* and *love*'. He holds that the Cappadocians insisted on the Father, rather than the divine *ousia*, being the *arche* of personal divine being precisely because they wanted to avoid necessity in ontological causation. The divine being, God the Trinity, owes its very being to the 'free love' of the Father; it is the outcome of a personal decision in love. This reality instructs us not to attribute the ultimacy of being to a necessity inherent in the nature of a being. It follows that 'Being owes its being to personhood and ultimately becomes identical with it.'[55]

The connection between essence and necessity was at the centre of Arian reasoning. The Arian argument, that by introducing the notion of *homoousios*, the Orthodox made the generation of the Son necessary for the Father, was simply rejected as irrelevant by St Athanasius of

Alexandria. He insisted that the Father generates the Son 'willingly' and 'freely'[56] without any detailed demonstration of the Arian argument's invalidity. Is there any vacuum in his formulation, apart from not being embedded in an absolute personalistic rationale? For the Alexandrian bishop to dismiss the very premise of the Arian argument – the association of essence to necessity – would suffice. Nevertheless, instead of simply rejecting it, he does present a logical counter–argument: Nature precedes will, and it is by nature that the Father is good, although what He is, is also His pleasure, for 'who is it that imposes this necessity on Him?' Thus, 'To say, "The Father wills the Son", and "The Word wills the Father", implies not a precedent will but genuineness of nature and propriety and likeness of essence.'[57] Quite clearly, Athanasius' theological framework would not embrace the oppositional separation of essence from person.

However, the patristic writings are utilised to establish a personalistic ontology. Indeed, the supposedly Cappadocian contribution to the solution of the problem seems to derive from an interpretation of two patristic references.[58] The first refers to the trick set by the Arians in employing the notion of 'willingness' or 'unwillingness' in the Son's generation by the Father.[59]

> He [the Father], they say, either voluntarily begat the Son, or else involuntarily. . . . [I]f it was involuntarily, He was under the sway of some one, and who exercised this sway? . . . But if voluntarily, the Son is a Son of Will; how then is He of the Father? – and they thus invent a new sort of Mother for him – the Will – in place of the Father.

In order to invalidate the argument, Gregory applies it to the relationships between creatures and between God and creation.

> You yourself, . . . were you begotten voluntarily or involuntarily by your father? If involuntarily, then he was under some tyrant's sway (O terrible violence!) and who was the tyrant? You will hardly say it was nature, – for nature includes also chastity. If it was voluntarily, then by a few syllables your father is done away with, for you are shewn to be the son of Will, and not of your father. But I pass to the relation between God and the creature . . . Did God create all things voluntarily or under compulsion? If under compulsion, here also is the tyranny, and one who played the tyrant; if voluntarily, the creatures also are deprived of their God . . . For a partition is set up between the Creator and the creatures in the shape of Will. And yet I think that the Person who wills is distinct from the Act of willing; He who begets from the Act of begetting . . . Thus the thing willed is not the child of

will, for it does not always result therefrom; nor is that which is begotten the child of generation . . . but of the Person who willed, or begat. . . . But the things of God are beyond all this, for with Him perhaps the Will to beget is generation, and there is no intermediate action.

Then, the Cappadocian ends with rhetorical questions concerning the cause of the very Divinity:

The Father is God either willingly or unwillingly; . . . If willingly, when did He begin to will? It could not have been before He began to be, for there was nothing prior to Him. . . . And if unwillingly, what compelled Him to exist, and how is He God if He was compelled – and that to nothing less than to be God?

Now, Zizioulas employs Gregory's distinction between 'will' and the 'willing one', to sustain the notion of the ontological priority of the person – here, the willing one.

Gregory distinguishes between 'will' and the 'willing one'. The significance of his position for our purpose here is twofold. On the one hand, it implies that the question of freedom is a matter of *personhood*: God's being ultimately depends on a willing *person* – the Father; and, on the other hand, it indicates, as indeed Gregory explicitly states, that *even the Father's own being* is a result of the 'willing one' – the Father himself. Thus, by making a person – the Father – the ultimate point of ontological reference, the αἴτιον, the Cappadocian Fathers made it possible to introduce freedom into the notion of being.[60]

However, Gregory proceeds to that distinction not because he is concerned with presenting personhood as the ultimate ontological category, but because the heretics gave the Father's 'will' ontological status, making it a 'mother', an intermediary that acted out the generation of the Son. The Cappadocian simply says that the essential powers do not actively move without the impulse of the willing subject – which, after all, includes the person and the essence. He rejects any connection of nature (even created) with necessity and argues that the adverbs 'willingly' or 'unwillingly' are irrelevant to God's being as God. As Maximus the Confessor comments, the birth of the Son is beyond willing.[61] For this reason, Gregory crowns his thought with a very important statement: 'What belongs to God transcends all these cases.'[62] Any personalistic argument does not appear to be in context here. On the contrary, when one correlates the above Gregorian statement with the more elaborate elucidation of the younger Gregory, the mind is directed towards a different, more holistic image:

We neither reject from our doctrine the 'willing' of the Begetter directed to the Son . . . nor do we break that inseparable oneness, when 'willing' is regarded as involved in the generation. . . . In the case of the simple and all-powerful Nature, all things are conceived together and at once, the willing of good as well as the possession of what He wills. For the good and uncreated (ἀΐδιον) will is contemplated as operating (ἐνεϱγόν), indwelling (ἐνούσιον), and co-existing (ἐνυπόστατον) in the uncreated Nature, not arising in it from any separate principle, nor capable of being conceived apart from the object of will. . . . The will, which always indwells the good Nature, is not forced out nor excluded by reason of this inseparable conjunction.[63]

No less inappropriate seems to be the use of the Basilian statement that everything in God begins with the 'good pleasure' (εὐδοκία) of the Father.[64] For it is clear that the Cappadocian refers solely to the economy, namely God *ad extra*, as Gregory does when he says that God 'subsists in three greatest "entities" (μέγιστα), that is the cause, the creator, and the perfecter'.[65] As mentioned above, the prepositions *ex, per* and *in* do not reveal the way the immanent Trinity exists.[66]

Summing up the patristic tradition, St John of Damascus affirms that the generation of the Son is beyond the Father's volition.[67] There is no precedent personal will in the Trinity. The Son is not of the Father's will, say the Fathers, countering the assertions of the Arians, and this definitely does not deny the Father's 'pleasure' in the generation of the Son. The statement that the Father 'εὐδοκεῖ' means that He rests upon the Son, that the Son is His beloved. But He is His beloved with the same love with which the Son loves the Father. God the Father, as the willing Person, derives His will not from being the Father but from His Godhead, as Maximus the Confessor clearly states. Sharing the same nature, and having 'their being simultaneously', the Father and the Son also share one single, simple and indivisible will, so that the Father's willing presupposes the existence of the Son.[68] As Athanasius explains, 'The Son wills the Father by the same will that He is willed by Him.' For will, and love as well, are not personal attributes.[69] Neither the Son nor the Spirit is a 'work' of a 'purpose', nor is the person of the Father the manufacturer of divine nature.[70]

Now, let us see how Basil of Caesarea becomes involved in personalism. Speaking of the Trinity, he reads *arche* in the sense of the beginning of being, with regard not to time but to cause or principle: 'Father is the one who has given the principle of being to the others . . . Son is the one who has had the principle of being by birth from the other.'[71] It has been pointed out that the Cappadocian speaks of *einai* (being) and not of *ousia* (essence). But one begs the question if one asserts that being *is* the person. Zizioulas employs the analogy of the generation at the human level: Human beings derive their being not from a common substance but from the person of Adam. Equally, it is God the Father and not divine *ousia* that is likewise the principle and foundation of divine being. Thus, God as person makes the one substance to be that which is: the one God.[72] In fact, such a rationale would appear odd to Basil, who displays no care to affirm a hypostatic cause of being. He uses the example of lineage to disprove the identification of divine essence with the hypostatic characters; put otherwise, to say to Eunomius that knowing 'whence' a person has its cause reveals nothing of what it is.[73]

Similarly, the radical personalist takes God's disclosure to Moses as proving the ultimate priority of the person. The 'One who Is' is identified with the person of the Father, above and beyond essence. This is supposedly buttressed by the statement of St Gregory Palamas: 'When God was conversing with Moses He did not say I am the essence but I am the One who Is. Thus it is not the One who Is who derives from the essence, but essence which derives from the One who Is.'[74] But it is clear that in the thought of Palamas as well as that of his predecessors, the name of 'being' includes the essence, the unchangeable core of a thing, the person or hypostasis, the essential energies and, in the created being only, the accidents. In other words, 'being' encompasses the whole of existence.[75]

Indeed, the claim that God the Father 'as a person' is above and prior to His existence would be meaningless for the patristic mind. Should we argue that God exists not simply because He exists but because the Father as person wills God's very existence, we present divine will as a personal, not an essential, attribute. It thus becomes *gnomic* will, which is defined by the person. And as we shall see in due course, the gnomic will cannot be predicated on the divine Persons. But, by nature, God is God and man is man, and the community of will is intimately joined to the community of nature.[76] Moreover, in the Cappadocian mind, being is often identified with essence. The essence is 'the very being of God'; it 'indicates the very existence (εἶναι) of anything, so far as it does exist'.[77] Only God possesses existence by virtue of His own nature, and on this account He is referred to as 'the Being' (ὁ ὤν), since He is the only one to exist apart from participation.[78] And 'in Himself God contains all being . . . like some great sea of essence, limitless and unbounded, transcending all conception of time and nature.'[79] Here, being is identified with the unfathomable essence, 'summed up' in God as Trinity. After all, the principle (*logos*) of every nature is its essential existence and indicates its perfection.[80] Of course, God's essence is supra-essential; it tolerates no kind of analogy with the creaturely level of being, as the radically Other, radically seamless ontological category. Together with its energies it is 'the hidden and inseparable supreme foundation of a permanence which is beyond ineffability and unknowing'.[81]

Zizioulas admits that Gregory Nazianzen seems to use the term *monarchia* in the early sense of 'one rule, will and power'. As such, the Cappadocian applies it to all three persons of the Trinity:

> a monarchia that is not limited to a single person, for it is possible for unity if at variance with itself to come into a condition of plurality; but one which is constituted by equality of nature, and agreement of opinion, and identity of motion, and by the convergence to the one of the things that come from it . . . so that though numerically distinct there is no division of ousia.[82]

Gregory employs 'monarchy' in the sense of one will and concord, that is, in the old 'moral' or functional sense. The emphasis is placed on order as opposed to disorder, and on common will. Yet, he is not unaware of the ontological meaning which he expresses in the term *monas*. This he applies to the Father. The ontological sense of *monarchia* comes with the text that immediately follows, showing the dynamic character of the divine nature:

> For this reason the one having moved from the beginning to a dyad, at the Trinity came to a halt. And this is for us the Father and the Son and the Holy Spirit.[83]

According to Zizioulas, it is now a question not of a 'moral' unity, but of how the Persons relate to one another in terms of ontological origination. The text equates the One with the Father, for it explains itself immediately by saying, 'the one [moved] as the Begetter and Emitter'. One may even discern in the Cappadocians some departure from the Athanasian idea of the 'fertile substance' of God. For they give ontological primacy to the person by stressing that the Father is the one God. In brief, great emphasis is placed on the person over the common nature; and yet, not on all three Persons. In this kind of monarchy only one person is basically active, the Father, the only giver of otherness.[84]

The Cappadocians are not, in fact, afraid of essence-language, nor do they anchor monotheism to a single hypostasis. On the contrary, going beyond the earlier strategy of referring to the Father as the indivisible source of derivation, they insisted on the indivisibility of the divine essence or nature, considered as common, 'undivided monad', commonality of 'being', 'distinct' from the person of the Father, circumscribed in (and constituting) the hypostases, and exemplified by each Person.[85] Monarchy is not the monarchy of the 'person of the Father' above and beyond the common nature. There is not a hierarchy of 'a first, a second and a third', but there is monarchy related to 'the one form which is seen in God the Father and in God the Only-begotten, imaged through the undeviating character of the Godhead'.[86] When Gregory is prepared to name the Father 'union' of the other Persons, it is because he recognises in the Trinity a simple nature and identity of being, which means no space or grade within the will or power. It is precisely this that differentiates created from uncreated being: in the created state, one may rebel not only against others but also against one's self. Nowhere is in the divine mystery a reference to the cause without a simultaneous reference to the identity of nature. This is clear also for the Irish theologian: there is nothing temporal or spatial, nothing superior or inferior in the Trinity, but one everlasting God.[87]

We have already observed that the term 'monarchy' carries some negative connotations, when it is identified with strict Judaic monotheism, or even in a trinitarian context, whenever divinity is considered to be circumscribed by one Person. Such a perception would suggest 'poverty' and 'pettiness' in deity,[88] which easily becomes the metaphysical basis of claims for absolute authority. On the other hand, true monotheism should not be endangered by any misconception of the internal divine 'richness'. That is why the Fathers pay such great attention in utilising the notion of the monarchy to figuratively express divine abundance and reach the golden mean between the disorder of polyarchy and the tyranny of singularity.

Monarchy is not limited to a single person. This Gregorian thesis is reiterated by Maximus the Confessor and also glossed by him in combination with another relevant passage of Gregory. Maximus' holistic thought, without implying any distinction between a 'moral' and an 'ontological' sense of monarchy, defines monarchy as the 'three-personed monad'. The one principle is 'not limited to a single person... without the Word and the Spirit'; God as one principle is contemplated in the Three.[89] Maximus points to another passage by Gregory, in which the above thesis is rephrased. Gregory speaks again of the 'monad which has moved on account of its abundance, the dyad being transcended, since it denotes corporeal matter and gender, and the triad being defined on account of its perfection'.[90] Indicating the absolute identity of the two citations, Maximus proceeds to say that *our* monarchy 'is comprised of a Trinity of persons co-equal according to nature . . . whose richness is the consubstantiality and the one burst of effulgence'. So, the supra-essential cause of beings is simultaneously a Monad and a Triad. A real Monad, as one enhypostatic entity of a co-essential Trinity, not subject to natural emanation; and a real Trinity, not compound but indivisible, as an essential subsistence of a three-person Monad. Maximus sums up with a succinct statement aiming for consolidation: The Triad is truly a Monad, because that is *what it is*, and the Monad is truly a Triad, because that is *how it subsists*.[91] The Trinity as a Monad is identified with God's being. The one Divinity exists monadically, whereas It subsists triadically. Accordingly, the term *Thearchic existence* 'refers to the divinity which is recognized in three hypostases'. Certainly, this divinity has no logical priority over the Persons; for 'it reveals Itself through the proclamation of the three persons'. Indeed, it is the unity of the Persons that allows the attribution of 'thearchy' to the one divinity.[92]

The Deity is moved in the intellect, teaching the principle of oneness. But the 'movement' of the Monad towards the Trinity is interpreted by Maximus in revelatory and epistemological terms: it refers rather to God as cause of the human movement towards Him: The Monad, as uncreated and infinite, cannot be moved, but moves everything as the cause of all beings. How then does Gregory introduce a Divinity in motion? He does this because, as the cause of all beings, It may receive all the attributes of the beings that It moves and draws back to Itself. Thus, God is said to be moved insofar as it is the cause of the mind's search and because of His progressive manifestation. For first, we are illumined by the principle of His being, after which we are enlightened regarding the mode of His subsistence; for the fact of being is always grasped before the manner of being. Apart from that, Gregory does not assume the 'cause' of the Holy Trinity's being, which is 'above cause'.[93]

One might say that Maximus appears to contradict himself when he asserts in another context that God the Father, as 'cause' and 'source' and 'the begetting divinity', 'in an atemporal and loving movement has proceeded to the distinction of the hypostases, … the cause and source of all was multiplied to a three-person thearchy'.[94] However, is this truly a contradictory statement? One could argue that for Maximus, as for his predecessors, the Father is the cause in the Trinity, but the divine supra-essential essence, or simply Divinity, bears the fecundity of the Father's 'incomprehensible progress'. It is the divine nature that, in its very immovability, moves in the co-inherence of the hypostases.[95] Thus, the one that has 'moved' as the Begetter and Emitter is nothing but the Father's essence. Accordingly, the 'richness' of the Trinity is for Maximus the connaturality as well as the common energy—the outflowing of one radiance. This is the inseparable 'community of nature and of energy'.[96]

We may infer that God the Father is the 'principle' or 'cause' of the other Persons, to whom He communicates His whole essence, but the divine being includes the essence with its natural energies as well as the incomprehensible Persons. Although Maximus is very

concrete in distinguishing the Persons, he is also very careful not to
jeopardise the mysterious divine unity. The knowledge of God in
His essence and personhood remains inaccessible to all – angels and
men alike – and He can in no way be known by anyone.[97] Employing
a number of negations, Maximus tries to delineate, or rather to
safeguard, the mystery of Triadic Monad. Trinity and Monad are not
to be understood as something within something else, nor as one and
the other, nor as one through the other, 'for there is no mediation of
relation as from effect to cause between what is entirely identical and
absolute', nor as one from the other, 'for the Trinity does not derive
from the Unity, since it is without origin and self-manifesting'.[98] With
such outflow of exclusions, it becomes clear that no priority of any
kind is intelligible in the immanent Trinity, not even on the grounds
of causality. Prioritization comes out of a brain that discounts the fact
that God is beyond both unity and trinity, indeed 'beyond ineffability
and unknowing'.[99]

A person comes from a person; a Self from another Self,[100] as the
Son and the Spirit proceed in a different manner from the Father.
They do not proceed *de unita natura*, as the Carolingians advocated.[101]
Among these, Ériugena was particularly cautious, asserting that 'the
Father is Father not of the *nature* of the Son, nor is the Son Son of the
Father's *nature*: for they are of one and the same nature.'[102] Certainly,
in this very 'progress', the essence is the fount of the generation of
co-essential entities. But the essence is neither caused nor 'possessed'
by a person, nor is it a 'bundle' of persons; it is simply manifested
through them. Gregory of Nyssa draws clearly the subtle distinction:
'Neither generation nor absence of generation can any longer be
supposed to constitute the essence, but the essence must be taken
separately, and its being, or not being begotten, must be conceived
separately by means of the peculiar attributes contemplated in it.'[103]
In short, 'fatherhood is outside the circle of the essence . . . His
ungeneracy is made to mean something outside the essence'.[104] Thus,
as Fr John Romanides puts it, 'The manner by which the uncaused
Father exists, and by which the Son and the Holy Spirit receive their
existence from the Father, are not to be confused with the Father's
communicating His essence and energy to the Son and the Holy
Spirit. It would, indeed, be strange to speak about the Father as
causing the existence of His own essence and energy along with the
hypostases of the Son and the Holy Spirit.'[105]

Gregory Nazianzen insists on the uniqueness of the Persons while
emphasising the oneness of divinity and essence. This was the urgent
need of his times, so it became a priority for him to protect the doctrine
from any unbalanced emphasis. In a magnificent description of his
encounter with the transcendental reality, he insists on the

one Godhead and power, found in the Three in Unity, and comprising the Three separately . . . Each God, when considered in Himself; as the Father so the Son, as the Son so the Holy Ghost; . . . the Three One God when contemplated together; Each of them God, on account of the co-essentiality; One God, because of the Monarchia. No sooner do I conceive of the One than I am illumined by the splendour of the Three; no sooner do I distinguish Them than I am carried back to the One. When I think of any One of the Three, I think of Him as the Whole, and my eyes are filled, and the greater part escapes me. . . . When I contemplate the Three together, I see but one torch, and cannot divide or measure out the Undivided Light.[106]

This is the Gregorian – indeed the Cappadocian – baptismal confession. In the above credal context, first, the co-essentiality sanctions the clear distinction of Persons and the attribution of the name and reality of God to each Person, and second, monarchy applies to the contemplation of the Three together, the undivided light of the one torch. The monarchy is the Three, because the Three is the One God. The patristic thought can be delineated in the following correspondences:

Each One, God (Θεὸς ἕκαστον) ←→ Co-essentiality (ὁμοουσιότης)
God the Three (Θεὸς τὰ τρία) ←→ Monarchy (μοναρχία)

This is the One with respect to essence, power, mind and will.[107] When all Persons are considered, they point to the single divine nature, as for example in the vision of Isaiah, where 'the Cherubim, who unite the Three Holies into one lordship, indicate the primal essence'.[108]

At times, Gregory focuses more on the Persons, presenting in detail their particular identities. He says that the Son is referred to as 'God' on account of the nature. But when He is mentioned together with the Father, He is referred to as 'Lord' on account of the monarchy.[109] At the outset, the focal point is the definition of divine uniqueness: He knows one unbegotten God, the Father and one begotten Lord, his Son. Until the end, he insists on their personal characteristics, which, in the case of the Father, is the cause or principle. Even so, each Person is unique and complete, because the unique properties converge in the one, namely the uncreated divinity. They are absolute properties in a nature which is one.[110] That is why Gregory seems to present both Father and the Trinity as the cause of all:

The Godhead exists undivided in separate entities. It is as if there were a single intermingling of light, which existed in three mutually connected suns. When then we look at the Godhead, and the primal cause, and the sole sovereignty, we have a mental picture of the single whole, certainly. But when we look at the three in whom the Godhead exists, who derive their timeless and equally glorious being from the primal cause, there are three whom we worship.[111]

May we not conclude, then, that one compromises God's simplicity and transcendence when one suggests that the person is 'itself primary and constitutive'[112] of its essence, thus introducing an ontological priority? We should not dispense with the fact that the notion of causality in the immanent Trinity pertains to the level of distinctions but not to the level of union, which is the common divine nature. Indeed, the Father generates hypostases 'of his essence', but it would be biased or even meaningless to say that He, 'as a person', is the cause of His own essence, as if there were within the Father something which causes and something which is caused or, in other words, as if there were two ontological phases in the realisation of being. But the *aition* here has rather the sense of the gateway through which we enter into the divine mystery; for the essence is revealed only through its hypostases.[113]

Eventually, Gregory's twofold way of understanding monarchy is summarised as follows: 'God is one, on account of the Son's and the Spirit's relation to one cause, . . . and also by virtue of the one and the same movement, so to speak, and will of divinity and the identity of essence.'[114] He says the same elsewhere in his typical literary vein, namely that by looking at the Divinity we acquire a mental picture of the single entirety.[115] The ground of the divine unity is both the monarchy of the cause *and* the monarchy of the common Divinity. The Persons, being incommunicable distinctions, cannot but refer to one Person – the Father – when they are considered from the viewpoint of their unknown, uncreated, immediate and atemporal generation and spiration. Again, as we shall see later, the very communion of the Persons – their union – lies in their connaturality and shared 'essential' movement or energy; and so oneness is recognised in what is totally shared, in the whole and total presence. This is why the Persons are 'divisions' within or around (περὶ) the essence, and the personal distinctions 'are detected in the essence' (ἐπιθεωροῦνται τῇ οὐσίᾳ), as different particular modes of existence of the whole and common.[116] Accordingly, one can affirm of the Christ-Logos that 'He essentially subsisted (κατ' οὐσίαν εἶναι) in the first and blessed nature Itself, thus proclaiming aloud, In the Beginning was the Word and with God, and God and Light and Life.'[117]

As already evident from the above cross-references, the other, more philosophising, Cappadocian, Gregory of Nyssa, expresses the same truth. For him the word 'God' refers either to the one essence or the one cause along with what he causes.[118] And 'the word "one" does not indicate the Father alone, but comprehends in its significance the

Son with the Father, inasmuch as the Lord said, "I and My Father are one."'[119] Accordingly, monarchy is identified with the commonality of essence, while the one principle of the one deity is described as the 'concurrence of the similars'.[120] The Father is God, not on account of his being Father. There is one and the same God, because there is one and the same essence. Right belief 'observes a distinction of persons in the unity of nature', and it is the nature that secures unity, 'so that the state of monarchy is not split and cut up into differing Gods'.[121] The unity of the Three lies not in any personal relationship; each Person is joined to the other by virtue of their uncreated nature. Their power resides in their nature. And by virtue of this 'superior nature' and 'native dignity', and not 'by an arbitrary act of capricious power', God governs the universe.[122]

Gregory's older brother, Basil of Caesarea, exposes in lapidary language the depth and weight of the connection of the particular Person to the common essence. He explains that 'as the Son exists from the Father by way of generation, and has the Father by nature imprinted upon Him, he saves on the one hand the unchangedness, as he is an image, and on the other hand he saves the co-essentiality, as an offspring of Him.'[123] What warrants the identity of the Persons is the common nature and divinity.[124] That is why Basil explicitly connects monarchy not with a specific hypostasis but with the unity of the essence: 'We both confess the distinction of the Persons, and at the same time abide by the Monarchy . . . because one Form, so to say, in the invariableness of the Godhead, is beheld in God the Father, and in God the Only begotten. For the Son is in the Father and the Father in the Son; since such as is the latter, such is the former, and such as is the former, such is the latter; and herein is the Oneness. So that according to the distinction of Persons, both are one and one, and according to the commonality of nature, one.'[125]

The picture is completed by one of the most influential theologians, St Cyril of Alexandria, who confirms, if not enhances, the former expositions. As in fire and glow, sun and ray, soul and mind, the divine Persons are distinguished 'ἐπινοίᾳ' (i.e. in thought), as a result of human reflection on the mystery of the Godhead. Such *epinoia* is necessary to avoid confusion of the hypostases; yet distinctions in God have a transcendental character, as they are applied to the timeless and uncreated.[126] The personal properties that differentiate the Persons refer to the cause and effect relationship and the mode of being. However, although the principle of causality remains unquestioned, Cyril perceives the full significance of the fact that the generation of otherness is atemporal, of equal glory and undivided.[127] Thus, the notion of causality is always combined with that of co-essentiality to signify the one God.

The unity of the Godhead is beheld in the essential oneness that conjoins the Persons. But when Cyril envisages the one Deity from the point of view of the hypostases, there forms in his mind the notion of inter-penetration or mutual indwelling. In fact, it is by virtue of this common essence or divinity that the Persons co-inhere 'naturally'; they are 'one' (John 10:30); they are equal on account of their co-essentiality.[128] Like Athanasius, Cyril dismisses the question of the association of the Son's generation with the Father's personal will as an absurd and misleading invention. Will does not precede essence/existence, and this aphorism does not in the least introduce a necessity in God.[129] To want to grant mercy is an inherent property of the Father's nature, in which the Son subsists, displaying the same mercifulness and all that is good arising from the same nature in a simple, uncompounded manner. God's nature is fixed to God's will to be what He is.[130] In fact, more than simply willed, the Son *is* the essential and hypostatic will of the Father, or the wisdom and word in whom the Father's will lies, according to Cyril, who is not reluctant to say that the Persons *are* in each other 'both naturally and necessarily'.[131]

The principle that safeguards the hypostases is their common nature. For that reason (long after the Cappadocian 'personalistic revolution'), the term 'Only-Begotten' is interpreted as the Son being generated from the Father's essence, the 'natural character and image' of the Father's essence.[132] Cyril clarifies that the Son and the Spirit own all that belongs to the Father 'essentially, according to nature', not by participation or communication, even though it is said that all has been given by the Father,[133] so that the most subtle and refined notion of separation or subordination would be warded off. This is why Gregory Nazianzen, referring to the immanent Trinity, says that the Spirit was 'ever being partaken, but not partaking'.[134] And Gregory of Nyssa observes ironically that Eunomius tells the truth unintentionally when he argues that the Father 'does not *impart* His own glory to the Son'. Strictly speaking, 'the term "impart" (μετάδοσις) is used in the case of one who has not his glory from within, whose possession of it is an accession from without, and not part of his own nature: but where one and the same nature is observed in both Persons, He Who is as regards nature all that the Father is believed to be stands in no need of one to impart to Him each several attribute.'[135]

Thus, the common essence, wherefrom equality of the Persons and identity of will and power derive, makes us confess and praise the one God and the one humanity.[136] Causality itself in divinity is impalpable and unknown; it furnishes the distinction between the hypostatic properties, only to ensure that no kind of priority is acceptable within the Deity. For that reason the reference to the cause by Gregory is balanced, if not overshadowed, by the emphatic characterisations of the Spirit, which are not personal properties, but common – namely essential – attributes. This emphatic language is also employed by the other Cappadocians: 'sovereignly, and not as a minister'; the Spirit, no less than the Son, 'serves the bestowal of the gifts . . . according to His will'.[137] In other words, they are very careful to refine the affirmation that the Father is the 'root and source' of the Son and Spirit, by emphasising the perfectness, wholeness and self-sufficiency of the being of each Person that resides 'in their nature', 'in full divinity'. Moreover, perplexing phrases such as 'God is spirit' (John 4:24) or 'Spirit of Christ' (Rom. 8:9) testify not to a confusion of the Persons but to the commonality of nature.[138]

Let us bring to the stage another prolific writer of the fourth century, St Epiphanius of Salamis, who averts a polytheistic understanding of the Trinity by stressing the unity of the Godhead. It is not quite clear whether he identifies the 'one God' with the omnipotent Father, but what is noticeable is that the monarchy of the Father is turned into a monarchy of the Father and the Son and the Spirit, due to their one nature, will and operation, as proclaimed by Christ Himself: 'Because I am in the Father and the Father in me, we are both one, to wit, one divinity, one will, one rule.'[139] Explaining the scriptural trinitarian terminology, Epiphanius says that attributing the phrase 'one God' to the Father 'deprives the Son of nothing', so that the terms 'God' and 'Lord' function as a kind of synonymous parallelism. Hence, ultimately the 'one God' is the 'co-essential Trinity'. And, as Gregory says, it is by virtue of the common that we 'properly declare the Divinity to be one, and God to be one, and employ in the singular all other divine names'.[140] Both interpretations are fused by Maximus the Confessor, without any hint of logical discrepancy or effort at harmonisation. 'One God', he writes, 'begetter of one Son, Father, and source of the Holy Spirit . . . One God, for there is one divinity', and 'the Divinity is both wholly one and wholly three'.[141]

This is by no means a degrading of the person. On the contrary, the Greek Fathers are well aware of the role of the essence in the foundation and integrity of the distinct persons. The emphasis on co-essentiality safeguards the reality and perfectness of the hypostatic distinctions. As the Cappadocian explains, 'Nothing can be of one essence with itself, but with another.'[142] So, either, because the Persons 'are united in essence, they really preserve an unalterable relation to each other; or else they stand apart in essential unlikeness'.[143] The essence is participated in totally by the person, and this total participation is the presupposition for a person to be genuine. Ultimately, the very appellation 'Son' is given because of the communion in the begetter's nature.[144] Consequently, otherness is contemplated only in the identity of nature. As Basil affirms, 'This is the character of hypostatic properties, that they show the otherness in the identity of essence.'[145] Thus, nature – in particular, connaturality – proves to be not only the ground of sameness and unity but also the *terra firma* of otherness, fullness and equality. Each hypostasis is 'perfect', so that we may understand one uncompound perfect essence, existing in perfect subsistences.[146] According to Maximus' statement, 'The co-essential entities are in every way distinct according to their hypostasis; and those that exist in a hypostatic union are of different essence.'[147] And the Cappadocian explains that 'in the communion of the essence we maintain that there is no mutual approach or intercommunion of those notes of distinction perceived in the Trinity'.[148]

Hence, the causal relationship needs some qualification; it is the commonality of nature that introduces the perfectness of the notion of the persons in communion. Gregory perfectly combines the two inseparable aspects of Sonship: from the viewpoint of personal origination; and from the viewpoint of essence. 'In my opinion He is called Son because He is identical with the Father in essence; and not only for this reason, but also because He is of Him.' That is why the Son is called 'a concise demonstration and easy setting forth of the Father's nature'.[149] As a person the Son is from the Father. As an essence He is identical with the Father. The Cappadocians always return to the identity of nature as their vantage point for the twofold proof of simultaneous oneness and otherness. For the Persons 'should rather be called identical than like'; and what else could safeguard this very fact of identity but the common nature?[150]

We may also view the concept of cause through a different lens, namely the patristic theology of *imago*, inherited from Paul (Rom. 8:29; Phil. 2:6; Heb. 1:3) and enriched by the Greek philosophical legacy. The Son is the natural image of the Father – the image of the essence of the Father.[151] This special relationship between the image and the prototype prevents us from considering a kind of increase from the one Person to the many. Thus, we confess 'God of God'; we affirm the distinction of the Persons, and at the same time abide by the monarchy. And this monarchy rests in the fact that in God the Father and in the only-begotten Son we contemplate one form, depicted in the invariability of the Godhead. The same applies for the Spirit of the Father, so that each person 'is not one of many, but One'.[152]

So, what is the connection between the concepts of cause and image? They both designate the gnosiological succession. As Basil says, fixing our eyes on the beauty of the image of the invisible God, namely Christ, through the image we are led up to the beauty of the archetype, while the Spirit, the image of the image, gives that very power of beholding, in Himself leading on to the full knowledge of the whole; as it is written, 'in thy light shall we see light'. Basil's final remark is most relevant: 'Thus the way of the knowledge of God lies from the one Spirit through the one Son to the one Father, and conversely the natural goodness and the inherent holiness and the royal dignity extend from the Father through the only-begotten to the Spirit. Thus there is both acknowledgment of the hypostases and the true dogma of the monarchy is not lost.'[153]

The theological tradition described above was summed up in the seventh century by the scholastic redactor of the Greek East, John of Damascus. According to him, the divine Persons derive their being 'from the essence of the Father'; and the fact that the generation is a 'work of nature', and not a 'work of will', precludes the application of created categories to the divine mystery.[154] But in his case something unusual is apparent that should not be overlooked. Although the monk-sage of Damascus handles with perfect knowledge the patristic theological abundance, and thoroughly shares in that living past, he prefers not to expose ontological dimensions of the notion of the person; instead he seems content with a 'logical' exposition.[155] This draws us back to an interpretative device used by the Fathers so that a limit might be set to analytical speculation; the distinction between two complementary modes of experiencing different aspects of reality. First, in an initial phase, we experience and perceive something in actual fact (πράγματι); parallel to that is the way we perceive, identify, name and describe the distinct properties of the same reality through afterthought, in the sense of the activity of reflection, conjecture and conceptualisation based upon experience (ἐπίνοια/*epinoia*). The latter also grants an accurate knowledge – 'the very philosophy of being and the contemplation of intelligible things' – but since it relies on concepts developed by human consciousness, it should not be considered as a penetration into the ontological dimension of things, a dimension that 'takes to flight before we have conceived it'.[156] Human language itself, as a limited vehicle and medium, is a substantial product of *epinoia*. The Fathers know that 'the more we take flight upward, the more our words are confined to the ideas we are capable of forming'.[157] Men have a right to such word-building, says Gregory of Nyssa, adapting their appellations to their subject; for 'God is of Himself what also He is believed to be . . . but He receives His appellations from what are believed to be His operations in regard to our life.'[158] Thus, it is evident that all distinctions within the Godhead – including the concepts of inter-trinitarian cause and principle or even order and succession – are professed as expressions on the gnosiological level, the level of the 'stated being' corresponding to that of 'being'.[159]

So far, the concept of 'cause' in the Trinity has been demonstrated as vital for the patristic triadology, for it offered a valuable philosophical key to the understanding of the divine unity that avoided heretical

extremes. It also refuted the Arian understanding of Christ's saying
that the Father is 'greater'. Gregory Nazianzen re-emphasises the
Father's hypostatic property of being the originator, from whom
'flows both the equality and the being of the equals'. But this does
not justify 'precedences of honour', which would be an 'insult' to
the Source. At the same time, in the face of tritheism, he offers 'this
good thing, the unity in the Three', which is the common essence.[160]
This is the trinitarian horizon of the Fathers, rendered figuratively by
Gregory of Nyssa:

> Like colours seen in the rainbow, the peculiar properties of
> the hypostases flash their brightness on each of the Persons . . .
> but that of the proper nature no difference can be conceived as
> existing between one and the other, the peculiar characteristics
> shining, in community of essence, upon each.[161]

Now, if we turn to the theological production of the *mundus
extremus*, we find ourselves in the same interpretative milieu. Irish
theology moves largely in the realm of divine economy and very
rarely enters the sphere of the immanent Trinity. In contemplating the
one Principle, Ériugena venerates the Unity and understands the three
substances of the Unity by observing that this Unity does not consist in
any singularity or barrenness.[162] We may suggest here that *singularitas*
points to the one person monarchy, while *sterilitas* refers to a natural
'poverty', quite close to the Cappadocian formulations. When the
anonymous luminary addresses himself to the matter of numbering
gods in the Trinity, he does not have recourse to the language of
causation, though he has already presented the Father as 'the fount
of the Godhead'; rather, he turns to the 'shared fullness of divinity'.[163]
The Irish cultivate a strong sense of unity as well as of distinction.
First, the person is never considered as an ontological reality
separate from or prior to its essence. That is why the Son is 'ex Patris
substantia', 'from His nature . . . from the medulla of His divinity'.[164]
Ériugena concludes that the hypostasis of the Father is the cause of
the hypostasis of the Son, making it no less clear that the Son is 'ex
corde, ex secretis sinibus Dei et Patris'.[165] And that is why we can say,
without eliminating the Persons, that 'the Son subsists in the Father',
'ex secreto essentiae'.[166] At the same time, the Son is equal with the
Father not because of the Father's will, but in virtue of *divinitas*, whose
hidden mysteries He revealed in the incarnation.[167] From this nature
springs 'one and the same will, one love of the three Substances of the
one essential Goodness by which the Father moves Himself' to create
everything in the Son and perfect it in the Spirit.[168]
When the Irish Fathers encounter the mystery of the Trinity, they see
oneness in the inseparable essence and uncreated divinity, insisting at

the same time on the unique character of the Persons. The Persons are equal and coeternal not by virtue of a personal will but because of their co-essentiality.[169] The Irish commentator on the Psalms insists on the one power, will and glory, the common property that pertains to the one divine essence. Accordingly, the names *Deus* and *Dominus* are a common property and thus can be both interchangeable and used separately for each Person, presenting the 'aequalis gloria', where there is nothing minor or major, nothing prior or posterior.[170] In safeguarding the unity in the Trinity – 'the one in the many' – St Columbanus does not have recourse to the concept of the cause and principle; he instead nurtures the wonder before the *mysterium trinitatis*, expressed in the equal attribution of the name *Deus* to each Person and the experience of the common glory.[171] For this reason the theology of the image has a rigorous presence in the Irish mind. And as the Irish sage believes, the image–archetype relationship indicates the fact that there is no distance between glory and glory, light and light, for there is one nature and one essence.[172]

Even in the sphere of divine dispensation the scriptural evidence, according to the Irish exegete, points to a reciprocal – one could also say symmetrical – movement from the Father to the Son and vice versa. Not only does the Son lead to the Father, but the Father leads to the Son, and this fact stems from their commonality of nature and essence.[173] In a similar fashion and on scriptural grounds, Basil speaks of this symmetrical interrelationship even at the level of economy, as expressed in the mutual intimate glory of the divine Persons: the Son glorifies the Father, and is glorified by the Father, the Spirit glorifies the Son and receives of what is His, and is glorified by the other two.[174] We could also apply this interchange of glory to the domain of will. This will is viewed in respect of God's presence *ad extra* and in respect of the immanent Trinity. Thus, we may espy reciprocity also on the level of the inter-trinitarian causality; for the Son is not simply the 'willed' one, but the one who 'wills the Father by the same will that He is willed by Him'.[175]

One could argue that the Irish Fathers feel uneasy with the concept of the monarchy of the Father; for, commenting on John 1:1, the unknown sage is eager to state that if the Father is *principium*, the Son is also *principium*; and a *principium* has no *principium*.[176] We also find the same articulation in Gregory of Nyssa: the One Who is in *principium* has no *principium*. This is not a denial of the first cause. But there is no confusion between the essential relationship and the hypostatic origination. There is one principle, and not two principles, not because there is a prior person of the Father, but because the Son is 'seen' or eternally subsists indivisibly within the Father.[177] This is an expression of the common authority, the affirmation of the mutual indwelling of the Persons and their equality in essential divinity. For, as we see also in Ériugena, *principium* may refer to the immanent relationship, but also to the beginning from which and through which all created being was brought forth.[178]

Meanwhile, when speaking of distinctions and interrelations one should never lose sight of the critical function of *epinoia*. Is there a distinction between the experience of the actual fact and the product of *epinoia*? What is the relationship between the experience of transcendental realities and language, given that the Word 'runs ahead of Himself through riddles, words and figures'?[179] The Irish commentator knows that in speaking about God 'these are human words'.[180] This conviction also lies at the substratum of Ériugena's theological experience and discourse. What we say about the transcendental realities is constituted not in themselves but in our minds, which conceive such knowledge of them as is permitted by them.[181] The spiritual experience of Columbanus should be summoned up here: 'The threeness is proved by being named, and the unity by being witnessed.'[182] The saint 'witnesses' the unity and 'names' the distinctions within the Godhead. The depth is venerated in solemn silence and wonder. That is why the Irish and the Greek traditions are especially marked by poetical predication 'connected with apophatic discourse, the use of metaphors, illustrations and images'.[183]

ii. Subordination or a wonderful plot

To conceptualise the relation of Christ to God the heretical groups fully exploited the schema of subordination. Zizioulas himself acknowledges that with the identification of God's being with a person, 'theology accepted a kind of subordination of the Son to the Father', without downgrading the Son, thanks to their shared essence. In similar lines, Catherine LaCugna seeks to rehabilitate some form of subordinationism and, like K. Rahner, she equates God's original being (unity) with the unoriginated, equated with the Father.[184]

Let us turn to the Greek Fathers' approach to this particular question. Among the key principles of patristic thought is a clear distinction – but not a violent disjunction – between the economic and the immanent Trinity, dictated by the creature's restricted capacity to perceive and encompass the divine mystery in its revelation. There are diverse ways of speaking about Christ in a human fashion. One of them, applied 'after the union' of Godhead and manhood in the incarnation, is the manner 'according to appropriation and relationship' (κατ' οἰκείωσιν καὶ ἀναφοράν). In this category belongs the Christological schema of 'subordination', introduced by St Paul: 'Then shall the Son also himself be subject unto him that put all things under him, that God may be all in all' (1 Cor. 15:28). In fact, as Cyril of

Alexandria clarifies, 'there is no need [for the Son] to be subordinated to the Father; for since He is God, He is equal to the Father, and neither is He opposite nor subordinate.' After all, only in this way does the last clause 'that God may be all in all' make sense. But in this schema Christ appropriates our own person.[185] We can really see the sovereign act of subordination within the person of the incarnated Christ, in whom the natural human will subjects itself to the natural divine will. All the Christological references to obedience indicate the submission of the 'servile form' to God and not an aspect of the inter-trinitarian relations.[186] Subordination is a category of the 'economy of manhood', for the subordinated constrains and submits his own will to another's will, whereas there is a sole will in the Deity. St John Chrysostom, pointing to scriptural details, strongly insists on the Persons' equality by saying that 'there is one will of the Father and the Son, hence what the Son willed, was that in which the Father was pleased'.[187] Indeed, even at the level of economy a linear hierarchical Trinity (with its implicit subordinationism) is belied by certain references: the Father always hears the Son, the Son Himself speaks *in* the Spirit (Who is not just sent by the others),[188] and the Spirit is sent with the consent of the *three* of them.[189]

Subordination cannot find justification in the 'order' in which the divine Persons are presented, says Gregory of Nyssa, who deeply investigated the matter. After all, this order is itself changeable, not to mention that in Gregory's exegetical writings a structured order is blurred in a shower of poetic trinitarian analogies.[190] From the point of view of mutable human nature, submission to God and salvation are tautological. Apparently, this, as well as all contingent social schemata, does not pertain to the case of the Son. Gregory notices the eschatological thrust of the future tense 'ὑποταγήσεται', used by the apostle. The meaning is that Christ will subordinate Himself as the first and best of humanity, having appropriated all that belongs to created nature. Thus, human nature, liberated from all rules and powers, will accept only God's 'life-giving authority'. The so-called subordination of Christ is offered in His body by Him on behalf of us, since the whole lump of our nature shall be incorporated in His body, the body with which He has mingled and which is the Church. The whole of creation achieves harmony with itself, it becomes one body, His body, in which all of us have been incorporated through mutual obedience, and which is subordinated to God the Father.[191] Furthermore, Gregory prevents any abuse of language of authority by saying that subordination means not a 'servile subservience, but kingship and incorruption and beatitude'.[192] One admires how the semantic value of terms is altered by the Fathers so that the infinite 'richness' of the uncreated life may be expressed.

It is clear that we cannot transfer any kind of subordination from the field of the history of salvation to the immanent Trinity. Christ makes our condition His own as Head of the whole body, says Gregory Nazianzen. In this manner He Himself will also have fulfilled His submission, bringing human nature, which He has assumed, to God. Thus, subordination is a 'drama' with cosmic consequences and 'a wonderful plot devised on our behalf', and cannot be applied to the relationship of the Son to the Father.[193] Anthropomorphic expressions implying subjection of the Son, such as 'The Son can do nothing of Himself, but what He seeth the Father do' (John 5:19), should not mislead us through inapt interpretations of familiar words that bear many related senses; they in fact demonstrate 'the commonality and the equality of honour'.[194] And the other Cappadocian adds that 'He Who shines with the Father's glory and expresses in Himself the Father's person, has all things that the Father Himself has . . . Not that the right is transferred from the Father to the Son, but that it at once remains in the Father and resides in the Son.'[195]

Gregory Nazianzen, with a view to preventing the abuse of generic terminology, makes a meaningful distinction between the Father as the point of origin, and the Father as the holder and giver of life and being for the Son, considering the latter concept unseemly. He explains that although 'the Father impresses the images of the divine acts', the Son brings them to pass, yet not in slavish fashion, but 'in a masterly way, or, to speak more properly, as a Father', in respect to the equal authority.[196] Nor should anyone misuse the assertion that 'the Son has come not to do His own will, but the will of Him that sent Him' (John 6:38; Matt. 26:39). The true sense is that the Son executes the one common will; for as there is one Godhead, there is one will. Will, as well as truth, goodness, wisdom, immortality and all that are summed up in the word *divinity*, are attributed not to a person but to the common uncreated nature. In fact, every scriptural sentence proceeds upon the basis of a common Godhead.[197] Commenting on the above Gregorian clause, Maximus the Confessor states that the command and its acting out are appropriate for beings in motion, namely mutable, but not to the uncreated being whose nature is to be still. So, by assuming obedience or subjection the Word takes the shape of something alien to His nature.[198] When St Paul says that Christ will submit to the Father, he uses a metonymy, to name all that has been created from Him, through Him and for Him.[199]

The same rationale is applied to the Holy Spirit, when the heretics urged for its subjection to the personal will of the Son. Gregory of Nyssa does accept that the Spirit accomplishes the good pleasure of the Son. But this is the consequence of their natural will. 'For the community of nature gives us warrant that the will of the Father, of the Son, and of the Holy Ghost is one, and thus, if the Holy Spirit wills that which seems good to the Son, the community of will clearly points to unity of essence.'[200] That being so, the Spirit is presented by the Cappadocians as self-moving, with free-will, self-powerful, all-powerful , 'ever being partaken, but not partaking'.[201]

Now, the Irish view on the particular subject is worth mentioning. The Irish sage interprets the words 'my Father is major' not by using the notion of causality, but from the angle of incarnation. Hence, the Son is 'minor' 'in carnaliter', that is in His human nature, which suffered the whole human drama, excluding sin.[202] When Peter says in the context of the Lord's Transfiguration that Christ accepted honour and glory from the Father, he alludes to the deified human nature of Christ. The proclamation of God the Father that He is 'well-pleased' in Christ indicates not an asymmetrical relationship but the common treasure, the sharing in natural majesty and glory.[203] Furthermore, the commentator wishes not to restrict the subject of the verb 'pleased' to God the Father only, but he includes also the person of the Holy Spirit.[204] And for the Irish bard, the Spirit proceeds from the Father and the Son to the creation 'with the consent of all'.[205] Even within the field of economy, the Irish refuse non-reciprocity in the Trinity and take pains to avoid any hint of subordination.

iii. Godhead: the Father's prerogative?

But God is the Father, it has been argued, since we confess 'one God, the Father Almighty', and a personalist may elaborate on the conviction that the very term 'Godhead' refers to the person of the Father. In fact, this statement, considered as cornerstone, is at variance with the patristic teaching, which is less one-sided. Although the biblical expression 'ὁ θεὸς καὶ πατήρ' survives in many patristic writings, indicating a usage that recalled an earlier close association of the terms 'God' and 'Father',[206] one detects in a Father as early as Irenaeus a resolution to redefine the title. Thus, searching through patristic literature, one sees that although the name 'God' in some cases is allotted to the Father, it is mostly assigned to the divine nature. The faith in God the Father together with His Word and His Spirit needed a clearer form to safeguard oneness and threeness, one less open to more than one interpretation; the drastic step being that of the First Ecumenical Synod.[207]

'The Godhead is common', Basil insists; 'the fatherhood particular. We must therefore combine the two and say, "I believe in God the Father." The like course must be pursued in the confession of the Son; we must combine the particular with the common and say "I believe in God the Son," so in the case of the Holy Ghost we must make our utterance conform to the appellation and say "in God the Holy

Ghost." Hence it results in a satisfactory preservation of the unity by the confession of the one Godhead.'[208] After all, the name 'God' is not a personal attribute, so it does not grant, nor is it associated with, any kind of precedence within the Deity. If 'there is one God, being the Father', the Son is the same one God, 'by virtue of the identity of Son with Father'.[209] This is also evident in Irish trinitarian formulations modelled on St Paul's language expressing the *mysterium trinitatis*: 'O one God, O true God, O chief God, O (God) of one substance'.[210]

In his most 'monarchical' statement, Gregory Nazianzen says: 'In the Three one nature, God. And the Father is the union, from Whom and to Whom the rest converge.' But since the marks of distinction are 'around' nature, the ground of oneness is 'the simple nature and identical being'.[211] The Godhead cannot be identified with the person of the Father, precisely because we have to emphasise the equality and perfection of the Persons. Thus, 'the mind can separate the inseparable, acknowledging each person as Godhead', whereas the Godhead, as their common name, is recognised by the identity of movement and nature.[212] According to Gregory, the 'one', as in 'one God', first and foremost refers to the common. Particularly in the following context the monarchy as a prerogative of the person of the Father is rather dim: 'To us there is one God, for the divinity is One; and all that proceeds from the One is referred to the One, though we believe in Three.' This One is 'undivided in separate Ones'.[213]

The example of the three reciprocally inherent suns, a rather 'anti-monarchical' conception, combined with a reference to the first cause, is indicative of Gregory's all-encompassing train of thought, shared also by Ériugena. For 'there is one mingling of light, as there is one undivided divinity, seen in distinct subsistences.'[214] An anonymous Irish treatise moves on similar lines. 'One Almighty God' is the Holy Trinity, while each Person distinctively 'God Almighty', having everything in common with the other Persons save its unique inexpressible hypostatic property.[215] Considering the name of God, far from any personalist inference, Ériugena refers explicitly to the Greek tradition, which allows him to elaborate on the 'energetic' relationship between the created and the uncreated. The name 'God' is given to the divine essence, the theophanies and the creative 'motion' of the divine nature.[216]

The etymology of the word Godhead (θεότης), Gregory of Nyssa suggests, points to the power of contemplation or beholding; so by this operation, we judge whether the word belongs to one of the Persons or to all of them equally.[217] But Gregory could also adopt 'the view of the majority' and state that the name God represents the common nature (although divine nature is not subject to a signifier), hence it is attributed equally to each of the Persons 'in an absolute and identical manner, without the conjunction *and*'.[218] Most remarkably, the Cappadocian explains that the Father's otherness – His being the Father of the Son – is not the foundation of His being God; for that would subscribe to the ontological deficiency or subjection of the Son. God is not God because He is a person, the Father; 'but because there is a certain essence, of which there is Father and Son, and for which the Father is God and the Son is God and the Holy Spirit is God'.[219]

Gregory firmly argues that oneness and sameness derive from one and the same essence, while at the same time each Person himself bears the whole essence and divinity. Although the distinctiveness makes the threeness, the identity according to nature makes the oneness; and this identity of nature makes the Persons identical. Thus, the name God indicates not a person, but the essence – not in the sense that it reveals the unapproachable 'what' of that unnameable nature, but in the sense that it intimates it through an essential characteristic.[220] His line of argument against the pagans is based on the premise that the name God is not a privative attribute. The words 'God', 'Good', 'Holy', 'Saviour', and all the divine names, are employed in the singular, in accordance with the singular nature.[221] For this reason, fatherhood in the Trinity does not give us the right to call the Father 'God of the Word', unless we refer to the incarnate Word, namely to the economy.[222] It is noticeable that the Cappadocian feels the need to compensate for his 'essentialism' by reaffirming the principle of causality: he counterbalances common essence and causality as the two pillars of the divine being; the former referring to the 'what it is', grounding absolute oneness; the latter indicating the 'how it is', in the differentiation of the unique hypostases.

Gregory Nazianzen preaches that the term 'God' encompasses unity and distinction at the same time, that is, the One and the Three; 'Three from the point of view of properties or hypostases . . . or persons . . . One in respect of the essence or the divinity'. In the three he sees the Godhead; or, 'more precisely, the three are the Godhead'.[223] Having associated the Oneness with the divine essence or divinity, Gregory proceeds to the scriptural scheme describing the divine order in the work of creation and salvation: ἐξ οὖ (from), δι' οὖ (through), ἐν ᾧ (in). 'For to us there is One God, the Father, of Whom are all things, and One Lord Jesus Christ, by Whom are all things and One Holy Ghost, in Whom are all things.'[224] He explains that the above prepositional phrases 'denote the properties of a nature which is one and unconfused. And this is evident from the fact that they are again gathered into one'. Thus, it is plain that the term God cannot be ultimately attributed to the Father except only as a *terminus technicus* corresponding to the hypostatic names.

Likewise, we observe that the order of the appellations of the Persons is not unchanged, says Gregory, with a view to gainsaying the idea of inequality. First, the facts themselves do not depend upon the order of their signifiers. Even so, as the same things are counted in Scripture at an earlier or a later stage, 'the same goes for the names *God* and *Lord*, and for the prepositions *of whom*, and *by whom*, and *in whom*, by which you describe the Deity according to the rules of rhetoric, attributing the first to the Father, the second to the Son, and the third to the Holy Spirit. Yet, these expressions . . . are used of all the persons, as is evident to those who have examined the question.'[225] Our teacher is Paul, he says elsewhere, who sometimes 'counts up the Three Persons, and that in varied order, not keeping the same order, but reckoning one and the same Person now first, now second, now third; and for what purpose? Why, to show the equality of nature . . . and at times he separates the Persons saying, "One God, of whom are all things, and we in Him; and one Lord Jesus Christ, by whom are all things, and we by Him"; at other times he brings together the one Godhead, "For of Him and through Him and in Him are all things."'[226] In this passage Gregory offers the necessary qualifier. We can speak about God's being in a twofold way: from the viewpoint of distinction, where the name God is used of the Father, and from the viewpoint of unity, where all the hypostases are 'brought together' in the common divinity and essence. To employ the terminology of the Areopagite, all names are ascribed totally to God in His entirety, except the non-interchangeable attributes that specify the Persons.[227]

Again, John of Damascus lucidly and creatively sums up the previous tradition. He espouses the etymological interpretation of the name 'God' as describing the activity either of 'running' (because He courses through all things), or of 'burning up' (as fire consuming all evils), or of 'beholding' (for He is all-seeing).[228] Quoting or rephrasing the Cappadocians, after having referred to the one cause, he gives the image of the 'three suns cleaving to each other without separation and giving out light mingled and conjoined into one'.[229] He is also quite clear in his distinction between the natural and the personal notes of character.

> The name God is applicable to each of the persons, but we cannot use the term Godhead with reference to person ... For Godhead implies nature, while Father implies subsistence just as Humanity implies nature, and Peter subsistence. But God indicates the common element of the nature, and is applicable derivatively to each of the hypostases, just as man is.[230]

Furthermore, as mentioned above, there is a substantial difference between the created and the uncreated regarding the cognitive approach to essence–hypostasis distinction. In the case of all created things, the distinction of the hypostasis is observed in actual fact, while community and unity are apprehended by thought. In the case of the uncircumscribed Deity, it is quite the reverse. 'For there the community and unity are observed in fact, through the co-eternity of the hypostases, and through their having the same essence and energy and will and concord of mind, and then being identical in authority and power and goodness – I do not say similar but identical – and then movement by one impulse. For there is one essence, one goodness, one power, one will, one energy, one authority.' And it is by thought that the difference is perceived, in terms of manner of existence. Each one of them is related as closely to the other as to itself. The hypostases dwell in one another according to the word of the Lord, 'I am in the Father, and the Father in Me.'[231] Now, what is the exact meaning of this mutual indwelling or co-inherence of irreducible persons? Is this a kind of loving relationship constituting a social trinity of persons? The answer is implied in the above citation, but we shall wrestle with this question in due course. For at this point we need to discuss further the notions of person and nature in the patristic tradition.

Nature is understood as a complex of properties that together make up the essence of a being; the 'common' that pertains to and substantially unites all beings of the same species, and the whole created reality.[232] Person is identified both with hypostasis, and with *atomon* (individual), which means the undivided entity.[233] Hypostasis is nature with characteristic properties. And more than that, it is the particular human being, who is distinct from other human beings.[234] The person should not be identified either with relations or with the mode of being. The appellations are indicative of mutual relationship and of the mode of being, so one can speak of the *habitus* (condition) or *relatio* between the persons, whereas each person is perceived *per se*.[235] It is characterised and distinguished from other hypostases by a conflux of attributes, qualifications that differentiate from the common and general mine: origin, matrix of relations, personal history, external form, feelings, beliefs, memories, particular talents. It is the unique fusion of these properties – not in themselves unique – that makes for personal otherness.[236] In psychological terms, the person possesses interiority, conscious and unconscious, a most complicated web of internal and external relationships; all that makes it a unique entity. With regard to its connection with *physis*, Gregory of Nyssa explains that there is no a-personal essence beyond its hypostatic manifestations: When one says 'Paul', one sets forth, by what is indicated by the name, the nature subsisting ('hypostasised'),[237] although the latter verb should not be understood in the sense of 'being made' or 'originated' but in the sense of 'being circumscribed' or 'being manifested as subsisting'.

More simply, Paul shows that human nature particularly subsists. But the continuity of nature is never rent asunder by the distinction of the hypostases.

In the trinitarian context one may discern more clearly a special dimension of the person. 'What is from the essence of the Father', says Athanasius of Alexandria, 'and proper to Him, is entirely the Son; for it is identical to say that God is wholly participated [by the Son] and that He begets [the Son]'.[238] And for Gregory the appellation Son indicates His identity with the Father in respect of essence. The appellations make known a genuine and intimate relation, and this relation is the identity of nature between Him that is begotten and Him that begets. Thus, the Persons' 'essential relationship to each other, expressed by those names, indicates that nature', and this is the meaning of the words 'I and my Father are one.'[239] So, as has already been said, the person totally participates of the essence, and, conversely, otherness is contemplated in the identity of nature.[240]

In the theological ideas of exclusively person-oriented thinkers personhood is the ultimate ontological category and constitutes the whole being. Unquestionably, 'person' is a relational term, and the very term 'Father' implies the same inherently relational character. As mentioned above, while the word 'God' signifies nature, the word 'Father' signifies essential relationship with his Son.[241] This seems to show that even the divinity of the Father is not independent of his relationship to his Son. But however assuaging is this appreciation of the element of mutuality', it hardly seems to match the insistence on ascribing the very being of God to the personal will of the Father, which, accordingly, constitutes an internal asymmetrical relationship. The Father is allegedly the One who constitutes the other Persons, even though He is also conditioned as Father through His eternal relationship with them. After all, essence itself is somehow repressed to a derivative level and subsidiary function, inasmuch as it derives from the 'personal' will and freedom of the Father.[242]

Contradicting the thesis that derives from a specific understanding of the 'cause', another model, the social trinitarian model, emphasises the reciprocal relations of the equal Persons, relations constituted by the force and bond of mutual love. Yet, both models tend to ignore or lower the significance and function of divine nature. In the first case, the person of the Father is considered to be the one God and the principle of unity; in the second case, the principle of unity is a personal relationship, and the Trinity is perceived in the image of a confederation. In the first instance, the divine being is identified with the person of the Father, who is God's mode of existence as love. In the second instance, the depth of love is seen in the mutual co-operation of the Persons as separate centres of action, and the unity can only be understood as the wonderful product of the free wills of the Persons themselves. The divine mystery itself is defined as communion, the latter providing 'the hermeneutical criterion of all that has existence'.[243] This approach is undoubtedly appealing and maybe useful for an ethic of mutuality. But as it has been rightly observed, however attractive the idea of analogical continuity between the Trinity and human relationships may seem, a far-fetched connection remains improper due to the utterly dissimilar realities of the created and the uncreated.[244]

iv. *Perichoresis* and essential unity

To be is to be in communion, since God *is* a Trinity of Persons, and this appears to accord with the views of the Church Fathers. But, as we will see, communion within the Trinity has different connotations in modern and post-modern interpretations and expositions of the Christian mystery. When the Fathers pondered over the mystery of union and distinction within the Godhead, apart from the relations of the Persons in terms of origination, they introduced the concept of *perichoresis* (interpenetration, co-inherence or mutual indwelling), the biblical bedrock being Christ's witness: 'I in the Father, and the Father in me' (John 10:38). That means that 'all three, without forfeiture or mutual dissolution of independence, reciprocally interpenetrate each other and inexist in one another'.[245] In the words of John of Damascus, the Persons 'are made one not so as to commingle, but so as to cleave to each other, and they have their being in each other without any coalescence or commingling'.[246]

Perichoresis, involving each Person as a centre of action internal to the other Persons, is sometimes considered to be an *alternative* to divine nature as the source of unity. This is suggested for ecclesiological reasons, since the common essence is falsely taken to represent the universal Church as the point of reference for the local Churches – obviously with underlying demands of universal jurisdiction. That is why Miroslav Volf insists that 'the unity of the triune God is grounded neither in the numerically identical substance nor in the accidental intentions of the persons, but rather in their mutually interior being'. Thus by the power of love the Persons constitute themselves in their unique and complete union.[247] Yet, the same scholar seems to separate by force person from nature when he questions the compatibility of the ideas of *perichoresis* and co-essentiality. He fears that with the premise of the identical substance the only content of divine Persons consists in their relations of origin, in which case co-inherence of Persons would mean the blurring of the personal properties. He even criticises John of Damascus for coupling the two ideas, *perichoresis* and co-essentiality, since John asserts that God is one with regard to the *homoousion* and mutual indwelling of the hypostases.[248]

We are invited to understand 'person' – indeed, reality itself – only as *schesis* (relation): as *schesis* which is constitutive of a particular being and in which or by virtue of which natures are such a particular being – or beings – and thus exist at all.[249] In this statement an Augustinian conception appears on the scene; for according to Augustine the person is relation and the divine names either refer to essence or are relations.[250] Now, the modern personalist view steals a march on Augustine's tentativeness, for it sets the essence aside and makes the person an ontological category. As for the Greek Fathers, they do not appear to assume that the Persons are identical with relations of origin, nor that *perichoresis* expresses simply personal relations. According to Maximus, the name of the Father 'says how the Father is towards the Son and how the Son is towards the Father'.[251] It is clear that the names Father and Son are indicative of a relationship, which is not to be identified with the Persons themselves. Nor is the person identified with the mode of existence, which is denoted by the hypostatic attributes 'begotten' and 'unbegotten'.[252] As we have already seen, the Persons remain no less incomprehensible and unknown than the divine essence.

Christ's proclamation 'I am in the Father, and the Father in Me' remains the most plain and vivid expression of unity or oneness, where 'the One in His entirety is in the Other in His entirety', the One not superabounding or being deficient in the Other.[253] But what do we mean by saying that the Persons are receptive and able to mutually contain one another? What is this uncreated *locus* that both totally occupies and is totally occupied by the Father and the Son and the Spirit in their distinctive perfection? How do Persons 'contain one another', since there is not a vacuum in the container to be filled, and by no means does the container fill the contained? First, one must exclude the case of a hypostasis *within* another hypostasis, since the hypostatic properties are incommunicable.[254] Gregory offers a powerful and balanced example from the psychological reality by likening *perichoresis* to the simultaneous existence of two or more disciplines in the human soul, where they can cohabit without mutual constraints, but rather in a mutual coexistence; in the same way the Father and the Son fill the same place, differing only in appellation and hypostasis and indwelling in each other. 'Like the fragrance of myrrh, the sunlight or the winds – though all created paradigms are exceeded by the divine nature – you will find the distinct to be one in essence and consonance, and the one to form Father and Son as hypostases and appellations.'[255]

The chapter of John of Damascus challenged by M. Volf implies the mutual indwelling as essential quality, and that is why *perichoresis* is ranked with all the common attributes:

Owing to the three subsistences, there is no compoundness or confusion: while, owing to their having the same essence and dwelling in one another, and being the same in will, and energy, and power, and authority, and movement, so to speak, we recognize the indivisibility and the unity of God.[256]

It seems that in the mind of St John – as well as his predecessors – the two ideas are overlapping and concentric. He considers the subject from its two angles, from the point of view of person and from that of essence, knowing that the removal of the one would imperil the reality of the other. Thus, in respect of essential oneness, he employs a combined function of two 'grammars'. This is not to say that language substitutes reality, but that different semantic images can furnish the same polychromatic reality. Particularly interesting is the rephrasing of *perichoresis* offered by John: 'For each one of them is related as closely to the other as to itself.'[257] The meaning of the term is qualified by the fact that in the uncircumscribed Deity the mind 'recognises no void interval wherein it may travel between Father, Son, and Holy Spirit . . . neither is there any vacuum of interval, void of subsistence, which can make a break in the mutual harmony of the divine essence'.[258]

According to the Greek Fathers, the communion between the Persons, or their mutual indwelling, lies in the perfect and total communion of nature. The scriptural notion of *perichoresis* implies the identity of the essential energies, 'mind', power and the essence itself as expressed in the words of Christ, 'I and the Father are one'. By this 'union' and the statement of a mutual and total indwelling of him and his Father Christ asserts the identity of divinity and the unity of essence.[259] Such co-inherence of the Persons does not signify 'a relational unity', a concord of will, opinion and love between personal entities , but the absolutely indistinguishable essence and nature.[260] As Maximus the Confessor confirms, it is the divine nature that in its unmovable stillness seems to be moving eternally in the indwelling of one another.[261] At the same time the concrete reality of the hypostases is safeguarded by the difference of the appellations.[262] Thus, *perichoresis* in Godhead is the common divinity, which the Persons totally share in an undivided way; for each Person is entirely within the others, because there is one and the same essence, power and activity of the Father and Son and Holy Spirit. And this is precisely the vision of God granted to the saints: in the Spirit they see Christ, and in Christ they see the Father (John 14:9), and this is what makes them so reluctant to represent the Trinity in images.

As for the so passionately defended 'will' of the Father, it is not a personal attribute prior to, or exempted from, such natural *perichoresis*. On the contrary, it is the natural outcome of co-essentiality. The Father's will is not something *followed* by the Son's will (let alone the Son's generation), for it is the very same will of the Son, the very same 'good pleasure' (εὐδοκία) wherewith the Persons are the objects of one another's pleasure and honour. Even God's 'creative will', though operated by the Persons, is 'the outcome of the essence beyond creation'.[263] God's will is not produced by a person, who thus expresses his absolute freedom, but it adheres to the utterly free divine essence; and by virtue of that connection 'is beheld as like and equal, or rather the same, in the Father as in the Son'.[264]

The indissoluble and continuous communion of the Persons is not simply that which emerges from causality or any vague idea of indwelling of independent centres of consciousness. The Greek word κοινωνία (*koinonia*) is frequently skewed to represent a 'community' of persons. However, to be in communion means to share in a common essence, otherwise persons are incommunicable *qua* persons. Should persons be in communion at the level of personhood, they are confused, and the Father is the Son and the Son is the Father. One should not be misled by the interaction between corporeal identities. As Gregory remarks, in the case of a spiritual nature, the term 'connection', with reference to persons, signifies the union and blending of what is spiritual with what is spiritual through identity of will.[265]

Even the hypostatic origination means total participation in the same essence and all its properties. The Logos is one with the Father because He is generated from the Father's essence. Likewise, the Spirit proceeds from the Father's essential depth.[266] On the other hand, as the element of its proper distinction is its 'procession' from the Father, the phrase 'Spirit of Christ' is to be understood not in terms of hypostatic origination, nor simply in terms of economy, but as an intimation of essential affinity.[267] Such uncreated affinity is meant by the 'conjunction' between the Father and the Son, the Son and the Spirit, a conjunction without interval of time or space.[268]

The key principle for the above is that the divine will and energies are essential qualities, and they are not derived from the individual existence or the Persons in 'relation'.[269] God's will resides 'in the spontaneity [ἐξουσία] of the divine nature' and the ontological reality behind God's properties are the activities, the power and the essence.[270] Thus, there is no coincidence between three centres of action or three wills in co-operation, but one essential will, power, and energy operating *ad extra ex patrem per filium in spiritu*. In created hypostases one may see distinct wills in spatial and temporal distance. But in the Trinity communion and unity is considered *in reality*, because of the sameness of essence, will, energy and the one thrust of movement.[271] In fact, the idea of *perichoresis* is complementary not to the idea of consubstantiality but rather to the concept of monarchy, so that it can be seen as the monarchy of the Three.

The Son is totally in the Father according to essence, because He is wholly God by nature.[272] Therefore, the one nature should be evaluated as the buttress of perfectness and uniqueness of the Persons in their co-inherence. Essence, on either the uncreated or the created level, is not an abstract universal but an immanent principle of community.[273] That is why Gregory of Nyssa argues – and one should not hesitate to repeat his argument – that only persons who share a single nature maintain authentic otherness, having their being in each other without coalescence or commingling: 'In the communion of the essence we maintain that there is no mutual approach or intercommunion of those properties perceived in the Trinity, whereby the proper particularity of the persons is set forth.'[274]

When we relate *perichoresis* to love and advocate an ontology of love as replacing the ontology of essence, we give rise to some confusion. If we speak in terms of relationality, 'loving and being loved' above and beyond the essential ground of oneness, either we ontologise love and person or we refer to a moral, volitional relationship between the Persons, something that echoes views championed by Arius. Any love–essence dialectic, in particular the arbitrary identification of the Person of the Father with freedom and love, means that freedom and love are absolute predicates of the person. In this case – if love is a privative property or a 'mode of existence' – the Persons in the Trinity would somehow communicate not according to nature, but through their distinct properties of freedom, love and, indeed, individual will. As Cyril of Alexandria concludes, this is a 'kind of relational and not natural union . . . the manner of the union being to love and to be loved'.[275] It is a sort of solidarity soothing a nature split into persons, which have appropriated and proudly possess this nature. This might be regarded as impressive, yet the Fathers would espouse neither the inference nor the premise.

Three:

Person and Grace

1. *Chasing* Ekstasis

In the mystery of mutual indwelling, we perceive the total and perfect communion of nature. But there is a problem with nature in the mindset of radical and romantic personalism, the formulations of which are characterised by indicators of severance. In these oppositional terms nature lies in, or rather forms, the dark, injurious, tragic, godless reality, a reality that cannot be transformed. It is discredited as it is more or less identified with the Fall and all that that implies. On the other side, high up in the clouds, stands the authentic person, far and above any reality of sin, identified with love, freedom, grace, and being itself. And, obviously, there is only one way for someone to reach it: by escaping from one's dark mother.[1]

Now, what is the case concerning God's nature? In the personalist outlook, the divine essence inevitably maintains an unspecified, subsidiary role in the being and life of God. The divine Person transcends its very nature, thus proposing the way and the mode of being an authentic person. Because nature is coupled with necessity, as it imposes certain irreversible laws and insuperable limits, it must by definition impart the burden of a tragic existence. Fortunately, Zizioulas argues, 'When we say that God *is*, we do not bind the personal freedom of God – the being of God is not an ontological "necessity" or a simple "reality", but we ascribe the being of God to His personal freedom. God as Father, and not as substance, perpetually confirms through "being" his free will to exist', thus proving the divine being to be unconditioned by any necessity of existence.[2] Accordingly, communion is a product of freedom as a result of a person, the Father. Communion and essence come from His free choice.[3] This is the ecstatic character of personhood – a version of the Heideggerian *ekstasis* – an escape and liberation from the confines of an impersonal nature to constitute the very being as communion.

The consequence is all the clearer in Christology. Christ Himself, according to the personalistic interpretation, is supposedly above His natural qualities.[4] Confined in dialectical dichotomies, such interpretation overstates the 'free person' of the Logos, seriously degrading the mystery of the union of God and Man, that is of the uncreated and created natures in Christ. This tends to disarm the fervently advocated patristic notion of the *communicatio idiomatum*, namely the community of natural attributes by virtue of the interpenetration of the two perfect natures in Christ incarnate. *Communicatio idiomatum* is neither a metaphysical concept nor a useful theological device, but the very core of the mystery of salvation/deification in Christ: Christ acts uniquely in both of His two perfect natures; He acts as God by nature and as man by nature, simultaneously and inseparably. The exchange of the natural properties designates the ineffable, unconfused union of divinity and humanity, the inflowing of the deifying fire which effects the deification of the created nature.[5]

From another point of view, if one attributes Christ's will to His person, so as to safeguard His 'freedom', then one must recognise one will and one single energy in Christ, and not the union of two natural wills and energies, corresponding to the double nature of Christ. Thus, all orthodoxy falls into the most rigid monophysitism. In strident contradiction, the Fathers, as we have already seen, associate what is common with nature or essence, leaving the unique and incommunicable properties to the hypostases. Accordingly, on the trinitarian plane, as John of Damascus argues, 'If the will . . . is hypostatic, the Son must thus forsooth have a different will from what the Father has: for that which is hypostatic is characteristic of the person only.'[6]

Now, let us turn to the patristic approach to nature. The concept of nature is a keystone in the spirituality of the Greek East as well as of the Irish West. The Fathers never accepted an ontological association of nature with necessity. We see that Gregory of Nazianzus does not hesitate to say that it is absolutely impossible and inadmissible for God *not* to exist; clearly he does not see in this assertion any limitation of God's absolute freedom.[7] A personal will is not the cause either of divine essence or persons or activities, says Cyril of Alexandria, and this does not at all introduce a necessity to the uncreated being; for God exists apart from anybody's will, including His own.[8]

Whenever we say that the Trinity is love and light and justice and goodness, we know that we refer to essential characteristics of God. In this sense we would not be far from the truth in saying that God's energy, His active presence in creation and history, is determined by His nature, which nonetheless is not an object of enquiry. God is good according to nature and Creator according to nature and God according to nature, and yet all these things that 'belong to' and 'define' His nature do not subject Him to necessity.[9] Although His essential attributes (goodness, benevolence, holiness) are not products of His will, they are far from being unwilled.[10] Thus, nature/essence 'moves voluntarily and sovereignly' through its energies, which are not external but the very 'movement of nature', or else 'God-in-activity'.[11] If all divine energies are ascribed to the common divine essence, will and freedom should also be perceived as the common trinitarian life. This nature is supra-essential; it neither precedes nor succeeds being or Persons. Accordingly, God's ontological freedom is not freedom from His own nature; God's freedom means that God is the sole self-subsisting and reigning uncreated reality, which is the fundamental law and principle of everything else – of all that belongs to the category of created nature.[12]

Now, what is the case with created being? Here again, the personalist says that real humanity is 'hypostatic' in being 'ekstatic', that is, free from its natural garb. Freedom is not identified as conformity with nature but in contrast with it.[13] Human nature *per se* is considered as separated from God. Yet, such an assumption can hardly be corroborated by patristic testimony. In the created order, our experience is that intelligible nature is capable of good as well as the reverse. Its position on the 'borderline' has the meaning of the liberty of choice,[14] beyond any necessity, and beyond any ontological inclination towards the abyss from which it emerged. Many terms, more or less synonymous, have been employed to render this mystery of freedom: προαίρεσις, αὐτεξούσιον, ἐλευθερία, ἐξουσία, θέλημα.[15] In its pre-lapsarian state, as natural will or the noetic appetite of the soul, it was directed towards God.[16] This is a power belonging to nature and being used by the person. The nature of man – possessing its perfection by virtue of its proper principle[17] – was created to share in the divine light and glory and any other quality observed in the divine nature, including eternal existence as its inherent faculty. And this has been shown in the comprehensive utterance of one phrase: that man was made *in the image of God*. This image and likeness is 'a summary of all things that characterize Deity':

> For as the eye, by virtue of the bright ray which is by nature wrapped up in it, is in fellowship with the light, and by its innate capacity draws to itself that which is akin to it, so was it needful that a certain affinity with the Divine should be mingled with the nature of man, in order that by means of this correspondence it might aim at that which was native to it.[18]

Ériugena follows the same lines when he says that the trinity of human nature (falling under the ontological terms of essence, power and activity) expresses in itself the image and likeness of the creative Trinity.[19] One finds it hardly justifiable to agree that the notion of the image of God 'cannot relate to nature . . . but to personhood'.[20]

On this point the personalist invokes John of Damascus for support. According to the sage of Damascus, the human being differs from non-rational beings by 'leading nature rather than being led by it', whereas the animals are subject to necessity.[21] Yet, reading the chapters on the physiology of the human being, from which the foregoing citation is taken, we see something different. St John's exposition includes the term 'nature' both in its broader sense, as the essential ground of humanity and all beings, and in its narrow sense, as the specific laws that circumscribe the bodily aspect as well as the unintelligible (passive and appetitive) part of the soul. It is in this narrow sense that the human being is called to lead nature and not to be led by it. But man is created with 'nature visible and invisible', namely with a body and an intelligible and noetic soul, the latter being identified par excellence with the divine image, where freedom springs and blossoms. 'For the phrase "after His image" clearly refers to the noetic character and free will, whereas "after His likeness" means likeness in virtue so far as that is possible for human nature.'[22] It is the soul (mind being its purest part) that 'enjoys freedom and volition and energy'; and all these natural qualities 'it has received of the grace of the Creator, of which grace it has received both its being and this particular kind of nature'.[23] And, as Maximus says, the soul – being the very image of God and deified by means of the power of love – takes care of the body and acquaints it with God, 'itself mediating to the body the indwelling presence of its Creator'.[24]

The movement of the soul is spontaneous, precisely as nature is spontaneous, Athanasius asserts.[25] And Maximus, citing a fragment from Clement, remarks that 'will is a natural power, which desires what is in accordance with nature . . . a natural appetite, corresponding with the nature of the rational creature . . . a natural spontaneous movement of the self-determining mind.'[26] That is why we can state that 'the nature of logical beings is not bound to necessity'; for '*according to nature* the intelligible part of the soul rules over that which is void of reason'.[27] Given that the nature of the human being always remains incomprehensible, one may wonder how free will has to be excluded from such mystery. John of Damascus concludes:

> The will is natural, and we hold not that it is dominated by necessity, but that it is free. . . . For it is not only the divine and uncreated nature that is free from the bonds of necessity, but also the intellectual and created nature. And this is manifest: for God, being by nature good and being by nature the Creator and by nature God, is not all this of necessity. For who is there to introduce this necessity?[28]

Gregory of Nyssa juxtaposes the conspicuous contradiction of the original state 'that it was good' (Gen. 1:31) with the 'present condition of things', whose external observation induces attacks against human nature. Still, nothing abnormal in this present condition, no ugliness or imperfection, no tendency to misery, no evil manifestation, seems to divert the Fathers' acute sight from that royal origin and perspective. The Creator 'incorporated in human nature the principles of all that is excellent', including the gift of free will. 'For if necessity in any way was the master of the life of man, the "image" would have been falsified in that particular part, by being estranged owing to this unlikeness to its archetype. For how can that nature which is under a yoke and bondage to any kind of necessity be called an image of the reigning nature?'[29] Nature possesses, as a precious endowment, the self-ruling and independent principle, and this is what enables the participation of good.

And yet, if this be so, how is evil engendered from within, springing up in the will? Here is the rub. Nature, 'inasmuch as the subsistence itself of creation had its rise in change',[30] carried the potentiality of returning to the logical opposite of goodness, namely to the state of non-being, from which it was called. But to close the eyes to the sun lies not in the eye's specification, intrinsic quality or essential entelechy. Evil has its origin in activity on our part that opposes nature. Thus, the ancestral man 'on his creation', but certainly not *because* of his created state, 'through an initial movement' perverted natural longing and began to experience life in a way that is contrary to nature. The fall of everything was a result of personal, deliberative will, or rather a co-operation of personal wills, that of the fiend 'craftily mixing up badness in man's will' and that of the human person. Nature's fall followed on from the person's sin.[31] The personal use of natural power can either urge towards the divine model, or provoke evil, which is a deprivation of natural energy. The person can use all natural capacities against its very nature. And the cause of such a vicious cycle should be traced not in the perfect natural will, but in the 'gnomic' will, a kind of weakened, autonomous, self-directed will, the expression of the egocentric individual, which stems ultimately from an impetuous desire for divinisation without God.

Hence, nature is subject to a double reading: as either the implacable power to whose alleged laws (or 'lusty stealth') man's corrupt purpose and inventions are bound; or conversely, as the mother whose 'offices' are blessed and fruitful, but who is scourged by the effects of personal malice. In the first case nature is used in the sense of each one's nature – that is to say, the person, whose idiosyncrasy perceives, appropriates and uses what is universal. Such abuse is what puzzles Shakespeare's King Lear, who wonders in agony if there is any cause in nature that makes a hard heart! No doubt, he would agree with Maximus the Confessor that human nature is bound to sin and decay only because of the personal *gnome* – the use (or rather misuse) of free choice.[32] In the long run such abuse of the inner powerhouse fabricates a 'second', false nature that counterfeits and violates the authentic one. Therefore, if there is something that imposes necessity to human nature and the human person, this is the passions – parasitic weeds spawned in the hotbed of the gnomic will. On this account, when the spiritual man 'separates what is natural from what is opposed to nature', he 'surpasses that power which endeavours to subject freedom to slavery'. But the Creator 'never subjected mankind to the yoke of a strong compulsion'.[33]

Furthermore, in the cosmic dimension there is a kind of deep affiliation of the whole of creation – the subservient nature – to the uncreated nature. This is due to uncreated grace pervading every created being and sustaining its very existence in an unending creative activity. This grace – this grandeur with which the world is charged – is imprinted on every essence. Nothing is 'without its portion of divine fellowship . . . the lower nature being mingled with the supramundane'.[34] This is a field where Irish theology offers its best. For the Irish this natural world, with all its personal and impersonal entities in their very concreteness and reality, is not only the locus of the benign power of God but is also empowered by this life-giving grace. Therefore, when the Irish invoke the natural elements in their poetry for protection or praise, it is because they recognise within them the all-encompassing divine energy.[35] There are two ways of expressing this reality, both of which are to be found in Irish and Greek exegesis. The first, and closer to the 'Celtic' mentality, is the scriptural statement that the life of everything is the uncreated life that was in Christ before all ages, according to the Johannine phrasing 'Quod factum est in ipso vita erat' (John 1:3–4). As the Irish catechist asserts:

> Neither heaven, nor earth and all that are in them . . . dwells in itself but rather in Him, that is, in God . . . The life of whatever has been created is in Him; . . . Thus, the creature always remains in the Creator . . . For before they were created, they were life in Him, and that life was not created but is itself Creator . . . because the Word is God, then, the life which is in Him is God, and in that life is the light of men and women.[36]

It is fascinating that the anonymous catechist insists particularly on the uncreated nature of life that is 'within' God (i.e. not identified with essence or person) and at the same time God and Creator, which becomes the very life of beings in perpetuity. This is the 'one single life penetrating all things in a manner that meets each one's premises and capacity of participation', according to the Greek Fathers.[37] But the Greek mind is more philosophical. It proceeds to a second expression of God's immanence in creation, which is the omnipresence of Christ as the *logos* of everything. The term *logos* – a borrowing from Greek philosophy – was first applied to Christ in St John's Gospel, possibly because it bears a wide range of connotations: word, utterance, immanent rationality, meaning, and principle with teleological nuances. It thus became a term intrinsically connecting the divine Word with the quintessence of every particle of creation. Every being carries the *logos* of its essence – an act of will instituting the natural condition, in accordance with which a creature participates in being – which is contained, from all eternity, in the divine *Logos*. Everything is within Him and He is the One in all the *logoi* together, and the *telos* (the ultimate purpose) of everything. The Logos, who was incarnated in the last times, is an ineffable, supernatural and divine fire present, as in the burning bush, in the being of everything that exists. He is immanent as incarnated through the *logoi* and as participated through 'a greater measure of the divine activity'.[38]

This Christological dimension has a pneumatological corollary: this indwelling life of creation is the Holy Spirit, says Maximus. Or, more precisely, 'the Holy Spirit vivifies or activates the inner *logoi* of all things in accordance with their nature'; what he later calls 'the natural seeds'.[39] And this is why creation functions as a pointer to God. Through the natural activity of created beings we discern the power that gives created beings their life, and God's presence is clearly proclaimed.[40] In the Irish mentality, nature, as the whole created reality, blesses God in its inescapable return to Him; and along with God it is the sole teacher of the human being.[41]

Among the Irish, the absorbent and eclectic mind of Ériugena, drawing on both Eastern and Western streams, and expanding the affirmation that 'the divinity beyond being is the being of all',[42] holds that every thing exists as a 'creative word', conceived within the Word above time and space. Christ, 'the divine ray . . . is beautifully multiplied' and 'diffused' into beings, so that they may subsist and return to their source. He is in a deep and real sense 'the light and life of all things', for no essence or substance exists or can be contemplated but within Him.[43] Ériugena follows the common Irish stream, where Christ is the only life of all things; as Logos, without diminution He sustains and penetrates every creature, which is 'life in life', so that 'the wood and the stone are alive in God'.[44] Accordingly, for Columbanus, 'the Trinity fills heaven and earth and every creature',[45] not simply figuratively or in an extrinsic manner: Trinity embraces all things from within. Its uncreated activity or will becomes the being of all created being, so deeply and truly, that the divine nature is also considered to create itself in the creature, as the Logos is born in human beings.[46] In this sense, all creatures are 'theophanies', says Ériugena, citing Romans 1:20, although not equally.[47] All the same, as the Greek Fathers conclude, the divine nature 'touches every being in an equal manner, keeping everything within it through the all-encompassing power', 'permeates all . . . illumines land and sea and mingles with the air', and 'the healthy mind believes that God fills everything', as the soul pervades all the members of the body, interior and exterior.[48]

Thus, even in its post-lapsarian condition, nature is at work in man, because it has an actual participation in God's being. The human being is part of it, it is expecting its salvation with the human being, the moment when it will glow with the fire of Divinity – a gift already given through Christ's salvific economy.[49] Then, creation and salvation are blended in divine unified activity. A thorough reading of Maximus' Christological insights shows that 'if creation as well is due to grace, then salvation must consist in a kind of enhancement of the original grace' and that 'every divine act in relation to the cosmos has the mystery of Christ in view. This means that the created status and the redeemed status are not to be separated into two unrelated dimensions.'[50]

On this account the Greek Fathers insist on the naturalness of spiritual life. The notion of *physis*, in its potential and in its destiny, has been indicated as a key to Basilian asceticism, according to which God does not demand a moral régime at odds with the essential qualities of beings, even though ascetic effort is needed for these qualities to be brought to light and fruition. So it is by nature that man brings his mind to bear upon the appetites, to channel thoughts and have control over emotions, and no less natural is the capacity for and intensity of love.[51] For in the very nature of the soul God's love and creative will is beheld, since the longing for the noetic image is an essential attribute of the human being.[52] Therefore, the human being's perfection is not a sort of amputation of his nature (involving body, senses, imagination and the other dynamic drives of human existence) through any kind of skilled artistry.[53] That is why in the Byzantine liturgy the supplicant prays not for release from his physical senses, with a view to reaching a state of apathy, but for the liberation of his own physical senses 'from the deadly passions'.[54] Thus, the imitation of divine nature, far from truncating human nature, is a restoration of true human nature.

We see this in the allegory that Maximus finds in Moses' passage through the Red Sea. Moses breaks up the deception caused by the fluidity of the sensible realm and makes visible to the people (and the individual) the 'firm and unshakeable ground beneath their feet', by which he means 'the foundation of nature that is concealed below the level of superficial sensation'.[55] Below the surface lies a pure and stable nature, charged with love, looking towards its destiny and disclosed through ascesis. This natural 'seed' of good is cultivated by the 'spiritual' man 'in a natural movement of ascent and conformity to his own origin and principle'.[56]

What the spiritual life seeks is 'pure nature' dispatched and liberated from the unnatural state of vicious passions.[57] This nature, given by God and filled with His grace, is the content and the ground of the person, and no less reveals the authentic person, insofar as that person follows its nature. That is why, according to the Irish commentator, the 'conversion' of a human being to himself in the act of repentance and self-awareness is equivalent to conversion to the goodness of nature. The exhortation 'go to your home' means 'go to your good nature', which is the goldmine whence free choice, ascesis, prudence and wisdom are drawn.[58] Therefore, if we wish to surmount the *logos* of being – namely its measure and condition of existence – in an illusory flight of ecstatic transcendence from nature to a 'relational ontology', we simply become irrational and we lead existence to its fall.[59] On the contrary, if a being moves according to its logos, which exists in and with God, it comes to be in God.[60] Man's salvation is not a salvation *from* nature, but the salvation *of* nature, whether insensible and intelligible. For the human being – as the index of a great volume – recapitulates in it the whole of creation.

Thus, it would be inappropriate to present the authentic person as a transcendental ontological category, realised in the very act of transcending nature. This is quite clear in the patristic approach to the Triune Divinity, where, while the person is a relational entity, *schesis* (relation), signified by the very names of the divine hypostases (the Son's eternal relationship to the Father), indicates the essential conjunction.[61] Let us consider the most essential quality of the Trinity, Love itself, which finds its supreme theological expression in John 14:20, where the Son is said to be in the Father and in us, and we in Him. Love points to the divine Persons' natural oneness, and we could not make of it a personal property, i.e. the love/freedom identified with the person of the Father. In the same vein, the Spirit cannot be called love hypostatically, but love is its essential energy.[62] A kind of love that originates from the particular person, or, being identified with personhood, precedes nature, would just create, invent or fabricate no more and nothing deeper than defective asymmetrical relations, an external unity of relational entities. On the contrary, for the Greek Fathers, love is a fruit and an expression of essential relationship. That is why the Alexandrian Father says that 'the manner of the union is not defined by the law of love'.[63] God is Love, Light and Life, but these are not hypostatic, but rather the essential energies. The One, Triune God is active and willing and loving. That God is love, explains Maximus, means that God is the originator and emitter of *agape* and *eros* to creation, for these exist within Him.[64] The existence of love and will, as well as their content, is determined by nature,[65] albeit they are personally manifested.

Not the person as such, but nature, is a movement toward communion. And this movement is free, for God's nature is not subject to limitations, and freedom is also an endowment of human nature, since the latter has 'the principle of all excellence' and participates in God's essential properties as His image.[66] Although natural and historical reality is now a determining factor for the human being, the whole of creation is to be transfigured, that is glorified in God's holy fire, whose sparks and warmth is already present and felt. Indeed, within this essential movement the person becomes a universal reality: it bears within itself the whole of human nature, without appropriating it; in other words, it includes all other persons within itself and thus is a unique reflection of them all. But at the same time human nature, in its richness, includes and unites all particular entities, so that we can say that there is One Man. Philosophically speaking, 'the more universal a principle is, the greater the degree to which it embraces and unifies the more particular principles.'[67] Absolute ontological freedom does not properly characterise a transcendental person, but is the grace to be granted eschatologically to the whole of creation. It is not the person, in its transcendentalist sense, but the human being as a whole who is not of this world, by virtue of the uncreated grace sanctifying the entire human nature.[68] The whole of man is to become 'not of this world' (John 15:19) in the sense not of escaping from the world but in the sense of receiving the deifying grace in a unique manner from the uncreated reality.

At the same time the human being is a particularity determined by space and time. This is supposedly Man's tragedy as biological hypostasis, one remains caught in one's individuality as a result of one's specific created constitution.[69] But here a painful question looms: what exactly is the individual – the particular human being – before reaching the state of 'being not of this world'? Is it something deprived of God's spiration? Is it a being ontologically inferior to the 'authentic', 'ecclesial' being? We need to consider that the image of the imperceptible divine essence is engraved on and shines in human nature and in each particular person from their creation – an image that was never extinguished, never turned into a mass of perdition, even in stains of transgression.[70] Also for the Irish commentator, the human being is the royal palace (*aula regia*) of God, containing, as a microcosm, not only the 'light of virtues' but also the 'shades of vices'; that is, before the realisation of one's potential of sanctification to which one is called.[71] This is the reason the Fathers identified the person with the ordinary individual, while speaking of the deification of the whole human being in its entirety and integrity: flesh, intellect, heart, volition, energy and one's whole spectrum of qualities.

As we saw earlier, in the Irish environment the person–nature dialectical approach is nowhere to be found, any kind of ontologisation of the person is entirely unwitnessed, and nature is wholly affirmed as the good work of the Creator, sanctified and glorified through the incarnation of the Logos. Christ is emphatically presented as 'verus homo natura', from the nature of His mother, a man in 'ratione, carne et natura'.[72] Although the 'glowing coal' of human 'good nature' was extinguished by the first-born of this earth, it was illuminated again by the Holy Spirit through the incarnation.[73] Nature is by no means truncated but released from bondage. In the Paschal mystery the eschatological destination of nature is connected with the renovated human nature.[74] That is why the whole of creation expresses empathy for the passion of Christ and rejoices in the resurrection.[75] In his lyrical vein Gregory also portrays the scenery of a cosmic salvation in unity with the risen Christ: nature is illuminated, it exhibits clearer outlines, creatures exploit to the greatest possible degree their natural qualifications and properties; everything – including man – comes back to its state of harmony and liberty. 'The dolphin leaps up blowing in delight' and 'the proud horse, having broken his chains, is swimming in the river'. And from the hymn of creation humans are inspired to offer their own hymn.[76] For the Irish commentator the very event of the incarnation verifies that humanity cannot be saved – we cannot become whole – apart from the *mater terra* that we come from, and apart from the earth of our body. On the contrary, our body is the earth that produces the fruit of sanctity and is wrapped around by the celestial vestment of mysteries.[77] This salvation is the result of the union of Godhead and Manhood in Christ, in whose incarnated hypostasis the interchange of natural properties took place. As God He gave grace, and He received that grace as man and on behalf of all men.[78]

It is true that in our minds freedom and love are immediately connected with the person, while sometimes they do give a sense of transcending or, conversely, being pinioned by natural constraints. The reason is that the person is the agent who has at one's disposal all this innate treasure. But the suspicion lurks that a person who chases its priority as if it were the ultimate source and generator of love and freedom and enjoys their primacy over their own natural ground as a Kantian extra-terrestrial subject, a person who exclusively grants otherness to others or passively receives otherness from them, is in danger either of being lost in a universe of external determination[79] or of being absorbed with a transcendental ego, constituting its own narcissistic reality in self-love and illusory relationships. Is that being not on the threshold of self-deification in the very act of communion, taken up into a theatre of vainglory, ambition and coercion?

2. Deification and Personhood

'The being made God'[80] is the ultimate goal and uncompromising longing of every human being. Every one has been called to become partaker of divine nature, as created 'in the image and likeness' of God. Created nature bears a substratum of deification – the *ad imaginem Dei*[81] – or, according to the Greek expression, the character of the godlike image. This is the potentiality and destiny of human nature, enriched by the abundant divine nature, from which it welcomes not only its very life, but also the qualities of the uncreated, while still on earth. In other words, the human being is invited to become god, according to the divine precept: 'Ego dixi dii estis.'[82] Deification is not just a symbol for man's external – ethical, sentimental or legal – relationship with God. Although it is not always present in the texts as a term, its numerous substitutes express in a polychromic spectrum of descriptions a real union that transcends all and each of them. Participation in God (μετουσία Θεοῦ) emphasises the most 'important aspect of all participation in God's perfections: the presence of God Himself . . . in the participants'.[83]

'The being made God' was fulfilled through God's incarnation.[84] God's being made flesh heals human nature, says the Irish commentator, so that it may contemplate the divine glory.[85] For the True Light 'darted the beam of His Divinity through the whole compound of our nature . . . and so appropriated humanity by means of His own light, and took it up and made it just that thing which He is Himself'.[86] Thus, what is Christ by nature we become by the gracious participation in the energy of the divine nature, by virtue of the hypostatic union of Godhood and Manhood. Christ incarnate restores the laws of truly divine creation and grants nature the supra-natural grace, namely deification. By being united or commingled with the Divinity, His humanity was made divine.[87] For 'as God became partaker of human nature – *contra naturam* – in the same way the human being became partaker of divine nature, against natural laws'.[88]

Nonetheless, deification is not a theme only to be found in the New Testament, signs can be found in the Old Testament tradition of theophanies. For every theophany, rather than merely transmitting a piece of information from above, entails the transformation of the human being. This is also conditioned by the abiding presence of Logos–Christ in creation and His divine activities in history. As Maximus the Confessor says, encapsulating the theological experience of the Greek and the Irish Fathers, the ineffable divine fire, which Moses beheld in the bush, 'is present . . . in the being of every thing that exists. I mean God the Word, who in the last times shone forth from the Bush of the Holy Virgin and spoke to us in the flesh'.[89] In this way creation, history, and ecclesiology are connected; they cohere together in one economy. The personal God, the cosmic Christ, is revealed in the theophanies of the Old Testament, speaking to patriarchs and prophets, visiting them in the form of three men, even 'fighting' with them. He is the fire in the bush, says the Irish Isidore, the 'columna nubis' and the 'columna ignis', the serpent and the 'stone of honey' and the 'heavenly bread distributed to the saints'.[90] The Logos imparts His life – the energies of the Holy Spirit – to every part of creation according to each part's preordained capacities and receptivity.

A question arises as to whether the union of which the scriptures speak is a union of persons, communicated by the divine Persons. Let us follow the personalistic thread: The event of communion with God has no 'natural' or essential dimension; it is an interaction between persons. All issues of human capacity can be determined either at the level of nature or at the level of relationship, that is, of personhood. And the union of man with God is not to be understood in terms of the uncreated divine nature, for that would leave humanity without any hope of attaining the goal. This is possible only at the level of the 'mode of existence', that is, the person.[91] Consequently, if man cannot be God by nature, he can become a person; in other words, he can become God by being an 'authentic' person.

Personhood, Zizioulas opines, is what the Greek Fathers have called *theosis*. The call to deification is the call to transcendental personhood, which is beyond nature. Only the mystery of personhood makes possible man's union with God, while any 'natural' perspective invokes natural reservations. Since *theosis* does not mean participation in the essence of God, it must mean participation in the hypostasis of Christ.[92] Thus, personhood indicates the gift of deification itself, inasmuch as personhood is identified with ontological freedom and is equated with the ecclesial hypostasis, namely the human being reborn, as a person, through baptism and the Eucharist.[93] One cannot help feeling that in this approach something *essential* is missing, leaving the direct communion and assimilation with God unfulfilled. This makes adoption and filiation to be comprehended in a 'modal' way.

According to this tenet, the anthropological significance of the union *in* Christ is in becoming a 'son' of God by transforming one's hypostasis through a relationship identical with that of the Son with His Father. As it is affirmed, 'unlike the notion of *communicatio idiomatum* [i.e. the exchange of properties between the two natures in Christ incarnate], that of hypostatic union aims at giving ontological priority to the person rather than to the natures of Christ.'[94] In Christ 'our hypostases are . . . transfigured, or rather constituted, in the relationship which Christ has with the Father'.[95] Undeniably, in Christ we are transformed into sons of God. Yet, what we draw from the patristic sources as the meaning of the hypostatic union in Christ is not the imprint upon us of 'filiation' as the personal mode of being of the Son in His relation to the Father. Maximus the Confessor does not focus on the special and incommunicable hypostatic property of the Son, his 'filial' relationship to the Father. Rather, he revolves around 'the great mystery' of Jesus' 'physiology': that is, the coming together of the two natures and their energies, the divine properties manifested in the composite hypostasis of Christ, and the exchange of the Divinity and the flesh.[96] In Cyril's trinitarian language, this union of the 'flesh' with the Logos – 'Who is one with the Father in terms of nature' – is the foundation of the mystery of our baptism 'into the holy Trinity Itself'.[97]

In similar fashion, Maximus' Irish adherent confirms that to be a 'son of God' by grace and by adoption means to become a participant of the divine nature.[98] And Christ reveals to all in His human nature 'the secret mysteries of divinity', that divinity which makes Him equal with the Father, and in which we participate.[99] Besides, one needs to safeguard the apophatic stance by presenting the personal properties only as marks of distinction, and by avoiding perforating the mode of relationship between them, for instance that of a 'filial' mode of being, characterised by or even identified with love or obedience.[100] Eventually, one might ask: How does the hypostatic union give priority to the person, if the person/agent performs the activities proper to natures *from* which and *in* which He is constituted, and also carries out a divine dispensation that is originated in the Trinity's essential goodness?

Reflecting on the realism of divine–human communion, one is justified in enquiring whether it is adequate or meaningful to speak of a personal relationship vis-à-vis any other kind of external relationship, either ethical or sacramental. If salvation is described 'as the transformation of being into true personhood *in* the person of Christ',[101] how can we be in the person of Christ as persons? It is clear that the Fathers would reject the concept of hypostasisation of one in the Other, since the hypostatic properties are incommunicable. We are the body of Christ not because He passes into us in His person.[102] A union of two persons contravenes this fundamental premise, and thus any reference to 'union of persons' becomes a vague statement, or an oxymoron.

And then, if the human being is called to a personal relationship with God, and if this communion is effected by the personal God, what really does bring about our union with Christ? And in what sense do we become 'partakers of the divine nature' (2 Peter 1:3–4)? Certainly, we have to exclude participation on the level of natures, for that would invalidate the absolute ontological distinction between the created and the uncreated. Likewise, one should not follow the medieval scholastic line, according to which one participates through the medium of a created grace; the latter points to a merely external and moral mode of communication. The patristic mind rests on a different approach. Christ lives in Paul (Gal. 2:20) not hypostatically, but because He confers upon Paul the abundance of Triadic activity. The mind of Christ comes 'not as essentially and personally passing over into our mind, but rather as illuminating the power of our mind with its own quality and bringing the same energy to it'.[103] Since God's supra-essential being is absolutely transcendent and imparticipable, the only way in which there can be a relationship with creation is through the 'movement' or radiance of the divine essence *ad extra*. For the essence is not static but dynamic and energetic.[104] This natural movement, which becomes the *logos* of every thing, is the multiple and innumerable energies; for the energies, although they need and manifest a personal agent, are ascribed to nature and not to the privative properties.[105] It is through the energies that human beings participate in the divine nature; it is through them that God relates to creation, since to move is to relate, and thus 'grace is in fact a relationship', as Gregory Palamas acknowledges.[106]

Divine energies or activities are not merely created works of God, as Aquinas implies.[107] They are God Himself in some definable way, participated in by creatures, or, put differently, the uncreated Being itself, which becomes the being of beings. Each divine activity – although distinct from the divine essence – signifies God in His indivisibility and absolute simplicity. In this sense God is immanent in every particular thing, without being divided, yet sustaining the diversity of creation and becoming truly all things in all.[108] Divine activity is that which 'returns them [creatures] to its own simplicity'.[109] As Gregory of Nyssa argues in a trinitarian context, it is not an accident 'following' an essence externally, moving between 'cause' and 'effect', while also residing in the result. At the same time, no natural necessity compels the energy to follow the essence.[110] It is God Himself freely operating in all theophanies and through the incarnated Son. Only this uncreated grace wondrously bridges the ontological gap separating God from creation and grants deification, namely God Himself in His activity. This philosophical notion and empirical fact permeates the whole patristic tradition. Although we are unable to participate in either the essence or the hypostases of the Trinity, yet we are able to share in God's nature via its energies, the 'heavenly fire', which always remains in and out of the human being.[111]

A similar perspective in quite dissimilar language appears in Ériugena, who writes under the shadow of Augustine. He employs the concept of primordial principles, the nature *creata et creans*, standing between God and creation, and he insists on its subsistence within the only begotten Word.[112] For Ériugena, however, 'created' does not convey an identical meaning with that of Augustine or, later, of Aquinas.

Rather, it has more affinity with the statement of Maximus about the 'works of God which have no beginning in time, the participated beings, in which participate all beings by grace' (such as goodness, life, immortality, simplicity, infinity), 'such things which are essentially contemplated in regard to Him'.[113] Accordingly, one would say that the 'abyss' of the primordial principles is a real participation of the one Cause, not an effect of it.[114] As the water wells up in the source and then flows forth, so the divine Goodness and Essence and Life through the primordial causes descend in an ineffable way to the universe and then flow back again.[115] This is what we call the 'ineffable motion' and 'manifold power' of the threefold Goodness, His 'providential acts' worked within Himself.[116] There is a power (virtus) logically distinct and inseparable from the superessential unmanifested Essence, like the natural power of the magnet, manifested in ways that can be accommodated by our natural capacity.[117] This activity is manifested in theophanies. Although forms created by Him (Ériugena here wishes to safeguard the absolute transcendence of the super-essential essence in the reality of panentheism/'all-in-God'-ness), still God Himself is revealed in them after a wondrous fashion and the creature takes on the dimensions of creative nature.[118] This is what distances Ériugena from the Augustinian and scholastic interpretation, in which a theophany is simply a vehicle of a message, a reference to God, with no transfigurative power.[119]

Nonetheless, one could insist that it is the person of the Spirit who communicates the love of the Father to us – and there is no mistake in that. But for a better understanding one must recall the teaching of Athanasius that the Spirit is the energy of the Son;[120] not in the sense of being pure energy itself, but with a view to conveying the meaning that creation is 'acted upon' or 'energised' by the Spirit, and that all we receive from God – even the power to will – are energies imparted to us by the Spirit, essential processions mediated through the hypostasis of the Spirit.[121] Undoubtedly, in speaking of communion with God, one speaks of relations with the Persons. It is so, because according to the ancient Fathers (at least before Augustine) and the entire Eastern as well as Irish tradition, Christ is the author and the subject of all theophanies, with whom holy men come 'face to face'.[122] But it is through the transforming divine energy that Christ is manifest to participants. Each divine Person remains inaccessible according to its very hypostasis, being approached only by imparting the uncreated gifts of the Trinity. In the light of the scriptural testimony, as interpreted by Maximus the Confessor, the Word is indeed 'known through the energies'.[123] Notwithstanding Persons as agents, they are united in terms of essence and the essential energies. In the trinitarian context, divine Persons *are* in each other precisely because they totally share common essence and energies, and not in a blending of Persons or simply the sharing of 'personal' love. As we saw earlier, the union of the divine Persons is not simply a power of love – a kind of 'personal' will – but the common essence. But since there is no essential affinity between the created and the uncreated, only the divine energy or grace, which is the essential vivifying procession of God to creation, unites us with God.

God is personal not *in spite of* the operation of the essential energies. One cannot presume that the distinction of essence-energies affords less room for trinitarian thinking; nor that the energies reveal that God exists and nothing more.[124] Maximus the Confessor, examining the proposed ways of approaching God, indicates the way of essence and the way of those around the essence, without any reference to a third way.[125] The same Father refers to the infinite activities as being the transcendent way in which God relates to His creation.[126] And this is a personal contact. For the divine activities – the fire that goes before God, burning up or enlightening – like goodness, philanthropy and meekness, 'characterize God's person',[127] thus demonstrating not the predicates of the divine Persons but the personal character of the encounter between the Trinity and man. At the same time, one sees no personalistic nuance in Maximus' comment on the Gregorian figurative description of God's internal movement.[128] Reflecting on and expanding the meaning of Gregory's saying, Maximus speaks of Divinity as an active and immovable power, which is the cause and the end of everything. Maximus applies his mind to the field of economy, to say that if Divinity moves, it is rather that He pulls creation to Himself, as the word produces art. Immovable in respect of essence, He exists as a *logos* in the created essences and, therefore, He providentially prompts and moves each creature according to its *logos*. In this respect, He 'moves' in producing an inward relationship of love. The immovable Divinity moves as energy in the receptive intellect to teach through this illumination the mystery of the Trinity in the 'perfect monad', which is the one essence, divinity, power and energy.[129] The energies reveal not only that God exists; for they are 'the three-splendoured light', they point to the trinitarian mode of existence and not only to the divine nature. God's essential activities imply the 'that is' and the 'how it is' of God, leaving the nature of the Person(s) in utter silence.[130]

As has been often repeated, the complete union of God and Man was brought to pass in the person of Christ. The concurrence of natures was realised in the hypostasis of Logos. But although hypostasis is the principle of the union, this is not to say that the union is 'personal' as opposed to natural. The very fact of human nature being assumed into union with the divine Logos was the outcome of the divine activity. Natures are in a state of co-penetration through their properties and energies. In Christ, the mystery of the exchange or 'co-inherence' of properties means that Christ's created and subservient nature – as will and energy – operates in a godly mode, while his divine nature – as will and energy – operates by means of created nature, through which it is manifested, thus presenting an indissoluble union of the two, a 'theandric' (godly–human) activity. The declaration 'all became new' means, according to Maximus, that 'all have become one; say that in terms of nature or energy, it is up to you'.[131] Maximus speaks of a concourse of humanity and divinity, 'according to an essential union, namely true and real', through which Christ accepts a composite hypostasis. Christ unites the *logos* of being of human nature with the supra-natural 'how' of divine being, so that 'nature be granted the newness of manners'.[132] John of Damascus recapitulates the views of his predecessors when he says that the Lord's flesh – that is human nature – was endowed with the divine energies by virtue of its thorough union with the Logos, without suffering any fall from its natural marks.[133] Human nature 'suffers' the Divinity and divinity acts through human nature; 'for although we hold that the natures of the Lord permeate one another, yet we know that the permeation springs from the divine nature'.[134] Christ causes human nature to participate in divinity. And this flesh receives deification in Him through His peculiar glories, as the verb 'ἐνεργῶ' indicates in the Christological context.[135]

Therefore, what deifies human nature in Christ's own hypostasis by virtue of humanisation is the fullness of the essential divine activity. This grace, in which we are invited to participate, is not an external supernatural bonus. It is the divine nature 'that penetrates and permeates all things'.[136] It is Divinity itself given 'partly' to a created being.[137] It is the 'uncreated power and divinity' (ἀΐδιος δύναμις καὶ θειότης) that deifies beings under God's providence.[138] The divine mystical activity effects the elevation of the human being above all heavens and his assimilation with God, save the essential identity. Man becomes 'wholly God in soul and body owing to the divine radiance of blessed glory', which irradiates nature and raises it above its natural limits. He becomes wholly God, insofar as the gifts imparted 'pertain essentially to God'.[139]

Deification refers primarily to nature (body and soul), the person being the vehicle of nature and the recipient of this mystery.[140] Union with and in Christ means that in each of us the same concurrence of natural energies takes place by virtue of our communion with the Body and the Spirit of Christ. The hypostatic union of unconfused natures occurred once only and uniquely in the person of Christ. Henceforth our union with Christ occurs on account of our incorporation in his body through the same divine energy effecting our own deification.

This is the meaning of union in the Eucharistic context. Eating the heavenly bread indicates not a reception of a hypostasis within our own hypostasis, but the assimilation in the field of energy through likeness of the prototype.[141] It is the same energy that makes us partakers of this salvific mystery of the body of Christ. It is that very energy that makes Him bread and wine for us and, thus, it cultivates, like rain on a fertile ground, our eternity-conferring association with Him. In the sacraments, light-conferring theophanies take place through the sanctifying activity of the Holy Spirit. Christ's presence in the Holy Gifts, as well as in us, is an 'energetic' presence. Through this energy the Church is the Body of Christ in an ontological sense. The fact that the Irish theologians introduce the '*transfiguratio*' formula in referring to the change of the species in the Eucharist may not be fortuitous; no less relevant and indicative is their preference to speak of the 'transformation' of Christ into bread and wine rather than vice versa.

The event of the Lord's Transfiguration on the top of the mountain witnesses that, if we can confess to a certain degree a direct knowledge of the Logos, this knowledge is granted through the uncreated light emanated from the Lord's presence.[142] In Christ's Transfiguration it was the divine activity that transformed the senses and strengthened the spiritual perception of the three disciples, so that they might have a direct encounter with the divinity hidden and concentrated within Jesus' body, the very divinity that would operate within them. In this trinitarian light one becomes capable of an intimate relationship with His Person, which still remains unknowable in its highest revelation.[143] The Cappadocian is unambiguous in his minimalist description of a relevant experience:

> I went up into the Mount, and drew aside the curtain of the cloud, and entered away from matter and material things, and as far as I could I withdrew within myself. And then when I looked up I scarce saw the back parts of God, although I was sheltered by the rock, the Word that was made flesh for us. And when I looked a little closer I saw, not the first and unmingled nature, known to itself – to the Trinity, I mean; . . . but only that nature which at last even reaches to us . . . the majesty and glory.[144]

This is a reflection of a theophany experienced upon the biblical model of the Lord's Transfiguration. The effulgence at the event of the Transfiguration revealed what had already taken place in the Word incarnate: as if lighting a lamp, He had made His own flesh shine by the light of His own divinity. This event illustrates the fact that in Christ's hypostasis the divine energy has wholly infused human nature; and this energy grants real communion of things distant in respect of essence, like firewood, which blazes not according to its proper natural energy but on account of its participation in the energy of the fire that has been united with the firewood.[145] In the Transfiguration – as in the Eucharist thereafter – the disciples were joined to the glorified body of the Son by having their whole being – both spiritual and corporeal senses – transfigured in the radiation of the divine glory.

The event of the Transfiguration was the realisation of Christ's beatitude, which informs us that to participate means to see.[146] Gregory of Nyssa proceeds to explain that such vision is not merely a sensory perception, an intense sentimental state or a rational meditation. Rather it 'is purity, sanctity, simplicity, and other such luminous reflections of the divine nature, in which God is contemplated'.[147] As we have already seen, virtue, wisdom, goodness, life, love, holiness, beauty, immortality, incorruptibility, infinity, simplicity, are not personal attributes but the essential movement in which persons are revealed; essential energies with no beginning, no end, offered for participation.[148] And everyone's soul is invited to imitate the properties of God's nature, 'the immutable and beneficent of his essence and activity', through the firm and irremovable habit of being in goodness.[149]

Naturally, this is not a mechanistic operation. As already implied, the ever-progressing union with God is the result of theophanies, which raise the responsive recipient to the transcendental realities, bestowing likeness to God on all those who are returning to Him in imitation.[150] The identification of the participating human being with the uncreated God takes place through likeness to the prototype, that is, by the ongoing transformation of the very self, receiving, as much as possible, by grace the qualities of Godliness or the perfections of the divine existence (Phil. 2:5; 1 Cor. 2:16; Rom. 8:29; 2 Cor. 3:18; Phil. 3:21): deification is given to those who deserve it, for it is the identity of energy through likeness.[151] Yet, it is God who becomes embodied in man's spiritual life. It is the divine Logos who is 'the essence of all virtues'.[152] Goodness, and all that it includes, 'although by nature uncreated, allows itself to come into being through us', so that we may be deified.[153] The uncreated virtues become human virtues, and vice versa; the natural faculties are established in a divine mode of activity, because the divine activity becomes the driving force in man. Through the participant's sharing in these divine energies – the divinity glowing in the Trinity's splendour – the personal reality is known. Christ did relinquish the world bodily, but not 'in respect of His divinity'.[154] From then on, one participates in that divinity which makes Christ present within the human being and is expressed in the activities of the human agent.

In the perception of deification as a metonymy of personhood, nature and person are again dragged into the arena as adversaries.

From the anthropological perspective of John Zizioulas, the 'natural' human being is not truly a person. The very image of God in man is not to be traced in nature; rather it is personhood itself. Being 'not of this world', personhood becomes a transcendental category; in theo-ontological terms, personhood is divine 'grace' that comes from above to replace the *natural I* with the *ecclesial I*, which is the human being in its relational realisation. As has been pointed out, 'here we have not only a full ontologization of the person . . . against nature, but also an identification of it with grace'.[155]

Yet, in the patristic mind, it is clear that God asks nothing with which human molecules (material and spiritual) cannot reciprocate. Thus, the Divine draws to Itself 'all things that are capable of desire and love' or 'according to the principle (logos) by which each one is naturally moved'.[156] The Holy Spirit 'stirs' the essential principles of beings in accordance with their prescribed potential or natural endowment, which Christ elevated to perfection by assuming flesh endowed with soul and intellect. Thus, 'the human being by no means goes beyond its nature in being deified'.[157]

And yet, according to the succinct expression of Gregory of Nyssa, 'the human being exceeds his or her own nature, by becoming immortal from mortal, incorruptible from transitory, uncreated from ephemeral and, as a whole, God from man.'[158] Indeed, a kind of crossing of borders is demanded. For the soul that remains in its nature, namely in its worldly state and in the illusory safety of its works, without the communion of the Holy Spirit, does not earn the eternal life of divinity. Like the air which is capable of receiving the light but not of generating it, nature itself is not the source of grace, nor the giver of *theosis*.[159] The foolish virgins remain 'in their own nature', in the sense of the autonomy of their own moral purity and sensory impressions, while the sensible ones accept that which is 'foreign to their own nature'.[160] This 'foreignness' indicates the ontological gap separating the created from the uncreated, a gap which is bridged by God Himself *in exitu*.

But this grace by no means cancels the power of nature; instead, it makes it operate again, after having been annulled due to the use of unnatural modes.[161] It is the property of grace to illumine nature in the supra-natural light and to make nature transcend its proper limits.[162] The human being resembles the iron that becomes fire in fire, without altering its essence.[163] Personhood does not ecstatically transcend nature, while deification denotes an enhancement of very nature by the divine essential energies: the subject, wholly circumscribed by God, does not wish to be known from his own qualities, but rather from those of the circumscriber. As Ériugena explains, 'To surpass nature is this: that nature is not manifest, just as air . . . when full of light, is not manifest because the light prevails alone.'[164] Thus, man sees beyond what is visible and comprehensible by discursive reasoning. This is an ecstatic experience, an *ek-stasis* or rising of the entire human being – nature, person, energies – above oneself, that is above one's limitations as a created being. Ecstasy means rather the widening and extension of nature in being enriched by and inflamed in the power of divinity. And this is the outcome of theophany, which is a transforming operation of God's energy that makes the uncontainable presence accessible and participable. Therefore, if we can speak of a transcending of nature, we do that in the sense of nature itself being elevated above its created limits, even beyond time and space. Christ, says Maximus, 'elevated nature to himself, making nature itself another mystery'.[165] Is it not remarkable that virginity, which becomes – *contra naturam* – fertile in the case of the God-bearing Mother, is listed among 'nature's greatnesses', as a means to deification?[166] Thus, created nature – no more fastened to death – becomes the gold hammered 'in God's holy fire'.[167]

The human being needs this 'grace of institution' to actualise its full potentiality according to the ultimate purpose of God, although the logos of being should not be isolated from the calling to the level of divine goodness and eternity.[168] The inherent *logoi* or principles that define the human being in its totality have a natural as well as a divine character, since they grant the orientation, movement and power or faculties for the human being to attain his purpose.[169] Divine grace cannot actualise its gifts unless there is a natural faculty capable of receiving them; and the proof that grace does not really suspend nature is the fact that 'the saints, after receiving revelations of divine realities, inquired into the spiritual principles contained in what had been revealed to them'.[170] As Ériugena states, echoing Maximus, the incomprehensible Light never ceases to illuminate human nature, or, more precisely, to shine *within* our nature,[171] restoring and deifying it. Human nature is the paradise, in the midst of which the 'Tree of Life' is planted, beyond and yet within the nature that was made in the image of God. After all, God '*habitat . . . in humana et angelica natura*', to whom He grants the power of contemplation.[172] Human nature, regardless of the event of sin, is not self-illuminated, yet is a receptacle of illumination, as space is a receptacle of light; for it is not light by nature but by participation.[173] For Ériugena, although there is a distinction between the good '*datio*', which is the natural endowment, and the perfect '*donatio*', which is the deifying grace or virtue, there is no dividing line. They both 'come down from above', for the Spirit bestows the gifts of grace and the gifts of nature through the same Christ.[174] This is the motion of the threefold Goodness, which *is* all things. The essential principles of creation in its primordial as well as its eschatological state lie within God's supra-essential being.[175]

Thus, human nature is transformed 'into something more divine'. As the hymnographer exults, the deification of our nature is 'its refashioning to a better condition, its ascent and *ekstasis* to realities which are above nature'.[176] For deification is deification of nature; not an abolition of nature but a negation of its unnatural impoverishment; not a transubstantiation into divinity – the arch-blasphemy of created existence – but an immersion of consummate, full naturality into the uncreated splendour of God's own life.[177] Deification as participation in the essential activity of God is often expressed by the Cappadocian: 'Come, give me yourself, and let us give ourselves to God, Whom you will receive after having been given. Such becomes the giver's nature.'[178]

As the sun is shone upon a tiny piece of mirror, 'in the smallness of our nature radiate the images of those ineffable properties of Divinity', meditates Gregory of Nyssa .[179] The image of God is traced in human nature, which is endowed with two divine attributes: being and eternal being. Correspondingly, goodness and wisdom are granted to the volitive faculty and correspond to the 'likeness' of God. God in the beginning created human nature similar to Him, a clear reflection of His own goodness.[180] The essence is the *logos*, reflected in the dictum 'according to image'.[181] This very constitution is not static but eminently dynamic.[182] And that is exactly what the Irish tradition affirms, namely that created human nature, constituted *ad imaginem Dei*, reserves the dynamics of deification: not only the created elements, but also 'the Holy Spirit and the Light of the World' make up the human being in his wholeness.[183]

But the call to likeness, which is the fulfilment of the potential of the image itself or the realisation of its essential relationship with the archetype, relies upon the particular person. The one that follows the ways of God 'adds to the natural beauty of the image the voluntary good of likeness'.[184] More precisely, likeness refers not to *hypostasis per se*, but to one's *tropos* or mode of life, characterised and imprinted by the divine virtues.[185] The authentic 'mode of the image' is the return of the individual will from the state of alienation to the primordial state of union and convergence with nature. Man is called to mould his will in conformity to nature and advance towards God according to nature, namely the principles of divine creation. He thus reveals in himself the way of being in the image and shows 'how excellently God created our nature in His likeness and as a pure copy of His own goodness, and how He made our nature one with itself in every way'.[186] The identity of individual wills corresponds to the unity of nature. Nature therefore takes precedence in being the deposit from which *gnome* (i.e. the mind's inclination and deliberative will) draws and uses every good thing from God.[187]

Thus, we are introduced to the fundamental concept of synergy. The role of each person in spiritual life is his synergy in the work of divine grace. It is a matter of response, sharing in and interacting with God's activity.[188] The notion of synergy brings to the fore one of the principal faculties which gives human nature its dynamic orientation towards God: free will, which is integral, according to the Irish theologian, to creation in God's 'likeness'.[189] For the Cappadocian, the gift of free will and self-determination has been granted to human nature, so that the participation in God's life may be an accomplishment of virtue.[190] As has been observed, the Greek Fathers (and I would add the Irish) 'did not confront the problem of the relationship between grace and free will, since this grace enters into the very structure of man, into the operation of his faculties'.[191] Nature, grace and freedom are conjoined with no division and with no confusion. Thus, free will and uncreated grace are both the ontological structure and enhancement of human nature. For grace assists what has already been irrevocably imprinted in creation, namely the twin movement of created being towards the fulfilment of its potentiality and the assimilation of absolute existence, through a real and direct participation in uncreated life, effected by its transcendental source.

Each person deliberately either 'chooses honour or accepts dishonour'.[192] As we have already seen in the context of evil, although the will or volitive faculty emanates from the essence,[193] it has also a personal dimension or 'version', the *gnomic* will, which could be described as the most 'human' feature of the human person. It is an 'arbitrary inclination', 'the self-chosen impulse and movement of reason towards one thing or another', potentially separated and deviated from the 'natural movement of reasonable nature'.[194] While the will refers to nature, *gnome*, as individual inclination and judgement, and *prohairesis*, as purposive choice, are distinctive marks of the person. Actually, as already observed, *gnome* corresponds to the mode of the operation of the natural will. Insofar as it follows its natural movement – the *logos* of nature – it moves in accordance with God, and thus *gnomic* will is identified with natural will.[195] It is clear that 'natural' does not imply the submission to a common will, the will of an undifferentiated mass; it means the spontaneous movement of the deepest heart towards good and God. In this case *gnome* commingles with the virtues, making one's mind a cosmos befitting to the uncreated beauty. Inequality of virtue among human beings is due to the voluntary inequality in operating what belongs to 'good and beautiful' nature; for 'we do not practise equally what is natural'. Otherwise, 'one virtue would be exhibited in us all, just as there is one nature'.[196]

Substantial information on this subject can be gleaned from the area of Christology. The *gnomic* will, being correlated with wavering judgement and equivocal choice, cannot be predicated on the person of Christ; for as He is God by nature, 'He is never changed by the impulse of choice', His choice 'never being severed from what is most excellent'.[197] In other words, Christ kept the human will in its purely natural condition, undefiled by individual separative partialities, 'wholly deified'.[198] Only the human person can be associated with this *gnomic* inclination as a source of sinfulness, and the way to salvation and likeness to God is through overcoming this division and rediscovering and recovering natural will, so that the world, inner and outer, will be one. For the gnomic will divides, and the natural will restores unity. For this reason, if we recognise a 'personal' will in the Father as the generative factor of God's existence, not only *gnomic* will is attributed to each of the divine Persons, but it is also presented as the most innate, irremovable and sacred component of human uniqueness.

That which makes a human being attuned to the divine Logos – and accordingly to the logos appropriate to him – is the identification of the gnomic/personal will with the natural will. Personal will must unite with the logos of nature and converge with it, since the logos of nature is a natural as well as a divine law.[199] This natural willing, completely deified in Christ, is a state to which we are also invited: a will that is ever drawn into God naturally and by God's grace.[200] In this state, which is pursued through the endless course of spiritual life, the will and energy of the human being is united with the uncreated divine power and energy. This accordance, bearing both a moral and ontological dimension, manifests the human being's transfiguration and glorification.

To further substantiate these thoughts one should focus on the patristic distinction between the 'logos' of nature (or principle of being) and the 'tropos' of existence, which can be applied for an orthodox understanding of the deification of the human being.[201] First, one must say that the concept of *logos* itself does not refer to a 'personalisation' of nature, for there are multiple singular and general *logoi* in each being, corresponding to its nature, qualities, energy, genre, species and unity with other beings. Now the logos of human nature is that it consists of a rational soul and body, whereas its mode is the order whereby it acts and is acted upon.

Maximus has figured out the sense of innovation, intrinsic in the process of deification, safeguarding the stability and immutability of nature. Every innovation refers to the mode of being of the innovated entity and not to the immutable logos of its nature, otherwise nature would be defiled. God, in the vast range of His interventions in history, that is, in His innumerable miracles, does not alter the nature of creatures – their perfect logos – but the way their nature moves and behaves to meet the divine purpose. Innovated tropos indicates nature energised and operating clearly beyond its normal scope. And physis is innovated according to its mode of activity, its direction and administration, as when Enoch and Elias were transported 'to another genre of life', and Noah was enabled to live unharmed amid wild animals.[202] That innovation was principally manifest in the very conception by the Holy Spirit and the birth of Christ, the new Adam, without corruption and pain – a paradox showing not the abolition of nature, but the renewal of 'the laws of the first and truly divine creation'.[203]

Thus, human nature remains whole and intact in the unprecedented mystery of its assumption by the Logos incarnate, while its mode of being is innovated.[204] Christ lives out the new mode of theandric existence without affecting the wholeness and integrity of each of His two natures, without changing their logos. This is clear also in the theological reading of the Eucharist, where the term *transfiguratio*, used by the Irish, indicates a change of the tropos of the species, rather than the alteration of their logos/essence into Christ's essence; precisely as in Christ, human nature attains a new mode of being.

The 'innovation of nature' according to its tropos cannot be translated as 'personal mode of existence'.[205] Reading the relevant reference of Maximus, on whom the personalist relies, one can see that the saint speaks of the ineffable mode of union (συμφυία) of the natural properties, and the coming together of the energies into one.[206] Christ circumscribes nature in an innovation of modes. As we saw earlier, this newness is the unprecedented and arcane mode of the manifestation of the essential energies of Christ revealing the interpenetration of natures, the exchange of the human and the divine. The innovation of tropos is not personhood, but the interchange of properties, which makes it possible for the Logos to accomplish human acts in a godly manner and divine acts in a human way. Wondrous even are His sufferings, for they are 'renewed by the natural divine power of the one who suffered'.[207] What characterises the new mystery is the *theandric* energy, the mode of natural co-inherence. A sword united with fire becomes fire, and at the same time that fire acquires a cutting edge. In other words, the quality of each nature becomes the quality of the other. Now, how is this 'newness' translated in our persons? The human being is not of a double nature, as Christ is. However, a person receives the essential deifying activity, in accordance with his intimacy with God incarnate. That is why the human being may be able to perform miracles and endure sufferings – things that are contrary by means of one and the same energy – as Christ did.[208]

For Maximus, tropos signifies *energeia*. It is the use of essential energy by the self-determinative power, according to nature or not, that one may be just or unjust, following nature or discarding it.[209] Accordingly, this tropos is not conceived by Maximus as the filial mode of existence, identified with that of the Son in His relation to the Father, in other words as a 'hypostatic mode', in which Christ submits His human will to the Father's will.[210] Instead, deification is envisioned within a trinitarian horizon. By virtue of the Logos incarnate and by revealing the common logos of beings, the deifying grace manifests the trinitarian God to all men, rendering it participable and visible to all who contemplate it – in all and in each one separately, like the natural abiding of the soul in the body and in each of its limbs.[211]

The dictum 'being made God' does not refer to the accomplishment of a personal mode of existence. The ancestral man enjoyed his personhood remaining with his Creator, but his destination was to reach union with God, and through such union to be enriched with *theosis*, 'in due course'.[212] Engraved like an excellent flower on human nature, deification was to be animated by the divine sap with the human consent. The first human being was 'in the image and likeness of God' before attaining the goal of deification. Already a person in his original condition, man was endowed with certain potentiality to 'become God', 'to ascend to heaven' and to possess 'divine eternity'.[213] When Maximus speaks of deification in terms of a change of the mode of being, he refers to the mode of God's activity, in and through which divine features are imprinted on the human being. This is a paradox: Man, originate in essence and hypostasis, becomes 'unoriginate' and 'infinite' by virtue of the uncreated life of the indwelling Logos,[214] who is our Archetype and our true self.

Part II

Subjectivity and Catholicity:
The Monastic Paradigm

My Eyes more and more
Like a Sea without shore
Continue Expanding,
The Heavens commanding,
Till the Jewels of Light,
Heavenly Men beaming bright,
Appear'd as One Man
Who complacent began
My limbs to infold
In his beams of bright gold.

William Blake

ONE:
The Individual and the Community

1. *The way home*

The relationship between the individual and society has, over the ages, followed an uneasy course, encompassing all forms of total absorption as well as aggressive opposition. At any rate, the two notions have been considered, in a dialectical setting, as two defined opposed entities in need of reconciliation. It was Christian philosophy that understood the particular and the total as two aspects of the same reality, refraining from attributing any precedence either to the particular and the individual or to the universal and corporate. After all, Christ had come to break down 'the middle wall of partition' (Eph. 2:14), to bring us back to the state of unity, that we may be again one.

One and yet distinct. There is an inward or vertical dimension in every human being as well as an outward or horizontal one. That means that I am partly accessible and partly inaccessible to others, as indeed others are to me. I have an I-consciousness and a deep interiority, while at the same time I am largely conditioned by an external, social feedback. Subjectivity is not a 'motionless identity with itself'.[1] There is no radical and transcendent otherness in the world; only the relationship between man and God is totally conditioned by revelation and epiphany. Kinship and difference mirror each other. I am not a pure disembodied and self-sufficient interiority, but an incarnated being in the cosmic network.[2]

Yet, this does not exhaust the mystery of the human being. The creative logos that lies within the human species includes the depths of self-mystery, hidden in the very life of God, as He is revealed to His creation in history. Although the person is a relational entity, and one realises oneself in and through the other, each human being is a person because each is fashioned 'individually' by God (Psalm 33:15), enjoying a unique relationship with God, who calls every human being by name (Gen. 3:9).[3] The wanderer in the winding roads of history returns to his home when he arrives at this true Self – which lies deeper than personhood – and the authentic nature in which all human beings equally share. So we shall be one, and one another's all.

This study will now explore the mystery of the person and the mystery of common nature that comprehends all persons and is instantiated in each person, the mystery of 'distinction in unity and unity in distinction',[4] as these realities have been experienced in the life of the Church, focusing especially on the monastic life and philosophy.

2. The trinitarian aspect

Christian anthropological conceptions are reflected in and drawn from the doctrine of the Trinity. Here, paradox is predominant. As a divine tongue described it, the awareness of the One takes place 'in the illumination of the splendour of the Three'.[5] This dynamic paradox became the deepest heart of Christian philosophy; not as a complex abstraction inviting inquisitive spirits to revel in it, but as the Way to divine perfection. God Himself in His very revelation, as well as His very unknowability, suggests His own being to the human being, since the latter is created in God's image and likeness. Divine being is oneness in threeness, one and undivided essence in distinct hypostatic realities. This underscores the interiority and uniqueness of the particular and at the same time its communal character that emerges from the common essence. We cannot have the awareness of the One other than in the common light of the Many.

As we saw in the previous chapter, the Fathers of the Church focus on divine oneness as well as on the distinct Persons. In his reading of the Dionysian phrase, 'within communion and unity' (κοινωνικῶς καὶ ἡνωμένως), Maximus the Confessor perceives that 'in the Holy Trinity unity is shared',[6] that the divine hypostases are one in essence as befits communicants; One they are, but not a single impersonal entity. And they are united not in a concurrence of autonomous consciousness, but in the communion of essence and essential love. Communion and oneness characterise the Godhead.

Now, far from being merely a theoretical statement that is irrelevant to life, in the mind of the Fathers, the communion and oneness that characterises the Godhead dictates a mode of being. As Gregory Nazianzen says, those who believe in and belong to God are 'one', as God is one in essence.[7] This does not allow for a personalistic or, rather, 'paternalistic' understanding of the 'one' in God, for such interpretation would be meaningless when applied to humanity and would not fit the pastoral concern of the writer. 'One' refers to the entire Divinity and not to a single Person, for 'the unified names apply to the entire Godhead'.[8] After all, Gregory himself explains in the same context that the Trinity is one God no less on account of concord than on the essential identity. The one in Trinity and in humanity is co-naturality.[9] But being one, God is three. This relationship between divine nature and the divine Persons can create a social analogy for humanity. It is precisely on account of the fact that human beings are fundamentally one because of the common essence that they are also co-equal and of the same spirit. Equality and dignity are clearly connected with nature; this is what nature in its purity and integrity enunciates. Common essence impels equality, considering that equal essence, expressed in mutual love, makes co-equal persons;[10] and the natural law itself grants equality to all men in accordance with natural justice (κατ' ἰσονομίαν), since it is interdependent with the 'spiritual law', which is similitude to God.[11]

Origen says, 'The Church is full of the Holy Trinity.'[12] For the Irish hymnographer, the whole Christian congregation moves towards the unity of the heavenly Church, which alludes to the unity of the Trinity, from which it springs: 'in the unity of the heavenly Church in the presence of the Trinity'.[13] Not only humans, but also the angels, receive their oneness by the Holy Trinity, 'since the Trinity is one God, no less for the concord than for the identity of essence'.[14] This points to the archetype, which the image – the Church – must imitate. The imitation of Christ is directly linked with the unity in the Church. 'The unity of the holy essence' says Evagrius of Pontus, is the 'inheritance of Christ'; hence, the 'heir of Christ' is he who participates in this inheritance and 'arrives in that unity'.[15] The proper mark of the Trinity is peace as the prevailing feature of unity. Such peace stems and flows from the depths of the Deity to the whole of creation, whose ornament is solidarity.[16] The Trinity is the perfect model of unity and the ultimate cause of unity for creation. Basil of Caesarea turns to the Trinity as to the archetype of this life. He presents the heavenly Father as the archetype of the father superior of the community, for in both there is no passion. Love unites the Persons above; love joins one another here.[17] And, as we have seen, love derives not from a person; it is primarily the essential power *per se*. The relationship is not simply one of loving in the sense of being emotionally attached to one another; love is the expression of the common, which always refers to the essence.

Yet, no one seems to draw extensively on the trinitarian theological repository. The Fathers appear to be highly diffident about illustrating analogies between the created and the uncreated. They are very careful in converting the trinitarian perception into ecclesiological ideas, lest they tamper with the inscrutable mystery of the divine through arbitrary correspondences. Hence, they avoid appropriations attempted from presumed patterns of relationship between the Persons and the Godhead. Logical construals of that kind, Colin Gunton admits, 'can be used to justify theologically the dependent status of the laity because it is supposed that the hierarchy is more directly a reflection of the Father or Son'.[18] There is an ontological gap between the divine Person and the human person. Thus, although the Trinity is used by Gregory Nazianzen for its rich ecclesiological implications on account of its proper quality of concord, he does not go so far as to fathom out or even to refer to inner-trinitarian relations with a view to seeking an analogy for the relations between the ecclesiastical leader and his flock. The earthly shepherd corresponds to Christ-Shepherd, the analogy being received from the plane of God's economy.[19]

In the patristic exposition of ecclesiological ideas, occasional allusions to intra-trinitarian relationships are restricted to the common, namely the essential features of the Godhead, and leave aside the incommunicable personal attributes. There are only references to the absolute harmony, peace and co-inherence. But while in God the essential undivided oneness in its uncreated simplicity is most perceptible, and while in the trinitarian being the bond of the essential oneness is perfect and absolute, in the human domain it remains a *desideratum*, something natural and yet something to be accomplished. For in the created world persons are perceived *in reality*, whereas oneness is considered in thought. On the other hand, in the uncreated Being, the one is approached *in reality* and the many as a result of thought. And this is what Dionysius implies by saying that 'in the divine realm unities have a higher place than differentiations'.[20] Whereas at the human level love leads us to the common nature, in God the one nature renders the archetype of essential love 'in reality'.[21] Human beings are led to the common nature through love or, rather, through fostering the innate, natural power of loving.[22] Human persons are characterised by delimitation, and yet they are one man, descendants of one man, participants in one unchangeable essence, in a common DNA that does not sanction any *ontology* of difference even if unlikeness is the conclusion of empirical observation. So, the human person receives an imperative call to follow their nature, realising all potentiality from their fashioning 'according to God's image and likeness'. Believers become 'one of the One'.[23] The mutually internal abiding or reciprocal interiority that intrinsically and essentially characterises the divine Persons is a demand also made on human beings, through the energies of the Spirit, and that returns human nature to unity.

To conclude: at the human level, persons cannot be internal to one another as subjects. Still, as will and energy are essential properties, human persons, in their natural state, have one natural will and energy, their personal traits being preserved intact. This is the work and at the same time the expression of love; and this is what makes the self become self-less, authentic, embracing or entering 'empathetically' into others. The restorative heavenly peace is given only 'in love of

God and the whole of community'.[24] Such love is not a moral category, but an essential 'procession' graced by the divine energy. As St Paul puts it, 'the love of God is shed abroad in our hearts by the Holy Ghost, which is given unto us' (Rom. 5:5). Thus, it is the indwelling of the Trinity in each person that makes the Church into a communion corresponding to the Trinity.'[25]

3. The image of the body

In patristic references to ecclesiology, the Pauline image of the body, rather than the triadological image, is preferred and utilised for its rich connotations and the safer ground it provides. The Fathers turn to the physiology of the body for the purpose of presenting an image of the relations between believers, and in particular, ecclesiastical relations; that is to say, the network of functions within the ecclesiastical community. No member can ignore another member, but all, through each one's special function, adhere to the law of nature, which bonds and nurtures them. This image, having little association with hierarchical concepts, offers the opportunity of stressing the most 'essential' factors of the unity of the Church, factors referring not to structure but to the common life and to the essential energies proceeding from Christ, its Head, to all members. All ecclesiological relationships are placed in the context of the image and reality of the body: 'neither does the hand neglect the eye, nor does the eye neglect the hand; neither does the head oppose the feet, nor do the feet separate themselves from the head . . . because this will lead to total confusion and annihilation. The members care for one another according to the order and the law of nature, which ties and preserves all through their interrelation.'[26]

The body image epitomises the notion of natural unity. Basil's argument in favour of the communal life is built upon human nature and the precept of love. But love is also an essential power, something we possess from the first moment of our creation, which anyone can discover of oneself and within oneself. Human nature causes us to be in need of one another, to unite with one another, while communion is the 'good according to nature', to which the monks 'return'.[27] Nevertheless, the union, or rather reunion, of human nature is accomplished in Christ. In this sense, it is, as the Irish poet says, a gift,[28] but it is also a virtue. Exalting the coenobitic life, Basil spells out the connection between the incarnation and the human effort for unity. 'This is the sum of the salvific divine economy of incarnation, the convergence of human nature to itself and to God, the recovery of the primordial union through the removal of the evil severance.'[29] Sin, namely adherence to the 'gnomic' will, generated division, cutting nature to pieces. Christ 'rejoined, like a perfect physician using effective medicine, the dispersed limbs of the body'.[30]

The body image not only allows the emphasis upon the unity of nature restored in Christ, but also gives the opportunity of referring both to a head, which is Christ,[31] and to a life-giving and unifying principle, which is the divine energies, translated into personal gifts bestowed by the Spirit, who initiates us to divine life. In this way, Christology and pneumatology are perfectly intertwined. According to an inspirational passage from the Macarian homilies, 'the entire Church of Saints is His body and members, and He is the Head of the Church. As there is one soul in the whole body, and each member of the body is governed by that very soul, in the same way all the Saints live in the Spirit of Divinity and are governed by it, and each member lives in the divine substance and soul.'[32] Christ, as head, is the unmediated source of being and principle of union for every member. Moreover, the presence of Christ is made known through His members, the saints.[33] In this image, the organic unity, springing from the one essence, and the interpersonal unity must be seen as one and the same. But if we dismiss the former, we may resort to a fantastical unity of persons who may be strongly interdependent through (or constituted in) a network of relationships, but not necessarily mutually internal. This society is just an interaction between isolated egos, dispersed and lost in projections and introjections.

Commenting on the ecclesiological reference to be found in Ephesians 4:4–16, John Chrysostom says that the illustration of the body, whose head is God Himself, signifies and dictates the indispensable conditions of unity, namely love and sympathy.[34] Love solders the members, making them inseparable in perfect union. In this way, the preacher prevents a possible totalitarian reading of the image. What he really draws from this image is the reality of, and demand for, the common sharing in the most substantial divine gifts or energies: immortal life, eternal glory, brotherhood. Therefore, in spiritual matters, namely the divine energies, we enjoy 'equality of honour'.[35] Although the distinction between the governors and the governed is present and functional, it does not turn into a hierarchical pyramid, nor is it founded on any personalistic understanding of a 'first'. Apart from the common spiritual gifts, there are also particular gifts 'for the edifying of the body' (Eph. 4:12), and in that list of charismatic functions 'pastors' and 'teachers' follow other forms of charismatic activity, represented by the 'apostles', 'prophets' and 'preachers' of the gospel (Eph. 4:11).[36] Having said that, Chrysostom is clear that in fact nothing lies between the head and the body, otherwise the head would not be head, nor would the body be body.[37]

Although the members of the body are considered equal, we should not think there is confusion between the orders.[38] Such equality contains a hierarchy of merit, but not a hierocratic ladder. We can learn much from the lapidary ecclesiological passage of Gregory Nazianzen:

> Now, just as in the body there is one member which rules and, so to
> say, presides, while another is ruled over and subject; so too in the
> Churches, God has ordained, according either to a law of equality,
> which admits of an order of merit, or to one of providence, by
> which He has knit all together, that those for whom such treatment
> is beneficial, should be subject to pastoral care and rule, and be
> guided by word and deed in the path of duty; while others should
> be pastors and teachers, for the perfecting of the Church, those, I
> mean, who surpass the majority in virtue and nearness to God . . .
> in order that both may be so united and compacted together, that,
> although one is lacking and another is abundant, they may, like the
> members of our bodies, be so combined and knit together by the
> harmony of the Spirit, as to form one perfect body, really worthy of
> Christ himself, our Head'.[39]

The notion of body inheres differentiations, but the Father of the
Church has in his mind a hierarchy of virtue whose function is to
perfect all in the very life of God.

The Irish theologians share the same insight. God's commandment
that we should be holy in love is a call to be in Christ's Body. Belonging
to Christ and being images of Christ means that we are 'in the union of
his Body'.[40] The change of water into wine mystically points to the union
of Christ and His Church in one body.[41] This is also something given
and demanded: 'Because they are in one body, let their unity be good.'[42]
The Irish commentator does not build upon a hierarchical pattern; rather
the prevailing distinction in his mind is that between practical and
contemplative life. The body image alludes not so much to a hierarchical
construction but to a loving affinity and mutuality, where there is no
schism, 'so that each member may do what the other desires'. Love makes
all the gifts of the Spirit be beneficial. For 'every member serves the other
. . . that the talent of every one of us should serve the other, for we are one
body in Christ.' Thus, 'every gift is given for the benefit of the neighbour
through love in a mutual way, and each one helps his brother by his
particular gift.'[43] When there is an allusion to hierarchical relationships,
a reverse pyramid is indicated, in which power turns to service in the
model of Christ. Thus, it is nobler for the most honourable 'to serve
the other members than even to serve themselves'.[44] The commentator,
pondering on Galatians 3:28, stresses equality in Christ, and attributes
the liberty from the yoke of bondage (Gal. 5:1) to the fact that we become
members of Christ, and are a body to Him.[45] Such equality is the result
of the energetic relationship between God and the cosmos. Truly, in that
body, all 'have drunk a great draught of the grace of the Holy Spirit'.[46]

What is most noticeable is the interweaving of the pneumatological
and Christological dimensions. Oneness as a divine attribute is not

afforded by created nature. All supplies, no matter whether minor or major, come from the Spirit, which 'equally acts and equally touches' everyone.[47] The Spirit united Mary with God by 'overshadowing' her. The Spirit has been given to humanity to unite us in the one body of Christ;[48] or it is the one soul that animates the members that Christ, as head, unites.[49] In this body each member carries all others within it and is itself carried by all the others, while each preserves its own special features.

4. The monastic model

The Church, although 'not of this world' at its very core, and an immense power of leavening influence in a society of oppression and antagonism, still, at the social level, did not avoid being partially corroded by societal secular standards, especially as soon as it embraced the masses of the Roman empire, and moreover, when it identified its borders with the borders of the empire. The criticism of the nominally Christian society made by the Fathers is often severe, while in most cases those spiritual leaders suffered ill-treatment or persecution by the ecclesiastical or political government, becoming living proof of their very denunciations.

In this process of relativising absolute evangelical standards, a new counter-culture emerged from the ecclesial womb and flourished all over the world. This alternative society did not inaugurate a new moral standard or new spiritual targets; it simply aimed at living according to the Gospel – the new mode of being – in an uncompromising way. Monasticism cropped up in the remote desert, demanded withdrawal from the 'world', sanctioned solitary life, and remained at the margins of established Christianity, while being at the centre of life.

It is true that the more a human mind is attached to worldly things, the more it seems embarrassed by the paradox of the correlation between the act of withdrawal and the state of communion and unity. An old view, still abiding in secular societies, regards monastic renunciation as a purely individualistic and selfish business, characterised by negation of life, or even disclosing avoidant personality disorders. This is surely a confusing false alarm, at least when we discuss Christian monasticism. When monastics make the vow of chastity or virginity, they do not scorn marriage, nor do they inhibit the natural powers of eros or friendship; on the contrary, they espouse the more inclusive 'institution' of spiritual marriage, and they perfect eros by directing it to the most loving and desired Absolute. In fact, monastics apply to themselves the first divine law, which was restored by Christ Himself through His conception, birth and way of life – 'a mystery of a great resonance brought to pass in the silence of God'.[50] Monastic renunciation is the radical reception of restored first things and the anticipation of the age to come; in other words, it is an act that has a protological and eschatological character. The deeper message of renunciation is the surpassing of the restrictive bonds of blood and the inauguration of a universal family tied together with the liberating vinculum of the Spirit. Monastics have neither parents nor children according to the flesh. In monasteries there is no birth, save the birth by the Spirit. (And, as Maximus indicates, that was the first law of divine creation, which governed the increase and multiplication of humanity.[51]) Thus, monastics leave their narrow families to enter the great family of God; and this is the meaning of the classic saying of the desert: 'The monk is he who is detached from all, yet joined to all.'[52] The monastic vows of chastity, obedience and unpossessiveness, are just the beginning of the journey to perfect unity.

In the monastic world, no precedence is given to either the individual or the corporate body. The individual and the community are not only conditioned by each other – that would not overcome the friction – but vividly and authentically are in each other, the individual bearing the whole and the whole presenting itself through the personal properties of the individual. The common is not a uniform mass, in which the individual becomes a fraction, and the one or the many are not egos in co-operation.

The notion of the body abounds in the monastic environment. Relying on the theology of the body, the Greek Fathers are imbued with the vision and experience of oneness – the one body and spirit 'in concord and perfect love' for the sustenance of the brotherhood.[53] A Macarian homily highlights the functional organic character of every deed pertaining to the whole body:

> Let him who is at work say of him who is at prayer, 'The treasure that my brother receives is common, and therefore mine.' Let him who prays say of the reader, 'The profit which he receives by reading is to my advantage.' Let him who is at work say, 'The service which I am doing is for the common good.' As the members of the body, being many, are one body, and help each other, and each performs its own function – as the eye sees for the whole body, and the hand labours for all the members, and the foot, as it walks, carries them all, and another member suffers with all alike – so let the brethren be with one another.[54]

Thus, 'much concord and peace and unity in the bond of peace holds them all fast'.[55]

For monasticism 'order' and 'being in order' (1 Cor. 14:40) refer not to structure and regulation, but to that animating force which conjoins the members of a living body; it means unity, accomplished and sheltered in self-knowledge, humility, and love.[56] For this reason the indolence of just one member imperils the whole body. The ascetic and solitary Nilus of Ancyra, a lover of stillness, draws on the Aristotelian definition of man to present it as a demand. Man has to be 'a sociable animal', imitating, through sympathy, the co-operation of the limbs of the body.[57] The saint displays in detail the physiology of the limbs of the human body, used as an image of the relationship between the members of the community. Each member seems to strive for the rest, but in reality it works for its own benefit; for whatever a member receives from the common labour, it converts it to its own quality.[58]

We can see this figuratively in an instructive Irish narrative. Constantine, of royal descent, and king of Scotland, gave himself to manual labour 'like any monk a-serving God'. One day, the story goes, he was in the dyke doing his work. The clerics dined but he was forgotten. Thereat he became angry. When Mochutu, the abbot, went to seek him out, he was sweating profusely from the pressure of his labours. The abbot put his palm on Constantine's brow and then on his own brow. 'Well, O cleric,' said Constantine, ' 'tis the sweat of one's own tonsure that heals every one.' And Mochutu replied, 'Thou hast injured thyself. If thou hadst not said that, even the dew of thy grave would have healed every one.'[59] The symbolic gesture of the elder, bearing deep ecclesiological content, indicates that one member's toil charges the whole body, and at the same time, the one body infuses its member with divine grace. Referring to the Pauline theology of the body, an Irish homily expounds the social aspect of martyrdom. When a member is sick, the whole body is sick. 'Thus it is fitting for us ourselves, that every suffering and every ailment that inflicts one's neighbours should inflame every part, for we all are members unto God.'[60] Thus, Aidus, abundant in love, took unto himself and suffered the headache of a layman, 'so that he may liberate the neighbour from affliction and endure crucial martyrdom for Christ'.[61]

Truly, the monastic community is the embodiment of the theology of the body, for it abides by the law of sym-pathy (com-passion). Each member, using the power given by nature, activates this power in supporting the weaker members. Paul refers to the compassion between the limbs of the body (1 Cor. 12:26), confirming that the exquisite features of love are to be concerned, watchful and caring for the beloved.[62] With such observance in the spiritual community, it is evident that the brothers and sisters really are 'the body of Christ and members in particular', in preserving for ever the 'harmony of conjunction' and the unperturbed union.[63] As the Macarian homily sums it up, 'the joining in love . . . grants the harmony of the diversity of gifts in the operation of the body'.[64] Love, simplicity and integrity means that each person, in his own duty and work, in his own minor or major spiritual status, receives profit and augmentation through the synergy and concord of the rest. Without such disposition the spiritual edifice is impossible. In this way the coenobites 'substantiate in everyday life the grace granted by God's incarnation, namely by bringing back to itself and to God the human nature, which was sundered and divided in numerous pieces'.[65] Love is the unifying bond and the theurapeutic treatment of the fragmented human being, who is brought back to one's natural wholeness and unity.[66] It is such love that gathers all things into one.[67]

The members of the physical body are conjoined due to the bond of nature – they are essentially connected, and they cannot separate from the body, for that would mean death for the separated limbs. In the Body of Christ the supreme unifying power is the essential activity of the Spirit. The monk, joined to a brotherhood with the solidity and harmony of the Holy Spirit, is not entitled to disjoin himself, otherwise he would be lacking the grace of the Spirit. This is not imposed as an external rule, but is the consequence of the activity of the Spirit that becomes nature. The bond of the Holy Spirit is much stronger than the bond of created nature; nature as such is not the *cause* of unity.[68] Real unity is the co-naturality of the divine Persons. But from this co-naturality love springs and flows *ad extra*, and, therefore, the Spirit enhances human nature in each person, so that unity may be accomplished. The heavenly man, the image of Christ, is portrayed in every one by the Spirit, 'out of the essence of light itself, the ineffable light'.[69] This is why ultimate unity is identified with the state of deification.

Although deification is not identical with personhood, still, it means that in the body of Christ each person is secured in its wholeness. This is perfectly expressed through the notion of personal gifts, which is emphasised by the image of the body. Bestowed by the Spirit, these personal gifts (*charismata*) are the results or manifestations of the divine trinitarian energies. Thus, a totalitarian concept of *Ecclesia* – in which a *primus* assumes and handles all gifts – would be awfully biased and alien to the patristic vision and experience. Following John Chrysostom's statement that the Spirit equally acts and equally touches everyone, the Irish commentator insists that the edification of the body of Christ 'comes therefrom through the multitude of the gifts in the multitude of the persons', 'through bestowal of the gifts of the Spirit on every one'. The divine grace has been given to every one.[70] The divine activity elevates every particular person, so that all may be one in their common essence, will and activity, although distinct in their personal properties and at the same time single in their interiority, that is fully personal, and trinitarian, that is, in essential communion and co-inherence. Personal gifts create and safeguard total harmony through and in the very affirmation of the particular. 'It is worthy of admiration', says Nilus of Ancyra, using a captivating metaphor from the realm of music, 'how you sound with one accord one composition of piety in vibrant notes, like a tuned harp. Each one of you succeeds in a specific genre, and nobody is in dissonance, thanks to the mutual obedience, which, by nature, joins the minds of those who are separate in bodies, making them one soul, combining, like a composer, the particular high and bass tones in a harmonious melody. That, which seems to be deviant from the norm, is precisely what creates the harmony, giving savour through the variant subtleties of sound'.[71] The freedom and diversity of personal expression in the practice of virtues and the manifestation of diverse *charismata* creates harmony and melody in the unity of the body. We should also discern the link to the teaching on the Trinity. The fact that the activity of the Spirit is the one and undivided will and energy of the Trinity, the ineffable light, means that in each particular gift all other gifts inhere and, in this charismatic way, persons live in one another.

Consequently, in what way and by what means does the totality live and be disclosed in the individual? Two intertwining notions figure prominently in patristic literature, presenting a reality which is given as well as demanded. It is the reality of, and demand for, a common mind and heart, and also for what appears as the reverse side of the same reality, the indwelling of the Spirit. A clear-cut distinction between the two would be flawed. First, because according to the patristic perception of divine energies, the Spirit is the creative and sustaining force of the whole of creation. Thus the Spirit, manifesting the common divine energy, is the One who dwells *by grace* within each person, granting them real unity of mind and heart. On the other hand, this is possible, precisely because nature is by definition the shared ground, from which natural energies flow, and it is, by its constitution in God's image and likeness, receptive of the indwelling of that absolute deifying Other. In this way all live in each one and each one lives in all.

5. *Different notes: the One and the many*

The foregoing is variously expressed in the two main forms of monastic life, seemingly different, yet built on the same philosophical basis: the coenobitic and the eremitic. It has already become evident that the coenobium represents the social implication of the theology of the body. But the solitary, entirely alone before the one God, is also invited to bear within him the whole of humanity, realising the oneness in total separation. That is why one is not entitled to undertake the solitary life before reaching the level of flawless communion. Eremitism – the sanctuary of the individual – and coenobitism – confirming the concern for the perfect oneness – were never seen in separation and isolation. Instead, each of those ideals and modes of life is understood in the illumination of the splendour of the other.

One of the hallmarks in the historical course of monasticism in the Greek East as well as in Ireland is the parallel presence and maintenance of hermits and communities in a functional relationship, with eremitism being especially applauded.[72] Eremitism is a permanent, strong and shaping stream in Ireland. Its most developed forms in the Celtic lands was a new and, to a certain degree, foreign practice for the Roman Church, a way not unreservedly accepted by the pope in the fifth century. We meet here not the instrumental monasticism of Western Europe but the contemplative ideal of anchoretic life.[73] It seems that in the Irish consciousness eremitism is the primary scheme that develops into a monastic community.[74]

On the other hand, the communal spirit is vigorous in the Irish world, primarily due to the unbroken bonds of kin. This spirit reinforces the coenobitic system, but at the same time it generates impediments to a person's development. Such impediments are overcome by the radical monastic philosophy that focuses on the free response to the Gospel, selfless love and personal gifts. The monastic *familia* 'is founded upon the unerring faith . . . perfect in love'.[75] Even in their quest for the tranquillity of the outer *eremus* in the remote ocean, the Irish monks used to travel as brotherhoods.[76] At the same time, there is an obvious penchant for the ideals the desert represents: the freedom of the spirit and the unmediated relationship with God. But the intense longing for solitude is not connected with the state of atomism and egocentric seclusion. Rather, only sin is associated with man's being alone, and in turn, that sin requires the restoration of repentance in withdrawal.[77] The solitary is not separated from confession and spiritual guidance, and the anchorite forms part of the monastic *familia*.[78] Even when Christ is presented as the archetype of withdrawal, the ship on which He sails is the Church, and, according to the Irish exegete,[79] when we leave the world, it is on this ship we embark. Eremitism and coenobium, 'like sea and land, by an interchange of their several gifts, unite in promoting the one object, the glory of God'.[80]

If the monastic Fathers subscribe to the community life, it is for fear of the ever-present danger of over-individualism, self-love and self-pleasing in the solitary life.[81] Basil's acclaim for communal life is based upon human nature and the precept of love.[82] Basil proceeds to a more analytical presentation of the *civitas* – an applied socialistic model founded on the deliberate offering of love and commingling of characters and souls:

> It is wondrous that men of different origin move towards perfect identity, so that we can see one soul in many bodies, and many bodies being instruments of one mind. They are servants of one another, masters of one another, and in this uncompromising freedom they exhibit perfect service to one another. Love subjects free men to one another, preserving free will in their deliberate choice. This is the coming back to the ancestral blissful state, an

annihilation of sin, which has cut nature to pieces, generating division and hostility among human beings. This way of life . . . has been constituted by Christ, who ordered everything to be common and made Himself equally participated by all. So, the way of monks, their abbot being a replica of Christ, is an authentic imitation of the life of the apostles and the Lord Himself.[83]

Also, if monks model themselves on the life of the angels, it is because they carefully nurture the spirit of communion, since everyone shares in all goods, and all treasure within themselves the totality of goodness. Yet, whereas the many are one and the individual is within the many, no hint is made of the possibility of all being in the one, unless this one is Christ. Love simply subordinates free men to one another.

Patristic literature is animated by the breath of the desert, leavened by its scent. To be alone with God is the monastic profession.[84] But this is not isolation, for the disposition and behaviour towards the others is of paramount importance. Everything points to gentleness, moderation and meekness.[85] So, when Basil refers to the spiritual fruits of a life of a solitary, he cites the typical features of man as a social being – how he uses speech, how he asks or answers, how he listens, how he is instructed and how he teaches, which is his soul's disposition towards the others.[86] Thus, it is not strange that the life of an anchorite might include service to the poor and needy.[87] Withdrawal becomes the cauldron of a catholic consciousness. This intertwining of community and solitude is also felt in the monastic environment developed around the axis of the stylite, the solitary living on a pillar, literally between heaven and earth. Around the stylite, who seeks excessive solitude in the remotest parts, a nucleus of disciples develops into a community.[88] It does not seem strange that Alexander the Sleepless was not only an uncompromising hermit but also a competent superior father, in whom negation of organisation was combined with ardent social care.[89]

The eremitic and the coenobitic ideal commingle and become consubstantial in the diverse cosmos of the monastery.[90] Even the superior of a huge monastery would remain 'a bird on a cliff', following the traces of hermits.[91] 'United in mutual unfailing love and unbroken affinity' with her fellow-monastics, the Irish abbess would remain a heroic hermit, a descendant of the archetypal hermits of yore.[92] Withdrawal and seclusion nurture communion and, vice versa, the coenobitic mind seeks ways of ultimate withdrawal and stillness.[93] Everywhere we see a *perichoresis* of the two ideals, a functional relationship and a mutual interiority. The spiritual route points to the outer desert, which is nevertheless a symbolic target within the community.

What is conspicuous in the monastic literature is the principle of diversity, the acceptance of various forms and the free choice between different ways of ascesis, in accordance with personal character, potential and desire.[94] There are even diverse forms of eremitism: the imitators of Elijah and John, who live beyond the reach of men, and those who, having become perfect in the coenobitic life, are deemed worthy of the purely contemplative life.[95] The desert, the community, worship, contemplative prayer, the ministry of spiritual gifts and social intervention, all make up an undivided whole, an intertwined synthesis. This is also expressed in the organisation of life in the monastic community. As is written on the iconic community of Mernoc, 'their housing was indeed scattered, but they lived together as one in faith, hope and love'.[96] The author juxtaposes the loose organisational structure of the monastery, which witnesses the significance of the particular, and the internal unity of spirit that charges the whole community. The monastic model is delineated as integrating spiritual unity into organisational minimalism. This is why the Old Irish Rules focus on relations and the inner equilibrium, and always return to the general principles of measure and love.[97]

As already illustrated, the personal element is merged with the community in the teaching on *charismata*. The spiritual gift is personal, but 'it becomes common to the fellow citizens'.[98] Christ's δόματα (Eph. 4:8), rather than being exclusive donations and private properties, conjoin and sustain the mystical body. Gregory Nazianzen spells out the basic ecclesiological principle according to which the grace granted to the pious spreads to all, as it is mingled with the natural law of friendship.[99] Thus, in the communal life, the activity which the Spirit operates in one individual passes equally to all. Through this distribution the particular gift is multiplied, and everyone enjoys the gifts of others as their own. In this way the energies of the Spirit restore the inward fragments in each person and reunite the dispersed limbs of humanity into their former natural state of oneness.[100] Again, this is not something automatically passed on, but something acquired through the work of the heart. Columbanus praises the value of *consortio*, which is the exchange of spiritual gifts and the virtues rooted in them.[101] And each one regards 'not the gift that has been given to himself, but the gift of his fellow monk',[102] thus evading self-idolisation and edifying the charismatic body.

Personal gifts create and nurture total harmony through the very affirmation of the particular. Beautiful sound is produced by different notes; and the freedom of personal expression in the practice of virtue creates the sense of harmony and melody.[103] In the compelling words of Macarius, the apostolic phrase 'let all things be done unto edifying' (1 Cor. 14:26) means that 'everyone enjoys the gifts of the others through unanimity and concurrence in love'.[104] This is how the subject is constituted by the community and the community is constituted by the subject. Otherness and community is verified in one another.

Yet, there is a 'first' in the monastic community. His role and position hardly points to the position of the Father within the Trinity, except that the heavenly Father presents an analogy to the father superior in respect of His passionless generation of the Son. Even so, not a person, but love is what unites the Persons on high and joins the terrestrial, says Basil.[105] To begin with, a hierarchy is acknowledged within the monastic body, yet it is a loose hierarchy of merit, a kind of distinction within the mutuality of affection and sympathy equal in degree, where the criterion is the extent of contribution and service to the soundness and perfection of the whole. But the need for a first is not justified in the immanent Trinity. It is justified by the failure of most people to come to an agreement as to what is right and useful, and in the danger of confusion resulting from each person conducting oneself according to one's private whim, which is found in the alienating operation of the darkened part of the soul wherein the gnomic will is born and bred. It is the need for the abdication of self-centred wills, the need of self-denial or liberation from deceptive impulses, that renders necessary the presence of one or more authorities in the community; but certainly not a transcendentally established (human) one, who constitutes the many. It is equally important that the person placed in authority 'has been declared in the judgement of all eminent in intelligence, stability, and strictness of life, that his good qualities may be the common possession of all who follow his example'. The writer elaborates this by turning to the archetype–image motif.[106] This definitely points to the dynamic archetype–image relationship between Christ Himself and every human being.[107] The role of the 'first' is to initiate and oversee the progress in this ultimate relationship.

The subordination of the Son to the Father fits this purpose and is frequently used, but it always refers to the obedience of the incarnate Christ to the Father; the framework of reference is the economic Trinity. Yet, even the phrases of subordination of the Son to the Father (John 6:38; 12:49) and of the Spirit to the Son (John 16:13) dictate not the obligation for subjection to a 'first', representative of the Father, but the maintenance of one heart and one soul, and the seeking by all as one of the will of Christ. Christ's 'obedience' to the Father prescribes the obedience of one to another.[108] As for the 'first', although obedience to him is 'unto death' (Phil. 2:9), yet it is defined within the unsurpassable and conclusive ambit of the Word. We will return to this point.

In the body pertaining to the monastic community, no less than to the local or universal Church, hierarchical structure is not central. Through the exchange of personal gifts, in simplicity of heart, equality is firmly established. One comes to the same conclusion: Equality, perfect communion and a person's integrity are generated from human nature, divine grace, and the love that derives from both. In the light of the above, the thesis that the communion-unity presupposes the one, and that the concept of hierarchy is inherent in the idea of the person, since communion can never exist without the one,[109] appears to be not entirely in tune with patristic reasoning.

6. Reaching the unity of the Monad

Monastic philosophy is built upon the vision of inner and cosmic union, and monastic life is textured with a view to attaining the ideal of oneness in Christ. According to the evocative portrayal of monasticism by the great Cappadocian, 'men of different origin move towards perfect identity, so that we can see one soul in many bodies, and many bodies being instruments of one mind.'[110] Life within the monastery is fed by the communal praise of God and the constant effort to make the individual transparent to the community,[111] so that all may be one (John 17:20–1). The monastic community is an image of the divine Trinity, pursuing, as far as is possible for human beings, the same 'virtues' that are revealed by God Himself as Trinity. Unity in diversity, otherness in oneness, is one of the optimal virtues pointing to the advanced stages of spiritual life.

But while 'virtue' in the divine realm denotes the very life of God in His absolute simplicity, in humanity the same word implies a double reality: a divine gift and a human activity. These determinative parameters are inseparable, forming a spiral rather than parallel lines; the monastic world is dramatically aware of the indispensability of both. Thus, the Eucharist offers the flesh and blood of Christ, yet the sacraments do not necessarily secure the participants' remaining in the body of Christ, unless they assume a 'crucified', self-sacrificing, blameless and magnanimous 'body' – His body.[112] As the Celtic catechist says, 'Only those who observe the eight beatitudes truly enter the unity of peace in the Ark-Church.'[113] The Church as a whole in each Eucharistic assembly, and in each particular person as a temple of God, is on the challenging journey to the Promised Land, continuously crossing the Red Sea, continuously persecuted by the Pharaoh or tempted by the illusory wealth of Egypt.

In what follows, we shall reflect on specific aspects of monastic life, internal and external, in which unity in diversity and oneness in otherness is fabricated in the Greek and Irish traditions.

i. From obedience to discretion

Saturated by the vision and experience of oneness, the monastic Fathers positively insist on the desideratum of one spirit in concord and perfect love for the sustenance of the brotherhood. This unity is safeguarded by the virtues of humility and obedience.[114] Included in the eight monastic virtues, obedience builds up a human personality in Christ.[115] Its fundamental function is the eradication of egotism and the cultivation of humility and real communion in love. Far from being a docile faith lacking individuality, it is a 'heroic activity directed to the end of personal development'.[116]

The monastic community is committed to eliminating the passion of pride,[117] which is the by-product of self-centredness and the cause of distance from God as well as from one's neighbour. Its opposite virtue, humility, maintains a central position in spiritual life, since it unites the lowly of heart with the humble God (Matt. 11:29). The device for the realisation of this ideal is the art and discipline of obedience. In the monastic world, there is a call to obedience to the spiritual father, namely the person who guides, and also to the whole community of brothers.[118] One has to take note of the vital character of obedience: according to the holy scriptures obedience is life and disobedience is death. Obedience 'works life'.[119] Life according to one's will is a negation of life, while the affirmation of life is associated with the loss of the self. This depends on our *prohairesis*, which retains its freedom.[120]

The demand for obedience is founded in Christ Himself, who provides the paradigm and the measure alike, and thus it becomes a *mimesis* of Christ, 'who being in the form of God humbled himself and became obedient' (Phil. 2:6). If the Lord Himself said 'I seek not mine own will, but the will of the Father which hath sent me' (John 5:30), we can infer how far every judgement based on one's own will is potentially erroneous.[121] Since this is Christ's message, namely that nobody should pursue one's own will, he who bears the cross sees that the will is not legitimate. Yet, does obedience in Christian terms entail the subordination of one's will to another's will? Although this may seemingly meet the requirements for a basic definition, it needs some essential qualifications to illustrate the whole picture.

Obedience has a personal character. It does not refer primarily to a law, rule or institution, but to real human beings, thus cultivating personal relationships. The requirement for this relationship is free will on the part of the person who obeys, and the ability to guide along the paths of God on the part of the person to whom obedience is shown. The personal character is expressed in the significance of the function of spiritual paternity.[122] It is also testified in situations where a senior brother commands something inconsonant with the monastic rule, thereby creating a serious dilemma. Provided that it is not an essential matter settled in the Gospel, Columbanus advises the maintenance of harmony in the context of immediate personal relationship, although the senior monk is subject to penitence.[123] For this reason obedience to the elders is often considered to be higher than the observance of the rules, even beyond ascetic achievements.[124] Without this personal character, not only does obedience become inhuman, it also nurtures what it tries to root out, namely pride. Yet, the outcome will be the same when failure of specific presuppositions occurs, since the personal relationship may entertain abuse of power, indeed the swallowing of the other as an object either of utility or desire or as a substitute.

Obedience is not a one-sided relationship, nor is it confined in a hierarchical conception. At the trinitarian level, this feature is mirrored in the relationship between the Son and the Father even in the field of economy: Christ does the will of the Father, while Christ Himself declares through His oral prayer that the Father 'always hearest him' (John 11:42). Besides, the superior of the community is animated by a disposition to be the solicitous servant of all with humbleness, which renders the teacher the disciple of his own disciple. As compassionate fathers of 'children of God', instead of dominating them, the superiors give themselves to the brothers, looking after them bodily and spiritually, aiming for the benefit of the soul of each one individually. They preserve in their outward appearance the office of the superior, so that confusion may be avoided, but inwardly they regard themselves as 'unworthy servants' of the brothers.[125]

In other words, obedience finds its true meaning in mutuality. This is implied by the fact that obedience is offered by everyone to the entire community of brothers. We are already familiar with the passage of Nilus of Ancyra, where the monastic leader expresses his admiration for the way in which those monks 'sound as one composition of piety, while each one succeeds in a specific part, and nobody is in dissonance, thanks to the mutual obedience, which combines, like a composer, the individual tones in a harmonious melody'.[126] This mutual obedience is not received as an instrument of uniformity, invariability and sameness but as a creative composer who gives value to diverse sounds; thus, in the context of mutuality, obedience does not eliminate the freedom of personal expression. Rather it uses personal gifts and talents, like the notes and phrases of a musical composition, to create the harmony of interdependence and interpenetration. No unity can be real without the hallowing of the particular human to the depths of its being. According to the representative and inclusive description of St Basil:

> Men of different origin move towards perfect identity, so that we can see one soul in many bodies, and many bodies being instruments of one mind. They are servants of one another, masters of one another, and in this uncompromising freedom they exhibit their perfect service to one another. Love subjects free men to one another, preserving free will in their deliberate choice. This is the return to the ancestral blissful state, an annihilation of sin, which cut nature to pieces, generating division and hostility among human beings.[127]

This is why Paul says: 'In lowliness of mind let each esteem other better than themselves' (Phil. 2:3), 'submitting yourselves one to another in the fear of God' (Eph. 5:21). Obedience to one another is a law of the Gospel, and is manifested in the service of the others.[128] It is remarkable that the superior is expected to pass to the others the knowledge of equality. Spiritual and monastic life is the discipline and art of 'piety and equality',[129] with equality comprising the social aspect of piety. The holy abbot Finnian, mirroring the Good Shepherd, gives a fine example of equality in love, detachment and humility: he would have accompanied his monks into the wood to cut trees, had they not prevented him from doing so 'because of the honour they held for him'. Still, he wholeheartedly submits to the contemptuous 'order' of the sub-prior to go and work hard, which naturally attracts the profusion of God's grace for the humble superior and magnifies his name.[130]

But, as is evident from the foregoing excerpts, nothing hampers the monk's freedom. It is significant that Brendan's disciples interpret his words in different ways, which urges him to have recourse to prayer. A spirit of freedom exists in the obedience to the superior, who shows condescension in cases of strong will on the part of his monks, leaving God's economy to act in a corrective way.[131] Yet, personal freedom is also associated with another guide, which functions as a supreme minister. This reverend and mysterious companion is conscience. Reflecting on the way of life of the ancient monks, which was based on equality and freedom from possessions, Nilus of Ancyra ascribes those features not to the organisational structure or the imposition of rules, but to the operation of conscience – witness and guardian of freedom and moral good simultaneously – which transcends the basic notion of justice. It encourages the testing of one's own judgements in the light of the judgement of one's true brothers, and can be rendered by the untranslatable Greek word *filotimo*, which describes the spontaneous and fervent response of a most sensitive heart. Eventually, the monks' humble and loving disposition created another kind of inequality.[132]

Obedience is reciprocal because ultimately it is obedience to God. The final recipient of obedience is God who reveals His will through the spiritual father or the majority of the brothers. The monk's aim is to follow not his own will, but 'the will of God's justice'.[133] The purpose shared by the superior and his monks, through the guidance of the former and the diligence of the latter, is to please God. This is not to say that the will of a superior is automatically identified with God's, or that it reveals it unconditionally. A healthy spiritual relationship entails a shared concern for finding the ways of God in each one's life. The monk puts the burden of his life on his spiritual guide, and the spiritual guide seeks in prayer and humility to utter words of grace that are pleasing to God. In other words, what is demanded is obedience to the authentic word of the holy man, and the closer a person is to God, the more his word springs from the Holy Spirit and conveys divine justice. God's word and will is mainly transmitted through fellow monks, but especially through the mouth and blessing of the holy man.[134] Principally the spiritual guide stands for the person of Christ, not by exercising any kind of absolute authority, but by ministering before God the salvation of those who follow him, by pointing them to Christ. God is the Person who receives the offering of one's soul.[135]

Such qualification introduces the issue of criteria in spiritual life and, particularly, in obedience to a spiritual leader. The first criterion is sanctity, namely closeness to God; the second is compatibility with scriptural testimony. Kierkegaard would say at this point that the judgement of men has validity insofar as it agrees with the word of God.[136] While the limits of obedience reach all the way to death, in the very fibre of this training the biblical criterion is activated. Basil of Caesarea accepts the possibility of interrogating the commands of the superior in the light of Scripture, circumscribing the 'unquestionability' of a command. Consequently, by no means is obedience encouraged in the case of heretical teaching or opposition to evangelical precepts. One should observe, even in danger of accepting death, those things that are according to the Lord's commandment or that direct to the Lord's commandment. As the flock follows the shepherd, ascetics must defer to their superior father, 'without being much inquisitive about his requests, when they are untainted by sin'. The example of the Lord, who became obedient unto death, applies to everyone's case, 'provided that the command cherishes piety'.[137] But one should not tolerate that which is against the word of God or simply distorts it. Basil clarifies that whenever uncertainty and doubt occur, there must be sound reason for it based on the scriptures. Should the instruction prove to be at variance with scriptural teaching, the harm shall be avoided for the benefit of all. And should it be proven to be 'according to the right word', the monk will liberate himself from vain and perilous doubt. Emphasis is given to the 'word' and 'discourse'. But when a disciple says to a holy man, 'speak a word to us', the latter utters words of scripture.[138]

The purpose of obedience is not subjection to mere human judgement that leads to a standstill. A command may be opposed to God or infected by a mingling of the Lord's commandment with sin; otherwise, it contributes to the Lord's commandment, even if this is not entirely explicit. One needs to observe that 'We ought to obey God rather than men' (Acts 5:29), since the Lord said, 'And a stranger will they not follow' (John 10:5). Nobody, neither an angel nor the most distinguished man, should be welcomed in demanding anything contrary to the Lord's word or in preventing one from following it.

Basil introduces personal responsibility before the word of God, thus framing the power of the superior or any other spiritual and administrative power. The disciple exercises obedience to a superior, once 'he is convinced' that the latter can receive and is willing to transmit God's knowledge.[139] At the same time the sincere quest for truth liberates one from any vain apprehension. This is why obedience is an expression of trust in those who have progressed in knowledge and discernment and who are able to weigh up and adjudicate on the issues in question.[140]

The rationale of obedience lies in the renunciation of one's own will, and this imperative and determining act is the bedrock of spiritual progress. Obedience aims at eradicating the 'gnomic', solipsistic will, the will that is based firmly on one's own reasoning, the will that springs purely and totally from the person, encapsulating 'the desires of the flesh and mind' (Eph. 2:3). Not only is every judgement based on one's own will potentially erroneous, but whatever is initiated and activated by one's personal will is an expression and symptom of egocentricity. Insistence on the personal will makes even ascetic life open to a charge of hypocrisy.[141] Even if the personal will appears well reasoned, it is in fact a temptation 'from the right', an attack clothed in a vestment of piety. Truly, nothing good can be regarded objectively as such, insofar as it is formed in the individual mind and outside the spiritual relationship.[142]

The patristic insistence upon renunciation of personal will is rooted in the thorough knowledge of human psychology and ontology. The Macarian homilies, with their tincture of depth psychology, dive to the bottom of the self to verify the imperative of surrendering the personal will. Here, we find an almost chilling picture, yet with a reassuring message: since the serpent became the lord of the house and a second soul beside the soul, Christ orders the negation of the self, the hate and loss of the soul (Luke 14:26; Mark 8:34; John 12:25). In other words, insofar as sin became a part of the soul, impure thoughts spring up in the heart, the will of which is followed by man. But he who subordinates his soul and fights wilful desires is he who raises himself to the measure of the Spirit, and who as a result receives 'the authentic man and becomes greater than himself'. He obtains a godlike character, receiving the heavenly sign upon his soul. Thus, renunciation of the will runs contrary to the track of the Fall; it becomes the counterbalance to the post-lapsarian disharmony.[143] It is important that the will is associated with sin, which has acquired the power of second nature; this sort of personal disposition has to be transcended by the spiritual fighter in order to find his authentic nature established within the Spirit of God. The same activity is outlined by Maximus the Confessor in his own characteristic language: 'gnome', having to do with the individual way of using the free natural will, needs to surmount, through disciplined training, its insecure post-lapsarian condition, so as to let man live in accordance with the logos of nature and to activate what is natural.[144]

Columbanus, meditating on the psychology and ontology of the will, describes it dramatically as a monster which devours the very person who gives it birth and serves it.[145] In the régime of corrupted *prohairesis* (where the reasoning is not true and the desire not correct) the human heart unceasingly breeds desires, thus generating passions. Their operation abolishes the inner freedom of the human being, and causes rupture and alienation in human nature. The Greeks and the Irish are aware of the tyrannical power of the passions over human nature. Such passions captivate the human body; they deceive the human heart. In order to be satisfied, not only do they defy God's will, they also brush aside man's will and indeed man himself. In their captivity man maintains no desire for learning, wisdom or dignity, no concern about his soul or the earth or the heavens.[146] Columbanus reflects upon this enslavement, giving the prerogatives of tyranny to the all-inclusive passion, namely self-love, in which the ensnaring fiery circle closes. Such enslavement is not just a matter of ethics; it indicates submission to falseness and insensibility, since the passions seek only the satisfaction of blind desires, thus creating a state of bewilderment as to the real purpose and nature of things.[147]

The Fathers emphasise the internal conflict and abnormal situation of self-love, wherein the human being acts in ignorance against itself. As the Irish saint states, 'We are too hardly assailed . . . by ourselves, while each loves himself ill, and in the act of loving hurts himself; . . . he who makes terms with his foes is not said to love himself aright. So it is a great misfortune, when a man hurts himself and does not know it. For while a man is at feud with himself, it is not the gift of all so to pacify him that one should love himself truly.'[148] Thus, the will expresses not true love for the self, but a perverse passion of unreasonable destructive attachment. Self-love, his contemporary Maximus concurs, 'has so extended the insensibility . . . that our nature, divided in will and purpose, fights against itself'.[149] Following one's personal will is not only a moral failing, but an inconsistency akin to mental disruption, since the patient indulges conflicting attitudes: while submitting himself to the doctor, does not accept any therapeutic treatment. As Basil says, 'Whoever refuses the remedy applied by the superior acts inconsistently even with himself.'[150] Awareness of this situation is the point of departure of ascesis. The target of monastic life is the fight against self-love and the elimination of deception or false knowledge, which feed on the impassionate and insatiable 'will',[151] a will that replaces the natural will of the deep heart.

Wilfulness is considered to be not only a morbid state of the psyche, but also a disruption of social harmony. For it is the tension of the will which resists the natural logos that caused human nature to revolt against itself, introducing unnatural laws, dishonouring that which is by nature of equal honour. Its source, self-love, 'alienating men from one another … has cut our single human nature into many fragments'.[152] We certainly stand at the spiritual roots of the 'brand-new world', the forerunner of our modern greatness, which was portrayed by Charles Dickens as the grotesque outcome of the deceitful disease of self-will: as the soulless opportunist in *Hard Times* reminds his former teacher, 'the whole social system is a question of self-interest'.

Such 'gnomic' otherness, namely self-centred wills and strong opinions – the seed of the man who made freedom, love, and human nature personal properties – must be removed. 'Gnomic' will can be thought of as wanting something for my own satisfaction, albeit a refined kind of satisfaction. And 'personal' love can be thought of in a similar way when, for one reason or another, I choose to love or am captivated by somebody, or something that satisfies my impulses and needs, and refuse to offer my love to someone else. Here, will is but a fragment and love is partial, both no more than instances of self-love. Conversely, humanity becomes 'one', when 'in will men are perfected into one, this union of wills conforming with the connexion of nature'.[153]

Now the Fathers know that willingness is often disguised, underlying the desire for departure from the community on the pretext of godly solitude. But what is individual, self-reliant and unwitnessed is perilous. There are illegitimate forms of spurious withdrawal, based on human passions rather than on the love of God.[154] Therefore, to follow the way of solitude, one must first have acquired sociability as a quality of soul through the suppression of one's egocentric passions. Basil is categorical in safeguarding this principle, and quite uncompromising in its application. Thus, before the danger of hidden mistrust and the scandal of defiance, he advises the expulsion of the person who persists with his egotistic will.[155] As Columbanus writes to his monks, liberty of will entraps in the slavery of vices and militates against unity. On the contrary, mutual obedience fosters the unity of the body and its salvation through harmony and love.[156]

The highest manifestation of monastic devotion, something the Irish call the 'blue' martyrdom, is identified with the mortification of the will and transformation of self-love, the 'loss' of soul (Matt. 16:25). Such mortification is revealed as humility, peace and gentleness.[157] Laying aside the swelling growth of pride, 'if we all choose to be humble and poor for Christ's sake . . . as it were with the causes of discord and difference abolished, all the sons of God shall mutually enjoy between themselves a true peace, and entire charity, by the likeness of their characters and the agreement of their single will.'[158] The loss of self – where self is identified with the personal will – is, paradoxically, an affirmation of life, the real life of the self. For it springs from natural *prohairesis*, which preserves its freedom.[159] Its power overcomes the power of death.[160]

The aim of obedience is neither administrative discipline and uniformity, nor submission to a human will; it is the free identification of one's will with God's will. But since God's will is an expression of His love, perfection in obedience means perfection in love (Eph. 5:21). Obedience, as an antidote to self-love, is substantially associated with the categorical precept of love, which is the bounteous disposition towards one another; what was earlier defined as mutuality. It is a sequence and a fruit of love. The monastic Fathers know that 'uprooting one's own will amounts to changing self-love into love, to detoxifying the soul of its pathogenic disposition called, so appropriately, self-will, in order to make a person into the perfect image of God through the "blessed passion of holy charity"'.[161] In love, obedience finds its true meaning and also its very surpassing.[162] Outside a loving relationship in truth, obedience would be repugnant no less than inhuman. Indeed, Christian obedience is the other side of love, as illustrated in a moving narrative from an Irish saint's life. Fintan's spiritual father blesses his disciple's cup and gives him a rule not to drink anything but water during his absence until they meet again. But this becomes impossible due to the elder's demise. Fintan considers it wrong to break the rule. Many years later, the abbot of the monastery happened to sip from Fintan's cup and realises that his water has the taste of perfect wine. Fintan tells his superior that he will leave the earth now that his secret has been discovered. And he confesses that he has been experiencing this sweetness from the day of his elder's passing.[163]

Being love's counterpart, obedience is not blind and devoid of desire. 'I wish to do only what you wish,' said the mute girl to St Brigit, when she was asked by the holy abbess about her preferred way of life. But such a relationship presupposes freedom, as expressed by Brigit in her question, 'What do you desire?'[164] In Brendan's conduct with his monks we also notice the 'democratic' spirit of mutuality, which harmonises the whole in the quest of God's will. The yearning of Brendan's heart makes him seek out the will of God and the brothers' advice. But the brothers are also sons of obedience, since they have renounced everything for one purpose – to seek God's will. The love of God dictates the willing offer to the superior, who in turn accomplishes the convergence of wills.[165] It is the same love that dictates the superior's self-offer to his fellow monks.

Love itself does not vindicate its own name, if it is not founded upon the truth. While the Fathers speak of unwavering obedience, one should bear in mind, first, that the Greek adjective ἀδιάκριτος (in its old usage) does not indicate indiscriminate or blind behaviour, but rather conduct free of mistrust, disquiet and resistance; second, that the raison d'être of obedience is the need for discernment.[166] Obedience is not an end but a means: 'The brothers are . . . in need of much pedagogy' and 'those who set out for the heavenly kingdom always need guidance from the advanced and discerning, until they are rooted in grace and become unperturbed and free from stumbling.'[167] The spiritual guide, 'conforming his precepts to the laws of God', appeals for 'unwavering' obedience in providing guidance. But this request, far from indicating a totalitarian relationship, is justified in the context of the learning procedure by which monks become 'disciples'.[168] Basil ponders over the question: Does inner information suffice or do we need to submit our thoughts to others' judgement as well? He answers that 'it is crucial to entrust ourselves to like-minded brothers, to those who have given proof of their faith and understanding, so that the erroneous may be corrected or the right be confirmed.'[169] These are the 'gnostics', who carry the lamp of true knowledge, who can trace the hidden ambushes of wickedness, and whom we should follow. The parasite of self-love, which steals true judgement, makes self-knowledge and therapy quite difficult.[170] Therefore, obedience, drawn into the course of spiritual learning, becomes a route to authentic knowledge and discernment. After all, the students of an art need to obey their master, and so do the novices, enrolled in the courses of piety and equality, since they are convinced that they can receive from their superior this discipline.[171]

Providing the epistemological basis of obedience, Nilus of Ancyra touches on the relationship between true knowledge and conviction through phenomena. Will he who entrusts his salvation to a person of knowledge not vouchsafe his thoughts to the art of the specialist, having been convinced that the master's knowledge is most reliable? What appears to the inexperienced to be fair or foul is not necessarily so. Therefore, everything has to be entrusted to the knowledge and 'economy' of the art master.[172] Yet, the path towards learning is not through observance of commands, but through imitation of personal examples.[173] The superiors initiate the brethren into the knowledge of God's good will through their example, in which there is no split between belief and real life.

Mark the hermit helps us reach the deeper meaning of obedience as communion and the path to knowledge. He who wants to follow Christ bearing His cross needs to labour for the acquisition of 'knowledge' and 'understanding'. This is accomplished, first, through unceasing introspection and, second, by addressing servants of God who are of the same will and spirit and who can provide support. The self-reliant monk walks in darkness, without divine knowledge and guidance, regardless of how laborious it may be; self-reliance, self-confidence, indiscretion and non-receptivity of profit from his neighbour not only make all labours unsuitable, but also cause the 'loss of wits', that is, absolute surrender to fallacious reasoning, the impaired ability to perceive the truth and to focus on the right point.[174] After all, as Maximus time and again explains, knowledge of the truth is not the result of scientific and experimental procedures or discursive thought that often ministers to vainglory, but a spiritual sense which is born by the active Word, accompanied by the blessed passion and perfect virtue of love.[175] Truth is an event rather than an idea.

Thus, obedience in the whole scale of ascetical life is a means by which the eyes are opened to the truth and to the freedom which God grants – a means of discernment. Through *subiectione* and *oboedientia* Patrick, the enlightener of Ireland, learned, loved and practised knowledge, wisdom, purity and every good disposition of spirit and soul.[176] But as we see in an Irish desert narrative, as soon as the 'disciple' reaches the summit of virtue, his spiritual guide sends him away to build his own stronghold of ascesis and contemplation; for he 'must be not in the hands of a man but in the hands of God only'.[177] This is an expression not of isolation and singularity, but of optimal maturity in Christ.

The following story is quite revealing of the 'circle' of love and freedom in knowledge of truth: while already in the midst of the Irish Sea sailing towards Ireland, Aedan seeks to return to Britain, for he has forgotten to ask St David about his new spiritual father. When his disciples refuse to turn the boat around for fear of the sea, he sets out to walk upon the water. An angel rebukes his audacity, but Aedan says that he trusts not his judgement but God's benevolence. The angel's final remark is very important: 'You do not need a confessor save God only, Who knows your pure conscience. But if you want someone, go and find Molua.'[178] When discretion governs matters, man is peaceful and hits the mark. Discernment in Christ is a city that a man conquers through the practice of virtues. The temple of this city is the edifice of the soul and body made by God, and the altar is the arcane and true room of the heart wherein Christ dwells.[179] When the disciple reaches this state of the 'sacrifice of the first-begotten thought' to God, obedience as discipline is fulfilled; and as a means to an end, it is absorbed by essential love, which makes one 'one' of the many, and sanctions the one among the many.

In conclusion, how can those who believe in Christ achieve oneness (John 17:20–1)? This is the prayer of the Lord and the greater obligation of the Church; to restore everything to unity. Mutual obedience in love is the 'translation' of common faith and experience in everyday life. Having one heart and one soul means that 'no individual puts forward his own will, but all together in the one Holy Spirit are seeking the will of their one Lord Jesus Christ'.[180] In the monastic environment, the evangelical notion of negation of one's soul is the renunciation of one's individual will, so that one may hang on God's creative word. The will of God is done on earth as it is in heaven when we are one, participating in simplicity, love and peace, when we are subject to one another, in honour preferring one another (Rom. 12:9).[181] The renunciation of one's will aims not at the demolition of the willing faculty, but at its proper operation through compliance with the divine will, which is love and equality. It follows naturally that this does not mean suppression of a person and his irrational submission to either a personal or an impersonal authority; rather it is the fulfilment of the person in love, which makes the many one and each one embraced by all in one's otherness. The ascetic act of suppressing willingly the egotistic will is the way to the 'essential person', the person that follows its nature and becomes aware of its royal entitlement. Through sound judgement and nobility of intelligence one's will is moulded in conformity with nature, and thus one realises and reveals the grandeur and unity of human nature as a 'transcript' of uncreated Goodness.[182]

On this road, the experienced, 'those who . . . have their senses exercised to discern both good and evil' (Heb. 5:14), can supply the guidelines. These bearers and witnesses of the sanctifying energy of the Spirit shape a unifying tradition, because the rules and laws of spiritual life are distilled from their common experience, which is participation in God's grace in history and creation. These persons have created the apostolic succession of spiritual fathers and mothers, rings of a 'golden chain'.[183]

ii. Spiritual paternity

We should focus a little more on a unique contribution of Greek and Irish monasticism to Christian spirituality: the mystery of spiritual paternity, or soul-friendship as it is called in the Celtic tradition. The concept of spiritual paternity is already present in Paul and in the writings of the very early Fathers.[184] Although there is a tradition connecting paternity with the office of the bishop, it became a prerogative mainly of the monastic superior,[185] but also an acclaimed characteristic of the holy anchorite. Still, regardless of the office, location or particular pattern of life, fatherhood (or motherhood) on a universal scale is a quality of a holy person, who is called spiritual father (or mother) of all, over time and place. Thus the range of paternity transcends the borders of the monastery.[186] And if the notion of paternity alludes to guidance, maternity, attributed both to males and females, injects the idea of spiritual birth; it qualifies 'the virgin mother who by the operation of the Spirit conceives the deathless children'.[187]

As spiritual guidance is indispensable, obedience of the monk to his spiritual father is repeatedly praised in the Irish lives.[188] The fact that Maedoc – famous for his spiritual gifts and powers – leaves Britain not only after a divine call but also with the blessing of St David, indicates a profound relationship which lies at the foundation of the spiritual mode of existence.[189] It is a life-giving mystery with a therapeutic power. The man of obedience can perform miracles in the name of God through the power of his spiritual father's prayer. Death itself cannot violate this spiritual bond, as is illustrated in the persistence of Fintan to adhere to his spiritual father's temporary rule even after the latter's sudden passing away, and such faith was abundantly rewarded by God's grace.[190] The second Litany of the Irish Saints commemorates twelve young monks who ascended with their father Molasse to the heaven without illness, the reward of obedience.[191] Not unexpectedly, the Celtic term *anamchara* implies a treasury of sensitivity and abundance of tenderness that is also found in the Greek tradition. He is regarded as the 'physician', who cares for the sick man, as the 'judge', who can discern, and as the person who can journey with his child.[192]

The spiritual father or mother functions as a unifying centre for the whole monastic community, although without any transcendental justification. This father or mother is a guarantor of unity, by imitating the pastoral care of the arch-shepherd and teacher – Christ.[193] It is said about Macrina, the great abbess and sister of Basil, that she was 'the safety of the monastics' life' and 'the conjunction of concord', the point of reference of all.[194] This spiritual attachment leads to proximity and union with God through a sublime relationship: We shall attach ourselves to him who has delicate spiritual senses (cf. Heb. 5:14), who lives with apostolic discipline and self-denial in pains, whose life is in tune with his good words; we shall accept him as our father and teacher and brother and faithful friend.[195] It is a relationship of unceasing reception of life, loftier than the reception of material food. The aim of spiritual fatherhood is the communion of the spiritual child with Christ, through discourse and paradigm. This is symbolically expressed in the Eucharistic context, in which the monks deem it right to receive Holy Communion from the hands of their *anamchara*.[196] One could say that it is not the bishop that possesses *ex officio* fatherhood, but any person dedicated to God, any person who can stand as a signifier of God's virtue and regenerate others through that intimate relationship. Such a person, even if he does not preside at the Eucharist, is paralleled with a head for his spiritual progeny.[197]

Pastoral care in general entails the principle of individualisation. The concern, care and respect for the person are evident in the early literary output of Christian Ireland and, particularly, in the monastic Rules and Penitentials. Here 'remarkable emphasis is laid on the degree to which people differ, and on the consequent necessity for individual judgement and responsibility. The uniqueness of each human being's experience of life is recognised as an essential aspect of the approach to God.'[198] Thus they share in the categorical features that characterise the Basilian Rules, namely individualisation and personal responsibility. The Irish lay emphasis on the principle of personal responsibility in one's relationship with each other and with God.[199] But the reality of the particular person reaches its unequivocal sanction in the relationship between the *anamchara* and his spiritual children. In the mystery of confession, either sacramental or simply the unveiling of the heart to a spiritual father who is not necessarily in Orders, we encounter the mystery of the person and the personal character of the ecclesiastical life. This 'personalism' protects the disciple against legalism and slavish submission to laws.[200]

Therapy is the work of the *anamchara*. As Gregory states concerning pastoral duties, 'Our office as physicians far exceeds in intensity . . . that which is confined to the body; and moreover, because the latter is mainly concerned with the surface, and only in a slight degree investigates the causes which are deeply hidden.'[201] Three factors are crucial for therapy: love and experience on the part of the father, desire for healing on the part of the spiritual child.[202] Private confession and guidance, directly associated with spiritual paternity, were introduced in the environment of monasticism, and eventually replaced in the wider Church the conventional practice of public confession and penance. Although the therapeutic process included penances, and in the Celtic world this created a penitential code that elicited much criticism, we need to consider that a penance is not imposed as an impersonal penalty, but is offered as a healing remedy and an opportunity for more spiritual effort, always within the ambience of personal contact.[203]

Such healing character conditions individualised treatment, for neither the same treatment nor the same nutrition fits all. All the Fathers articulate the principle of diversity in caring and the need for the *anamchara* to be many-sided and adaptable for the direction of those who obey him in faith and love. Respect for personal otherness and the estimation of different situations prescribe differentiation in pastoral practice. Not all advice is suitable for all, since human beings differ widely from each other. Individualised therapeutic practices are applied for the healing and guidance of the particular person, for the superior knows 'everyone's morals and passions and psychic inclinations, so as to adapt his care to each one's needs separately', and treats each one in Christ's mercy, according to one's personal profit.[204] Thus, particular demeanours do not justify generalisations and fixed patterns, since they should be interpreted within the framework of pastoral individualisation. The compassionate fathers, as physicians, begin from the uniqueness of a person and his special needs in the same way that God provides for the benefit of each one individually.[205] The only absolute standard is the activity of love, which is the cornerstone of spiritual life as a whole. However, this is not the love that is generated from the person. Love generated from the person, according to Columbanus, is no less 'dangerous' than is hatred, insofar as it forges exclusive relationships, and therefore in such a kind of love 'integrity perishes'.[206]

The salvation of the person is safeguarded in the integrity of nature, through the substantial act and delicate art of love, recognition and reciprocity, in which the self-will is peacefully and willingly united with the shared natural will. This is fostered through this intimate relationship, which discloses the special and sacred identity of human beings in their initiation into the mystery of God's uncreated love. Once the spiritual child has grown up, spiritual paternity evolves into a sublime diaphanous relationship reminiscent of the Holy Trinity itself, leading to the union of hearts equally filled with God. It is 'a paradoxical intimacy, equally composed of detachment and attachment, because detachment itself, by freeing the soul from every trace of self-love, gives attachment a strength, a serenity, and a certainty that belong only to the divine order of charity'.[207] It is a love that makes us one with God and ourselves.

iii. Introversion and *Nepsis*

The spiritual father provides support and help in our struggle in the inner arena. In this field, the monk remains 'single' with his soul, while at the same time nourishing communion with the others. To be more precise, he nourishes communion insofar as he remains single with his soul. Acquisition of 'knowledge' and 'understanding' is accomplished not only through instruction by the expert, but also through unceasing introspection.[208]

Remaining and working in the field of the heart is the unerring road to unity. Here lies the altar, the innermost, arcane and true chamber, where Christ abides. The heart is the deepest core of personality, where the mystery of inherence and union of man with God takes place. The *templum sanctum*, in which God is enthroned, is the body and the heart of the saints. And the believer is called to become God's atrium, so that He may dwell in it.[209] According to the Irish teacher, the heart shelters God, as God is man's dwelling. Long before him Macarius had noticed this mutual indwelling: 'The throne of the Godhead is our mind, and again, the throne of our mind is the Godhead and the Spirit.'[210]

'The union of flesh and spirit, receiving the Spirit of God, brings about the spiritual man' says St Irenaeus of Lyon.[211] But if God made the first marriage, that of soul and body, man made the first divorce.[212] Thence Man turned into a deep wound, maintained in history through personal sin, where sin is not simply a transgression, but an orientation, nay rather disorientation, of personal existence, with innumerable manifestations and symptoms, clear or unseen. In this state the human self is divided, disintegrated, fallen apart, enslaved in a struggle to maintain a certain image. First of all, the distance between appearances and being, between a persona and the true person, calls for introversion and internal striving against the generative passions that fracture the unity of human nature: ignorance, self-love and tyranny.[213]

The call to repentance does not impel bodily actions, but appeals to the inner man, who is led by his heart. The unfathomable abyss of the heart is the battlefield, where victory is secured only through Christ's intervention. The medical treatment of the heart lies at the heart of primitive monasticism, both Irish and Greek; for the desert Fathers – centuries before the achievements of psychoanalysis – were aware that the will to power and all related liabilities often exist underneath the skin of consciousness. In this method a diagnosis is necessary, so that the 'first causes, causes which are deeply hidden', the roots of sin, may be eradicated. As Gregory explains, 'The whole of our treatment and exertion is concerned with the hidden man of the heart, and our warfare is directed against that adversary and foe within us, who uses ourselves as his weapons against ourselves.'[214] The monk enters his 'captivated mind' and behind it, in the chambers of the soul, he confronts the nested snake, which kills through the principal faculties of the soul. Only in this way can he avoid false identifications, illusory self-images and narcissistic relationships. Thus, in the secret workroom of the heart, the monk sets out on the route to purification and illumination. A saint is one who is purified and sanctified in the inward man. Purification is the epitome of all the philosophers, and the law, and the prophets, and the coming of the Saviour.[215] But even in this interiority no man is an island. He discloses and places the secrets of his heart before 'those of his brethren, whose office is to exercise a compassionate and sympathetic solicitude'. And 'by the practice of such co-operative discipline, one shall gradually attain perfection'.[216]

The heart houses an intrinsic impartial judge: conscience. This judge must be upright and unblemished, peaceful and radiant. Such pure conscience is the fruit of the soul's therapy. And vice versa, should we seek our therapy, we need to take care of our conscience, so that we may do as it dictates. As in a circular motion, pure conscience is gained through prayer, and pure prayer is obtained through conscience; for they are naturally interconnected. For this reason the process of descending into the self, investigating the movements of the intellect, and exploring and checking conscience, is a *sine qua non* of spiritual progress.[217] The *anamchara* is an assistant to the conscience, helping it to probe the depths of awareness.

Conscience has nothing to do with personal will; rather, it is a 'natural book', summoning us back from our personal inclinations, but also lying beyond and above the superego, as it reflects on ties and values themselves. The person who studies it actively receives the experience of divine aid. One's conscience and God alone know one's secrets and provide correction.[218] Thus, the monk stands always before his freedom and responsibility, and with his inner eye, which sees and judges, is invited to see the world and to listen to and decode his own inward voice in a course of purification and communion with God, where, all deceptive echoes being isolated, the soul is no longer rebellious against its own nature. This is why Macarius stresses that 'those who wish to achieve a Christian life with any great thoroughness must before anything else cultivate . . . that faculty of the soul which discerns and discriminates.'[219]

Since both the Greek and Irish traditions agree that spiritual struggle undertaken in total withdrawal clears the inner power of sight, offering the opportunity for the uprooting of the passions, *hesychia* (stillness, quietness) is presented as the beginning of the soul's purification. Without doubt, the term refers not to an outward but to a spiritual condition characterised by vigorous movement, an intense inward activity also known by the term *nepsis*, which indicates watchfulness, sobriety and readiness. The act of following Christ is not only external, but also 'noetic', insofar as it focuses on the continuous purification of the inner man and his unceasing prayer.[220] 'As the eyes of the captain are stable and unperturbed in the waves, the mind, when it is watchful, is stolen only a few times.'[221] A wandering eye cannot see the object, and a mind held down by many concerns is unable to contemplate the truth. But a monk is an eye with an undistracted clear vision.[222] His main duty is the cultivation of inner quietness, the sobriety and alertness of the spiritual senses. He is on a good course for perfection if he is watchful, his intellect being concentrated in introspection, his whole existence oriented towards one bright summit.[223] That is why the cell of a monk is likened to 'the furnace of Babylon, where the three children found the Son of God; and the pillar of cloud, from which God spoke to Moses'.[224] It is a place of struggle, self-knowledge and theophany.

Thus, the urging towards introversion is not exhausted in the awareness and uprooting of internal sinfulness; more than that, it is an initiation, a mystagogy, having its roots in the image of the human being as microcosm which sums up all created elements, as well as his purpose to unite with God. This is beautifully expressed by Nilus of Ancyra: 'You are a *cosmos* of the cosmos [the Greek word meaning 'world' as well as 'ornament']. Therefore, always contemplate the whole of creation within you, and perceive everything as referring to you. Do not look outwards, turn your mind entirely inwards to the noetic room of the soul, prepare a temple for the Lord without idols',[225] wherein the idols are primarily the illusory images of oneself. The sacrifice is prayer itself in the bountiful desert of dispassion or detachment.[226] Pure nature, revealed through purification of the heart from evil thoughts, words and deeds, is the inner dwelling place of Christ. Having obtained pure senses, man proceeds to the deepest heart, with a view to reaching the love of God. He gives his entire mind to God, offering the sacrifice of the first-begotten thought. His soul, perfectly pure and made steadfast according to nature, becomes clear-sighted. Not only does the soul see, it is also able 'to transmit to itself the entire visible world in which God is hidden' and thus create 'a world of spiritual beauty within itself'. Purification and lustration of the optical organ of his soul leads to contemplation of God.[227] No wonder that introversion is said to 'cover the two thirds of piety'.[228]

Nilus of Ancyra defends the superiority of the monastic profession on the basis, first, of the importance of the inward man, and, second, of the strategic discipline of spiritual warfare. Any criticism of monasticism by secular society disregards the dynamic reality of the inner microcosm and the necessity of the purified heart.[229] Along these lines, one may argue that any downgrading of interiority in favour of an over-emphasis on the sacramental or structural dimension of the Church tends to ignore that the Kingdom of God and the decisive battles for the regeneration of man take place within the inner realm. The need for this inner activity is urgent not only in a monastic's private quarters but also during communal worship. As a holy abbot remarks, echoing the apostle Paul, 'What is the profit if I chant with my spirit, but my understanding is unfruitful?'[230] Physical participation in or belonging to a structural body is neither the main point nor the whole story. The *atrium* and the *domus Domini* is understood on two levels, that of the heart and that of the visible congregation.[231]

There is no definition of monastics as inclusive and succinct as the one articulated by the Areopagite: 'They are called therapeutae or solitaries, from the pure service and worship they offer to God, and the single undivided lives they live as they strive for simplicity in a sacred folding together of all division into a God-like unity and perfection of the love of God.'[232] The most comprehensive virtue, love, is presented as the by-product of the tranquillity of the mind, which comes from the renunciation of worldly things. How can he who is conquered by torrents of thoughts see what is hidden beneath them, the fog and darkness of soul? How can he who cannot see seek his purification? How can he who is not purified find 'the place of his pure nature'?[233] When free from the turbulence of the passions, the mind contemplates beings according to their natural *logoi*, and in their unity in the Logos.[234] *Nepsis* is not a negation of external activity; neither is renunciation an explosion of materiality. They are viewed within a holistic understanding of the human being, and because of that, they aspire to the perfection of love.

iv. Love and sympathy

Passion is the real thing. Desire is not to be buried within us, and The Christian and monastic ideal of dispassion (*apatheia*) should not be misinterpreted as lack of sensitivity or deadening of the passionate part of the soul. It is 'the immobility of anger and desire in relation of what is contrary to nature . . . and for this reason it signals the consummation [telos] of what can be practised'. It is fashioned from courage and temperance. Some call it dispassion, others gentleness.[235] If the dispassionate monk is expected not to show concern for himself and the transitory matters of earthly life, he is nevertheless meant to co-suffer with his neighbour. The sweet pain of the heart, not as a sentiment, but identified with God's remembrance, charges the spiritual man. This kind of person is not afraid of lamenting and of tears, which are primarily shed before God's sacrifice for His world. Dispassion is acquired from compassion, which is to walk towards God in a godly manner.[236]

True discipleship and communion in Christ is manifested not through signs and extravagant powers but through mutual love (John 13:35), which finds its measure in God's self-sacrifice. 'Once for all, love is the full measure of the law,' according to the concise Pauline maxim, modified by Diadochos of Photike with the significant introductory phrase, 'once for all'.[237] Love of God and one's neighbour is the perfect work, the all-inclusive criterion of sanctity: 'It is when full of charity that one is holy. He proceeds with charity.'[238] The recognition of the divine 'image' in the person of the neighbour restores that very image in the subject who loves.[239] Thus, love safeguards the meaning of creation and fulfils the potential of human nature as created in the image of God.

Love is 'naturally hidden' and found in the righteousness of God, in contradiction to being hidden in one's own righteousness.[240] It is a property of nature, first divine and then human. In Christian love, as expressed in the monastic world, human beings of different origin move towards perfect identity, free men and women who deliberately submit to one another, surpassing their own egos. In this environment and mode of life souls are recast and commingled, restored to the natural state of primordial harmony. Thus, Christian love is the return to an authentic and natural state, the purging away of sin that has cut nature to pieces, generating division and producing this red earth. Love, the outcome of divine economy, returns human nature to itself and to God, and offers the recovery of union through the removal of the evil severance.[241] This 'narrow way' (Matt. 4:14) begins with the suppression of the will so that one is able to reach the level of compassion and love for one's enemies.[242]

Through natural, that is, essential, love, persons exist in one another either on the created or on the divine level. Although in the Trinity every aspect remains unknowable, yet that extraordinary distinction and union in divinity is the model of humanity. As Maximus wonders, in paralleling divine and human existence, 'what is so extraordinary about a man being both united with and separated from a man as the Son to the Father and nothing more?' The rising above the tyranny of the passions, he continues, matches love's perfection, and love's perfection looks to the one human nature, which means the transcendence of any distinction between human beings whatsoever and in any respect, whether of faith, social class, sex, nationality.[243] Since God is love (1 John 4:16), the Celtic catechist argues, love makes the thing possessed by one to be shared by all; a reality that will be more evident in the eschatological glory.[244]

This principle leads to an earnest concern for the application of the concept of equality as derived from triadology and Christology. In the system of monasticism that developed in the West in the twelfth century, community was rigidly stratified into an upper and a lower class, with no communication allowed between them. In the old Irish monastic rules and lives, however, there is no evidence of any substantial division based on the criterion of social status. Spiritual relationship liberates man from attachment to that kind of physical bondage that creates group features such as gender, class, family and race. The monks also bypassed the Irish law according to which a person of high rank was not allowed to do physical work. It is highly significant that for the deeply class-conscious Irish society, menial work, at least in principle, was undertaken by all for its spiritual benefits: labour, vigil and prayer are the 'three things which drive out the spirit of instability, and make the mind steadfast'.[245] Physical and spiritual work, and sharing in all goods, is what the coenobitic custom and rule prescribes for all, although personal abilities or gifts would inevitably create a sort of division in an organised community. However, the Fathers well knew that the observance of the rule presupposes the mortification of self-love and love of earthly treasures.[246]

Accordingly, love transcends the bonds of natural kinship. The Irish rule demands the mortification of the monk insofar as the physical bonds of kindred are concerned.[247] Thus, the monk is called to liberate himself from narrow natural kinship, to whose laws the wealthy man adheres, striving to reach another level of consciousness, that of catholic kinship that emerges from two sources, namely common nature and divine grace. This is extraordinary, especially for Irish culture, wherein the individual is confined within the unbreakable matrix of family and clan. This revolution is mainly expressed in the philosophy of eremitism, the ideal of the 'stranger' and the practice of self-exile.[248] In a society where the person is entirely dependent on the community, the striking phenomena of eremitical life and self-exile become not merely acceptable, but even more so, they give back to the 'stranger' precisely that which has been renounced – namely social status – yet this time on account of his universal sanctity.

The same overturning of social conventions is even clearer in the Greek sources, where every social distinction is explicitly condemned. The man who wants to enter into God's life must become, like Melchizedek, without father or mother or genealogy.[249] For women this was a real revolution. A typical example was St Macrina, a female pioneer who converted her huge estate and household into a nunnery, making her former servants 'sisters and equal in honour', with whom she would share every good thing. She thus abolished every differentiation based on social value and status.[250] Alongside the secular concept of aristocratic ancestry, Gregory Nazianzen emphatically juxtaposes true gentleness in the sense of imitation of God.[251] Aware of the power of social conventions and custom, Basil trains the person who has enjoyed any of the higher positions in society, and who aspires to imitate the humility of our Lord Jesus Christ, by prescribing for him 'tasks which may appear extremely humiliating to worldlings', as tests of his resoluteness to be a worker for God.[252] And we should not leave aside that hermit, abbot and bishop, who, having kept his extremely austere régime, committed himself to providing care, supplying advice, serving the brothers and discharging all humble duties.[253] Only in the offering of disinterested, unconditional and undivided love does equality find its true meaning and full content. Love must be equally given to all, whereas partial love is injustice. Oneness, substantiated by love, is distinguished 'by the beauty of equal value of all men'.[254]

Since God Himself is Love (1 John 4:16), love is the 'common salvation', and the offering of one another to God constitutes the charismatic community.[255] Using the etymology of the Greek word πλατυσμός combined with 2 Cor. 6:11, the Irish sage Aileran introduces the idea of expansion and broadening of the heart to brotherly and catholic love, and expansion of the human spirit to the virtues.[256] It is an expansion of the self towards the other, an ecstatic movement, yet not in a fashion in which self-love encloses and swallows up the others within its narcissistic 'monarchy'. If we accept, along with Adam

Smith, interest and concern for oneself (even in their most delicate form) as the main drive of fellow-feeling and interaction with others, then relations are condemned to be no more than an interchange of individual perspectives, a counterfeit of true and real communion.

Love is sometimes coupled with the almost equivalent term 'compassion' or 'sympathy', denoting a unique form of intentionality, encompassing tenderness, deep awareness and a strong inclination of consciousness embracing all creation, enabling us to participate in another's life. We also call that distinctive mode of consciousness 'empathy', a word that bears the tinge of identification with the other and expresses our fundamental relationship to others. It is not merely a way to access emotions, desires and the beliefs of others by imagining ourselves in their situation, nor is it a thematic encounter between isolated egos wherein one is trying to grasp the emotions or experiences of the other.[257] Empathy indicates the humble (even self-emptying) and loving entrance into and inherence in the psychic world of the other, in the whole drama of his life and existence. It is not just a sympathetic disposition but deliberate identification, since Christ identified Himself once and for all with the person of the least brother. This divine act of identification was comprehended by the Fathers not only symbolically, but also in a pragmatic manner; for God truly assumed human nature, becoming the least brother Himself, becoming co-natural with any lowly person, giving the rule and the measure of compassion. Empathy in this context does not have the psychological sense of over-identification; it designates the existential feeling, or rather state, caused by the awareness of the common nature shared by human beings, that same nature which was assumed by God Himself and deified through this divine act. Christ's compassion, which culminated in the incarnation, means exactly this: that the absolute Other brought about the union of His own uncreated nature with created human nature, restoring the unity of scattered human nature and opening the way to the fulfilment of creation in God's image and likeness. The utmost and inexplicable union was an act of compassion. The substratum of unity is the power of compassion, rooted in human nature and proceeding from divine nature as the 'divine law', through which the powers of the soul reach their entelechy:[258] a laborious work no less than a gift.

Sympathy is the natural behaviour of humanity, a reality which is also conveyed in the body image. According to the Irish homily that displays the social character of martyrdom, each believer is called to take up his cross, meaning that when one member is sick, the whole body is sick. 'Thus it is fitting for us ourselves, that every suffering and every ailment that inflicts our neighbours should inflame every part, for we are all members unto God.'[259] For this reason, taking another's sins upon oneself is among the basic monastic virtues.

Compassion is embodied in mercy, clemency, caring, bearing sins, trials, passions and the illness of others.[260] Strange as it may seem, Christian renunciation dictates deep concern for the neighbour even beyond the commandment: 'How can I, having renounced the world, put on clothes while my brother is frozen?'[261] As we have already said in the context of the body image, the 'order' and 'decency' in the Church, which Paul commands (1 Cor. 14:40), is interpreted as unity accomplished and sheltered in self-knowledge, humility and love. Such unity cultivates the state of spiritual responsibility for one another. The success or the fall of one member affects the whole body. Bearing the burdens of one another, displaying self-committing solidarity, and sharing in the responsibility for the progress of all the members are integral elements of the monastic community.[262] While prayer is offered for all, even for the persecutors, the communion of prayer is of particular importance.[263] Prayer on behalf of the other returns as grace to the praying subject; and the offering of one another to God restores the image of oneness in threeness.

It is interesting how sympathy transcends the letter of the law and human justice, thus introducing the principle of economy. For the Irish exegetes, *justitia* is 'to love God with all your heart' and to love your brother.[264] Justice is identified not with an ethical code but with the practice of love. He who works justice resides in eternal life, for this justice – namely concern for the neighbour – indicates absolute disinterest, which is not to be found to this extent in other virtues. Justice desires the wealth of others, in imitation of God's justice, which is 'the perfect and unchanging love of the Spirit . . . which holds within it all gifts'.[265] Thus, 'the abridgement of the law is love, and the fulfilment of the commandments is love.'[266] This interpretation is very important for a comprehensive understanding of the status of the person in monastic and Christian society. Compassion, leniency and the use of economy feature in the Irish stories, in spite of the fact that the Irish Church is predisposed to canon law.[267]

'Sympathy in brotherly disposition' is included in the cardinal virtues of life according to the Gospel. It is articulated in the 'golden rule' (Matt. 7:12), through which one may grasp the terms of the love of neighbour. The monk preserves the chastity of the body and the candle of faith, and carries the oil of compassion in his pot. It contains *ascesis* and is contained within it. It is the horizontal manifestation of love, and for this reason, it is a distinctive mark of Christian life.[268] Sympathy, though an essential trait, calls for digging and clearing and watering the land of the inner self, which suffers in the disparaging of human nature. In this therapeutic procedure, love 'brings together those who have been sundered and begets in them an effective union of will in unanimity [*sym-pnoia*, literally, taking breath together]'.[269]

Thus, sympathy is the spontaneous behaviour of the expanded soul, regarding 'all men with singleness of intention and purity of eye, so that it may become like a fixed law of nature to despise no one, to judge no one, to abhor no one, to make no distinctions between anyone'.[270]

Sympathy is the underlying foundation of the value of hospitality in Greek as well as in Irish culture, not only within the communal life but even among the anchorites. Christ Himself, in His act of condescension and identification, became the Stranger coming from the desert, and remained as such in the world of human affairs; thence, every stranger – the most remote neighbour, who lacks all political rights and legal status – should be welcomed as Christ.[271] The divine law of hospitality overruns ascetical discipline. This act of welcoming the most distant neighbour, the act of becoming a neighbour to him who approaches us, the act of recognising the 'image' of the archetype Christ in the person of our fellow human, restores creation 'in God's image' to the subject of love.[272]

Being a natural trait, compassion is even presented as having an exclusive salvific value. Without mercy and compassion the human being is called an animal, beast or serpent, since he intends to become, through wickedness, that which he is not by nature and thus he sinks from natural decency into vulgarity against nature. In the process of alienation man fabricates a 'wilderness' for himself.[273] Even in the context of the Eucharist and participation in the Eucharistic gathering, the 'tree of knowledge of good and evil' is to be found, namely the absence of compassion, the empirical distinction between good and bad, which deprives the mind of sympathy. It is worth mentioning that this tree stands also in the new paradise, namely the Church.[274] The Eucharist is the workshop of corporate love, continuously edifying the body of Christ through the divine activities, continuously working against the dividing powers, but surely it is not an automatic reflection of the eschatological Kingdom in a structure, office or ritual.

Compassion, as the horizontal dimension of love, is a prescription of nature as well as a demand of the Spirit. Even if the written law of God had not required charity, nature itself would be an instructor of empathy, legislating compassion out of sharing in the same ontological condition.[275] Besides, human nature is innately sociable. Need brings closer to one another those who have been united by the law of nature. The impetus of love is a natural property: 'Man is a civilized and gregarious animal, neither savage nor a lover of the solitary state. Nothing, indeed, is as compatible with human nature as living in communion and in dependence upon one another and as loving our own kind.'[276] The Lord Himself gave us the seeds of these qualities in anticipation of His requiring their fruits.[277] At the same time, compassion is a demand of the Spirit. What else does the Spirit that dwells in us (James 4:5) desire and long for but the union and concord and mutual affection of the brothers?[278] Thus, common nature invokes sympathy, pointing to the 'inner glory of the image', which is the divine energy that enhances and fulfils nature.[279]

The gift of the Spirit guides Christ's followers to the one pure nature 'in the image and likeness of God'. It guides persons to oneness. This is the distinctive feature of holiness, the universal or catholic consciousness, the intimate awareness that mankind is all one. 'All we brethren who sit here have but one image and the one character of Adam,' says Macarius.[280] The person who has received the gift of the Spirit prays for all Adam, since mankind is all one, and his tears are bread, and his mourning is sweetness and refreshment for himself and for all. One of the inward manifestations of sonship and indwelling of Christ is this catholic love as the appropriation of Adam's lamentation.[281] The Spirit illuminates and encourages us to the 'natural will', which is not a hypostatic feature but the 'movement' of the one essential Manhood manifested through the distinct persons. As is repeatedly stated, this is a gift that calls for ascetic effort. It demands leaving one's own righteousness, and seeking God's righteousness, so that love may be found hidden in nature. 'Well,' says Macarius, 'have we in secret also, in the things within, one purpose among us all, and one heart? Are we all one, good and godly?'[282]

v. Unpossessiveness

Compassion is the polar opposite of avarice, one of the eight 'deadly sins'. Avarice, the always insatiable desire, which seeks to seize anything that comes into sight, is the cause of slander, maltreatment, robbery, plundering, blackmail and pretexts under whose cloak evil acts are justified. Avarice is a formidable conniver and turns things upside down.[283] On this account the monk undertakes an ascetical effort to overcome any feeling of acquisitiveness, which severs him from real communion. As Columbanus asserts, 'greed must be avoided by monks, to whom for Christ's sake the world is crucified and they to the world, when indeed it is reprehensible for them not only to have superfluities, but even to want them'.[284]

The backbone of monastic life (both eremitic and coenobitic) is the ideal of common possession or, rather, the principle of unpossessiveness. Monastic life is organised around the axis of real need, which demands moderation in everything. According to the monastic rules, the surplus – what exceeds the need – must be given to those who really need it.[285] More than that, the monk nurtures in his heart the conviction that he owns nothing in this world and takes himself only as a distributor of those goods that happen to be at his disposal. The beginning of apostolic life and devotion, according to the Lord's demand, is unpossessiveness, because of the perils of wealth to the immature mind. But he who considers any thing as his own alienates himself from the Church and the love of God, since God taught us in word and deed to give even our lives for our friends.[286] As G. Harpham observes, the Biblical narrative which stands behind the paradigmatic conversion in Christian history culminates with the Lord saying to the rich man: 'If you would be perfect, go, sell what you possess and give to the poor, and you will have treasure in heaven; and come, follow me' (Matt. 19:21). Shattering all self-sufficiency, this passage 'calls on the essential "perfect" self, setting it against "possessions", worldliness, inessentiality of all kinds'.[287]

The negation of individual property and the common sharing of everything is the highest expression of the renunciation of the gnomic will and the most compelling manifestation of the one body possessing one heart, one will, one desire. The aim is clear:

> Whenever a group of persons aiming at the same goal of salvation adopt the common life, this principle above all others must prevail among them, that there be in all one heart, one will, one desire, and that the entire community be, as the Apostle enjoins, one body consisting of divers members. Now this cannot be realized in any other way than by the rule that nothing is to be appropriated for anyone's exclusive use – neither cloak, nor vessel, nor anything else which is of use to the common life –, so that each of these articles may be assigned to a need and not to an owner.[288]

The perfect society is founded on common possession, one mind, one faith, wherein the many are one and the one stands not alone but in the many. But without the renunciation of individual property the discourse on common mind and faith remains in the sphere of theory and creates suspicion of insincerity.

The virtue of unpossessiveness or detachment is connected to another quality of spiritual being, that of simplicity. The fragmented and dispersed state of the soul's faculties causes a complicated and conflicted manner of thinking and behaving, a painful diversity within the person, expressed in the matrix of his relationships. As Kierkegaard states, the one who wills the Good only to a certain degree is double-minded, has a distracted mind and a divided heart.[289] Simplicity derives primarily from the sense of sharing the same origin and having the same destination, since all human beings are fashioned from the earth and the grace of the Holy Spirit, which forms Christ's image. From then on, simplicity is fulfilled in the purification of the inner man and the re-activation of the simple divine grace, which renders man capable of participating in the life of God.[290] The human being needs to return to the state of simplicity, through inner work, focusing on God's love and imitating God's virtues; for simplicity itself at its highest level is a property of the Uncreated. Analogically, the monk (no more, indeed, than any true Christian) experiences peace in all things and holiness by simplifying himself, and the content of this simplicity is the 'undivided identification' of his will with God's will, by transforming the irrational powers of the soul, namely anger and desire, into love and joy.[291]

'What is best for piety? Simplicity and simplemindedness.'[292] Simplicity of heart is the marrow of virginity, an indispensable goal for every monk. Simplicity, together with humility and love, proves prayer to be fruitful, and is considered to be one of the cornerstones of brotherhood.[293] Virtue, as expressed in simplicity and resignation, is real power. It evokes the parallelism of a monk to the anvil, on account of his stability and perseverance.[294] Thus in goodness and simplicity of heart St Patrick acquired knowledge, wisdom and purity.[295] This means that the heart must be released from the gear of egotism – either individual or group egotism – and not be delivered up to its own illusory devices.

vi. Liturgy *versus* asceticism?

The locus of unity is nature (including natural love) and faith, as the shared contemplation of truth. Their most immediate expression, and the device that functions par excellence as the weaving mill of spiritual life, is worship.

Elaborate liturgical *typica* and hymnography of incomparable beauty were handed down to the Church by most austere monastic communities, like that of St Sabba, the Studium, and Bangor, and this is indicative of the aptitude and zeal of monastics in liturgical prayer. The monastic is a worshipping being, living with the longing and practice of assiduous, unceasing, even sleepless hymnology.[296] Doxology makes the person who offers himself to God an imitator of the angelic chorus, shaping their eschatological identity.[297] It is a response to God's gifts, culminating in the offering of His Body and Blood.[298] Its importance is witnessed even among the hermits, who not only recite the canonical hours but also do not neglect their participation in the common gatherings.[299]

The Irish *Navigatio Sancti Brendani* appears as the most inclusive source here. Brendan sails with his monks to visit the 'Promised Land' of the saints. He visits many lands, meets holy men, confronts with demons, and contemplates God's mysteries in the vast ocean. In the voyage (which offers an allegory of spiritual life) of Brendan, progress is to be understood in a liturgical context, 'comprising a cyclic, annual celebration of the mysteries of the faith',[300] where the Eucharist is at the centre, an integral part of the undivided whole. It is not the Eucharist only that circumscribes the divine office, nor are the liturgical Services simply a preparation for the Eucharistic event. The whole space–time continuum is transformed into liturgical time and space, sanctified in God's energetic presence.

It is true that in the early monastic mental and physical environment there is no sharp distinction between 'liturgical' doxology as communal and 'private' doxology in one's cell.[301] Anthony and Paul in their legendary meeting are being committed to liturgical prayer in the desert. With the bread between them, in the famous depiction on the high cross in Monasterboice, they point simultaneously to the Eucharist, to prayer and study in a most intimate relationship woven in the loom of solitude.

Referring to the desert Fathers of Egypt, Columbanus associates the rhythmic harmony of worship with the harmony of communion among the brothers.[302] This connection of worship with the ethos of unity and the trinitarian faith is implied by the biographer of Alypius the Stylite. Standing upon his column, this formidable stylite praises the Trinity, surrounded by the three 'choirs' of his holy synodia – the choir of his fellow-recluses, the choir of the female monastery and the choir of the male monastery – all of them spiritually conjoined in a universal hymnody, which becomes a dramatic performance watched by the heavenly hosts.[303] God becomes the immense centripetal force that gathers everyone at the divine centre.

'Today the grace of the Holy Spirit has gathered us', was the chant at the Vespers of Palm Sunday, when the monks of Palestine would return to their monastery after total solitude in the desert during Great Lent.[304] Here one may see the absolute *perichoresis* of the ideals of withdrawal and community, of the desert and the coenobium, of private and common prayer. The more one gets closer to one's deep heart, alone with God, the more one is able to be in communion with the other 'self'. Within the physical synaxis of the worshippers it is the identity of prayer of the heart, and the attachment of the mind to God, that open the gate of spiritual perfection[305] – and there is no need to charge the scriptural word 'perfection' with elitist vibrations.

To reach the threshold of unity in Holy Communion, one is required to walk through the desert of trial and purification. Feasts and celebrations are accompanied by fasts and long journeys, vigils and vigilance, trials and perils, hardships and wonders, and contemplation of the mysteries.[306] For this reason, the Irish Fathers are austere in dealing with sins that harm love and unity.[307] One cannot sunder the liturgical from the ascetic aspect, precisely because they are 'aspects' rather than 'ways' of spiritual life. Nor is one right in inferring unbalance or separation between the two in the ancient monastic world. The whole training programme, including liturgy and prayer, is the foundry of the believer's union in the resurrected Body of Christ.

Liturgy and asceticism are associated with the perception of time and the world. In the Irish context, it has been argued that emphasis on liturgy (supposedly the heart of *The Voyage of St Brendan*) expresses a positive world view, in which time is considered as intrinsically sacred, whereas emphasis on ascetic effort (unambiguous in the Celi De texts) betrays a negative approach to time and the world, a view that goes back to Paul, in whose epistles time is taken as part of the fallen world.[308] However, can one really receive time and nature as a gift, if one does not realise the consequences of the Fall and the need for redemption? Again, does the idea of intrinsic goodness contravene or blur the fact that nature suffers from the sin caused by human free will? The fundamental work of liturgy is to transform secular time into a window to eternity. In fact, whatever is done or is repeated in time and is of truth (either liturgy or ascesis or any pure movement of the heart) extends beyond the created borders; it becomes a participation in the one liturgy offered by Christ the Lord (cf. Heb. 10:14).

The ascetic struggles, as understood and prescribed by monastic leaders, are not an alternative to liturgical attendance, nor do they correlate with a negative appraisal of time and the world. Negation in Paul (2 Cor. 7:1) and the ascetic tradition refers to the secular *phronema* and not to the human nature; and the *contra mundum* indicates the fight against those forces that spoil the intrinsic goodness of creation. Thus, ascesis aims at cutting off the deformity of vice through participation in the divine beauty.[309] What else could 'the change of the whole world' (Matt. 13: 31–2) mean than the foretaste of the coming of the Lord in glory?[310] God's love and beauty is the driving force and the end of ascesis, which becomes the expression of a restless desire for union with the loving God.

On the other hand, nothing at all indicates the absence of the view of *fuga mundi* in the 'liturgical' *Navigatio*, since the whole setting in it is monastic from the beginning to the end. A statement that salvation is a gift freely given, not to be arduously attained by effort, chanting and penitential exercises, would sound odd to the ears of ancient monastics. For them the free gift would justify the most extreme asceticism, since ascetic effort was in fact not penalty or payment, but 'training' or response to God's love: 'What sort of bed had the King of the world? A fist-full of straw and dress and two fist-fulls of branches.'[311] On the other hand, the desert Fathers know that the physical practice of asceticism does not of itself create virtue, but merely manifests it.[312]

We come to the same conclusion: we should avoid (mis)reading marked by the monopoly of dialectical relations in which the modern mind suspects radical opposition, division or unbalance in diverse approaches to the same reality. The result could be the monism of a single, strictly defined constituent of reality, which thus ceases to be reality. Practical life, liturgy, ascesis, reason and contemplation are not parallel and autonomous parts of the human person but aspects of spiritual life, which is the one fruit of the Spirit.[313] Accordingly, a Eucharistic monism is most likely to introduce a 'light' Christianity, no matter 'low' or 'high', in the sense that nothing really matters before the overwhelming sacrament and its solemn performance. On the other hand, the monism of ascetic struggle may lead to a gloomy, grotesque and spiritually confined life. But this is not evidenced at least in the Greek and Irish patristic sources; and to project our inclinations and fears on monastic records is not the best way to learn something from them.

vii. Triadic and monadic in virtue

As the centre of the circle precontaining the principles of the radii originating from it, the Logos/Christ is the origin and also the goal of creation; the beginning and also the end, which is the place where everything began. It is from this beginning that a person receives being and participation in what is naturally good, and it is by conforming freely to this beginning that he hastens to the end. Now the way from the origin to the end is through participating in the One Wisdom, Beauty, Righteousness, Love, Holiness, which is the Logos Himself. Seen from another angle, this way is the revertive movement of human beings to the one Logos. As the essence of every human virtue, He is contemplated indivisibly in the multiple virtues which arise from Him, 'which is to say that anyone who through fixed habit participates in virtue, unquestionably participates in God'; for it is written, 'He that sanctifieth and they that are sanctified are of one' (Heb. 2:11). Such a person has shown 'that the beginning and the end are one and the same'.[314] Thus, perfect virtues, as reciprocally entailing properties of God's simple and uncompounded nature, make the human being a partaker of the divine simplicity and oneness.[315]

Maximus gives an epic picture of the universal convergence on both macroscopic and microscopic levels, based on the ontology and ethics of virtue. Mirroring the divine simplicity and oneness means accepting the gift of Christ's economy, which is the recapitulation of all creation in His Body (Eph. 1:10; Col. 1:16) and the restoration of the first rules and purpose of divine creation. God incarnate was the first to unite the natural fissures and to bind together all things in peaceful friendship.[316] He removed all the existing divisions: between male and female (showing us in our most fundamental and basic humanity); between paradise and the inhabited world; between heaven and earth; between the intelligible and the sensible; even the absolute division between created and uncreated. That was the restoration of the first and unchangeable purpose inherent in created nature. Christ reopened this way for man. And man, as microcosm possessing all the elements of creation, was called to make 'of his own division a beginning of the unity which gathers up all things in God, in whom there is no division'. The removal of all divisions takes place by means of a dispassionate condition of divine virtue, through a holy way of life.

The way to unity, in which the soul creates a beauteous and spiritual world within itself, can be adumbrated as follows:

The presence of the two general virtues, namely wisdom and gentleness or dispassion, makes the faculties of the soul and the respective senses apprehend the *logoi* of beings. This leads to a unified knowledge, not marked by gaps of ignorance; and this knowledge endows the worthy with a concept of God that is beyond understanding. Finally, it is through love that created nature is united with the uncreated, 'the whole man wholly pervading the whole God, and becoming everything that God is, without, however, identity in essence'.[317] This mystery of synergy of man and God in the innermost self indicates the process leading to universal unity.

The soul acquires the virtues – graces manifested through the body – as soon as it is freed from its irrational movement around sensible objects and pleasures. Its confinement in the transient reality corresponds with the 'material dyad'; the dyad of matter (including temporal properties, such as 'father' and 'mother', or 'genealogy') and form. Beyond that state lies the perfect unity which is perceived in the Trinity.[318] When through liturgy, prayer and ascesis the faculties of the soul – intelligence, incensive power and desire – are concentrated and unified around the divine simplicity, then soul and body, pervaded by the ever-moving divine energy, are united in Spirit, and love uncreated arises, and 'awareness is given to man of the equal value of all men', 'and all unlikeness to the divine utterly vanishes'.[319] The soul is led to the contemplation of the truth that God has become all things in everyone, and that through all things He is present to all. Thus, in the power of virtues the soul grows in likeness to God, leading its connatural body to the same deification and the unity of all creation in God's presence.[320] In the language of Ériugena, the river that flows and becomes virtue in human beings and returns again to the Source, brings forth 'all unity, all equality, all difference'.[321] In other words, the virtues, as the embodiment and multiplication of God's Being and Wisdom, make a man 'triadic' and 'monadic' in God's likeness. Thus, virtues are the way to unity, both inward and outward, and the monastic rules are signposts on this path.

At the same time the original state of unity, expressed in each individual virtue, signifies a particular person's wholeness and integrity, the verification of its uniqueness as a separate creation and not its expiry within a mass culture of any kind. In the monastic milieu, the value of the particular person is expressed in the individualisation and differentiation in the practice of devotion and in spiritual discipline, provided it is carried out under the guidance or the blessing of the superior or spiritual father.[322] The Irish maxim is very apt: among those things contained in holiness is 'division together with equality', that is to say the recognition of personal traits together with the avoidance of elitism or privilege.[323] Although monastic texts are often seen as 'codifications of self-abnegation and rigorous conformity',[324] the practice of private penance, the place of thorough introspection, the intimacy with a spiritual father, the diversity in the expression of monastic dedication and the variety in the patterns of life, informed by the recognition of personal *charismata* and the sensitivity to personal needs, all those features that paint a vigorous spiritual life, indicate that personal creativity and spiritual freedom are integrated in the ascetic insight into human identity, whereas only a perverted asceticism or theology would encourage the opposite.[325] From the life and teaching of monastic Fathers, we learn that spiritual growth is hindered by the suppression of creativity and uniqueness.

This concern and respect for the individual has nothing to do with modern perceptions of individualism. Respect for the individual has a pneumatological foundation. It derives from the awareness and experience of the energies of the Spirit, who confers gifts, which are personal, since the Spirit co-operates with our innermost self, and prays, as Heavenly King, within each of us. For 'the grace of the Spirit is one and immutable; but it acts on each one as it wills'.[326] At the same time, the Spirit confers on human nature the very life of God, 'the energies of God's essence', coming forth from God's nature like sun rays, among which are 'wisdom and light and righteousness and life',[327] leading human nature to its destiny. Working in such a personal manner, the Spirit continuously creates and renovates the whole as one undivided edifice. The monastic Fathers focus particularly on the energies of the Spirit, praising harmony in the coalescence of particularities. According to their favourite metaphor from the realm of music, the freedom of personal expression in the practice of piety can create the tonic key that gives the sense of harmony and melody in the unity of the body. 'The union of many, achieving harmony from polyphony and dispersion, becomes one divine concert, following one dispensator and initiator, and resting on truth itself, saying "abba, the father".'[328] In this context of grace and responsibility, a person in priestly orders is supposed to imitate Christ. In the words of Columbanus, the cleric 'will need to be moulded to the example of his redeemer and the pattern of the true shepherd, Who first preaching humility, and adding seven beatitudes to the first, which is poverty of spirit, taught man so fully to follow His footsteps, that by following after righteousness he must attain to the true circumcision of the eighth day'.[329]

We see that in both traditions the unity of the body is not founded on impersonal identity and uniformity. Human existence is sanctioned in the relational (and essential) nature of love, so that true freedom is characterised as 'slavery' to God and to the brethren. 'The foundation is your neighbour', the desert Fathers say; 'for on him depend all the commandments of Christ'.[330] But love is an enemy rather than an ally of uniformity. The angelic life on earth, the will of God in heaven and on earth, is a co-joining in love, peace and simplicity, and considers our neighbour's progress as our own profit. This grants harmony in the diversity of gifts in the operation of the body.[331] The teacher of this love is God Himself. For the whole of creation is 'participations' in Him, by which 'participations' or 'distributions' all things are unified in universal Love.[332]

If there is something otherworldly in the life of a monk, this is not his person – personhood is not coming down from a transcendental domain – but his virtues, which are God's virtues, bringing human nature to its entelechy and being manifested through the particular person. Such a person receives from God divine characters, 'for to the beautiful nature inherent in the fact that he is God's image, he freely chooses to add the likeness to God by means of the virtues.' Then, 'wholly transformed', the spiritual man receives 'all the qualities of God which we may take as the meaning of being likened to the Son of God'.[333] This is clearly expressed by Eriugena in language echoing Maximus, in a glowing paean of praise of human nature as the created Paradise, in which a continuing transmission and embodiment of the uncreated grace operates for the unification of all in Goodness; not through a kind of obscure mysticism but through the transformation of the whole life, personal and social, inward and outward. In Eriugena's allegory, the spiritual rivers, the virtues, burst forth from the uncreated Fountain to water human nature:

> First, arising in the secret recesses of humanity, in the most hidden channels, as it were, of the intelligible earth they issue in invisible virtues: then they spread out into the manifest effects of good actions and produce innumerable kinds of virtues and acts. For from them every virtue and every act proceeds and into them returns: but they themselves proceed from the Divine wisdom, and into It return.[334]

The transcendental element is neither the person nor the office, but the activities of the Spirit, which co-operate with man in weaving the gleaming fabric of the virtues. The fruits of the 'island of strong men' are rich and sweet,[335] and these are the one fruit of the Holy Spirit. Through the virtues the monk appears to manifest God's attributes and, consequently, informs his environment about the works of God in history and creation.[336]

Trinity and Monad is the paradox of the ineffability of God.[337] One and three: one essence, three subsistences; one power, three persons; one nature, three names. One from Three, One in Three, and Three recapitulated in One.[338] And the peacemaking *militia Christi*, the monks, are guided to the blessed and magnificent dwelling of the Triadic Monad. Following Christ and observing his commandments in Spirit, they are initiated into the life of the Trinity.[339] Monastics are called 'triadic' and 'monadic', manifesting in their lives this trinitarian paradox. Their mode of being is trinitarian and single. They all live as one, in a *perichoretic* fashion, in one essence, and consequently with one natural will, power and activity; and each one lives as called individually by God, with a unique name given, as hypostasis and person, sustaining within oneself a corresponding unity with the divine will. What makes the many one is common humanity in its blissful state; that is, ennobled and enhanced by the essential grace of the Trinity. And as the Trinity is the one God, in the same way the trinitarian community of human beings recapitulates the one Man, who has become the one and deified body of Christ – a reality that outshines all human identities. This is an experience that anticipates the eschatological reality, as expressed in the visionary words of Macarius:[340]

> They are clothed with the habitation from heaven, not made with hands, the glory of the divine light, as being made children of light . . . for all alike are changed into a divine nature, being Christs, and Gods, and children of God. There, brother will then speak peace to sister without confusion, for all are one thing in Christ. At rest in one light, one will gaze upon another, and in the gazing will forthwith shine back in truth, at the true contemplation of light inexpressible.

But even in this earthly life, after the sign of the cross has appeared in light and fastened itself to the soul, 'the man no longer condemns Greek or Jew, sinner or worldling. The inner man regards all men with a pure eye, and the man rejoices over all the world, and wants to venerate and love all, Greeks and Jews'.[341]

7. The locus of unity: a Person?

The Celtic *Alphabet of Piety* concludes its first section with a reference to the vital condition of virtue, which is to be in union with the catholic Church.[342] Every act can be evaluated by the extent to which it is undertaken in the unity of the Church. In his last words to his disciples, Daniel the Stylite underlines the desideratum of unity with the 'Holy Mother', the Church.[343]

Unity needs a centre, just as all points from the periphery of a circle meet in its middle. This centre indicates the criterion of the ecclesial identity. There is a visible centre, John Zizioulas maintains; and this is the person of the bishop, since the person is the ultimate ontological category, the cause of everything. Strangely enough, the concept of person points to a structure as the deepest reality. Because the person can exist only in communion, and, as Zizioulas takes for granted, communion can never exist without the one, the concept of hierarchy inheres in the idea of the person.[344] After all, this is supposed to be a reflection of the putative divine structure at the level of created beings. The communion-unity of God presupposes the one. The theoretical background of this episcopocentrism is the conviction that the person precedes the essence on the trinitarian as well as on the anthropological level: the oneness of God, the one God, and the ontological cause of the personal-trinitarian life of God, lies not in the one essence, but in the person of the Father. Transferred to the hierarchical scheme, that means that the bishop is the person who constitutes all the other persons with their charismata in the ecclesial community. Therefore, as 'the One', the bishop stands above the community, which means that through him the Spirit is bestowed and the Church is constituted. As 'the many' he can never be considered outside the community. As *alter Christus*, he unites the Church in one body and at the same time he produces diversity within the unity, by distributing the functions and orders in the Church. In and through the bishop, the One Christ becomes the Many (the community) and the many become 'the One'.[345]

We tend to overlook the fact that there is an absolute disparity between the uncreated and the created. It is a consequence of this fact that the relationship of the One with the Many in the Trinity, while offering a mirror for humanity, cannot correspond automatically to existing relationships between the members of the Church. This is because in the first case there is an absolute identification of essence and will between the One and the Many, while this cannot be considered to be so in the second case, since the members of the Church are not identified ontologically with the divine nature of Christ, nor with His will.

Scanning the patristic evidence, one reaches the conclusion that the basis of unity resides at two levels. First is the level of common nature. In the human being who disciplines his mind towards the precepts of God, the power from above reveals the faculty of the pure nature. This is what has been given to all of us by God from the first moment of our creation, culminating in the innate power of loving and the desire for divine beauty.[346] It is not nature considered apart from its Creator. God Himself is its archetype and model. God Himself is its very being, as the One Logos multiplied in all things. Yet, the fact that the whole of creation is a constellation of *logoi* steadfastly fixed in the One Logos is the foundation not only of unity, but also of distinction and otherness; for 'the one Logos is many *logoi* (according to the creative and sustaining procession of the One to individual beings) and the many are One (insofar as the One gathers everything together).' The more we fail to move in consistence with our divine principle of nature, the more we slide into fragmentation and disintegration.[347]

Unity is mysterious. It is not mere loving, just as the relationship between the divine Persons is not simply one of love understood as a personal trait. In the co-essential Trinity, each divine Person has the whole Deity and not simply a part of it, without being considered as autonomous, independent of the other Persons. For as divinity is the common essence, by virtue of which the Persons co-inhere 'naturally', so humanity, as the image of the divine oneness, is the place of human beings' mutual indwelling.[348] The love of the divine Persons is a movement and offspring of their common uncreated nature, and on this trinitarian model one has to establish any effort for the union of the believers as well as of the Churches. This reaches its climax in the act of union of the two natures in the Person of the Logos. In His hypostasis, and by virtue of the exchange of natural properties, the common human nature receives the divine *propria* and acts in a godly manner. This is the gift granted to men, requiring their own personal consent. Hence the allegory that Christ's flesh is the faith and His blood is the love.[349]

Therefore, the locus of unity lies also on the level of faith. The monastic *familia* 'is founded upon the unerring faith ... perfect in love'.[350] The monastic archetype is delineated as combining organisational minimalism and spiritual unity; unity of faith, hope and love. This is the spirit of a typical Irish monastic community: 'Their housing was indeed scattered, but they lived together *as one in faith, hope and charity*. They ate together and they all joined together for the divine office.'[351] Faith is unequivocally the ground and content of unity in the Church, the uniting principle. As Columbanus states, 'whatever has been said by one orthodox Christian, who rightly glorifies the Lord, the other will reply Amen, because he also loves and believes alike.'[352] Because faith 'brings the mind to the contemplation of the Holy Trinity', unity of faith follows the trinitarian archetype: 'We are of the same opinion and mind in what concerns Divinity, no less than Divinity is in concord in Itself, though it seems far-fetched, and so we have become one mouth and one voice, opposite to the way we were, building the tower.'[353] Concord has direct reference to the inner Divinity, and it also pertains to the communion of faith. In this way doctrine is connected with ethos.

Unity has no transcendental reference to any person, even when there is a parallelism with the immanent Trinity. When Evagrius shows the way to unity through Christ, he alludes to the divine essential oneness not only as the highest model, but also as the treasure and fount of unity: 'The inheritance of Christ is the Unity of the holy essence' and the heir of Christ delights in this mysterious contemplation with Him.[354] But faith is not just a system of beliefs, requiring simply a cognitive acceptance and behavioural conformity. It is the 'mighty wind' that empowers the dispassionate human being, giving the water of knowledge (the knowledge of God's being wholly in and through all things) and the fire of deification.[355] Unity, much more than a structural edifice, is contemplation of God, the mind's and soul's concentration and unification around the Divinity. Faith as right belief, knowledge as contemplation, and virtue as participation in divine properties, is a spiritual Trinity. It witnesses that we have become flesh and bones of Christ, that is, the great mystery of marriage;[356] or that Christ has become flesh within us, that is, the mystery of divine maternity: Brigid became 'mother' of the Lord, through ascetic contemplation and 'the noble faith of the Trinity'.[357]

To be one is to have reached the unity of faith, which means thorough knowledge of the 'bond' of union, Christ Himself.[358] Christ is the 'perfect faith',[359] and the repetition of the phrase 'ἐν Χριστῷ' – distinctive of the writings of St Ignatius of Antioch – presents Christ as the centre and the foundation of unity. Still, because the Son abides in human beings through the Spirit, and because the Spirit is the Person who initiates human beings into divine trinitarian life, the unity of the Church is grounded in Christians in the interiority of the Spirit and consequently in the interiority of the other divine Persons. It is not the mutual *perichoresis* of human persons, but rather the indwelling of the Spirit, namely the indwelling and operation of the uncreated sanctifying grace of the Trinity, common to everyone, that makes the Church into an image of the Trinity.

This is a goal demanding spiritual assiduity, so that one may reach the fullness of Christ within oneself and the whole Church may maintain the unity of the Spirit in the bond of peace.[360] As we have seen, this grace is not an undifferentiated power, but the multiplicity of personal gifts. A Macarian homily emphasises unity as the participation in God's nature through the diverse gifts of the Spirit: 'As all vessels are made of the same wooden nature, by which men sail the bitter sea, in the same way the souls of Christians [are made] of the one Divinity's heavenly light, the diverse gifts of the one Spirit.'[361] The Church is rooted in the unity and communion of the Holy Spirit; the ground of the unity, therefore, cannot but be trinitarian. This is the common source of all gifts, which creates unity in diversity.[362]

Revisiting the body-image, we see that it is quite instrumental in pointing to the source of unity, since every member separately and the body as an undivided whole is dependent upon the head, which is Christ. Within this reality every hierarchy is relativised, being recognised in terms of membership as limbs of the body. The function of hierarchy is understood within the reality of virtue, enlightenment and initiation, that is, the transmission of God's knowledge, for the edification of the body, whose head is Christ.[363] Faith is the nervous system, the body's electrical wiring, connecting the members with their centre and bringing all to an integral whole. And the life dispensed through the nerves is that very life of God, the uncreated activity. Truly, there is no schism in the body (1 Cor. 12:25), insofar as the members 'are animated by one soul dwelling therein',[364] and not because of the constitutive presence of the one person within the congregation. The body of Christ, Basil says, means that 'the one and the only true Head, Christ, exercises dominion over and unites the members, each with the other, unto harmonious accord'.[365] In a different context of imagery, the clergy and the laymen are the flock of the 'above pastor'.[366] Thus, as the Celtic catechist comments, the phrase 'He stood in the midst' (John 20:19) denotes the closeness of God to all the saints who abide by the unity of faith. To them God gives spiritual peace, as He gave it to the apostles, to whom he said 'peace unto you', for it was peace for them to contemplate Christ.[367]

Admittedly, ecclesial unity is inconceivable without the one. But can a created person, notwithstanding his symbolic function, be the centre of unity? The course of history and patristic writings do not seem to justify the human one as the criterion of belonging to the Body of Christ. For Basil, most alarming is the fact that he finds 'the very leaders of the Church at such variance with one another in thought and opinion, showing so much opposition to the commands of our Lord . . . and so cruelly confounding His flock, . . . men speaking perverse things', although their presence does not discredit the abundance of the Holy Spirit.[368] Beside anarchy and rebellion, John Chrysostom recognises a third evil – the most notorious one – that of the bad Church leader. He takes it as much worse than anarchy, for it has to do with authoritarian guidance; in such cases, Chrysostom continues, self-reliance is preferable to obedience, because, although hazardous, it does not abandon a person to the destructive effects of blind submission. When Paul urges us to obey our superiors, he refers to those whose life is witnessed as a model for imitation.[369]

There is a situation in which one can separate from the bishop but remain within the body of Christ. The bishop is not truly a bishop when he is guilty of teaching perverted notions with respect to the grace of Christ Jesus. The moment St Hypatios realised that

Nestorios, Patriarch of Constantinople, had spoken 'against Christ', he removed his name from the Church, saying that he has no more communion with him, 'for he is not a bishop'.[370] Orthodox faith is the condition of apostolic succession, and a bishop falls from his office if he proves to have fallen from the true faith. One may just recall the 15th canon of the first/second Synod of Constantinople, according to which the interruption of communion with a heretical bishop not only does not disrupt unity but saves the unity and integrity of the body.[371] One may also bring to mind the non-compliance of both monastics and laymen with the large episcopal assembly of Hieria (AD 754), which sanctioned the Emperor's iconoclasm. The main criterion of reception remains the truth that a leader or an assembly of leaders embodies. Apostolic succession (often thought of as the historical line of ordinations) is identified with the apostolic tradition, namely the 'teaching of truth', preserved in the life of the local churches.[372] The vertical connection of each church and its bishop with the apostolic truth is the foundation of the horizontal unity. This is the reason why ancient canon law requires the suspension of the ordination of a bishop where there is a disagreement about the candidate's orthodoxy and life, until such time as the reasons for such disagreement have been removed.[373]

If ecclesia is to mirror the Trinity, this ultimate One cannot be part of the ecclesial community itself, while at the level of creation a created 'one' should function simply and seriously as a worker of unity, admonishing his flock to union with God. At the same time, there is no hierarchy whatsoever in the Trinity (either immanent or economic), where the second and the third are equal and co-original;[374] and, as we have already observed, if there is a hierarchy in the Church, it is a hierarchy of virtue, enlightenment and, therefore, initiation. The gift of unity takes place in the name of Christ only, who is entirely present in His Church and does not need any representative. The bishop 'reflects' Christ, expressing the pastoral divine activity. Without doubt, it is a specific task of the bishop to serve and preserve unity, as is evident in the letters of Ignatius of Antioch, and he is in a position to preside within the Church 'in the place of God'.[375] But to ensure the unity within his pastoral function is different from being himself the locus of unity, as a reflection of the supposed position of God the Father in the trinitarian order.

Ecclesial unity does not depend upon blind subjection to a visible centre. Conformity to the centre may fabricate cemented 'spiritualities', but does not necessarily vouchsafe real unity. The bishop does not provide in himself personally the criterion of one's belonging to the body of Christ. It is worthy of comment that when the Patriarch of Constantinople called St Daniel the stylite to his mansion, to consider whether he should leave him unbothered in his place of ascesis, it was the holy man's orthodox confession that prompted the bishop's respect and acceptance and not any confession of obedience.[376] Columbanus' reaction against the pope is justified in his professed triple axis: zeal of faith, love of peace, Church unity. Thus, any person not professing the orthodox faith is to be excommunicated, 'no matter his order, position or rank; for none should honour a man in despite of God'. Far from being a unifying centre, such a person tries to separate people from Christ. Consequently, spiritual authority is recognised in the hands of a bishop just so long as his 'ratio' remains 'right'. In this sense, unity is not a mechanistic scheme, but a spiritual achievement. It resides not in the person of Peter, but in Peter's right confession. Such unity of faith 'has produced in the whole world a unity of power and privilege, in such wise that by all men everywhere freedom should be given to the truth'.[377]

Ignatius of Antioch, among the apostolic Fathers, is thought to be a most rigorous exponent of the bishop as the centre of gravity, presenting his person as standing 'in God's place' and as 'a symbol (τύπος) of the Father';[378] where 'Father' is viewed in his personal 'monarchy'. First, as it became clear in the light of patristic evidence, the connection between monarchical personalism and immanent Trinity is arbitrary. Second, although Ignatius sets out to safeguard the authority of the bishop's office, which was then a subject of dispute, the parallelism should not be overstated. In patristic literature the bishop is also presented as image and symbol of Christ.[379] If Ignatius insists on the closeness of the believers with their bishop, it is because their bishop is the one who expresses and defends the divine truths. Only 'in Jesus' mind' may he operate the gift of unity in the name of Christ.[380] At the same time, Ignatius himself, on his way to Rome, avers that Jesus Christ alone, and the Romans' love, will have the oversight of his Church, having been now left without a bishop.[381]

The emphasis on the person of the bishop is not irrelevant to the notion of the Eucharist as the sole and exclusive medium of communion with God. According to this perception, the life of the triune God is mediated exclusively in the Eucharistic event, in which case doctrine holds, if any, a secondary place, as the criterion of the apostolic succession and as the basis of unity. The bishop, even if he does not take part in the sacrament, remains the centre of the Eucharist.[382]

In the first place, one must underline that the Eucharist is a Trinity-centric event, celebrated in the name of the Trinity and not in the name of a bishop. Any emphasis on the authority and power of the bishop over the trinitarian character leads inevitably to episcopomonism. One may easily be led to the conviction that for the achievement of catholicity the cardinal and most decisive role is that of the bishop[383] and that his ministry is the ultimate expression of the unity of the Church and, consequently, the Eucharist is considered as one of its functions. Even if he is taken as a type and image of Christ, he takes precedence over the Eucharist itself. Such views are consonant with the Roman Catholic views of universal ecclesiology. In the second place, although the Eucharist is unequivocally associated with the unity of the Church,[384] can it be considered as the sole indispensable feature expressing the notion of the Church and its unity? Should one understate the significance of the orthodox faith for ecclesiology, one presents the Eucharistic unity of the Church in a mechanistic way. Yet in some cases the Eucharistic unity may even express and foster division, while the unworthy participation in it separates from Christ and from one another.[385] How can the Eucharist *per se* make the Church, if it cannot secure the membership of a person in the Body of Christ? For it is 'audacity to call members of Christ' persons for whom the master is the wisdom of the flesh, where dissension, strife and rivalry sunder the harmony of the Spirit.[386]

The Church is founded on the confession of Christ: to be a member of the Church is to be Christ's and to bear his name. Such confession entails what humanity has received from the witnesses to the truth: the apostles and the holy Fathers of the Church.[387] Thus, unity in faith has not only a synchronic dimension. It is also unity with the past, a diachronic unity, the unity of tradition. This tradition has been shaped not by pious customs, human conceptions and societal values, but by the theophanies in history, and it has been handed down through the unbroken chain of saints and in the continuity of worship, ascesis and teaching. It waters life as the 'spring' of the Spirit, not as the 'torrent' of the letter.[388] Its characterisation as 'sacred' derives not merely from its ancestry but from its truth, namely what is accepted as true and godly by the innumerable chorus of saints over the ages. Sacred tradition embraces the liturgy and right belief, which is expressed in the ascetic ethos of love. Undoubtedly, the liturgy as a succession of acts may occasionally turn into typolatry and confinement to the tangible and immediate. It is no less a possibility that orthodoxy may lapse into mere ideology, grasped either by the hypertrophic brain of the rationalist or by the adamant teeth of the fundamentalist! Thus it would be more precise to say that sacred tradition is Christ Himself. It is the manifestation of the Holy Spirit that makes it sacred, that makes faith, liturgy and ascetic ethos the seedbed of unity. But when we see the Eucharist in itself as the Church, the Kingdom and goal of spiritual life, the way is open for the reduction of unity to a horizontal accord along structural lines and, consequently, to submission to a visible centre.

Maximus the Confessor at his trial was pressed on the fact that he was not in communion with the throne of Constantinople, a charge that touched his ecclesiological sensibilities. But communion, for Maximus, is genuine only if it is communion in the truth, so he justifies his stance by reciting the ways in which the Patriarch of Constantinople has rejected the faith defined by the synods. At the same time and on the same grounds the confessor and martyr praises Rome's primate for his proper confession of Christ during the hard days of monothelitism. Rome had endorsed and defended the faith founded on the apostles and the Fathers, a faith declared and confirmed in the sufferings of those who endured persecution and those who shone forth in the ascetic life. In response to the accusation that he has split the Church by his stubbornness, Maximus says: 'If the one who states what is in Scripture and the holy Fathers splits the Church, what does someone do to the Church who annuls the teachings of the saints, without which the Church's very existence is impossible?'[389] Eucharistic communion presupposes full unity in all the basic aspects, like baptism, faith and love.[390] It is the one, simple and indivisible grace and power of faith that makes the Church and the Eucharist a place effecting the 'simple, whole and indivisible *schesis*', where no one is separated from the community and even the existence of differences allows no division amongst men. The sole cause of disorder is variance in faith and incompatibility with holiness.[391]

Unity is accomplished as soon as we have in our hearts the right faith, that is, as soon as we are able to contemplate the mystery of creation and the divine mystery. Unity is contemplation of the Trinity, since contemplation is participation in the divine energy; when the soul and mind will what is proper and fitting, controlling and chiding the body, and abiding in serenity, then 'they enter the natural contemplation. They see the venerable Holy Trinity, as far as possible, pondering over the inaccessibility of divine glory on account of its stunning radiance.'[392] In truth, it is a cosmic unity manifest in human nature. For when in practice and contemplation the soul grows in likeness to God, leading the body to the same deification, then, the Creator of all is manifest as One, encompassing all things in (and through) humanity, in which all beings are drawn together into a unity.[393]

As a general ecclesiological remark, we may say that the local scattered Churches of Christ hold their catholicity insofar as they are united *internally* by the same *confession* and *life*, while externally this unity may be preserved with variations in organisation.[394] That is why Columbanus' exhortation combines faith with organic membership in Christ in a dynamic process towards perfect manhood, in which all are one:

We are all joined members of one body, whether Franks or Britons or Irish, or whatever our race be. Thus let all our races rejoice in the comprehension of faith and the apprehension of the Son of God, and let us all hasten to approach to perfect manhood, to the measure of the completed growth of the fulness of Jesus Christ, in Whom let us love one another, praise one another, encourage one another, pray for one another.[395]

Pure nature, which is the common endowment implanted by the Creator, and faith, which is eventually and essentially the enhancement of nature with God's activity revealing that very nature, form the ground of unity and distinction alike, the locus of sameness and otherness, apart from any structural element and hierarchical conception. Christian philosophy initiates the human person into the mystery of the one in the many and the many in the one through a spiritual method and a pattern of life, which aim at the transcendence of all division in a Godlike unity and the integrity of each person within this unity. Within the unending intertwining of nature and grace, which resembles Celtic lace, the human will operates either in a unifying or in a disrupting way. It is to these issues that we will now wend our way.

Two:
Institution and Charisma

1. Identification and distinction

The Church, both in its origins and in essence, is a charismatic institution, being constituted and preserved by the Holy Spirit. '*Charisma* and *energeia* and *diakonia* are one thing, differing only in names.'[1] Thus, all ecclesiastical institutions are charismatic manifestations of the one Body of Christ, in which the energies of the Spirit work out the salvation of the world. Meanwhile, certain manifestations of the Spirit have never been identified with institutional patterns, and these can be called 'charismatic' par excellence. The charismatic phenomenon of monasticism became institutionalised over time. In this sense, one may speak of the monastic institution, or even use the oxymoron 'the institution of the desert'. But other aspects of spiritual life remain by their nature outside the sphere of institutions, including private prayer, holy fools, eremitism, or even some extraordinary gifts. Without doubt, the divine 'processions' transcend the limits of the institutional zone, offering abundance of life to the undivided Body of Christ.

Can we possibly – beyond wishful thinking – deny any distinction between the terms 'institutional' and 'charismatic'? Such identification, though, can be meaningful in a prescriptive rather than a descriptive framework, otherwise every ministry and sacrament, every institutional element should be taken as existing and operating automatically.

Although the Church as a single body is constituted by the Spirit, yet the particular ecclesiastical ordinances – identified with spiritual gifts in their genesis – run the risk of objectification in their historical course through the reinforcement of their external and formal elements and the neglect of the charismatic dimension of religious life. Undoubtedly, every ministry or ordination is a gift of the Holy Spirit no less than any extraordinary charisma. Nevertheless, Basil of Caesarea insists, the renewal of the Church is the by-product of the renovation – in Spirit – of the *mind* of *each* member of the body.[2] As the Irish holy fool intimates to the wise bishop, worship is of no avail if it is not fuelled by an inward disposition, and the external image of the cleric has no dignity if it is devoid of any content.[3] In other words, observance of external forms is not necessarily an indication of the presence of the Spirit.

Each of the energies of the Spirit carries the one fruit of the Spirit, granted to all persons according to the measure of each one's faith. Now, if in a specific ministry – established by the energy of the Spirit – the fruit of the Spirit is not present, then we may speak of a discrepancy between the person who serves the ministry and the ministry's charismatic essence. And if such discrepancy and alienation exceeds its personal character, receiving sanction in the course of time, then the institutional dimension (whether ritual, office, ministry or sacrament) assumes a bureaucratic character and a mechanistic, mediatory or even quasi-magical authority, which extinguishes the flame of charismatic life. Then, institutions appear to constitute formal relationships and cease to function as living bearers of theology. Consequently, theology is led into secularisation or is frozen in conservatism – two sides of the same coin. Charismata have a relational character. They are integral parts of the body or they designate specific relationships, and in this sense they establish institutions. The primary relationship, though, is that between the human being and God. If there is a flaw in it, any other relationship will be external and conventional, unable to create communion except for fibres of power and submission.

2. Essential realities and institutionalism

The aforementioned qualifications are witnessed in the institutionalised charisma of spiritual paternity, which is not constituted by any bureaucratic office. The sacrament of spiritual paternity cannot lead to the sphere of God's grace, if specific demands regarding the spiritual condition of the minister are absent. In coenobitic monasticism the charisma and institution of spiritual fatherhood are identified in the person of the superior. The hegumen, as a descendant of Peter and all the succession of apostles and teachers, shoulders the pastoral care of his community, bearing the gift of 'binding and loosing'.[4] Still, the gift of the Spirit surpasses institutional boundaries. For this reason, although every priest, and especially the bishop, is entitled *ex officio* to fatherhood, spiritual paternity, as we saw earlier, is considered to be a quality of the person who is guided by the Holy Spirit and thus can offer a way of life.[5]

This is why much emphasis is laid upon spiritual guidance and its prerequisites, and not simply on formal confession and absolution.[6] Instead of being content with a reconciliation and atonement, which a cleric in orders can provide, the believer must assiduously seek out the right spiritual director or physician. Gregory Nazianzen associates the office of the bishop with spiritual guidance, and this association prescribes the highest standards. For even if a man has reached the greatest heights of virtue, no knowledge or power justify him in venturing into this office on is own volition, since the guidance of man, the most variable and manifold of creatures, seems to be the art of arts and science of sciences.[7] All offices and sacraments – ordination, monastic habit, the bishopric itself – are gifts offered by God according to one's progress in the spiritual life. Accordingly, the canons themselves are the servants of spiritual gifts.[8]

Institution does create objectified securities, though it is not meant to do so. Regarding the institution of episcopacy, Zizioulas claims that the episcopacy's charismatic character provides with the office's limitations. According to him, although we can even attribute infallibility to a bishop, such infallibility is 'a charisma, and as such it is constantly subject to the epiclesis of the community'.[9] In this way he acknowledges a dynamic *perichoresis* within the body, where each man can bear witness to the Truth. However, should we accept that all divine gifts pass exclusively through the office and person of the bishop as the 'infallible' (even with qualifications) head of the Church, and should we claim that he *constitutes* the community, while 'none else can give the Spirit to the community'[10] save him, then one cannot help suspecting how easily the emphasis upon the person turns into a personal totalitarianism, which is no better than an impersonal institutionalism, in fact if not in theory. If the person is 'the cause of being',[11] then the bishop is identified with the principle and cause of the very being of the community, a concept that might give rise to every kind of whim and arbitrariness, perhaps comfortably sanctioned by the institution.

In a way, the centrality of the person of the bishop is a natural consequence of the absolute exclusiveness of the Eucharist. Here, a question arises: Is the Church made, and is it becoming what it will eschatologically be, merely by virtue of the Eucharistic event? Does the Eucharist *per se* and what stems from it alone pertain to the true identity and mystery of the Ecclesia?[12] Does the Eucharistic event – with its structure, episcopacy and distinctions – necessarily involve the other essential features of true discipleship and true union in Christ?

Here, Dionysius the Areopagite points in the right direction. Our participation in the Eucharist, he explains, 'is an icon of our participation in Jesus', conveying His very presence; but it fulfils its function as long as it leads to 'the mind's intelligible fulfilment', 'the harmonious habit of mind' and 'the immaterial gift of light'.[13] In the words of another mystic, if the mystical activity of the Spirit is not 'accomplished on the altar of the heart',[14] then every event remains incomplete and ineffective. This illustration of the Church involves the irresistible invitation to a journey towards purification and illumination through the suppression of the passions and cultivation of the virtues, namely through a therapeutic process. If one focuses upon the text of the liturgy, one will notice that in the moment of consecration of the bread and the wine the celebrant prays and implores: 'Send down your Holy Spirit upon us and upon these gifts.' And after the consecration he again asks God to 'send down upon us in return his divine grace and the gift of the Holy Spirit'.[15] This repetition is intended to remind the participant of the fact that communion with God is a dynamic relationship and that the divine energetic presence is not restricted to the change of the Eucharistic elements. After all, the Spirit does not 'descend' save 'in love'.[16] Although the Spirit constitutes the Eucharist and the Church, it does not descend into unloving and unclean hearts. For it is the 'joyous shared love' that unites the members of the body and 'ensures for the whole hierarchy the beauty of its conformity to God'.[17] Nilus of Ancyra is eager to shift the emphasis from the external, conventional and superficial level to the inner and essential. Neither miraculous signs nor rank redeem man, but virtue, namely participation in the life of God.[18]

The Fathers insist on the charismatic aspect of the offices, focusing not on ritual performances but on spiritual requirements. Those who claim episcopal jurisdiction, they stress, rely upon the promise of the keys to Peter as the justification of their actions. This, Origen continues, is correct in so far as the bishop himself is like Peter in his life, and can in fact pass judgement with the same degree of authority. But if he himself is 'entangled in the snares of his own sin', he binds and looses 'to no effect'.[19] This is exactly Columbanus' thesis to the pope, where he associates spiritual power with orthodoxy. In the Irish tradition the case of Brigit indicates the prevalence of charisma over canonical rules. Bishop Mel, drunk with divine grace, reads to Brigit the service of the ordination of a bishop instead of the monastic tonsure; and the office is the crowning of her virtue. The supreme authority of the Irish abbess derives from her miracles, her lowliness of heart and purity of mind, her moderate life and spiritual grace.[20] The Irish tradition insists upon the demand for personal sanctity.[21] This is why the biographers of all the holy bishops, from Finnian onwards, attribute greatest importance to their value and role as ascetics, monastic leaders or hermits. The holy man is a continuing presence in the Irish monastic milieu, although never separated from the Eucharistic context.[22]

Let us delve a little deeper into the patristic mind and experience regarding the external elements of the religious life. The Macarian Homilies present ecclesiastical order, canon law and ritual as types and shadows of the hidden realities. As the Eucharistic institution is not accomplished without communion of the holy flesh and blood, likewise the soul's progress is impeded, and every work is invalidated, without the communion of the Spirit in the altar of the heart, all the more so consciously. Sanctity, the endless end of Christian life, is not an individual achievement or the realisation of individuation or simply personhood. It has a relational character, but this relationality presupposes inner communion and intimacy with God. Equating the inner man with liturgy and hierarchy, the Greek mystic exposes the ecclesiastical order and canon law as an image of the spiritual sequence in the soul's progress.[23] All the visible realities are types and shadows of the hidden ones. The visible temple corresponds to the temple of the heart, the priest to the true priest of the grace of Christ, the ecclesiastical rite to ascesis and virtues, and the Eucharist and communion to the mystical activity of the Spirit in the heart. Institutions are regarded not only as types of the eschatological Kingdom, but also as types of the inner Kingdom. The Church event is internalised:

> Well, the word 'Church' is used of the individual soul, as well as of many. For the soul gathers all her faculties and is thus a Church to God. For it was fitted for communion with the heavenly Bridegroom, and mingles with the heavenly One. This is observed both of the many and of the one. Thus the prophet says of Jerusalem, I found thee desolate and naked, and I clothed thee and so forth, as if he spoke of a single person.[24]

The rational soul is 'the living and true Church of God . . . For the Church of Christ and the temple of God and true altar and living sacrifice is the man of God.'[25] As Evagrius states, 'the temple of God is he who is a beholder of the sacred unity, and the altar of God is the contemplation of the Holy Trinity.'[26] Gregory the Theologian alludes to that inner temple and altar when he says that no one is worthy of God, who is both sacrifice and arch-priest, except he who has presented himself to God a living, holy sacrifice; only then can one offer the external sacrifice, the *antitype* of the great mysteries.[27] This double interpretation is given by Basil too. The *atrium* is the Church, but more precisely it is a spiritual state. Without the heavenly life no one is able to venerate in the holy atrium, even if one considers oneself worthy of participating in the physical congregation.[28] This view is echoed by Columbanus. Man worships in the sacred atrium of God, widening his heart in perfect sanctification, where God dwells, that is in the Church; also, one venerates God in one's consciousness. The Irish theologian operates on both those two levels, that of the Church and that of the consciousness.[29]

Yet, types and hidden realities are two dimensions of a single reality. The 'visible' are means for approaching what is 'concealed' and not immediately discernible. The mystical and the sacramental dimensions are interconnected. The priestly offering is no less 'mystical' than the inward activity of the Spirit. But the external form of the sacrament points to a deeper layer.[30] Not that the visible liturgy is a mere pointer, just a shadow containing nothing but messages; for its substance is the Comforter, who deifies the participants.[31] And yet, it is a shadow in the sense of the anticipation of an ever-present reality that is still hidden. Ultimately, 'the living activity of the Holy Spirit is to be sought from God in living hearts', Macarius says, 'because all visible things and all present arrangements will pass away, whereas hearts alive in the Spirit will abide.'[32] All visible arrangements and orders should be considered not as transcendental realities but as instruments guiding human souls to their fulfilment as true temples containing the uncontainable. It is worth noting that Macarius uses in this context the word *metabole* (μεταβολή), change or transformation of the soul, which is the same term signifying the consecration of the Holy Gifts on the visible altar. It has been rightly noticed that 'the consecration of the sacred elements is an anticipation of the eschatological transformation of the believer and of the world.'[33] But the theme of the inner temple of glory is not a novelty of later centuries; it is rooted in Paul (1 Cor. 3:16) as in the Transfiguration accounts that describe the experience of participation in the trinitarian light through the 'resplendent flesh'[34] of Christ (Matt. 17:1–9, Mark 9:2–13, Luke 9:28–36).

We are already in the domain of what we call mysticism or mystical life, within which features par excellence the charismatic dimension bearing on the personal immediacy of God's presence. This should be considered not as a strand in the Christian tradition, but as that very tradition, since the ultimate *mystikon* or *mysterion* – a secret told yet unutterable – is Christ Himself (cf. Col. 3:3), who remains the sole initiator into the mysterious being of the uncreated. From this perspective, one may understand that the sacramental and the mystical do not designate different approaches: the institution is a *mysterion* and the mystical communion is a sacrament. Or, as Andrew Louth has pointed out, the ecclesial and sacramental dimensions are intrinsic elements of the mystical, not to be contrasted with it. Mysticism 'refers to the lived reality of Christianity itself', not 'an individualist quest for "peak" experiences'.[35] But to live on the surface is to betray the very content of ecclesial institution, to lose the meaning that the institution enshrines, thus effecting a fragmentation within spiritual life.

3. *Charisma in monasticism*

If we now throw into sharp focus the monastic world, the haven of mystical life as defined above, we may recognise the charismatic aspect in the prophetic sap and the apostolic texture of the monastic profession, both clearly present in the Greek East and the Celtic West alike. The monastics are presented as descendants of the apostles, copying and imitating the 'perfect life' handed down to the apostles by Christ, which is the rising above the passions and the renunciation of the secular turmoil. Through possessionlessness, perseverance, equality, spiritual strife and compassion for their fellow men, they have made their life an impress of apostolic virtue.[36] Thus, the monastic schema is called 'sacred and apostolic' and if Anthony, 'our father', has been seen among the apostles, then the monk becomes a link in the chain of apostolic succession.[37] Furthermore, the apostolic vocation is bound up with the prophetic gift. Gregory praises the virgins of his territory as the 'enlightened eye of my court'.[38] Such gifts shape the universal or catholic person, the saint, who puts fire to the whole country, who possesses the whole world in his light. The saint is the basic chord of the harp. For he is a prophet, a messenger, an interpreter and a teacher, and also 'the physician' of the people around.[39] On the other hand, strange though it may appear, the origins of the episcopacy cannot be understood in terms of any identification of bishops with the apostles. 'Prophets' and 'teachers' are dignified as 'hierarchs' in the Didache. The apostles, who were acting as ecumenical bishops, were succeeded by the wandering prophets and teachers –also named apostles – who were disciples and immediate co-operators of the apostles and who acted as supra-regional bishops.[40]

One of the reasons of the mingling of the monastic profession with the notion of holiness or sainthood is the virtual identification of the monk with the martyr. The martyr is the perfect human being who follows Christ on the path of passion and victory over death. The monastic profession was considered above all, a martyrdom of conscience. This is a *topos* in patristic literature and expressed, in a characteristically Irish manner, in the scheme of the three martyrdoms.[41] The zeal for martyrdom, a zeal that is commingled with the ethics of heroism, led the Irish converts to the monastery.[42] Thus, as the martyr embodies the highest ideal of dedication to God in his very act of giving his blood for the love of God, an act that is another baptism enacted by the sanctifying Spirit, in the same way the perfect dedication of the monk, through an act that outreaches the visible limits of institutions, expresses the utmost union with God, namely sanctity. The monk is identified with Christ's Cross.[43] It is the monk, as martyr, who preserves the eschatological perspective of religious life, by living fully the confession of Paul that his life is hidden in Christ and that we do not have a permanent city in this earthly life (Col. 3:3, Heb. 13:14).

If we now cast our eyes upon the everyday life of the monastic world, we will see the charismatic element expressed and nourished in the freedom and spontaneity that paint a flexible pattern of organisation in both the Greek and Irish world, although more unequivocally in the latter. It is noteworthy that notwithstanding the Irish penchant for laws, monastic leaders seemed not to be eager to fix canonically a certain organisation of spiritual life.[44] Although a legal approach to spiritual life would be more than expected in Ireland, on account of its hierarchical stratification and its attachment to the Mosaic law, yet we meet a somehow flexible society, with deep respect of personal otherness, loose organisation and diversity in ascetic expression. Equally important is the high esteem in which the eremitic life is held. The charismatic dimension in the Church is secured mainly by the force of eremitism, and the recognition of the priority of the charismatic element is manifested in the practice of receiving advice from wise hermits.[45] Indeed, in the ascetic and intensely spiritual climate of Irish monasticism, the ecclesiastical grade is deemed subsidiary to personal response to the Gospel.[46]

In the plurality that characterises the Irish tradition, one may see the proportionate function of the charismatic and institutional dimensions of the Church. This is clearly shown in the constitution of synods. Whereas synods on the Continent were normally assemblies of bishops, in Ireland membership was wider and included bishops, *excelsi princeps, doctores*, scribes and anchorites. Unlike its Frankish counterpart of the sixth and seventh century, the Irish synod shows a Church that allowed for several sources of authority: the orders of a bishop; the prestige that flowed from being the abbot of a major monastery; the learning of the scholar; the asceticism of the anchorite. Because it allowed for distinct sources of authority deployed by men of equal rank, it was obliged to give the synod an even more central position than in Francia or in England.[47]

In both Greek and Irish traditions institutionalisation did not eliminate the non-institutionalised area of spiritual life, which fosters freedom, spontaneity, personal relationships and personal responsibility. The charismatic dimension of spiritual life secures the freedom of the person from institutional objectifications that tend to enslave it. Some expressions of the freedom of the Spirit in personal life are exposed by Macarius, who renders a multidimensional portrayal of the Spirit-bearer. The energies of the Spirit may be diverse and interchangeable in the existence of those who have become children of God, in a compass that extends from the more conventional forms to the bizarre state of folly for Christ.[48] The sense of freedom reaches a peak in the case of the holy fools, in whom we acknowledge the charismatic form in its extreme and marginal expression. Here lies the paradox: The fool is recognised as an idiot and simultaneously as a man plentiful in knowledge and the grace of the Spirit.[49] In the Irish milieu we recognise two supplementary forms of spirituality: on the one hand, the normal and prevalent form of the wise and incorrupt; on the other, the liminal form that transcends all institutional limits. The first voluntarily bows to the second, on account of the second's total dedication to God and neglect of human affairs.

The charismatic dimension not only secures respect for the particular person but also acknowledges God's freedom in His relationship with creation. The Spirit is likened to the wind. Clearly, it blows in the direction of Christ; but It blows not as a Person subordinated to another's personal will, nor in the direction of a Christ considered in an hierarchical scheme of submission and power. The freedom of the Spirit belies the claim that all divine manifestations pass through ecclesiastical structures. When the Irish biographer refers to the missionary effort of Palladius, the first bishop sent to Ireland by Rome (431), he attributes his total failure to the fact that no one can receive anything from this world, if it is not given to him from above.[50] We realise that the biographer does not acknowledge an institutional (papal) authority and universality, from which the divine gifts or the revelation of the divine will would emerge. The gift is given or refused directly from above, according to the ultimate freedom of God, whose ways are inscrutable.

4. Holiness and sacramental efficacy

A thorny question that arises within the framework of dialectics between institution and charisma is, How deep is the connection between holiness and the performance of the sacraments? Patristic language concerning this point seems somewhat nebulous, and one can detect a degree of intentional ambiguity. On the one hand, the grace of the Spirit does not accompany impure or evil men to the height of their thrones, states Gregory Nazianzen.[51] On the other hand, the Fathers endorse the paradox that the Spirit operates through institutions irrespective of the inner condition of the minister, and regardless of his personal participation in God's grace. In other words, even in the case of incompatibility between office and virtue, grace remains active through the sacraments in the participants in spite of any deficiencies of the institutional agent.[52] This is not because the ritual act has a drastic power in its ceremonial acting, but because of the real presence of Christ in the Spirit, and by virtue of the presence of real participants, that is, persons in real communion with God. John Chrysostom explains the matter sufficiently:

> Why wonder, if in the case of unworthy men these things are done for the other's sake . . .? There could not have been either Baptism, or the Body of Christ, or Oblation, through such, if in every instance grace required merit. But as it is, God even operates through unworthy persons, and in no respect is the grace of

Baptism damaged by the conduct of the priest: else the receiver would suffer loss. These things I say, lest anyone among the bystanders, busying himself about the life of the priest, should be offended as concerning the things solemnized. Man introduces nothing into the things which are set before us, but the whole is a work of the power of God, and it is He who initiates you into the mysteries.[53]

At the same time, Chrysostom takes it for granted that 'God does not ordain all, yet He operates through all',[54] transferring the focus from the validity of the ordinances to the personal responsibility and participation of the communicant. It is God's condescension that He operates through unworthy ministers, not because the performed acts have a quasi-magical power, but because the divine energies operate directly on the participants, initiating them into God's life. Yet, the same Father admits that when the bishop governs the people without the grace and peace of God, 'all is ruined and lost, for want of those helms. And though he may be skilled in the art of steering, he will sink the vessel.'[55] The fact of spiritual deficit on account of the priest is particularly emphasised in the life of Andrew the holy fool, in which the biographer, referring to a sinful celebrant, blames him for depriving the people 'of the grace of the sacraments'.[56] As for the other side of the world, the Rule of Patrick is very strict regarding the ordination of unworthy priests and imposes a grave penance on the bishops for such acts. It even ascribes the tribulations and destructions of people to such erroneous tactics, since there are no valid baptisms and chrismations.[57] In such cases the Fathers do not really refer to the power of the sacraments, but to the efficacy of episcopal authority and the obligation of edifying the *plerōma* of the Christian community.

Let us examine a short but very important text concerning this matter. In the famous epistle of Dionysius Areopagite to monk Demophilus,[58] which has had conflicting interpretations, the writer charges an unruly monk, a person of fiery zeal, with the sin of having broken into the sanctuary, chased the priest out while in the process of ministering confession and seized the consecrated elements in order to prevent their profanation. At the same time, Dionysius does not refrain from asserting that 'the unillumined priest is not a true priest', and therefore he does not fit the professed position in divine hierarchy. But what is at the heart of the story – and which has been overlooked – is Dionysius' reference to the reasons that forbid that monk's intervention and intrusion. Demophilus' inner being is as far from the truth as that of the priest. His duty is to establish order in *his own* temple by giving the proper place to the three faculties of the soul: appetite, emotion and reason. Such discipline will give him the virtues necessary to attain the vision of God, virtues like humility and compassion, which characterised Moses and David. Only such integrity can possibly supply him with authority over home, city and nation – and such a remark reveals a kind of ambiguity in the thought of Dionysius, a space for flexibility and mobility within the hierarchy. At the end of the day, what Dionysius really condemns is hatred, impatience and vengeance. One should never lose sight of the fact that the Areopagite never compromises his vision, which is *theoptia* (the vision of God) as the *sine qua non* of the higher orders, both the initiated order of monks and the initiating order of priests, although he does not go so far as to argue with Symeon the New Theologian and the great bulk of monastic tradition that authority belongs to those qualified by illumination irrespective of their order. The monk, being a true philosopher, has a high ministerial ability, for, according to John Chrysostom, he is indeed far more capable than an ordinary king in ruling with kindness over cities and men. After all, the true monk is a 'light to all', and for this reason he should not refrain from accepting the ministry in fear of jeopardising his contemplative life.[59] Nonetheless, Dionysius shares with the bulk of patristic literature the conviction that illumination is the condition for ministering the sacraments, even if judgement is not allowed for persons untouched by grace. Because the principle of hierarchy is not an impersonal principle, the link between the worth of the priest and the dignity of his office is imperative.[60]

Again, as in all cases, authority is seen against a backdrop of virtues and their by-product, the vision of God. Hence Dionysius describes, or rather prescribes, the hierarch as 'the inspired and divine man learned in all sacred knowledge, in whom his own (i.e. interior) hierarchy . . . is perfected and made known'.[61] The holders of spiritual office are set up against a definite theological ideal, by which they are measured. We, therefore, will not be far from the truth if we understand the Christian community 'as Paul, Irenaeus and others did, that is, primarily as a living, free cosmos of spiritual gifts in which every Christian can have his share even without the help of official mediators. Nevertheless, the normal and desirable thing is that the one who is endowed with spiritual gifts should also be appointed to the corresponding position in the Church.'[62]

5. The *vicarius* Christi *and the people*

The ardent refusal to distinguish the charismatic from the institutional aspect is partly grounded upon a total identification of the ecclesial community with Christ. In such identification John Zizioulas sees the causal roots of the theology of episcopacy.[63] In the bishop the Christological mystery of the one who is simultaneously the many becomes historically concrete.[64] The presence of Christ in the Church and the catholicity of the Church are mediated through the bishop. Despite the fact that the bishop is conditioned by the congregation, the situation of asymmetrical bipolarity remains between bishop and congregation. But, as we saw, this episcopocentric tenet not only seeks Christological ground but also sets the bishop in the place of the 'dictating' Father.

What is the impact of the foregoing on the life of the community? Obviously, an order of precedence implies a pyramidal pattern for ecclesiology. This order does not really emerge from the communion of love, but rather from the ontological priority of the person of the loving Father. One may consider how easily the relationship between bishop and congregation may turn into ideology (often an idolatrous one), fostering a coerced subordination of the many to the one. The priority of the person of the Father potentially constructs a totalitarian reality, in which each community, instead of living according to the internal authority of the choir or symphony, will have its own authoritarian *vicarius Christi*. Whether one or many bishops bear this power and authority makes no difference, since each one is considered a 'pope' within one's smaller or bigger territory. The argument that this *primus* is never to be understood outside the community is of little value, for ultimately no office or title can be meaningful outside the community, not to say that even narcissism is formed and displayed within a relational system.

Unsurprisingly, the lay members of the community are assigned a passive and submissive role, which is no more than an act of formal confirmation, very much restricted to rendering the word *Amen* in worship. This response is taken as the charismatic function of the laity, a single privilege of voting in the affirmative, the only function of their *ordo*. Moreover, the assumption that the particular person is led into a certain *ordo* in which he has a certain function counters any assertion about the uniqueness of the person. In this way the bestowal of charismata 'can only ground the distinction between various types of persons'.[65] Accordingly, if we accept the thesis that the Spirit guides and enlightens only in Eucharistic contact, we may well understand that the laity, apart from their liturgical responsorial role, have nothing to contribute to ecclesial government. On this point Basil of Caesarea makes clear that the governing of the Churches is carried on by those to whom the higher offices have been entrusted, but it has to be confirmed by the laity.[66] Obviously, such ratification includes the whole range of charismata and activities in the life of the local Church and not just the *Amen* of the worshipping congregation, so that the bishop may authentically represent the faith and life of his people.

Ignatius of Antioch verifies the unique mediation of Christ.[67] And John Chrysostom qualifies the concept of hierarchy by the immediate relationship between the head and the limbs.[68] Such immediacy is expressed by a rich imagery. After one has entered the gate of sincere introspection, Christ, the Light of the world, grants self-awareness and initiation into the divine mysteries. Reflecting on Christ's observations about the intentional eunuchs (Matt. 19:12), namely about renunciation and dedication to God, Gregory Nazianzen says that the cause of this movement may not be the teaching of a man, but the *logos* within oneself – inscribed in one's nature – that it is 'moved' by the subject, along with the free will that may kindle the spark of good. So Gregory praises those who decide on their own to dedicate themselves to God. And he advises: 'It is up to you to choose the part you will; either follow the teacher or be your own teacher.' Translated into the life of the body of Christ, this points to the fact that not everything comes from or through the bishop. No bishop or priest, or any other person commissioned to teach, is the exclusive channel of initiation for someone who seeks the truth.[69] Again, this process does not lead to isolation and individualism, for Christ is connected with the whole of creation, which becomes His body.

The uncreated energies of the Trinity make Christ entirely present in the Church, both in the Eucharist and beyond. Therefore, each charisma – including the pastoral – is a direct participation in Christ and derives not from an indispensable intermediary, who represents him, for each gift is Christ Himself in a particular and special enfleshment. For this reason salvation has to do only with God: it is bestowed by Him and not by a sacrament. There were cases where one single moment of deep repentance was enough to bring the Kingdom to a sinner, manifesting the liberty and bounteousness of divine activity. One may recall the example of St Mary of Egypt:[70] after forty-seven years in total isolation in the wilderness she meets elder Zosimas, from whom she receives the body and blood of Christ, reciting the words of Symeon: 'Lord, now lettest thou thy servant depart in peace. . . for mine eyes have seen thy salvation' (Luke 2:29–30). But even if Holy Communion is eventually brought to complete and crown the picture of the perfect hermit, what actually made her levitate over the ground, see things afar and prophesy the future, survive on such little food and cross the river dryshod before taking Communion? What else but the same transforming power which consecrates the Eucharistic elements and nurtures the Body of Christ?

6. Meanings of order

What has been said is not at odds with Paul's exhortation that all things should be done 'decently and in order' (1 Cor. 14:40). We saw that for Basil this is to be understood in the conceptual frame of concord and perfect love, as the effect of the animating and conjoining force of the body.[71] That very meaning of order in relation to the charismata is exposed by

Gregory of Nazianzus. In his defence of moderation the Cappadocian bases his argument not on a transcendental understanding of structure but on the notion and empirical reality of different charismata and personal abilities. To govern and be governed is not a reflection of trinitarian life, but a necessity generated by the variety of knowledge and experience among human beings and, consequently, by the need of initiation and guidance. Gregory does not refer to the oneness as the one person virtually incorporating the many but rather to the harmony and interrelatedness of the multiple charismata.[72] What prevails is the order of charismatic variety and plurality. Gregory reproves rude zeal, quarrelsome manners, superficial wisdom, and love of primacy, immoderation and indiscretion. The polar opposite of these estranging forces is order, which is to be found in all layers of creation.[73]

This order dictates the differentiation within the Church between those who are governed and led (namely the flock) and those who govern and lead (namely the pastors).[74] Such leadership should not be understood in terms of secular and political patterns, or ideas of administration. If order is lived out as sovereignty, it is no more than a masquerade of the deepest disorder, a play-acting pretending to reality, a religion of showmanship obscuring what was in the beginning. The purpose of the charismatic order of pastors and teachers is 'the benefit and illumination' of the rest. But there are other great charismata from the one Spirit that make up the body of Christ.[75] To be within the limits of one's particular charisma and order means to imitate a particular divine energy, in which the undivided God is hidden and revealed.[76] This dignity and order is conspicuous in the circle of the apostles and the Lord's behaviour towards them, with the Transfiguration presented as a striking example. Quite appealing is the remark that 'not the same thing is said by all, nor all is said by one, but each one speaks separately and in part', with humility and love being the underlying principles and drive.[77] Plurality indicates many voices, but not a confusion of voices and disorderliness. Each time there is only one voice transmitting a message and contributing to the edification of the body. Nor is it exclusively the voice of the bishop. 'There ought to be one voice in the Church always, even as there is one body,' John Chrysostom maintains. 'Therefore, he that reads utters his voice alone, and the bishop himself is content to sit in silence; and he who chants, chants alone; and though all utter the response, the voice is wafted as from the mouth. And he that pronounces a homily, pronounces it alone.'[78]

Equality and mutual respect mark the life of the ecclesial body. In fact, Gregory states that no primacy is to be found among creatures – all prerogatives belong to all creatures – and that the grace given to one is truly common to all. All gifts of God to His creation are common and co-equal, and creation itself is a witness to a common grace shared by all.

Now, there is an analogy connecting this distribution with the matters of faith: law, prophecy, testaments, grace, education, perfection, new creation, the Spirit's abidance, love of God and from God, illumination, insight of the Trinity – these are all common gifts, given according to one's volition.[79] Within this train of thought the role of the bishop is vindicated on functional grounds. According to John Chrysostom, it is a charismatic function within the body, wherein sovereignty and authoritarian behaviour are excluded: 'We do not exert dominion over your faith, my beloved, nor do we command in an oppressive manner; we have been committed with the task of teaching, not appointed either to sovereignty or despotism. Rather, we hold the rank of counsellors stirring you up.'[80] Otherwise, we must beware of the two dangers that constantly threaten the world: *l'ordre et le désordre*.

7. *Image and* mimesis

A magical brush tinges the statement that 'we cannot override the image to reach the prototype directly'; in other words, that 'we cannot pray directly to Christ without the intervention of His image, the bishop', otherwise, our communication with God will be carried out via imagination.[81] According to this dictum the existence of a 'mediator' mediating salvation to unredeemed people is mandatory. The God–man relationship is constrained to a single way, that of the image.

In this dictum an important distinction is disregarded. According to this distinction, two kinds of images or symbols are acknowledged: the natural and the technical. The first stands in congenital oneness with the archetype, where 'nature does not admit of the separation'.[82] Thus, in the divine Persons, all qualities of divine nature are attributed to the true image of the invisible God, which is Christ. The second kind, the technical image, is a mere representation conveying a message or pointing to the realisation of the true image–archetype relationship. With reference to the first, the natural image or symbol, there is no way of assuming an essential relationship between man and God, and therefore this type of iconology is not applicable, whereas the second type, the technical image, is one of the ways that lead to living personal relationships. In the created realm, the pictorial representation either of God incarnate or of deified human beings conveys something of the grace of their real hypostasis. With regard to the living image of Christ, the human being, this image is associated with the dynamic process of achieving the likeness of God, or *theosis*, since man is endowed with free will and has to fashion himself after the example of the true image of God.[83] If we say that the archetype is revealed in the bishop as image, we lose the dynamic relationship, and there is always a danger of idolatry in absolute and one-sided attitudes.

The bishop, along with the whole Eucharistic structure, remains an iconological representation of the eschatological Kingdom. This is a concept developed mainly by Maximus the Confessor:

> The bishop takes the place of the image of the God of all. In imitation, as far as possible, of God, as a symbol, abiding by his proper state, namely his ecclesiastical order, he moves along to those after him through loving providence . . . and then returns to the altar. Thus he symbolizes God, for although he moves providentially towards those after him . . . still he does not refrain from doing his proper work and from remaining in his own function, that is in the heights of God's contemplation.[84]

But, as Dionysius says that one comes to the presence of God as one passes beyond symbols and concepts, equally Maximus knows that symbols really work inasmuch as they lead the initiated beyond them. A 'technical' symbol as such is correlated with the ambiguity woven into the fibre of this life, and even in this life one may see the resurrected Word Himself 'clearly appearing without symbols or figures'. Every word and figure given in this present age is a 'forerunner' of something more perfect. And in the age to come truth will be free of any symbolic complexity (including the highest sacred offices!).[85]

On this account, insofar as symbolism in the very early sources is concerned, the use of symbols for representing ecclesiastical offices is fairly flexible, loose and malleable.[86] One must point to the fact that the relevant typology does not refer to the bishop only, but includes the other ecclesiastical orders as well. Nonetheless, the believers are also paralleled with Christ and the apostles.[87] This loose structure is evident in the New Testament and the apostolic era, where the terms *episkopos* and *presbyteros* appear to be synonymous and interchangeable. The *episcopatum* emerges from the council of the presbyters as a means of safeguarding co-ordination and unity.[88] And all the clergy are tested according to Jesus Christ, founded on the security of the Holy Spirit.[89] At any rate, as John Chrysostom explains, 'between presbyters and bishops there is no great difference. Both have undertaken the office of teachers and presided over the Church, and what he [Paul] has said concerning bishops is applicable to presbyters; for they are only superior in having the power of ordination, and seem to have no other advantage over presbyters.'[90] The plasticity with which Ignatius employs the image, the variation and interchanges in using symbols to describe the Church orders, and the fluidity of the images for the priestly grades, do not lead to the discrediting of those images and symbols, yet they reveal the Christological nature of all the grades (and all the gifts).[91]

In fact, as long as the Church is supposed to be identical with

Christ, it follows that it is identical with the Kingdom of God. But this identification has no place in the patristic mind. On this point we may recall the allegory of the Church-paradise, where the tree of knowledge indicates the fall to separative judgement.[92] Commenting on the passage about the Nativity, the Irish scholar says that 'the inn [where Christ was born] symbolizes the Church standing between paradise and the world. From there one may go to heaven and another to the world and sin, as it happened in the case of the pious thief and that of Judas Iscariot.'[93] Referring to the ship of the Church, the bishops and the rest of the officials, the Irish theologian transfers to the ecclesiastical area the dangers that a sailing ship faces: the devil's temptations, the wind of sins, the false brothers.[94] This is an image of a common treasury. As John Chrysostom advises, no matter whether the bishop is skilled in the art of steering, he will sink the vessel, if he is devoid of the grace and peace of God.[95]

Although Zizioulas does not refrain from asserting that the Eucharist is *identical* to heaven, at the same time he insists on the iconological character of the Church and the Eucharist.[96] But, as has been stated, when the image–archetype relationship is applied to humankind, we take for granted that the icon does not bestow upon the subject the features of the archetype in a magical and automatic manner. There is a dynamic character in the image, being on the way to its fulfilment in likeness of the prototype. Thus the self, through patient *mimesis*, becomes the painter, the paint and the image of that fairest form in accord with the character of the Archetype.[97] Should there be no effort and ascetic struggle for participation in the divine energies, the image is obscured and imperilled, and for this reason, the bishop needs continuous effort to identify his will with God's will.[98] Only by imitating Christ in word and deed does he become, by grace, another Christ for those who meet him. Accordingly, the order of the bishop is not an office – a prerogative granted by a Eucharistically situated event of ordination – but the state of contemplation of God, which is the flower of God's intimate and energetic relationship with the human being.

Therefore, the Eucharist and the Church are not a direct reflection of divine reality, a structural mirroring of the coming Kingdom of God, or an automatic achievement of deification here and now. The Church and each of its members have to act according to God's activities. There is a call for continuous imitation (in the sense of participation) of divine freedom and perfection, which is ontologically connected with love. There is need for a long, disinterested and kenotic struggle for the assimilation of grace. It is only with this presupposition that the Eucharist, the worshipping community and any office may be experienced as moving towards the Kingdom and not as ritualistic obstacles which hold claims of being the heavenly Kingdom upon earth. Participation in the Eucharist, as well as holding any position within the ecclesiastical hierarchy, has meaning only to the degree of the purification and illumination of one's intellect, desire and incensive power.[99]

Man's personal appropriation of salvific grace is not exclusively restricted to his participation in the sacraments. Macarius points to a deeper reality when he says that 'Christ, the good artist, for those who believe in him and gaze continually at him, portrays after his own image a heavenly man. Out of his own Spirit, out of the substance of light itself, the ineffable light, he paints a heavenly image . . . If a man does not gaze constantly at him, overlooking everything else, the Lord will not paint his image with his own light.'[100] One must read the image–archetype correspondence in light of this observation. Otherwise it leads to a frozen hierarchy, which tends to generate or justify an ideology of subordination. Although Christ is given in the Eucharist, a theophany is not confined to the sacrament; indeed Christ's revelation is not confined to any form, nor conditioned by any created law.

8. Amazing grace

What is the underlying theological principle of the charismatic life within or beyond the institutional context? It is the concept of the uncreated activities, which covers the whole range of life, and which lies behind all patristic anthropology and soteriology. A human being is deified by grace, through the person of Christ, that is, by the activities of the divine essence, which are genuinely God and not simply created effects of God's providence. The patristic distinction between essence and energies in God is not a metaphysical concept grounded on Aristotelian principles, but the verbalisation in theological terms of the reality of communion between God and the cosmos, since every particle of the world participates in God's creative being, according to its given potential. So, the distinction remains the interpretative key to religious experience. It gives us the right to say that a human being can act by means of an energy that does belong to his nature, and that God acts in him without imparting His essence to the creature.[101]

In the body of Christ growth is given to each member and through each member by the divine energies. This is the light that illuminates the soul and enables the body to participate in God's glory; 'the one ray' we receive 'from the one Godhead in Christ',[102] the light 'which is contemplated in the Father and the Son and the Holy Spirit, whose riches is Their unity of nature, and the one outleaping of Their brightness'. For 'God is Light . . . presenting Himself to our minds in proportion as we are cleansed; and loved in proportion to His presence to our minds; and again, conceived in proportion to our love for Him.'[103] That was the fire that burned the bush without consuming it, thereby showing its nature and declaring its inherent power. That was the light of the Old Testament's theophanies, the same light that shone round the shepherds, the star that went before the wise men to guide their way to Bethlehem. It was that Godhead that was shown upon the mountain to the disciples – 'and a little too strong for their eyes'; the eschatological Light 'to those who have been purified', the same Light that illuminates us in baptism.[104] According to the Celtic catechist, in this *splendore trinitatis* we see and participate in Christ's divinity.[105] For, as Diadochos says, unless the Spirit's divinity 'shines actively on the treasuries of our hearts we will not be able to taste what is good with an undivided sense'.[106]

The uncreated energies – God's holy fire – make us partakers of the divine nature, transforming us into Gods by and in grace. The divine grace becomes, as it were, 'the one energy of God and His saints', proceeding from the divine essence and becoming an attribute of the saints, permeating them 'by grace'.[107] Indeed, the number is mutually interchangeable from singular to plural, for the energies are both one and innumerable, and in each one the whole and undivided God is hidden and revealed in His procession to and activity in each and every particle of creation. It is the divine energy that safeguards the integrity of the whole, being the common creative foundation, and it is the same energy that dignifies the particular, since it calls for a personal response and provides the ground for a deep relationship between God and man.

God's presence is manifested on the one hand through the general grace which consists of His very life, namely eternity, glory, love and simplicity dispensed to all, the 'goodness' which 'comes into being . . . although by nature it is uncreated',[108] and on the other hand it is manifested through particular gifts which form specific functions. The latter include what we might now call institutional expressions (pastors and teachers) or charismatic expressions (apostles, prophets, evangelists). What substantiates and permeates all these is the energies of the Spirit, which transfigures each member according to one's measure, in other words, by conferring the essential glory and sempiternal life of God.[109] Therefore, God's life-giving presence, no matter whether manifested in or beyond institutions or structures, is always charismatic. The outcome is sanctity, by virtue of which God is active through the saints.

This is a mystery worked out in God incarnate on account of what we call *communicatio idiomatum*. For in Christ human nature, remaining totally human, received the one ray from the one Godhead.[110] For this reason we must not sideline the salvific mystery and paradox of the *interchange of properties* in order to emphasise the role of the person or even to build our ecclesiastical or social programme upon the person of Christ as such. This is why Maximus the Confessor, following the former tradition, staunchly defended the operation of two energies in Christ, 'from which and in which Christ the one God exists', the interchange and unconfused union of which made possible the deification of man.[111] The uncreated energy is from the essence and within the essence. The perfect work of love and the fulfilment of its energy is the interchange of the attributes and names of those natures that are united in love.[112]

How can the theology of the energies contribute to the desideratum of the unity of humankind? The tradition of the desert emphasises the unity of the Spirit not in the obedience to a person, but in the inner unity and the diversity of personal gifts, which are offered through partaking in the divine nature – the common energies: 'The souls of the Christians are made of the one Divinity's heavenly light, the diverse gifts of the one Spirit.'[113] God becomes light within the human being through the act of imitation; light manifested as virtue and knowledge. Because the energies of the Spirit are not autonomous operations but manifestations of the undivided procession of Divinity to creation, or the 'processions and manifestations of the thearchy',[114] each of them carries the undivided whole or, in scriptural terms, the one fruit of the Spirit, granted to all persons according to the measure of each one's faith and culminating in love. In this sense we have a mutual inherence of all gifts in each particular gift and, thus, a mutual inherence of all persons, a reciprocity of essential love.

9. Hierarchy and divine energy

Let us now return to consider the link or homogeneity between hierarchy and divine energy. This connection or identification guards the true meaning of the principle of hierarchy against authoritarian readings.

Hierarchy is the image of the divine beauty, not merely by radiating an aesthetic splendour, but also by mirroring God's virtues. Hierarchy, as understood in the Greek East, could never be separated from virtue as divine energy according to that bipolar relation, one pole of which is the characteristic imparted by God to His creation and the other its correlative within God. Dionysius, who gave the word a new content beyond its etymological overtones, defines hierarchy as 'a sacred order and knowledge and activity, the whole of which is assimilated as closely as possible to the divine, and uplifted to the imitation of God in proportion to the illuminations granted it by God'.[115] Its whole purpose is an activity, that of imparting the knowledge of God and bringing the initiated to deification.

The hierarchical distinctions are images of the divine activities. Through activity and imitation of those who are superior, one comes 'to look up to the blessed and divine ray of Jesus Himself', and will then 'be perfected and bring about perfection'.[116] This is the meaning of the 'structure' of Dionysius, who used the word 'hierarchy' without any tinge of suppression or subordination. Everyone, receiving the divine light, becomes transparent to those at a lower lever, but it is God himself who is 'the guide in all sacred knowledge and activity. Looking unwaveringly to His divine comeliness, the hierarchy receives his stamp as much as possible and makes its own members divine images, perfectly clear and spotless mirrors, receptive to the ray of the primordial and thearchic light'.[117] Deification is the work of hierarchy, both celestial and earthly,[118] a reflection of the workings of God. And although the hierarchical structure is not a mirror of the immanent Trinity, it concurs with the structure intrinsic to the divine *energeia*. God acts to purify, illuminate and perfect creatures, or rather is Himself purification, illumination and perfection.[119] For God has in a transcendent way the features that He imparts to others. Accordingly, the more one ascends to God, the more one realises that equality (one would say 'democracy' in the true sense of excellence) is real and permanent as a participated quality of God's nature, where cosmic levelling is validated.[120]

Since hierarchy is the structure of virtues, the divine characteristic is, in the first place, freedom from the passions that fragment the psyche.[121] If the hierarch is beheld 'a physician to others', it is 'by virtue of the dispassion of his own habituation (ἕξις)'.[122] Dionysius goes as far as saying that a fall from the charismatic contemplation of God, mainly expressed through seeking what is pleasant to God, means exclusion from the priestly order.[123] This statement, together with the striking absence of any allusion to hierarchy in his *Mystical Theology*, makes one realise that in Dionysius the Neoplatonic borrowings fail to impose objective intermediaries between God and man. Ultimately, nothing undoes the fact that truth cannot be received at second hand, that God reveals Himself directly to man in theophanies (even when such knowledge is mediated by angels), provided that one is not uninformed but is purified.[124] For 'the beauty of God . . . reaches out to grant every being, according to merit, a share of light', a participation in the One itself, 'which deifies everything rising up to it'.[125] Thus, everyone can participate directly in the godly union, reaching the holy unity of the monad. And every soul reflects the glow of the same sublime light. In God's love, which draws back everything into it, takes place 'the intermingling of everything'.[126] And this is the case in Dionysius' remote disciple, Ériugena, in whom the 'objective hierarchical scheme of nature is counterbalanced by an anti-hierarchical subjectivist tendency', which is the result of the ever-present ineffable light.[127] Thus, it is not far from the truth to assert that 'that which the Old Testament hierarchy was meant to foreshadow is not simply and directly the visible hierarchy of the Church's clergy but the new invisible hierarchy of the Spirit and of the Spirit's gifts, which Paul describes, and which at most is only manifested in the hierarchy of Church officials', who are supposed to stand at the higher stage of perfection.[128] Yet, hierarchies are not to be seen as ladders leading up to God, and thus immediate union with God does not entail ascent to the hierarchies.[129]

It is also very important that this hierarchy, the Church itself, refers to the corporate body as well as to the individual. The heavenly Church and the earthly Church meet in the Church of the inner man.[130] And it is only by the manner of life and the degree of God's contemplation that a simple believer can be moved to the rank and dignity of the disciple, and the disciple to the rank and dignity of the apostle alike, whatever his or her place in the hierarchy.[131] It is for this reason that the Irish episcopal synod equates monks and nuns with bishops and 'teachers' in respect of spiritual fruitfulness.[132] In a sense, the sincere believer in Christ has within oneself all the divine gifts collectively and only a careless observance of the commandments makes one feel excluded from the Holy Spirit's gifts.[133] This is a limpid expression of the unity of charisma and, respectively, a relativisation of hierarchy.

10. Ideals and accidents

In the historical course of Christianity, the degree of identity or rupture between the institutional and the charismatic aspects of ecclesial life appear to be analogous to the presence of the spirit of the desert within Christian communities. This is expressed in the adoption of the monastic ideal by the secular clergy and especially the bishops. The quintessence of Christianity is holiness, and holiness is expected to come – though not exclusively – from the desert. This is most evident in the Irish sources, which present many bishops under the direction of desert Fathers and monastic superiors.[134] The Church in ancient Ireland was a 'monastic' Church, if not in terms of organisation and administration, certainly on account of the spiritual and social centrality of the monasteries, some of which created a confederation of mother and daughter houses. Their extended ambit was principally a result of the holiness and fame of their founder and patron, whose spiritual calibre and pastoral abilities far exceeded the boundaries of the monastery. No doubt, the presence of the bishop remains extremely important for the maintenance of spiritual life,[135] but most often even the bishop is chosen from among the hermits.[136] The monk, the nun and the martyr represent the 'hundredfold fruit';[137] and thus, the monastic ideal is omnipresent, interpreting and shaping Christian life and consciousness, and the monastery becomes the actual and symbolic centre of the new creation. On the contrary, suspicion of monasticism hung in the air of Latin Europe, where an episcopate rivalling oligarchy was strong enough to shadow every other bearer of holiness.[138] Columbanus' letters bear ample testimony to his difficulties with bishops, while in Rome the pope was then opposed to any extension of monastic influence in the Church.[139]

A kind of opposition and rivalry is also detected in the East. This is partly because the East was the natural heir of the imperium Romanum, where the institution as such demands its right of domination, and the earthly monarch represents the monarchy of God the Father (especially as understood by the semi-Arian historian Eusebius). Not unexpectedly, the ecclesiastical office would face the temptation of being identified with the underlying power structure of the Empire.[140] Moreover, the state of triumph and safety experienced within the borders of an Orthodox oecumene would cultivate the sense of immediate satisfaction that compromised the eschatological spirit of the first Christian communities. Reacting to such degradation, Gregory Nazianzen laments the pomp and ceremony that accompanies episcopal elections.[141] Such high honours, John Chrysostom continues, adversely affect the motivation of episcopal candidates.[142] Yet, what was intrinsic to the Roman mind is somehow a drawback in the philosophically oriented Greek mind of the East, which is imbued by the sense of freedom. Thus, inasmuch as bishops follow the Roman ideology of strict organisation, they do not feel themselves to be accommodated in charismatic manifestations, although they do not appear as resolute as their western colleagues to 'tame' the Spirit.[143] On the other hand, many bishops come from the desert, and thus they love and respect monastics and also take advice from virtuous elders.[144] Constantinople develops into a big monastic centre. It is presented as the 'Second Jerusalem', because of holiness offered by the monasteries. And during the Byzantine era, abbots were summoned to participate in ecclesiastical matters.[145]

The Fathers present the model of the leader along biblical and monastic lines. Gregory of Nazianzus portrays the good shepherd in the light of virtues obtained through the practice of 'philosophy', namely monastic withdrawal and divine encounter. The life of Moses is retold as an illustration of preparation for leadership. But at the same time the vision of God epitomised by the Sinai theophany was the ultimate goal of monastic withdrawal and the mark of the true theologian.[146] The internalisation of the monastic ideal of withdrawal and the spread and influence of the monk-bishop ideal is best exemplified by John Chrysostom. The bishop's spirituality as an ascetic and holy man came to be the basis of episcopal authority.[147] As is dramatically illustrated in the description of an encounter between Basil and the emperor Valens, the bishop's spiritual power proceeds from his ascetic virtues.[148] They are the product of radical personal response to God's revelation in creation and history.

The emphasis placed on either the sacrament or the uncreated energies is relevant to the comparative observations of Peter Brown regarding the locus of divine power in Eastern and Western Christendom. Brown noted that in the Latin West the locus of divine power is exclusively the Eucharist and the bishop, while the East encompasses a major variety of cases. As a consequence, the Byzantine approaches to sanctity – and to the world – are characterised as being 'shot through with paradox'.[149] In this atmosphere we encounter the freedom of indefinability, which gives space to diverse manifestations of the Spirit. Brown seeks the interpretative key in the 'nature' of the 'holy' and its impingement on worldly matters. The holy lies outside the structures of power, it borders with the paradox, it marks the world of epiphany, where the divine presence is associated with illumination and *theoria*. In such an environment even an unordained man could receive 'the baptism of the Spirit' and serve as a director of souls.[150] Such moments of epiphany permeate the experiential spectrum of the 'Roman' of the East. Brown notes that in the West of the sixth and seventh centuries there is no parallel to the life of Symeon the Fool for Christ, where the paradox of marginal holiness is fully exposed.[151] Such an approach allows the possibility of immediate guidance in a personal relationship between God and man. For instance, in the life of Alypius the Stylite, the young ascetic is often guided by the heavenly world, and the initiative stages of his renunciation, in particular, are a sequence of revelatory messages. Although, as a deacon, he follows the bishop to Constantinople, he receives the message of St Euphemia, whom he follows without the bishop's knowledge. This is not to say that Alypios relies on his own thought and judgement, since, before he ascends the column, he is led to the hermitage on the advice of the 'elders'.[152] No less can it be admitted that emphasis upon the direct and personal experience of God proceeds from an anti-sacramental disposition. A most characteristic example – to be found also in the Life of Columba – is Symeon the New Theologian, whose vision of God occurred repeatedly during the consecration of the Eucharistic elements.[153]

The violent severance of the charismatic from the institutional aspect of ecclesial life is detected in the bitter complaint of many great Church leaders themselves against the law of unworthiness, simony and abuse of spiritual power. The deplorable state of the episcopate, as bemoaned in the writings of Gregory Nazianzen, allows us to speak of such a rift. Gregory was outspoken in censuring the abuses of the priestly office and the episcopate, while at the same time he outlined the portrait of the true leader, physician and man of God. His Orations reflect the ecclesiastical malaise of the imperial capital.[154] The Cappadocian strikingly presents the perils of not regarding personal virtue as the basic presupposition for the office of the bishop and gives an account of the problem in his days. The kind of promotion to 'the holiest of all offices', he says in an acute psychological description, makes it 'the most ridiculous among us'. For it depends

> . . . not upon virtue, but upon villany; and the sacred thrones fall not to the most worthy, but to the most powerful. . . We manufacture those who are holy in a day, and bid those to be wise, who have had no instruction, and have contributed nothing before to their dignity, except the will. So one man is content with an inferior position, and abides in his low estate, who is worthy of a lofty one, and has meditated much on the inspired words, and has reduced the flesh by many laws into subjection to the spirit: while the other haughtily takes precedence, and raises his eyebrow over his betters, and does not tremble at his position, nor is he appalled at the sight, seeing the disciplined man beneath him; and wrongly supposes himself to be his superior in wisdom as well as in rank, having lost his senses under the influence of his position.[155]

Gregory expresses his feelings on the disgrace and abuses of his time, when 'uninitiated souls intrude into the most sacred offices; … they push and thrust around the holy table, as if they thought this order to be a means of livelihood instead of a pattern of virtue, or an absolute authority, instead of a ministry of which we must give account'.[156] Such behaviour and customs not only express but also reproduce secularisation by adversely affecting the motivation of the candidates, indeed by imposing and feeding a new ethos within Christian communities. Adapted to this climate, Christians themselves seek pastors who will rival men of power, wealth and worldly status. And John Chrysostom, exiled by his fellow bishops, speaks of that thirst for domination and power that has so infiltrated the clergy that bishops are often no better than civil rulers.[157] Nor is the political ideology the only, or even the main, factor that affects this mindset. Delving into the abyss of the psyche, Chrysostom sees in the higher office the potential of stirring up psychic passions and exposing one's heart to ancestral inclinations such as egotism, ambition and vainglory, through the exaltation of a person invested with power, which becomes the strong citadel of will. In this way, the bishop, who ought to rule men with their own consent, makes his presidency tyrannical rather than popular.[158]

Some highlights from the instructions of Origen also give the same bitter criticism, although their hortatory nature prevents one from taking it at face value. Instead of acting as Christ-like examples and sympathetic physicians, he complains that most bishops are worldly minded, pursuing earthly occupations and affairs, allowing themselves to be flattered and corrupted, and often rival secular officials in arrogance and amorality, taking seriously only their advantages and privileges. Such men imitate the kings in retinues and presumption, superciliousness and isolation, abhorring any kind of equality. It is unsurprising that for those 'tyrants' 'the most sordid methods of intrigue and demagogy are brought into play as soon as there is a chance of snatching an office'.[159]

At the same time it is evident that the Fathers do not perceive the crisis to be within the institution *per se*. Ecclesiastical institution is nothing else than a crystallised gift of the love of God for the life of the world. Thus, the nature of the institution is to preserve the fundamental truth, albeit objectified. As John Chrysostom asserts, referring to the priesthood, 'the Paraclete himself instituted this order'.[160] If there is a severance between charisma and institution, it takes place within the person who ministers the institution. But we turn a blind eye if we say that such personal failure leaves a community unaffected, that it is irrelevant to the spiritual progress of a community. When the institution comes to pervade and dominate every sphere of spiritual life, the Church runs the risk of turning into, and operating as, a sphere of spiritual confinement. It may be right that what protects the truth of the Church from erring officials is 'our trust in certain signs', because 'true signs will always outwit our worst intentions'.[161] Truly, these signs are unshakeable pointers to the truths, and doors to mystical chambers of revelation. But though they function as constant reminders of transcendental realities, there is no little danger in reducing them to mute symbols, signifying nothing but sovereignty. This is the hard core of secularisation, when the signs/symbols lose or transform their initial content in order to serve worldly feelings, behaviour or purposes. A telling example in our time is the very peculiar interpretation of the monastic veil and mantle by some bishops, who take them as part and parcel of their episcopal office and more or less as insignia of exclusive pastoral and administrative power! It is unbelievable how many weird things the word 'order' can accommodate in its fluidity and multivalence.

In short, one cannot help detecting a discrepancy between the institutional and the charismatic dimension over the centuries. They are indeed identical, and yet they often divorce painfully, whenever and in whomsoever the inner link between the external and the internal, the objective and the subjective, is broken. But as a contemporary scholar opines, the observations found in patristic writings should not be pressed too hard in either direction, for the Fathers know that ambiguity 'constitutes, in fact, one of the fundamental antinomies of Christian existence *in statu via*'.[162]

Concluding Remarks

The place of the theology of divine energies in the life of Christian communities, or, in other words, the patristic perception of divine presence and activity within creation, establishes the intertwining of the charismatic and the institutional dimensions. According to the contrary contemporary position, the theo-ontology of the person appears to be congruent with the hypertrophy of the institutional facet, since structure is inherent in the concept of person if the latter is considered as the ultimate ontological principle, namely as prior to essence and energies. Paradoxically, in that case the person is virtually identified with the office, and is suppressed within a rank and prescribed relations. This process may end up in a coerced subordination of the many to a dominant one, who *constitutes* the body of the many and generates the others' personhood through his absolute will. This is the social and psychological repercussion of the concept of divine monarchy, if understood in personalistic terms, as an assertion of the ontological priority of the person of the Father. On the other hand, the personalistic substitute for this scheme – the concept of the 'social Trinity' from which a symmetrical distribution of power emerges – betrays an innate vacuum, should the trinitarian unity not be grounded in the common essence and produce common energies. Real love cannot but be essential.

Again, emphasis upon the energies means emphasis upon the personal encounter with God. In the energetic relationship between God and the cosmos, we all drink a great draught of the grace of the Holy Spirit. As Gregory of Nyssa meditates, 'every blessing which is bestowed on us by divine power is the operation of the grace which works all things in all.'[1] Only in this energy do we become receptive of God's knowledge. Only through the energy of the Spirit do we become gods by grace and limbs of the body of Christ. It is God's energy that saves human being, the energy that bears in itself and manifests the whole and undivided God. This deifying power is included in the 'unified names' ascribed to the entire divinity. That is why even in the hierarchical world of Dionysius the vision of God is open to all, and the monk, although belonging to the initiated order, can participate directly in the mystical union.[2] This may pose a challenge to a worldly ministry, when the ministers rely on their mediatory role through the sacraments, as happened in the days of Symeon the New Theologian. Accordingly, an exclusively Eucharistic understanding of the Church, nurturing the exaltation of institutional hierarchy, leads theology to abstraction, makes the knowledge of divine mysteries a prerogative of the higher officers, and tarnishes worship and prayer in frigid formalism.

The way to the Trinity in Unity, the only way to approach the trinitarian God in His utter simplicity and relationality, is by participating in the divine activities, properties that belong to God's nature and mark the creation of man in God's image and likeness.[3] Through the one ray from the one Godhead in Christ, we encounter 'that light, which is contemplated in the Father and the Son and the Holy Spirit, Whose riches is Their unity of nature, and the one outleaping of Their brightness'.[4] In the undivided presence of God we get a glimpse of the intangible Persons and we experience the unity of the incomprehensible essence. It is through participation in this life, given in the multiplicity of gifts, that we become one. And the one, who is simultaneously the many, is the one who imitates God by participating in His ineffable life. No doubt, this is a bishop's calling. But above that, and beyond certain institutional forms, this is a feature of the saint, the person who is charged with the divinity-infusing energy, the person who manifests the reality of the glory of the inner temple, stepping out of his humble hermitage like 'an initiate and Godbearer from a kind of sanctuary', to use bishop Athanasius' arresting image of St Anthony.[5] Thus, the more one participates in God's uncreated grace, the more one becomes a living signpost to the ways of God. In that person, the heavenly and earthly liturgies are present and mirrored as a microcosm. In his or her deified existence the true meaning of hierarchy – its status as diaphanous theophany – is demonstrated and condensed.

The way to holiness, like the way to authentic unity and distinction, is not a vague, floating-in-mid-air construal of weird personalities, nor an illusory state of consciousness. Like the making of an icon, the process towards holiness is the creative life of the natural human being in one's natural environment, made of cosmic dust and uncreated light, no less human than divine.

Last Prologue

The doric tunic
which your fingers touched and it swayed like the mountains
is a marble in the light, but the head is in the dark.

George Seferis

The patristic mind stands before God in wonder, abstaining from all inclination to solve the mystery. For this reason, patristic literature, in describing the encounter with the Trinity, preserves the apophaticism of the person as well as of the essence. Thus, it does not embark on a venture to root anthropology in the supposedly revealed inter-trinitarian relations. To ground social, anthropological and ecclesiological theories in the immanent Trinity is an endeavour in which lurks a danger of logical fallacy, and this is what happens when one attempts to support one's view by appealing to positive and desirable consequences.[1] Still, the trinitarian life is the archetype of the image. How can we learn from this reality without falling into fallacy?

The person is the cause of everything, including divinity, they say. And the personal mode of existence is the new creation, the 'essence' of God's revelation. God is God because the person of the Father freely *wills* both His own essence and the other Persons of the Trinity. Everything comes through a person and not through nature – and this repetition confines us in an 'either/or' state of mind. Nature and natural activities are severed from the person, which is entirely equated with the mode of being. Yet, as Maximus the Confessor maintains, 'the holy Monad is Trinity by reason of the hypostases *and* the mode of being'.[2] The mode of being of the Monad is its trinitarian character. We also found that the innovation of nature in Christ is not personhood *per se*, but the coming together of the created and the uncreated energies into one.

John Zizioulas one-sidedly elaborates on, and tarries over, the 'personal' aspect of the incarnation, namely the fact that the *person* of Christ works out the change of the 'mode of being'. This unbalanced maximisation of the hypostatic dimension of Christ undervalues some fundamental principles regarding God and the work of salvation. First, that the union of the two ontological categories – the uncreated and the created – is the ground of our communion with God. Second, that we are the body of Christ not because He passes into us in His person. It is the divine energy that Christ bestows naturally to His body and by grace to us; this deifying energy makes us abodes of the Trinity. Third, Christ Himself is God and Saviour not because He is a person but because He has a divine nature. Finally, that the life of the Logos, to which the logos of each being is bound, is not His personhood itself, but 'enhypostatic life' and 'essential power' – the life of the Trinity.

The ontological gap between the created and the uncreated is not bridged by an ontology of person. God relates to creation because His uncreated wills and activities become the essence or logos of beings. Definitely, God is not a physical object radiating loving energy. Nor, however, is He a subject expressing 'personal' love. He is a Trinity of Persons, whose divine power and energy flows forth from their supra-essential essence. A distinction is recognised in God's absolute simplicity. The essence–energies distinction (no less than identification) was experienced by the unbroken chain of the Greek Fathers and also by those of the Irish world, although the pens of the former offer a more explicit and concrete theological articulation. Indeed, it was considered as the 'mean' between the idea of an inactive essence and that of a composite Divinity. The same distinction appeared to be incompatible with the perception of God's simplicity in the Latin medieval mind, with the exception of some revolutionary luminaries.[3] Apart from any technical language, the patristic mind (not concerned with terms but with realities) sees 'unions' and 'distinctions' in God's being as the only way to explain the fact that God is truly participated in while remaining wholly imparticipable. This language aims not simply at advocating apophaticism of the essence, but at confirming the real communion between God and the world, the life-infusing energetic presence of God in all things, without breaking down the ontological gap between Creator and created. After all, apophaticism is not merely negative theology. Transcending all concepts, it expresses the wonder caused by the mystery of God's presence inviting us into His strange life, and it becomes 'an existential theology involving man's entire being . . . which obliges him to be changed, to transform his nature that he may attain true gnosis, which is the contemplation of the Holy Trinity'.[4]

Either by rejecting the existence or by undervaluing the role of uncreated energies, one inevitably comes to a rather institutional apprehension of the relationship between God and the world, and a respective ritualistic mindset, since uncreated activity is actually replaced by created means and mediators. It follows then that the Church 'at all levels is episcopal in its nature'.[5] Contrary to patristic teaching, the transcendental person becomes a substitute for divine grace, the association of personal charismata with uncreated energies is diminished, and deification is identified with personhood. Any particular charisma emerges exclusively from the Eucharistic assembly and, oddly enough, the charisma of the rank of the laity is limited to reciting the *Amen* in worship. What seems to be lost somewhere in this garden is freedom and responsibility, and what eventually appears is the peril of the absorption of the individual into the corporate body or even the corporate personality, namely the bishop. In this case person is used to validate a ladder of barriers between God and man.

Patristic teaching and experience affirms that *man reaches deification through theophanies.* This fact relativises any concept of hierarchy grounded in the category of person. The imperative of deification can be satisfied only by pursuing the path of the energies, which are the procession of divine nature *ad extra*, and in which the Persons are revealed. *Theosis* is indeed a matter of participating in God's glory and essential qualities. Now, only in a divisive mindset does this fact differ from the event of the incorporation of the individual into the only-begotten Son, for such an event is a product of the transfiguration in the divine trinitarian energy. After all, in what do we really participate if not in natural qualities, since the hypostatic qualities or attributes are incommunicable?

The divine energies in patristic writings function always in a context of gnosiology. The fact that the energies belong to the level of nature and to all three Persons does not fail to express God's personal presence: in the same way as one communicates with a family by receiving a gift from the family as a whole, even if one of its members is the actual emissary or mediator. It is the operation of the divine energies that creates a direct relationship between a human being and the divine being. For every particle of creation cradles its logos of being – the divine will which is the core of its nature – and, moreover, the gifts of the Spirit are personal. The energies not only reveal that God exists but also that they are the three-splendoured light, pointing to the trinitarian mode of existence.

Therefore, to emphasise nature and energies is not to say that we elude the concept of the person. The reality of the person is safeguarded by essential activities, of which it is the vehicle, and also by the principle of co-essentiality. Hypostases are integral and related entities by virtue of their common nature. Accordingly, it is not a person *as such* who can express real communion and otherness. Persons *qua* persons above their nature and energies cannot be in communion with one another, since the person is constituted by a unique whole or conflux of distinctive signs. Oneness and otherness is possible on account of the co-essentiality of persons, as in the divine Trinity the

'Logos or Wisdom' and the 'Sanctifying Power' are both co-essential and enhypostatic.[6] Therefore, in order to affirm the person, one needs to emphasise its essence within the essential unity of humanity. In this way the particular human being will be recognised as a real person and not as a constituent of a structure.

The relationship between the one and the many in the Trinity settles the issue of the relation between unity and diversity. Unity and diversity coincide in God's very being. But in what manner? It is clear that in his understanding of monarchy Zizioulas wishes to vindicate freedom and love in relationship. But the result is not a desirable one. For if the patristic notion of monarchy is interpreted in strictly personal terms, no room for reciprocity is allowed in the divine Trinity. Does this perception of monarchy maintain the intrinsic trinitarian character, if it be granted that 'any personal communion and relatedness in the Trinity flows from the Father *alone*', and if the Father, as person, constitutes His substance and makes it hypostases?[7]

Such apotheosis of the person, far from allowing the person to flourish, subjects it to reduction, and at the same time fosters oppressive forms of ecclesiastical life. Equality is abolished in the elevation of the particular one, while at the same time identity is blurred in the negation of interiority. Imagine what happens if the person supposedly constituting the other persons, standing in the place of God the Father, is dictatorial, small-minded, self-absorbed, indifferent or capricious. This sounds like a blatant monarchy, which overthrows the triune mystery. If the one constitutes the many in the matrix of relations ecclesial or social, if they receive their very being through their (one-sided) relationship with the one, then subjectivity is formed in the context of domination, power and authority. Recently, Nikolas Loudovikos[8] has convincingly argued that monarchy, understood in personalistic terms, implies a perilous notion of communion: to dictate or be dictated to in a non-reciprocal way. Indeed, granted that the ecclesiastical structure is considered to be a direct reflection of the divine structure, one can hardly find a more explicit sanction of totalitarianism, wherein reciprocity is proscribed and the slightest tinge of personal responsibility is ruled out.

Are we reasonable, or even legitimate, in trying to extract the notion of hierarchy (and consequently the bishop's authority) from trinitarian theology? We saw that Christ has no need to submit to the Father, for there is no personal will within the essential Godhead. What Christ does in His 'economic' subordination is to unite the human will with the divine will, so that we may all follow God's will. For His will is man's fiery principle. In the same way, the Father does not satisfy the personal will of the Son, although 'He heareth him always' (John 11:42). But even if we insist on the Father's monarchy based on His being the Cause and Principle within the Divinity, and if we insist on the bishop's correspondence with God the Father, problems still emerge from painting the whole concept in our own hue in its inappropriate application in ecclesiology. We tend to forget that there is no hierarchy or hierarchical grades within the Trinity. If the 'First' in the Trinity fully shares in the one divine fullness, and if 'the Father's status as principium is eternally exercised through His giving the fullness of divinity to Son and Spirit',[9] a truthful implementation in Church and society would mean a full sharing in power and activities, as well as in essence. After all, this is the reason why in the patristic mind the Father's monarchy is truly and not derivately a *triadic* monarchy.

The one and the many coincide in their common ground, which is Godhead, the common *ousia*. The Fathers do not appear as nervous as contemporary theologians before the concept of essence, considered as a monistic category. Maximus treats us with new wine in expressing the utter paradox: that the divine essence is signified by the number three, as glorified in a trinitarian formula, because of its three-personed existence. For the Monad is a Triad, being perfect in perfect hypostases, namely according to the mode of existence, and the Triad is truly a Monad in respect of the essence, namely the logos of being.[10] Only then the particular belongs to the one, and likewise, the one is fully manifested and embodied in the particular. Thus God the Father derives His will from His Godhead and not from His being the Father.[11] At the anthropological level, only in God's creative act is otherness granted to humanity, once and for all, in an asymmetrical way. Will, love, freedom are our common nature, fully shared by each and every person. And it is in such spirit that otherness matures and blossoms.

Reducing the importance of common essence leads to priority of person, structure and relations. Not surprisingly, in this way the significance of interiority is diminished and the person is seen primarily as *aliquid*. However, the relational dimension of the human being should not overshadow the dimension that encompasses the abyss of the soul and the orbit of consciousness. Within the created realm, the self has a profound interiority in its very essence, and by virtue of its intimate relationship with God. What shapes, by and large, the character of the authentic, that is to say, the undivided person, is the direct encounter and mysterious intercourse with the internal light, Christ Himself, who grants self-awareness, after one has entered the gate of introspection. Applying this perception in ecclesiology one may say that although we should not disregard the role of the Eucharist in the formation of the Church as a body, we also should never lose sight of the inner Church, worship and celebrant within the centre of personality, namely the heart, which is also the place of the decisive battle. It is here where God dwells and works out a universal consciousness. That is why a desert Father can say, 'He who has learnt the sweetness of his cell does not flee his neighbour.'[12]

Every human being *is* a person, not as *communion*, unless this communion is identified with the very act of his creation by the personal God 'individually', an act that posits the individual in an eternal energetic relationship with his Author. This person – fashioned within a set of cultural and historical conditions – is called to deification, with his natural qualities being transfigured in the divine energies, as happened to the three disciples at the event of the Lord's Transfiguration. Each person is called to union with God and union with one's fellow human beings through identifying one's gnomic will with the natural will, in order to cultivate the virtues, consummated and epitomised in love. He imitates Christ, who did not possess the will that acts by opinion or disposition, but the natural and simple will, which is to be observed equally in all human beings, and who summoned man to follow that natural will in the initiation to God's undivided and trinitarian life. In this way the person may become a catholic hypostasis, not by enclosing the others in his selfish aura or tightly binding them to his own axis, projecting every desire or inhibition upon them, but by adhering to the natural will, which allows dialogue and responsibility, the will which is orientated to, and illuminated by, the glory of the archetype.

It has been observed that in the one-dimensional models of the self, denials of the self's independence lodge together with its radical exaltation.[13] Something parallel, albeit more paradoxical, can be seen in the identification of being with the person. Its exaltation forges its very confinement, since there is an inevitable quest for the one. It magnifies the category but shrinks the natural subject, which eventually becomes absorbed into a matrix of dictated relationships. In modernity and post-modernity it was the undeviating appeal to a person's self that plunged the human being into depths of inhumanity by building cultures upon self-interest: the cult of the person has led that very person to destitution and disintegration. Our era has shown total inability to integrate otherness with the self and to overcome the long-existing tension between the individual and society. What remains is a 'dangling conversation', which designates the borders of alliance among human beings.

A 'koinonia' of 'persons', hotheadedly advocated in contemporary theological and sociological tenets, may in fact be no better than a community of solipsistic beings, even in Eucharistic communion, bearing *their own* freedom, *their own* will and *their own* love; that is, their own deceptions and narcissism. At the same time, if these persons' otherness is given by one particular person, then a group (or a troop) of 'empty' devotees are fostered, unaware of their inwardness, even lacking conscience. But a human being belongs first and foremost to God, who constitutes the self in its responsibility; and 'to relate oneself to God is precisely to have conscience'.[14] Now the idea that otherness *is* my being, and that being is a gift of the Other whose love grants me a unique identity, casts aside the fact that hypostasis is founded on a unique logos, which is its inner essence and an act of will within the divine Logos. Furthermore, the assertion that the Other must *always* have priority, even if this means going against one's own conscience, opens a chapter of accidents. For, if the Other is not the Archetypal image, namely Christ, then there is an imminent peril of betraying the real meaning of Paul's reference to one's submission of conscience.[15]

Such failure to integrate otherness in unity is partly the by-product of the severance between person and nature, a severance that caused a deep rupture and fragmentation in humanity. A positive substitute was offered: the *'ekstasis'* from a nature not just fallen but unredeemable. Nature is opposed to freedom, it is stated, as if natural laws were the impersonal operation of a cosmic clock (not divine activities manifested in the created sphere), and the person shall be liberated through an ecstatic escape from nature in order to find authentic personhood. Love and freedom cease to be considered essential attributes and are seen as notes of variation, the armament of the person before nature, which dictates its laws. Death is considered to be the sword of nature instead of its trauma or God's economy.[16]

It is in the framework of such dialectics between nature and person that the person of the Father *has* to be independent from His own nature in order to be free. That means that the divine nature, no longer 'life-giving', as Gregory of Nyssa calls it,[17] is now coupled with necessity. Even Christ's hypostasis has to be independent from His natural qualities, divine or human, as if God's economy is only secondarily relevant to the divine nature of Jesus Christ. At the level of the uncreated, it suffices to repeat Gregory of Nyssa, who states that the Father is God not on account of His being Father.[18] At the level of creation, Maximus is precise and instrumental in confirming that human nature is bound to sin and decay only because of the personal *gnome*.[19]

A substantial misreading lies in the identification of 'image' and 'likeness' with personhood. The human being is an 'image' and achieves likeness to God insofar as he receives personhood as a transcendental gift from above.[20] This perception, traced in modern European philosophical thought, is not to be found in the patristic understanding of spiritual life. The Fathers see the 'image' inscribed in nature; for the 'logos of being', which pertains to nature, is a divine art, 'firewood for the knowledge of divine mysteries', composed by a divine logos/will.[21] Nowhere in Greek or Irish sources is there the slightest evidence of the belief that the image of God or the grace of deification is personhood as transcending nature or leading it to its proper state. Man, especially his intelligible and noetic soul, is the image of uncreated nature.

We have seen that in the patristic mind, nature is a reality much broader than that which is restricted to biological necessities. The 'law of nature' directs to the one *logos* of nature, as opposed to the division caused by self-love. If the reason is not subject to carnal senses and will, the law of nature dictates love for those of the same nature. To those whose nature is crowned with reason, there will be one disposition, one ethos of life, one bond uniting all in communion, bringing them to the one logos of nature in one *gnome*.[22] Nature is endowed with a receptivity that surmounts death. Love and freedom are the quintessence of the endowment of human nature – created qualities calling for their perfection in the uncreated light of God's nature. As Gregory explains, 'when I speak of [human] nature, I am not slighting purposive will (*prohairesis*), but I suppose both—the aptitude for good, and that which brings the natural aptitude to effect.'[23] This is free will in its natural state, the natural will, which seeks after one thing; that which is good and is the purity of heart. Nature, for the patristic sensitivity, implies and dictates love and equality; it is the treasury of God's image, the vessel of God's grace, and the guardian of real persons, insofar as authentic personhood is associated with virtues, and virtues 'exist in all men because of their same nature'.[24]

Still, is ascetic discipline not a sort of 'violence' over nature, so that the person might be liberated from his natural confines? It would have been so, were nature no more than biological necessities, which it is not. The ascetic effort aims at the purification of the heart by eradicating all elements – the personal sinful elements – which maintain man in a fallen, disintegrated state, and at bringing him to the state of illumination and deification in the essential energy of God, which is love and freedom. Since there is no personal will in the Trinity, one's endeavour is to subject one's personal impulses, urges, desires or whims to one's natural will, which is oriented towards God and the common good. That is the 'self' that must be transcended: not the self identified with individuality or interiority, but with the egotistic realm of the gnomic will, fantastical relationships, and all the unnatural passions that are summed up in self-love.

The more the person takes precedence over the common underlying essence, the more it loses its content and dignity; for it receives its being by virtue of its place in a hierarchical structure, which actually and inevitably cultivates ties of domination and subservience. Subordinationism has a long history in theology as well as in social life. It goes hand-in-hand with the over-exalted person, who sides with the passions of pride and egotism, which are the very womb of all passions. When love, will and freedom become personal, they easily turn into caprice and sovereignty. Such love 'seeketh . . . to bind another to its delight'[25]; for the personal or gnomic will becomes the very core of being and the centrifugal axis around which the whole world is perceived to rotate. Thus, the passions cause disintegration in the soul or inner self, which subsequently can no more be in real communion either with itself or with others.

The need for the ascetic way is evident. Since we have a bodily selfhood, we are entities separated from one another in place and time, and that means that our acts of will and our opinions are different. Yet there is but one nature, so there is also but one natural will.[26] Again, this path is the most personal; it is the willing curtailment of the gnomic will. Since we communicate through our energies, the more these energies are purified by the expulsion of the deficiencies of the personal will, the more our inclinations are joined to nature; the more we are brought closer to our single nature and its uncreated Principle, the more we imitate and participate in divine life and come to a 'deiform unity and godlike oneness'.[27]

This perspective fosters absolute respect for the other's otherness, and at the same time it makes one advance towards real unity. Let us consider the etymology of the two Greek synonyms, which indicate the way to unity. The first is the word *syngnome* (συγ-γνώμη), which signifies compassion, remission, harmony and sharing of the same feelings. The second is the word *synhoresis* (συγ-χώρησις), meaning forgiveness and concordance. In the first word, the prefix *syn* (con) is joined to the word 'opinion' (or 'view', or 'belief'). The second is a derivative of the verb *synhoro* (συγ-χωρῶ), in which the same prefix is joined to the verb meaning 'to fit in one place/space'. Both words denote the ascetic way that leads to the co-inherence of persons, who renounce their personal will. The teacher and archetype is the trinitarian God.[28] Thus, the human being is invited to reach that concurrence and *perichoresis* that characterise the Trinity, through the absorption of the divine essential qualities. Maximus states that 'this is why there is only one God, Father, Son and Holy Spirit. For there is one and the same essence, power and activity of the Father and Son and Holy Spirit.'[29] But while God in His simplicity encapsulates the whole of creation in an undivided way, we need to engage in works of love, prayer and purification in order to find our deepest unity. And this cannot be accomplished but in God's grace, which enlightens nature, guiding one to the ineffable union with one's Creator.

God is the transcendental perfection of unity and trinity, and such perfection was given in the Person of God incarnate. Participating in

His flesh, blood and Spirit through the uncreated energies, the human being regains that state of integrity, in which all the powers of the soul converge and become one, producing authentic relationships. What takes place in God incarnate, namely the perfect communion of natures or, more precisely, the union and interchange of divine and human activities, also occurs in the human being by grace. Christ guides a person to the lost unity of nature. In Christ there is 'neither barbarian nor Scythian – that is, no tension of will pushing the single nature to revolt against itself'; 'Neither slave nor freedman – no division of the same nature by opposition of will – a division that makes dishonoured what is by nature of equal honour, having as an auxiliary law the attitude of those in power who exercise tyranny over the dignity of the image'.[30]

A thirst for unity remains the ultimate yearning of humanity; or, to be more precise, the quest for the unity that lies underneath all, and which is the common ground of all. This can hardly be found in political schemes and administrative patterns, much less in ongoing contemporary globalisation, which signals the annihilation of the person and the absolute fragmentation of the human psyche. It is also highly questionable that it can be achieved through a transcendentalism of personhood that sees nature and the self as enemies of communion and otherness. Eventually, the particular human will be evanesced in a culture that reveres the splendour of the void.

Arnold Toynbee, in his massive study of history, advocated *transfiguration* as the only way out of the deadlocks of a disintegrating civilisation.[31] The concept of transfiguration, with a much richer content, lies at the centre of the Christian mystery and spiritual life. It is the glorification of human nature, and nature in general, in the uncreated light of God. It is not simply a matter of withdrawal and return, a modification of the self through the cultivation of ethical virtues; more than that, it is a real union with God, an actual participation in God's life, in which the human and the divine energies bring forth not merely a mixture but the new creation of a wonderful amalgam. Within and above and beyond all structures and hierarchies, the charismata of the Spirit – the uncreated energies – in their mutual inherence express the unequivocal otherness in the deepest communion of essential love.

Such common nature is not produced by necessity or chance, for the inner principles of created beings are the divine wills. That is why a common brotherhood presupposes a common fatherhood (Col. 3:9-11). Consequently, the longing or need for a unifying orthodoxy is more profound, urgent and insistent than the quest for any institutional unity[32] and, I would dare say, the quest for a Eucharistic unity. Not because a system of beliefs functions as a unifying centre, but because one cannot live fully and be in real communion in falsity. Communion in truth is a constitutive element of the Church, indeed of humanity. Such orthodoxy should not be the adherence to a system of dogmas or the observance of an ethical code, but a transformative process, namely the encounter with God's *epiphany* in history and creation. It is the trinitarian being of God, as revealed in history, and described by an unbroken chain of holy witnesses, that proffers a mode of life encompassing the paradox of being one and many, after the image and likeness of divine Oneness and Trinity. This diversity in unity implies equality, and it is the consequence of the energetic relationship between God and the cosmos. Truly, as the Greek and the Irish Fathers state, in that body we have all drunk the same Spirit, we have enjoyed the same grace.[33]

Does what this study has laid forth from the patristic treasuries render the *mean* that we strive to achieve? We may answer, Yes. For *mean* is not simply what stands in the middle but rather the *means* through which we can grasp the *meaning* and achieve our purpose. This *mean* is characterised by a holistic approach, working out defragmentation and ruling out one-sided conceptions of being. For the Fathers the human being, by being created after God's image, indeed as a brilliant nature in innumerable hypostases encompassing the whole of creation, has to mirror God's ecstatic perfection through the saving experience of divine life, through the science of the unifying virtues, revealing one essence, one will and energy, one class and glory in unconfounded persons participating in the divine life; revealing the unity of the Trinity in the simplicity and single-mindedness of love, and fulfilling the abundance of natural potential, which is no less than deification itself, granted from within the depths of Triadic Monad, the principle and the *ariston telos* of everything.

Notes

Notes for Part I

ONE: The Quest for a Personalistic Ontology
(Pages 3–8)

1. John Milton, *Paradise Lost*, Book I.
2. For the various conceptions of 'person', see M. Carrithers, S. Collins and S. Lukes, *The Category of the Person*.
3. C.E. Gunton, *The Promise of Trinitarian Theology*, p. 87. J. Seigel, *The Idea of the Self: Thought and Experience in Western Europe since the Seventeenth Century*, p. 3.
4. J. Baudrillard (1996), *The Perfect Crime*, trans. C. Turner (London), p. 70. See his analysis of the consumer society in J. Baudrillard (2001), *Selected Writings*, ed. M. Poster (Oxford), pp. 32–59.
5. *CO*, p. 101.
6. The terms 'substance', 'essence' and 'nature' are conceived as equivalent to the Greek *ousia* or *physis*. They signify what something is, what is common and uncircumscribed in all the entities of the same genre. Initially there was no difference between substance and hypostasis; the latter signified that which subsists, and was rendered in Latin by the word *substantia*. The Cappadocian Fathers of the fourth century are credited with the clear distinction between *ousia*, as the common, and *hypostasis*, as the particular, the latter being identified with the person. In modern English, 'substance' became the standard translation of *ousia*. In the present study, rather than following the modern convention of translating *ousia* as 'substance', I have opted for the word 'essence' (Latin *essentia*) in order to avoid confusion with the term 'hypostasis' (Latin *substantia*). Both Byzantine and Latin theologians have drawn attention to this linguistic problem, which led to the misinterpretation of patristic sayings.
7. This is mainly the conception of Theodore de Regnon in his work *Études de Théologie Positive sur la Sainte Trinité*, vol. 1, p. 433. For a critical presentation of this 'antagonisme artificiel', see André de Halleux, 'Personnalisme ou essentialisme trinitaire chez les Pères cappadociens?'
8. *BC*, pp. 44, 87–8; *CO*, pp. 18–19.
9. *CO*, pp. 165, 277.
10. *BC*, pp. 41–4; *CO*, pp. 142, 66, 109–10; John Zizioulas (1996), 'The Contribution of Cappadocia to Christian Thought', pp. 23–37; Christos Yannaras (1996), *The Freedom of Morality* (New York), pp. 16–18.

11. *BC*, pp. 43–4, 49–53; *CO*, p. 102. See also Paul Cumin, 'Looking for personal space in the theology of John Zizioulas', 362–3. The 'either . . . or' formula (person vs. nature, person vs. individual, grace vs. history, philocalia vs. aesthetics) features in the philosophical work of Christos Yannaras. For critical remarks, see Chrysostom Stamoulis, Κάλλος τὸ Ἅγιον, pp. 209–24.

12. *BC*, pp. 49–65; Yannaras, *The Freedom of Morality*, pp. 22–4.

13. See Gregory Nazianzen, *Or.* 40, 41, *PG* 36.417 BC.

14. Evagrius, *Traité Pratique*, 3, p. 500. For the Trinity as experienced in prayer in the Greek patristic tradition, see J.E. Rutherford, 'Praying the Trinity in Diadochos of Photike'.

15. See, for example, Jürgen Moltmann (1981), *The Trinity and the Kingdom: The Doctrine of God*, pp. 149–50.

16. *CO*, p. 34.

17. *CO*, pp. 106, 121, 125.

18. *BC*, pp. 42–9; *CO*, pp. 106, 215.

19. *CO*, pp. 117–23, 195; Zizioulas (1983), 'The Teaching of the Second Ecumenical Council on the Holy Spirit', p. 45.

20. *CO*, pp. 119–20.

21. *CO*, pp. 161–2.

22. *CO*, pp. 35, 119–20.

23. See Gregory Nazianzen, *Or.* 29, 2, *PG* 36.76BC (where he explains that his purpose is to avoid notions 'by no means befitting our conception of Deity'); Maximus Confessor, Σχόλια εἰς τὸ περὶ θείων ὀνομάτων, *PG* 4.221A.

24. *BC*, p. 89. Zizioulas' synthesis, received by many as a panacea, has also been subject to serious criticism by non-Orthodox scholars through different lenses, as well as by leading figures among the young generation of Orthodox academics, including C. Stamoulis (1999), Φύση καὶ Ἀγάπη (Thessaloniki), N. Loudovikos (2009), Οἱ τρόμοι τοῦ Προσώπου καὶ τὰ βάσανα τοῦ Ἔρωτα (Athens) and J.-C. Larchet (2011), *Personne et Nature: La Trinité, Le Christ, L'Homme* (Paris). See also André de Halleux, 'Personalisme ou essentialisme trinitaire chez les Pères cappadociens?'; A.J. Torrance, *Persons in Communion*, pp. 283–306; M. Ludlow, *Gregory of Nyssa, Ancient and (Post)modern*, pp. 52–68; M. Volf, *After Our Likeness*.

25. *Wounded by Love: The Life and the Wisdom of Elder Porphyrios* (Limni, 2005), p. 87.

26. *CO*, p. 142.

27. *CO*, p. 143.

28. *OM*, p. 84.

29. *CO*, pp. 146–7.

30. *CO*, pp. 147–8; *BC*, pp. 153–4; *OM*, p. 284.

31. Elpidoforos Lambriniades (2009), 'Οἱ προκλήσεις γιὰ τὴν Ὀρθοδοξία στὴν Ἀμερικὴ καὶ ὁ ρόλος τοῦ Οἰκουμενικοῦ Πατριαρχείου', *Episkepsis* 698 (March), 25.

32. Volf, *After Our Likeness*, p. 112.

33. *CO*, pp. 121–2. See also the remarks of Tom McCall with reference to the Heideggerian notion of *throwness* in 'Holy love and divine aseity in the theology of John Zizioulas'.

34. *BC*, pp. 52–3.

Two: Monarchy and Trinity in the Greek and Irish Fathers
(Pages 9–47)

1. Nicomachean Ethics, II.6–7.
2. Gregory Nazianzen, *Or.* 20, 6, PG 35.1072.
3. Reg. III, *SCO*, p. 126.3–10; Reg. VIII, pp. 134–9; Ep. IV.6, p. 32.32. Also D. Greene and F. Kelly (eds), *The Irish Adam and Eve Story from Saltair na Rann*, p. 63 (verses 1581–1584).
4. Gregory of Nyssa, Λόγος Κατηχητικός, 3, *The Catechetical Oration*, pp. 16–17.
5. Πρὸς Ἀντίοχον, PG 28.597.
6. Gregory Nazianzen, *Or.* 38, 8 (PG 36.320); *Or.* 39, 11 (PG 36.344–8); *Or.* 42, 16 (PG 36.476).
7. Gregory Nazianzen, *Or.* 38, 7, PG 36.317BC. Gregory of Nyssa, Πρὸς Ἀβλάβιον, *GNO*, III, Opera Dogmatica Minora, I, pp. 52–3; Κατὰ Εὐνομίου III, *GNO*, II, p. 38.
8. For example Basil, Ep. 236, *Lettres*, vol. 3, pp. 47–56.
9. 'This is the character of individualities (idiomata), to reveal in the identity of substance the otherness.' Basil of Caesarea, Πρὸς Εὐνόμιον II, 28, PG 29.637BC.
10. *BC*, pp. 36–43. Much more complicated is Aquinas' thesis, which presents the Spirit as the 'Love proceeding' from the Father and the Son. See *Summa theologiae*, Ia. 36, 1–4; 37, 1–3; 27, 3.
11. John Donne, *Holy Sonnets*, XVI. The image of the knot implies the idea of strong unity and impenetrable oneness.
12. Gregory Nazianzen, *Or.* 6, 22 (PG 35.749); *Or.* 23, 11 (PG 35.1164); *Or.* 25, 16 (PG 35.1221).
13. Epiphanius, Ἀγκυρωτός, X, PG 43.33D–36B; Gregory Nazianzen, *Or.* 31, 9, PG 36.141C–144A; Athanasius, Κατὰ Ἀρειανῶν III, 4, PG 26.328C; L. Ayres, *Nicaea and its Legacy*, p. 295.
14. Gregory Nazianzen, *Or.* 20, 10, PG 35.1077AB. Cf. Basil, Κατὰ Σαβελλιανῶν καὶ Ἀρείου καὶ τῶν Ἀνομοίων 6–7, PG 31.612C–616B.
15. Gregory Nazianzen, *Or.* 20, 12, PG 35.1080A–C; *Or.* 6, 22. John of Damascus, Ἔκδοσις ἀκριβὴς τῆς ὀρθοδόξου πίστεως, 1.2, PG 94.792B–793B.
16. Gregory Nazianzen, *Or.* 23, 11, PG 35.1161C–1164B. He is more apophatic in *Or.* 6, 22, PG 35.749BC.
17. Basil of Caesarea, Περὶ τοῦ Ἁγίου Πνεύματος, 18, 46, p. 408; Basil (Gregory of Nyssa) Ep. 38.3; *Lettres*, pp. 83–4.
18. Basil of Caesarea, Κατὰ Εὐνομίου I, 15, PG 29.545–548; Κατὰ Σαβελλιανῶν καὶ Ἀρείου καὶ Ἀνομοίων, 6, PG 31.613A. No term that tells us only about something's origin tells us anything about what makes it the entity it is. See A. Radde-Gallwitz, *Basil of Caesarea*, pp. 129–30, 136.
19. L. Ayres, *Nicaea and its Legacy*, pp. 280, 295–6, 198–211, 357–9.
20. Maximus Confessor, Μυσταγωγία, PG 91.664C.
21. John of Damascus, Ἔκδοσις ἀκριβής, 1.4, PG 94.797B.
22. *CO*, pp. 9, 29, 74, 166–7, 214–5, 187; *BC*, pp. 44–6.
23. Maximus Confessor, Κεφάλαια διάφορα θεολογικά τε καὶ οἰκονομικά, I, 1, PG 90.1177A; Basil of Caesarea, Ep. 38.3–4, *Lettres*, I, pp. 84, 87.
24. Maximus Confessor, Κεφάλαια διάφορα, I, 12, PG 90.1184B.

25. Maximus Confessor, Περὶ θεολογίας καὶ τῆς ἐνσάρκου οἰκονομίας, II, 76, PG 90.1160C; Περὶ διαφόρων ἀποριῶν, PG 91.1048D–1049A.

26. Nilus of Ancyra, *Ep.* 216, PG 79.161C.

27. Gregory of Nyssa, Κατὰ Εὐνομίου III, *GNO*, II, p. 38; Εἰς τὴν ἡμέραν τῶν Φώτων, *GNO*, IX, I, p. 227. For the history of the distinction between essence and energy in God, both in pagan and Christian thought, see D. Bradshaw, 'The Concept of the Divine Energies'. For the concept of energeia, see T.T. Tollefsen, *Activity and Participation*, pp. 16–21.

28. O. Davies, 'An Introduction to Celtic Spirituality' in *Celtic Spirituality*, p. 11.

29. *ILH*, v. ii, p. 121. 'Praecamur Patrem', F.E. Warren, *The Antiphonary of Bangor*, II, p. 5. Patrick's Hymn, *ThPal*, ii, pp. 354–8. O'Kelleher, 'A Hymn of Invocation', p. 237. 'God be with me', G. Murphy, *Early Irish Lyrics*, pp. 23–5. 'Altus Prosator' A, T.O. Clancy and G. Márkus, *Iona: The Earliest Poetry of a Celtic Monastery*, p. 44.

30. *SCO*, Instr. I, 3, pp. 62–3; Instr. I, 5, pp. 64–7; Instr. III, 2, pp. 74–5; Instr. VIII, 1, pp. 94–5; Instr. XI, 1, pp. 106–7. Ériugena (Jean Scot), *Homélie sur le prologue de Jean*, XIII, pp. 266–8; also 'Litany of the Trinity', *ILit*, p. 79. M.C. Diaz y Diaz, *Liber de ordine creaturarum*, I, 2, pp. 84–6. D. Howlett, 'Rubisca', st. 15, p. 81.

31. See 'Litany of Confession', *ILit*, p. 3.

32. *SCO*, Instr. I, 3, pp. 62–3; I, 5, pp. 64–5. Ériugena, *Periphyseon*, v. II, pp. 74–5.

33. Broccán's Hymn, 18, *ThPal*, ii, p. 331. *SCO*, Instr. I, 3, p. 62–63. Cf. Comm. In Iohannem I.18, *SHM*, II, p. 109.

34. Ps. Isidore, *Liber de ortu et obitu patriarcharum*, 42.2, 42.5–8, pp. 46, 50–3.

35. See Ériugena, *Periphyseon* II, pp. 200–1, where he follows the Areopagite, Περὶ θείων ὀνομάτων, XIII, 3, PG 3.480D–481B.

36. A. Wilmart, 'Catéchèses Celtiques', V, 9–10, p. 59. Gregory of Nyssa, Πρὸς Ἀβλάβιον, *GNO*, III, I, p. 47.

37. Basil of Caesarea, Περὶ τοῦ Ἁγίου Πνεύματος, 15, 38, pp. 376–8.

38. See examples in Basil of Caesarea, Ep. 38.4, *Lettres*, I, pp. 84–7. John Chrysostom, Εἰς τὴν πρὸς Ῥωμαίους ἐπιστολήν, PG 60.513, 519. Macarius, Hom. 18, 5–7, *Die 50 Geistlichen Homilien des Makarios*, pp. 179–80. Dionysius, Περὶ θείων ὀνομάτων, II, 6, PG 3.644C. *SCO*, Ep. III, 2, pp. 24–5. Irenaeus, *Contra haereses* III, xxiv.2.

39. Ps. Isidore, *Liber de ortu et obitu patriarcharum*, 41.1, p. 44.

40. The Spirit of the Father reveals that the Son shines within human nature. See Ériugena (Jean Scot), *Homélie sur le prologue de Jean*, XIII, p. 266. Also *Periphyseon* II, pp. 84–93.

41. Confessio, chs 4, 20, 24, 25, 33 in A.B.E. Hood, *St. Patrick: His Writings and Muirchu's Life*. Also see the Litany of the Trinity, where each person is invoked separately with reference to one's common activity as well as one's distinct role in its cosmic dimension. For a general presentation of early Irish trinitarianism, see T. Finan, 'The Trinity in early Irish Christian writings'.

42. For the prayer-based model of the Trinity see S. Coakley, *God, Sexuality and the Self*, pp. 111-15, 126-7. Also, John Chrysostom, Εἰς τὴν πρὸς Ῥωμαίους ἐπιστολήν, PG 60.527, 662.

43. Dionysius, Περὶ θείων ὀνομάτων, II, 4–5, PG 3.641AD.

44. Περὶ θείων ὀνομάτων, II, 4 (PG 3.641B); II, 7 (644D–645B).

45. Gregory Nazianzen, 'On the Spirit', *Poemata Arcana*, p. 14.

46. L. Ayres, *Nicaea and its Legacy*, pp. 300–1.

47. Basil, Ep. 105, *Lettres*, II, pp. 6–7; Ep. 52.2, *Lettres*, I, p. 135.

48. *CO*, p. 120.

49. *CO*, pp. 117–18.

50. Gregory Nazianzen, *Or.* 42, 15, PG 36.476.

51. *CO*, pp. 121–2. C.A. Beeley (2008), *Gregory of Nazianzus on the Trinity and the Knowledge of God* (Oxford), pp. 215–16.

52. *CO*, pp. 126–7, 131. N. Loudovikos, 'Person instead of grace', 9.

53. Gregory of Nyssa, Ἀντιρρητικὸς κατὰ Εὐνομίου I, *GNO*, I, pp. 180–1. B. Tírechán [III]26(11), L. Bieler, *The Patrician Texts in the Book of Armagh*, pp. 142–3. The same goes in respect of divine energies. See Πρὸς Ἀβλάβιον, *GNO*, III, Opera Dogmatica Minora, I, pp. 51–2. John of Damascus, Ἔκδοσις ἀκριβής, 1.8, PG 94.808Bff; 1.14, 860B.

54. N. Loudovikos, 'Person instead of grace', 9. See Gregory Nazianzen, *Or.* 31, 14, PG 36.148D–149A.

55. *CO*, pp. 118–20; 218–9. BC, pp. 44–6. P.M. Collins, *Trinitarian Theology*, pp. 179–83. Zizioulas, 'Ἀπὸ τὸ προσωπεῖον εἰς τὸ πρόσωπον', Χαριστήρια εἰς τιμὴν τοῦ Μητροπολίτου Γέροντος Χαλκηδόνος Μελίτωνος, p. 299.

56. Κατὰ Ἀρειανῶν III, 66, PG 26.461C–464B.

57. Κατὰ Ἀρειανῶν III, 62, PG 26.453B–456A; III, 66, 26.461C, 464B. Cf. *CO*, pp. 120–1, 35.

58. See *CO*, p. 121.

59. Gregory Nazianzen, *Or.* 29, 6–7, PG 36.80–84. Translations of the Cappadocians are taken from *The Early Church Fathers* (Harmony Media 2000, originally published by Wm. B. Eerdmans, Edinburgh, beginning in 1867) with occasional amendments, unless footnoted otherwise.

60. *CO*, p. 108, n. 18.

61. See Maximus the Confessor, Περὶ διαφόρων ἀποριῶν, PG 91.1264B.

62. Gregory Nazianzen, *Or.* 29, 6, PG 36.81B.

63. Gregory of Nyssa, Κατὰ Εὐνομίου III, 6, *GNO*, II, pp. 191–2.

64. Basil, Περὶ τοῦ Ἁγίου Πνεύματος, 16, 38, p. 378.

65. Gregory Nazianzen, *Or.* 34, 8, PG 36.248D–249A.

66. See Gregory of Nyssa, Πρὸς Ἀβλάβιον, *GNO*, III, I, pp. 47–8.

67. Ἔκδοσις ἀκριβής, 1.8, PG 94.813AB. Also Maximus Confessor, Περὶ διαφόρων ἀποριῶν, PG 91.1264B.

68. See Maximus Confessor, *Disputatio cum Pyrrho*, PG 91.313CD; Περὶ διαφόρων ἀποριῶν, PG 91.1261B–1264B (*On Difficulties in the Church Fathers*, vol. 2, pp. 11–15).

69. Περὶ τοῦ Ἁγίου Πνεύματος 3, 66, PG 26.461C–464B.

70. Gregory of Nyssa, Κατὰ Εὐνομίου I, *GNO*, I, pp. 147–8. D. Bradshaw observes that the concept of an internal activity in the Trinity is not adopted by the Fathers (*Aristotle East and West*, pp. 157–60). This is clearly stated by Maximus: there is a kind of activity that enables beings to bring forth from themselves other beings absolutely identical to them. But not even that kind of activity can be applied to the Father and the Son, 'since it is far beneath the ineffable and inconceivable existence of the only-

begotten Son'. Περὶ διαφόρων ἀποριῶν, PG 91.1265D–1268B.

71. Basil of Caesarea, Πρὸς Εὐνόμιον II, 22, PG 29.561. Also Clement of Alexandria, Στρωματεῖς VII.1, PG 9.404C.

72. *CO*, pp. 131–2, 104–6; *BC*, pp. 39–49.

73. Basil of Caesarea, Κατὰ Εὐνομίου I, 15, PG 29.545–548.

74. *CO*, p. 215; *OM*, pp. 27, 29. Gregory Palamas, Ὑπὲρ τῶν ἱερῶς ἡσυ-χαζόντων, 3, 2.12, Συγγράμματα, I, p. 666.

75. Gregory Palamas, Κεφάλαια φυσικά, θεολογικά, ἠθικά τε καὶ πρακτικά, 135, Φιλοκαλία, IV, p. 182. For being, essence and accident, see John of Damascus, Κεφάλαια φιλοσοφικά, 4, PG 94.536C–537B.

76. Gregory of Nyssa, Κατὰ Εὐνομίου I, *GNO*, I, p. 171.

77. Basil of Caesarea, Κατὰ Εὐνομίου I, 10, PG 29.536. Gregory of Nyssa, Κατὰ Εὐνομίου I, *GNO*, I, p. 214. The term *ousia* in Gregory has an 'existential' – designating the existence – as well as an 'essential' sense, pointing to 'the being of beings'. See J. Zachhuber, 'Ousia', in L.F. Mateo-Seco and G. Maspero, *The Brill Dictionary of Gregory of Nyssa*, pp. 562–7.

78. Gregory of Nyssa, Εἰς τὸν βίον Μωυσέως, *GNO*, VII, I, pp. 4, 40. Also D. Balas, 'Participation', in L.F. Mateo-Seco and G. Maspero, *The Brill Dictionary of Gregory of Nyssa*, p. 585.

79. Gregory Nazianzen, *Or.* 38, 7–8, PG 36.317B–320.

80. Maximus Confessor, Περὶ διαφόρων ἀποριῶν, PG 91.1345BC, 1228A–1229B.

81. Dionysius, Περὶ θείων ὀνομάτων, II, 4, PG 3.640D.

82. Gregory Nazianzen, *Or.* 29, 2, PG 36.76AB.

83. Gregory Nazianzen, *Or.* 29, 2, PG 36.76B. Cf. *Or.* 23, 8, PG 35.1160.

84. *CO*, pp. 132-4, 161, 186-7, 106, 144.

85. Gregory of Nyssa, Πρὸς Ἀβλάβιον, *GNO*, III, I, 41.2–7; Πρὸς τοὺς Ἕλληνας, *GNO*, III, Opera Dogmatica Minora, I, pp. 19–20. Basil of Caesarea, Ep. 38.3, *Lettres*, I, pp. 82–4. The Cappadocians avoid the Platonic and Neoplatonic theories of participation. See Richard Cross (2002), 'Gregory of Nyssa on Universals', *Vigiliae Christianae* 56, 372–410. Only the Apologists take recourse to a subordinating hierarchy to align Christian belief with Middle Platonism. For the difference between them and Irenaeus, see J. Lashier, *Irenaeus on the Trinity*, pp. 208–9, 220–1.

86. Basil of Caesarea, Περὶ τοῦ Ἁγίου Πνεύματος, 45, pp. 404–6.

87. Gregory Nazianzen, *Or.* 42, 15; *Or.* 23, 11. *Or.* 20, 7. *Or.* 31, 16. Basil of Caesarea, Περὶ πίστεως, 2, PG 31.465C–468C. Gregory of Nyssa, Κατὰ Ἀρείου καὶ Σαβελλίου, *GNO*, III, Opera Dogmatica Minora, I, p. 81. Diaz y Diaz, *Liber de ordine creaturarum*, I, 2–3, pp. 84–6.

88. Gregory Nazianzen, *Or.* 38, 8, PG 36.320. Ps. Athanasius, Πρὸς Ἀντίοχον, PG 28.597C. Maximus Confessor, Εἰς τὴν προσευχήν, PG 90.892A–893A.

89. Maximus Confessor, Εἰς τὴν προσευχήν, PG 90.892A–C.

90. *Or.* 23, 8, PG 35.1160.

91. Maximus Confessor, Περὶ διαφόρων ἀποριῶν, PG 91.1033D–1036C. The three *are* the holy Monad. *Ibid.*, 1397C.

92. Maximus Confessor, Σχόλια εἰς τὸ περὶ θείων ὀνομάτων, PG 4.209D–212B.

93. Maximus Confessor, Περὶ διαφόρων ἀποριῶν, PG 91.1036C, 1257C–1261A; *Questiones et dubia*, 105, CC 10, p. 79.

94. Maximus Confessor, Σχόλια εἰς τὸ περὶ θείων ὀνομάτων, PG 4.200D.

95. Maximus Confessor, Σχόλια εἰς τὸ περὶ θείων ὀνομάτων, PG 4.196B, 212B. Cf. Anastasius Sinaite, Ὁδηγός, 2, PG 89.56A.

96. Maximus Confessor, Περὶ διαφόρων ἀποριῶν, PG 91.1036B, 1224D-1228A; Σχόλια εἰς τὸ περὶ θείων ὀνομάτων, PG 4.220AB.

97. Maximus Confessor, Περὶ θεολογίας καὶ τῆς ἐνσάρκου οἰκονομίας, II, 76, PG 90.1160C–1161A. Ériugena, *Periphyseon* I, pp. 68–9.

98. Maximus Confessor, Εἰς τὴν προσευχήν, PG 90.892CD.

99. Dionysius, Περὶ θείων ὀνομάτων, II, 4, PG 3.640D.

100. Adam 'ἐξ ἑαυτοῦ ἐγέννησεν ἄλλον ἑαυτόν'. Gregory of Nyssa, Κατὰ Εὐνομίου III, *GNO*, II, p. 30. We should not exaggerate the use of the term 'Self'; Gregory simply wishes to refute the Eunomian argument of the generation of essence.

101. Theodulf of Orleans, 'Libellus de processione Spiritus Sancti', ed. H. Willjung, *Das Konzil von Aachen 809*, p. 325. Cited in A. E. Siecienski (2010), *The Filioque: History of a Doctrinal Controversy* (New York), p. 97.

102. Ériugena, *Periphyseon* I, pp. 104–5.

103. Gregory of Nyssa, Κατὰ Εὐνομίου III, *GNO*, II, pp. 27–8.

104. Gregory of Nyssa, Κατὰ Εὐνομίου II, *GNO*, I, pp. 389–90. Also Basil of Caesarea, Κατὰ Εὐνομίου I, 14–15, PG 29.544–548. Gregory Nazianzen, *Or.* 29, 15–16, PG 36.93–96; *Or.* 25, 16, PG 35.1221A–C. A small phrase in *Or.* 20, 6 means in context not that the Father is the origin of the divine nature but that He is the cause of divine, equal to Him hypostases.

105. John Romanides (1981), *Franks, Romans, Feudalism, and Doctrine: An Interplay between Theology and Society* (Brookline, Massachusetts), p. 87. 'The hypostasis of the Son is generated from the unbegotten Father, but the essence of all three is the same unoriginated essence', T. Tollefsen, *Activity and Participation*, p. 54. Zizioulas shows a paradoxical affinity with a certain Augustinian mode of presenting the Trinity: the Father is the Father of His own essence in the same way as He is the Father of His own greatness. See *De Trinitate*, Book VI, ch. 2 (3); Book VII, ch. 1 (1). Still, 'Augustine very rarely ventures towards such statements', L. Ayres (2010), *Augustine and the Trinity* (Cambridge), pp. 247–8.

106. Gregory Nazianzen, *Or.* 40, 41, PG 36.417A–C.

107. See Gregory of Nyssa, Κατὰ Ἀρείου καὶ Σαβελλίου, *GNO*, III, I, p. 79.

108. Gregory Nazianzen, *Or.* 34, 13, PG 36.253A. Also *Or.* 33, 16, PG 36.236A.

109. Gregory Nazianzen, *Or.* 25, 15–16, PG 35.1220–1221.

110. Gregory Nazianzen, *Or.* 25, 16, PG 35.1221; *Or.* 29, 12, PG 36.89A–C.

111. Gregory Nazianzen, *Or.* 31, 14, PG 36.148D–149A.

112. *CO*, p. 220.

113. 'For everything that is regarded as subsisting [ἐν ὑποστάσει] is said, by the common custom of all who use language, to "be": and from the word "be" has been formed the term "being"', Gregory of Nyssa, Κατὰ Εὐνομίου III, *GNO*, II, p. 261. John of Damascus, Ἔκδοσις ἀκριβής, 3.6 (PG 94.1004A); 3.9 (PG 94.1016C–1017A).

114. Gregory Nazianzen, *Or.* 20, 7, PG 35.1073.

115. Gregory Nazianzen, *Or.* 31, 14, PG 36.149A.

116. Gregory Nazianzen, *Or.* 41, 9, PG 36.441. Also Gregory Palamas, Κεφάλαια φυσικά, θεολογικά, ἠθικά τε καὶ πρακτικά, *Φιλοκαλία*, IV, p. 182. Basil of Caesarea, Πρὸς Εὐνόμιον II, 28, PG 29.637. Also Gregory of Nyssa, Κατὰ Εὐνομίου II, *GNO*, I, p. 256.

117. Gregory of Nyssa, Λόγος ἀντιρρητικὸς πρὸς τὴν Εὐνομίου ἔκθεσιν, *GNO*, I, p. 352.

118. Gregory of Nyssa, Πρὸς τοὺς Ἕλληνας, *GNO*, III, I, pp. 19–20, 25.

119. Gregory of Nyssa, Λόγος ἀντιρρητικὸς πρὸς τὴν Εὐνομίου ἔκθεσιν, *GNO*, I, p. 321.

120. Gregory of Nyssa, *The Catechetical Oration*, 3, p. 16; Κατὰ Εὐνομίου I, *GNO*, I, pp. 179–80.

121. Gregory of Nyssa, Πρὸς τοὺς Ἕλληνας, *GNO*, III, I, p. 20; *The Catechetical Oration*, 1, pp. 6–7; 3, p. 16.

122. Gregory of Nyssa, Κατὰ Εὐνομίου I, *GNO*, I, pp. 179–80, 161–2, 107–8, 146–7. Accordingly, the name Son is given because of the communion in the begetter's nature. Gregory of Nyssa, Κατὰ Εὐνομίου III, 2, *GNO*, II, p. 89; Λόγος ἀντιρρητικὸς πρὸς τὴν Εὐνομίου ἔκθεσιν, *GNO*, I, p. 330.

123. Basil of Caesarea, Κατὰ Σαβελλιανῶν καὶ Ἀρείου καὶ τῶν Ἀνομοίων, 4, PG 31.605D–608A.

124. Basil of Caesarea, Κατὰ Σαβελλιανῶν καὶ Ἀρείου καὶ τῶν Ἀνομοίων, 3, PG 31.605AB. Gregory of Nyssa, Κατὰ Εὐνομίου I, *GNO*, I, pp. 170–1.

125. Basil of Caesarea, Περὶ τοῦ Ἁγίου Πνεύματος, 45, pp. 404–6.

126. See Cyril of Alexandria, *In D. Joannis evangelium*, v. I, pp. 44, 72, 191; v. II, pp. 507, 675.

127. Cyril of Alexandria, *In D. Joannis evangelium*, I, 5, v. I, pp. 69–71.

128. Cyril of Alexandria, Ἡ βίβλος τῶν θησαυρῶν, XI, PG 75.180A, 141; XII, PG 75.184–5; Περὶ ἁγίας τε καὶ ὁμοουσίου Τριάδος, III, PG 75.792A–796C; *In D. Joannis evangelium*, I, 3, v. I, p. 44.

129. Cyril of Alexandria, Ἡ βίβλος τῶν θησαυρῶν, VII, PG 75.84–85, 89, 96. Ousia and hyparxis are identified. See Maximus, Πρὸς Μαρῖνον, PG 91.205AB. Anastasius Sinaita, *Doctrina patrum*, p. 39.19–24.

130. Cyril of Alexandria, *In D. Joannis evangelium*, II, 7, v. I, p. 326. Περὶ ἁγίας τε καὶ ὁμοουσίου Τριάδος, II, PG 75.780B.

131. Cyril of Alexandria, Ἡ βίβλος τῶν θησαυρῶν, VII, PG 75.92AB; Περὶ ἁγίας τε καὶ ὁμοουσίου Τριάδος, II, PG 75.773D–776D; *In D. Joannis evangelium*, I, 5, v. I, p. 70.

132. Cyril of Alexandria, Περὶ ἁγίας τε καὶ ὁμοουσίου Τριάδος, I, PG 75.668B; *Ep.* 1, PG 77.16C, 17B, 36B; *In D. Joannis evangelium*, IX, v. II, p. 457.

133. Cyril of Alexandria, *In D. Joannis evangelium*, III–IV, v. I, pp. 253–5; Ἡ βίβλος τῶν θησαυρῶν, XXXIV, PG 75.593A–597C.

134. Gregory Nazianzen, *Or.* 41, 9, PG 36,441B.

135. Gregory of Nyssa, Λόγος ἀντιρρητικὸς πρὸς τὴν Εὐνομίου ἔκθεσιν, *GNO*, I, p. 364.

136. Cyril of Alexandria, *In D. Joannis evangelium*, IV, 1, v. I, pp. 494–5; v. II, pp. 414, 457, 638.

137. Basil of Caesarea, Περὶ πίστεως, 3, PG 31.472A. Concerning the Son, see John Chrysostom, Εἰς τὴν πρὸς Ἑβραίους, Hom. 27, 4, PG 63.189.

138. Basil of Caesarea, Κατὰ Σαβελλιανῶν καὶ Ἀρείου καὶ τῶν Ἀνομοίων, 4, PG 31.609AB. Gregory of Nyssa, Λόγος ἀντιρρητικὸς πρὸς τὴν

Εὐνομίου ἔκθεσιν, *GNO*, I, p. 330. We may say here that the patristic 'essentialism' does not lead to the *filioque* through a confusion between essential characteristics and the origin of the persons.

139. Epiphanius, Κατὰ Αἱρέσεων, II, 1, PG 41.1001–1004.

140. Gregory of Nyssa, Πρὸς Ἀβλάβιον, *GNO*, III, I, pp. 56–7.

141. Maximus Confessor, Κεφάλαια διάφορα, I, 4–5, PG 90.1180A; Περὶ Θεολογίας καὶ τῆς ἐνσάρκου οἰκονομίας, II, 1, PG 90.1124D–1125C.

142. Basil, Ep. 52, 3, *Lettres*, I, pp. 135–6. Cf. Κατὰ Σαβελλιανῶν καὶ Ἀρείου καὶ τῶν Ἀνομοίων, 4, PG 31.605.

143. Gregory of Nyssa, Κατὰ Εὐνομίου I, *GNO*, I, pp. 146–7.

144. Gregory of Nyssa, Κατὰ Εὐνομίου III, 2, *GNO*, II, p. 89.

145. See Basil of Caesarea, Πρὸς Εὐνόμιον II, 28, PG 29.637.

146. John of Damascus, Ἔκδοσις ἀκριβής, 1.8, PG 94.809A, 824B–825A.

147. Maximus Confessor, *Ep.* 15, PG 91.549B–552A.

148. Basil (Gregory of Nyssa), Ep. 38.4, *Lettres*, I, pp. 85–7.

149. Gregory Nazianzen, *Or.* 30, 20, PG 36.129A.

150. Gregory Nazianzen, *Or.* 30, 20, PG 36.128–129. *Or.* 31, 16, PG 36.152. John of Damascus, Ἔκδοσις ἀκριβής, 1.8, PG 94.808BC, 809A, 812A–C, 817A–C, 825A–828A.

151. Ps. Athanasius, Περὶ Ἁγίας Τριάδος, II, PG 28.1172A.

152. Basil of Caesarea, Περὶ τοῦ Ἁγίου Πνεύματος, 45, pp. 404–6; Κατὰ Σαβελλιανῶν καὶ Ἀρείου καὶ τῶν Ἀνομοίων, 4, PG 31.608.

153. Basil of Caesarea, Περὶ τοῦ Ἁγίου Πνεύματος, 47, p. 412.

154. See John of Damascus, Ἔκδοσις ἀκριβής, 1.8, PG 94.813AB. Gregory of Nyssa does not draw any far-reaching or speculative conclusions from his analogies. See T. Tollefsen, *Activity and Participation*, pp. 54–7.

155. For example, John of Damascus, Ἔκδοσις ἀκριβής, 3.4 (PG 94.997A); 3.11(PG 94.1021C–1024A).

156. Gregory Nazianzen, *Or.* 38, 7, PG 36.317BC.

157. Dionysius, Περὶ μυστικῆς Θεολογίας III, PG 3.1033B (trans. C. Luibhéid, *Pseudo-Dionysius: The Complete Works*, p. 139).

158. Κατὰ Εὐνομίου II, *GNO*, I, pp. 268–9.

159. That was the reaction of the Fathers against Eunomius' theory that the names designate the very substance. See Basil of Caesarea, Κατὰ Εὐνομίου I, 6, PG 29.520–4. For a more elaborate account, see Gregory of Nyssa, Κατὰ Εὐνομίου II, *GNO*, I, pp. 271; 255–6; 277–88; Πρὸς Ἀβλάβιον, *GNO* III, I, pp. 42–4. Also Gregory Nazianzen, *Or.* 38, 7; *Or.* 40, 5. On *epinoia* in the Cappadocians, consult S. Douglass, 'Gregory of Nyssa and Theological Imagination'. G. Maspero, 'Trinity' in L.F. Mateo-Seco and G. Maspero, *The Brill Dictionary of Gregory of Nyssa*, pp. 750–1. D. Bradshaw, 'The Concept of the Divine Energies', pp. 114–15.

160. Gregory Nazianzen, *Or.* 40, 43, PG 36.420BC.

161. Basil (Gregory of Nyssa), Ep. 38.5, *Lettres*, I, pp. 87–9. The same is expressed in the succinct phrase of the other Gregory: 'Light of Light, very God of very God, the one being all that the other is, save being that other'. Gregory of Nyssa, Κατὰ Εὐνομίου III, *GNO*, II, p. 33.

162. Ériugena, *Periphyseon* I, pp. 68–71.

163. Diaz y Diaz, *Liber de ordine creaturarum*, I, 4, p. 86. For the Father as source of divinity, see also *Breviarium in psalmos*, PL 26.1235AB.

164. Ps. Isidore, *Liber de ortu et obitu patriarcharum*, 42.4, pp. 48–9. *Breviarium in psalmos*, PL 26.135A.

165. Ériugena (Jean Scot), *Homélie sur le prologue de Jean*, VII, p. 234; *Periphyseon* II, pp. 74–5.

166. Ériugena (Jean Scot), *Homélie sur le prologue de Jean*, VI, pp. 226–8; *Periphyseon* II, p. 72.

167. Ériugena (Jean Scot), *Homélie sur le prologue de Jean*, XI, p. 258.

168. Ériugena, *Periphyseon* II, pp. 66–7.

169. Ps. Isidore, *Liber de ortu et obitu patriarcharum*, 42.3, pp. 47–8. Ériugena (Jean Scot), *Homélie sur le prologue de Jean*, VII, pp. 234, 238–40.

170. *Breviarium in psalmos*, PL 26.914D, 920D. Ps. Isidore, *Liber de ortu et obitu patriarcharum*, 42.3, pp. 47–8.

171. *SCO*, Instr. I, 2, pp. 60–63. *Breviarium in psalmos*, PL 26.1071D–1072A, 1070CD.

172. *Breviarium in psalmos*, PL 26.1069AB; 1070CD. Also *ILit*, pp. 80–1.

173. See *Breviarium in psalmos*, PL 26.1070CD.

174. Basil of Caesarea, Περὶ τοῦ Ἁγίου Πνεύματος, 46, p. 410.

175. See Athanasius, Περὶ τοῦ Ἁγίου Πνεύματος III, 66, PG 26.461C–464C.

176. *Breviarium in psalmos*, PL 26.1234B. Cf. Comm. in Iohannem I.3, *SHM*, II, p. 106.

177. Gregory of Nyssa, Λόγος ἀντιρρητικὸς πρὸς τὴν Εὐνομίου ἔκθεσιν, *GNO*, I, p. 360. Cf. Athanasius, Περὶ τοῦ Ἁγίου Πνεύματος IV, 1, PG 26.468BC. 'In this beginning the Son also is declared to be, being in His nature that very thing which the Beginning is'. Gregory of Nyssa, Κατὰ Εὐνομίου III, 6, *GNO*, II, p. 193.

178. Ériugena (Jean Scot), *Homélie sur le prologue de Jean*, VII, p. 232. For the Son as principle, see Theophilus, Πρὸς Αὐτόλυκον, II.13, PG 6.1072B.

179. Maximus Confessor, Περὶ διαφόρων ἀποριῶν, PG 91.1256A.

180. *Breviarium in psalmos*, PL 26.1070CD.

181. Ériugena, *Periphyseon* III, pp. 38–9; I, pp. 144–5.

182. *SCO*, Instr. I, 2, pp. 62–3.

183. This is what T. Tollefsen reads in the Cappadocians and Chrysostom; see *Activity and Participation*, pp. 39, 52–4.

184. *BC*, pp. 88–9. C.M. LaCugna, *God for Us*, p. 119. Also see P.D. Molnar, *Divine Freedom and the Doctrine of the Immanent Trinity*, pp. 132–3.

185. Cyril of Alexandria, *In D. Joannis evangelium*, V, 5, v. II, pp. 50–1.

186. See Ps. Athanasius, Κατὰ Αἰρέσεων, PG 28.1321–1322.

187. See John Chrysostom, Εἰς τὴν πρὸς Γαλάτας ἐπιστολήν, 1, 3–4, PG 61.617.

188. John Chrysostom, Ὑπόμνημα εἰς τὰς πράξεις τῶν ἀποστόλων, PG 60.95.

189. J. Carney, *The poems of Blathmac*, 197, pp. 66-7.

190. Gregory of Nyssa, Κατὰ Εὐνομίου I, *GNO*, I, pp. 82–6. For Gregory's apophatic turn in his later writings see S. Coakley, *God, Sexuality and the Self*, p. 288.

191. Gregory of Nyssa, Εἰς τὸ τότε καὶ αὐτὸς ὁ υἱὸς ὑποταγήσεται, *GNO*, III, II, p. 18.14–19. For the corporative character of Christ's subordination, see also Gregory of Nyssa, Κατὰ Ἀρείου καὶ Σαβελλίου, *GNO*, III, I, p. 78. For the selfsame argument offered by Origen, see I. Ramelli, 'Gregory of Nyssa's Trinitarian Theology'.

192. Gregory of Nyssa, Εἰς τὸ τότε καὶ αὐτὸς ὁ υἱὸς ὑποταγήσεται, *GNO,* III, II, pp. 27–8. Also Λόγος ἀντιρρητικὸς πρὸς τὴν Εὐνομίου ἔκθεσιν, *GNO,* I, p. 373.

193. See Gregory Nazianzen, *Or.* 30, 5–6, PG 36.108–109.

194. Accordingly, the affirmation 'I live by the Father' (John 7:57) does not mean that 'His life and being were kept together by the Father', but simply that 'He has His being from Him beyond all time, and beyond all cause'. Gregory Nazianzen, *Or.* 30, 11, PG 36.116C.

195. Gregory of Nyssa, Λόγος ἀντιρρητικὸς πρὸς τὴν Εὐνομίου ἔκθεσιν, *GNO,* I, p. 330.

196. Gregory Nazianzen, *Or.* 30, 11, PG 36.117.

197. Gregory Nazianzen, *Or.* 30, 12–13, PG 36.117–121. Anastasius, *Doctrina patrum,* pp. 115–16.

198. Maximus the Confessor, Περὶ διαφόρων ἀποριῶν, PG 91.1041BC, 1044B, 1076A–1076B.

199. Maximus the Confessor, Σχόλια εἰς τὸ περὶ θείων ὀνομάτων, PG 4.229D–232A.

200. Gregory of Nyssa, Λόγος ἀντιρρητικὸς πρὸς τὴν Εὐνομίου ἔκθεσιν, *GNO,* I, pp. 402–3.

201. Gregory Nazianzen, *Or.* 41, 9, PG 36,441. Gregory of Nyssa, Ep. 24, *GNO,* VIII, II, p. 79; Λόγος ἀντιρρητικὸς πρὸς τὴν Εὐνομίου ἔκθεσιν, *GNO,* I, p. 330. Basil of Caesarea, Περὶ πίστεως, 3, PG 31.472A.

202. Ps. Isidore, *Liber de ortu et obitu patriarcharum,* 42.4, p. 48. Quaestiones vel glosae, 60, *SHM,* I, p. 147. Ériugena follows the Greek interpretation of the cause. See *Homélie sur le prologue de Jean,* VII, p. 234.

203. In Epist. Can., II Petri I.17, *SHM,* I, p. 101.

204. In Epist. Can., II Petri I.17, *SHM,* I, p. 101. Comm. in Lucam III.22, *SHM,* II, p. 27.

205. J. Carney (ed.), *The Poems of Blathmac,* pp. 66–7.

206. It features mostly in Cyril of Alexandria. Also see Basil (Gregory of Nyssa) Ep. 38.4, *Lettres,* I, p. 85. Gregory of Nyssa, Epist. 24, *GNO,* VIII, II, p. 79. Basil (Gregory of Nyssa), Ep. 38.4. Maximus Confessor, Σχόλια εἰς τὸ περὶ θείων ὀνομάτων, PG 4.232B.

207. A. Louth, *St John Damascene,* p. 96. For Irenaeus, see J. Lashier, *Irenaeus on the Trinity,* pp. 209–12.

208. Basil, Ep. 236, 6, *Lettres,* III, pp. 53–4. Godhead pertains to the common *ousia.* Basil, Ep. 214, 4, *Lettres,* II, pp. 205–6.

209. Basil of Caesarea, Κατὰ Σαβελλιανῶν καὶ Ἀρείου καὶ Ἀνομοίων, 3, PG 31.605AB.

210. 'Litany of Confession', *ILit,* pp. 2–3. Cf. 'Litany of the Trinity', ibid., pp. 84–5. *Breviarum in psalmos,* PL 26.920D, 1071D.

211. Gregory Nazianzen, *Or.* 42, 15, PG 36.476AB. Also see Epist. 101, To Cledonius: 'as there is one and the same title, so there is one nature and one substance in the Godhead', *Lettres Théologiques,* p. 66.

212. Gregory Nazianzen, *Or.* 23, 11, PG 35.1164AB.

213. Gregory Nazianzen, *Or.* 31, 14, PG 36.148D–149A.

214. Gregory Nazianzen, *Or.* 31, 14, PG 36.149A. Cf. P. Rorem, *Ériugena's Commentary on the Dionysian Celestial Hierarchy,* pp. 181–2.

215. Diaz y Diaz, *Liber de ordine creaturarum,* I, 3–4, p. 86.

216. Ériugena, *Periphyseon* I, pp. 51, 61.
217. Gregory of Nyssa, Πρὸς Ἀβλάβιον, *GNO*, III, I, pp. 44–5. Περὶ θεότητος Υἱοῦ καὶ Πνεύματος Λόγος, PG 46.573C–576A.
218. Gregory of Nyssa, Πρὸς τοὺς Ἕλληνας, *GNO*, III, I, pp. 19–20. Πρὸς Εὐστάθιον, περὶ τῆς ἁγίας Τριάδος, *GNO*, III, Opera Dogmatica Minora, I, pp. 13–15.
219. Gregory of Nyssa, Πρὸς τοὺς Ἕλληνας, *GNO*, III, I, pp. 20–1. Cf. Basil, Ep. 8, *Lettres*, I, p. 35. Epiphanius, Κατὰ Αἱρέσεων, PG 42.13A, 248A.
220. Gregory of Nyssa, Πρὸς τοὺς Ἕλληνας, *GNO*, III, I, pp. 22–3.
221. Gregory of Nyssa, Πρὸς Ἀβλάβιον, *GNO*, III, I, p. 55.
222. Gregory Nazianzen, *Or.* 30, 8, PG 36.113AB. Maximus Confessor, Περὶ διαφόρων ἀποριῶν, PG 91.1268C–1269A.
223. Gregory Nazianzen, *Or.* 39, 11, PG 36.344CD.
224. Gregory Nazianzen, *Or.* 39, 12, PG 36.348A.
225. Gregory Nazianzen, *Or.* 31, 20, PG 36.156B.
226. Gregory Nazianzen, *Or.* 34, 15, PG 36.253C–256A. Also Gregory of Nyssa, Κατὰ Εὐνομίου I, *GNO*, I, p. 84.
227. Περὶ θείων ὀνομάτων, II, 1 (PG 3.636–637); II, 11 (649–652).
228. Ἔκδοσις ἀκριβῆς, 1.9, PG 94.836B–837B.
229. Ἔκδοσις ἀκριβῆς, 1.8, PG 94.829BC.
230. Ἔκδοσις ἀκριβῆς, 3.11, PG 94.1028A.
231. Ἔκδοσις ἀκριβῆς, 1.8, PG 94.828A–829A.
232. See J. Zachhuber, 'Physis', L.F. Mateo-Seco and G. Maspero, *The Brill Dictionary of Gregory of Nyssa*, pp. 615-20.
233. Gregory of Nyssa, Πρὸς τοὺς Ἕλληνας, *GNO*, III, I, pp. 23, 30–2. John of Damascus, Κεφάλαια φιλοσοφικά, 43, PG 94.613B. Ἔκδοσις ἀκριβῆς, 3.4, PG 94.997A.
234. Basil, Ep. 236, 6, *Lettres*, III, pp. 53–4. Basil (Gregory of Nyssa), Ep. 38.6, *Lettres*, I, p. 89. Maximus Confessor, Ep. 15, PG 91.557D; Πρὸς Μαρῖνον, PG 91.276AB. For the hypostatic principle in Maximus, see T. Tollefsen, *The Christocentric Cosmology of Maximus the Confessor*, pp. 128–37.
235. John of Damascus, Ἔκδοσις ἀκριβῆς, 1.10, PG 94.837C. Cf. Basil of Caesarea, Κατὰ Εὐνομίου I, 5, PG 29.516–17. Gregory Nazianzen, *Or.* 23, 8, PG 35.1160C. Ériugena, *Periphyseon* I, pp. 70–3. The mode of being of the essence of the Father is not the person of the Father but the ἀγεννήτως. Gregory of Nyssa, Κατὰ Εὐνομίου II, *GNO*, I, pp. 337, 339.
236. Gregory of Nyssa, Πρὸς Ἀβλάβιον, *GNO*, III, I, p. 41. Basil (Gregory of Nyssa), Ep. 38.3, 6, *Lettres*, I, pp. 82–90. Maximus Confessor, *Ep.* 15, PG 91.552B–D; Πρὸς Μαρῖνον, PG 91.276AB. Basil, Πρὸς Εὐνόμιον II, 4, PG 29.577–580. For the understanding of a person as a collection, congress or complex of properties in the Cappadocians, see L. Turcescu, '"Person" *versus* "Individual"', pp. 98–101.
237. Basil (Gregory of Nyssa), Ep. 38.3, *Lettres*, I, pp. 82–4. Nature is understood as 'a complex of properties which together make up the essence of a thing and are described by a defining formula, a *logos*'. For the word *physis*, see L.F. Mateo-Seco and G. Maspero, *The Brill Dictionary of Gregory of Nyssa*, pp. 615–20.
238. Athanasius, Περὶ τοῦ Ἁγίου Πνεύματος I, 16, PG 26.44D–45A.
239. Gregory Nazianzen, *Or.* 29, 16, PG 36.96A; *Or.* 30, 20, PG 36.128D. Gregory of Nyssa, Ἀντιρρητικὸς κατὰ Εὐνομίου, *GNO*, I, p. 170.

240. Basil of Caesarea, Πρὸς Εὐνόμιον II, 28, PG 29.637; Basil (Gregory of Nyssa), Ep. 38.5, *Lettres*, I, p. 89. Maximus Confessor, *Ep*. 15, PG 91.552BC.

241. Contrary to Eunomius' personal energy associating the Father with the Son. Gregory of Nyssa, Κατὰ Εὐνομίου II, *GNO*, I, p. 371. Ps. Athanasius, Διάλογος περὶ Τριάδος I, 25, PG 28.1153D–1156A.

242. Hence, Zizioulas' clarification that there is no priority either of substance or of person seems contradictory. *OM*, p. 22. Cf. *CO*, p. 220. M. Ludlow, *Gregory of Nyssa, Ancient and (Post)modern*, p. 59.

243. See P. Molnar, *Divine Freedom and the Doctrine of the Immanent Trinity*, pp. 249–50. For a criticism of the existential and social use of the concept of *perichoresis*, see R.E. Otto, 'The use and abuse of *perichoresis* in recent theology'. For a psychological interpretation of the social theories of the Trinity, see K. Kilby (2000), '*Perichoresis* and projection: problems with social doctrines of the Trinity', *New Blackfriars* 81, 432–5.

244. A. Louth, *St John Damascene*, pp. 114, 174. The human–divine analogy lies only in the relationship between nature and persons at both levels, thus pointing to the fundamental unity of human nature. See M. Ludlow, *Gregory of Nyssa, Ancient and (Post)modern*, p. 63.

245. K. Barth (1936), *Church Dogmatics* I/1, Edinburgh, p. 396.

246. Ἔκδοσις ἀκριβής, 1.8, PG 94.829A.

247. M. Volf, *After Our Likeness*, pp. 202–3, 210.

248. 'We speak of the three hypostases as being in each other, that we may not introduce a multitude of Gods.' Ἔκδοσις ἀκριβής, 1.8, PG 94.825AB. M. Volf, *After Our Likeness*, p. 210, n. 87. Cf. W. Pannenberg, 'Divine Economy and Eternal Trinity', p. 82.

249. *CO*, p. 239.

250. *De Trinitate*, Book V, 5.

251. Περὶ διαφόρων ἀποριῶν, PG 91.1265C–1268B.

252. John of Damascus, Ἔκδοσις ἀκριβής, 1.8, PG 94.816C–817A; 1, 10, PG.94.837BC. Cf. Basil of Casarea, Πρὸς Εὐνόμιον I.15, PG 29.545–548.

253. Gregory of Nyssa, Λόγος ἀντιρρητικὸς πρὸς τὴν Εὐνομίου ἔκθεσιν, *GNO*, I, p. 323.

254. See Maximus Confessor, *Ep*. 15, PG 91.552BC; Πρὸς Μαρῖνον, PG 91.249AB.

255. Gregory of Nyssa, Κατὰ Ἀρείου καὶ Σαβελλίου, *GNO*, III, I, p. 83.

256. Ἔκδοσις ἀκριβής, 1.8, PG 94.825AB. Also Gregory of Nyssa, Κατὰ Ἀρείου καὶ Σαβελλίου, *GNO*, III, I, pp. 79–80.

257. John of Damascus, Ἔκδοσις ἀκριβής, 1.8, PG 94.828C.

258. Basil (Gregory of Nyssa), Ep. 38.4, *Lettres*, I, p. 86. John of Damascus, Ἔκδοσις ἀκριβής, 1.8, PG 94.809A, 812B–813A, 816AB.

259. Gregory of Nyssa, Πρὸς τὰ Ἀπολιναρίου ἀντιρρητικός, *GNO*, III, I, p. 230; Κατὰ Εὐνομίου I, *GNO*, I, pp. 107–8, 170; Κατὰ Εὐνομίου III, 5, *GNO*, II, pp. 177; Κατὰ Ἀρείου καὶ Σαβελλίου, *GNO*, III, I, p. 79; Πρὸς Εὐστάθιον, περὶ τῆς ἁγίας Τριάδος, *GNO*, II, I, pp. 14–15. Epiphanius, Κατὰ Αἱρέσεων, II, 1, PG 41.1001–1004. Maximus Confessor, Περὶ θεολογίας καὶ τῆς ἐνσάρκου οἰκονομίας, II, 1, PG 90.1124D–1125C. Athanasius, Περὶ τοῦ Ἁγίου Πνεύματος III, 66–7, PG 26.461C–465A. Cyril of Alexandria, Ἡ βίβλος τῶν θησαυρῶν, XI, PG 75.180–181; XII, PG 75.185.

260. Cyril of Alexandria, Ἡ βίβλος τῶν θησαυρῶν, XII, PG 75.188; *In D. Joannis evangelium*, v. I, p. 44; v. II, pp. 261–2. For *perichoresis*, see N.V. Harrison, 'Perichoresis in the Greek Fathers'.

261. Maximus Confessor, Σχόλια εἰς τὸ περὶ θείων ὀνομάτων, PG 4.212B. Cf. Σχόλια εἰς τὸ περὶ τῆς οὐρανίας ἱεραρχίας, PG 4.76D–77A. Also see N. Loudovikos, Ἡ Κλειστὴ Πνευματικότητα καὶ τὸ Νόημα τοῦ Ἑαυτοῦ, pp. 272–3.

262. Cyril of Alexandria, *In D. Joannis evangelium*, I, 2, v. I, p. 25.

263. Cyril of Alexandria, Περὶ ἁγίας τε καὶ ὁμοουσίου Τριάδος, VI, PG 75.1053B–1056A; Ἡ βίβλος τῶν θησαυρῶν, VII, PG 75.88–89, 92. Athanasius, Κατὰ Ἀρειανῶν III, 66, PG 26.464A–C.

264. Basil of Caesarea, Περὶ τοῦ Ἁγίου Πνεύματος, 8, 21, p. 318.

265. Gregory of Nyssa, Κατὰ Εὐνομίου II, *GNO*, I, pp. 286–8.

266. Athanasius, Περὶ τοῦ Ἁγίου Πνεύματος I, 16, PG 26.44D–45A. Ps. Athanasius, Πρός τινα πολιτικὸν σύνταγμα, PG 28.1401–1404. Cyril of Alexandria, *Epist.* 1, PG 77.16C, 17B, 36B.

267. Although there is a linear movement in the economic Trinity, with the Father as the cause of the cause, and with the second cause, the Only-begotten, as the sender of the third person, any effort to found filioquism in such articulations of Gregory of Nyssa hardly seems convincing. What the Cappadocian declares with emphasis is the attachment of the two originated persons within the immanent Trinity and their causal relationship in God's revelation. A modified and moderated filioquism, as advocated by G. Maspero (*Trinity and Man*, pp. 149ff.), could be meaningful, yet the claimed participation of the Son in the existential origination of the Spirit is unqualified and obscure. The third person 'has its being attached to the Father, as cause, from Whom It proceeds'. 'It is known after the Son and together with the Son', but 'has its subsistence of the Father'. The Son 'declares the Spirit proceeding from the Father through Himself and with Himself'. Absolutely, 'in the communion of the substance we maintain that there is no mutual approach or intercommunion of those notes of indication perceived in the Trinity, whereby is set forth the proper peculiarity of the Persons delivered in the faith, each of these being distinctively apprehended by His own notes'. Basil (Gregory of Nyssa), Ep. 38.4. Thus, the Spirit 'united to the Son by the bond of uncreatedness, and deriving His existence from the Supreme, He is parted again from Him by the characteristic of not being the Only-begotten of the Father, and of having been manifested by means of the Son Himself'. Gregory of Nyssa, Ἀντιρρητικὸς κατὰ Εὐνομίου I, *GNO*, I, p. 108.

268. Basil of Caesarea, Κατὰ Σαβελλιανῶν καὶ Ἀρείου καὶ τῶν Ἀνομοίων 4, PG 31.609.

269. See M.R. Barnes' remarks on Gregory's psychology in 'Divine Unity and the Divided Self'', p. 52. Also Cyril, Εἰς τὸ κατὰ Ἰωάννην, v. II, pp. 493, 635, 733. For the essential character of energies, see Basil of Caesarea, Πρὸς Εὐνόμιον II, 29, PG 29.640A–641A. Gregory of Nyssa, Πρὸς Εὐστάθιον, *GNO*, III, I, pp. 10–11.

270. Gregory of Nyssa, Κατὰ Εὐνομίου II, *GNO*, I, p. 269. For the scheme essence–power–energeia in Gregory of Nyssa, see Εἰς τοὺς Μακαρισμούς, 7, *GNO*, VII, II, p. 150. Cf. Maximus Confessor, Περὶ θεολογίας καὶ

τῆς ἐνσάρκου οἰκονομίας, II, 1, PG 90.1124D–1125C. For the latter's ontological analysis of essence and activity, see T. Tollefsen, *Activity and Participation*, pp. 142–7. See also M.R. Barnes, 'Power of God'.

271. Gregory of Nazianzen, *Or.* 31.16, PG 36.152AB. Gregory of Nyssa, Ἀντιρρητικὸς κατὰ Εὐνομίου I, *GNO, I*, pp. 142–3. John of Damascus, Ἔκδοσις ἀκριβής, 1.8, PG 94.828C.

272. Maximus Confessor, Κεφάλαια διάφορα, I, 13, PG 90.1184CD.

273. See Maximus Confessor, Πρὸς Μαρίνον, PG 91.260D–261A, 264AB, 149B.

274. Basil (Gregory of Nyssa), Ep. 38.4, *Lettres*, I, p. 85.

275. Cyril of Alexandria, *In D. Joannis evangelium*, IX, v. II, p. 476. For some observations on the interpretation of love in Trinity and in anthropology, see Ch. Stamoulis, 'Physis and Agape'.

THREE: Person and Grace (Pages 48–76)

1. For example, *CO*, pp. 63, 224–5, 277, 24–5, n. 36.

2. *BC*, pp. 40–1; *CO*, pp. 18–19, 35–6, 215. For the origins of the necessity– freedom dialectics in the Kantian distinction (followed by the later western philosophers) between a free noumenal self and an unfree empirical self, see N. Loudovikos, 'Person instead of grace', 2.

3. *BC*, pp. 18, 44.

4. *CO*, p. 109.

5. For the significance of the union of the two natures, see Gregory Nazianzen, Ὅροι παχυμερεῖς, PG 37.959; Ep. 101, *Lettres*, pp. 48, 54–6; *Or.* 18, 42; *Or.* 22, 4. Gregory of Nyssa, Κατὰ Εὐνομίου III, *GNO*, II, pp. 126, 130, 132. Maximus Confessor, Περὶ διαφόρων ἀποριῶν, PG 91.1044C–1045A, 1053B, 1056B–1060A; Κεφάλαια διάφορα, I, 27–8, PG 90.1189BC; *Ep.* 15, PG 91.573B; Πρὸς Μαρίνον, PG 91.120AB, 189C–192A. Nilus of Ancyra, *Ep.* 102, PG 79.125C–128B. For the place of *communicatio idiomatum* in the Maximian Christology, see J. Larchet, *La divinisation de l' homme*, pp. 333–46. Cf. *CO*, pp. 37, 109.

6. Ἔκδοσις ἀκριβής, 3.14, PG 94.1040BC, 1036A.

7. Gregory Nazianzen, *Or.* 30, 11, PG 36.116C.

8. Cyril of Alexandria, Ἡ βίβλος τῶν θησαυρῶν, VII, PG 75.84–85, 89, 96.

9. John of Damascus, Ἔκδοσις ἀκριβής, 3.14, PG 94.1041B. Maximus Confessor, Pyrrho, PG 91.293B–296A; Περὶ διαφόρων ἀποριῶν, PG 91.1272B–1272C. Gregory of Nyssa, Κατὰ Εὐνομίου III, 6, *GNO*, II, p. 192. For the Christological aspect, see Maximus Confessor, *Pyrrho*, PG 91.289A–C.

10. Cyril of Alexandria, Ἡ βίβλος τῶν θησαυρῶν, VII, PG 75.88–89.

11. Gregory of Nyssa, Κατὰ Εὐνομίου I, *GNO*, I, pp. 87–8. Maximus Confessor, Πρὸς Μαρίνον, PG 91.281A. John of Damascus, Ἔκδοσις ἀκριβής, 3.15, PG 94.1048A. Also T. Tollefsen, 'Essence and Activity (Energeia) in Eunomius and St. Gregory of Nyssa', pp. 438–9. The term *ousia* in Gregory has an 'existential' – designating the existence – as well as an 'essential' sense, pointing to 'the being of beings'. See J. Zachhuber, 'Ousia', in L.F. Mateo-Seco and G. Maspero, *The Brill Dictionary of Gregory of Nyssa*, pp. 562–7.

12. See the counter-argument of Basil to Eunomius in Πρὸς Εὐνόμιον II, 31, PG 29.644B–645B.

13. *CO*, pp. 248, 39.
14. Gregory of Nyssa, Ἀντιρρητικὸς κατὰ Εὐνομίου I, *GNO*, I, pp. 106–7.
15. See G. Dal Toso, 'Proairesis' in L.F. Mateo-Seco and G. Maspero, *The Brill Dictionary of Gregory of Nyssa*, pp. 647–9.
16. Maximus Confessor, Πρὸς Μαρῖνον, PG 91.45B–49A.
17. Maximus Confessor, Περὶ διαφόρων ἀποριῶν, PG 91.1345AB.
18. Gregory of Nyssa, *The Catechetical Oration*, 5, p. 24.
19. Ériugena, *Periphyseon* II, pp. 93–7. For the connection of the Tree of Life with the human nature as imago Dei, see *Periphyseon* IV, pp. 182.23–184.9.
20. *CO*, p. 165.
21. John of Damascus, Ἔκδοσις ἀκριβής, 2.27, PG 94.960D–961A.
22. John of Damascus, Ἔκδοσις ἀκριβής, 2.12, PG 94.920B. Also Maximus Confessor, Περὶ διαφόρων ἀποριῶν, PG 91.1084A.
23. John of Damascus, Ἔκδοσις ἀκριβής, 2.12, PG 94.924B–925A.
24. Maximus Confessor, Περὶ διαφόρων ἀποριῶν, PG 91.1092B, 1096A, 1249BC; *Pyrrho*, PG 91.324D; *Ep.* 6, PG 91.429BC; Μυσταγωγία, 6, PG 91.684CD.
25. Athanasius, Κατὰ Ἑλλήνων, 32–33, PG 25b.64B–65C.
26. Maximus Confessor, Πρὸς Μαρῖνον, PG 91.276C.
27. Maximus Confessor, *Pyrrho*, PG 91, 293B–D. John of Damascus, Ἔκδοσις ἀκριβής, 2.12, PG 94.928B.
28. John of Damascus, Ἔκδοσις ἀκριβής, 3.14, PG 94.1041B. Also Athanasius, Περὶ τοῦ Ἁγίου Πνεύματος III, 66–67, PG 26.461C–465A.
29. Gregory of Nyssa, *The Catechetical Oration*, 5, p. 26.
30. Gregory of Nyssa, *The Catechetical Oration*, 6, p. 34.
31. Maximus Confessor, Κεφάλαια διάφορα, IV, 33, PG 90.1317C; III, 57, PG 90.1285B; Πρὸς Θαλάσσιον, 42, PG 90.405C. For Maximus, nature has become devastated as a result of sin, but nothing points to the fact that this course is a part of its very definition. Πρὸς Θαλάσσιον, 47, PG 90.424B; 64, PG 90.696D–700C. Gregory of Nyssa, *The Catechetical Oration*, 5, pp. 27–8.
32. Πρὸς Θαλάσσιον, 21, PG 90.312B–317A.
33. Gregory of Nyssa, *The Catechetical Oration*, 7, p. 40. Maximus Confessor, Περὶ διαφόρων ἀποριῶν, PG 91.1149A.
34. Gregory of Nyssa, *The Catechetical Oration*, 6, pp. 30–1.
35. This is a striking feature of the Irish Litanies. See *ILit*, pp. 102–7. The co-celebration and unification of the entire creation is rendered by the miniatures of the Book of Kells, which function as dynamic examples of transfiguration. See Suzanne Lewis (1980), 'Sacred calligraphy: the Chi Rho Page in the Book of Kells', *Traditio* 36, 139–59. But the most typical example is Patrick's Hymn. See *ThPal*, ii, pp. 354–8. For some theological observations, see N.D. O'Donoghue, 'St Patrick's Breastplate'.
36. A. Wilmart, 'Catéchèses Celtiques', V, pp. 59–60 (trans. O. Davies, *Celtic Spirituality*, p. 364). Also *Breviarium in Psalmos*, PL 26.1199AB; Comm. in Iohannis I.3, *SHM*, II, p. 106. Ériugena (Jean Scot, *Homélie sur le prologue de Jean*, VIII–X, pp. 236–69; *Carmina*, 5, p. 76.1–8, p. 76. Cf. J. Carey, *Teanga Bhithnua: The Evernew Tongue*, 18, p. 123.

37. Cyril of Alexandria, *In D. Joannis evangelium*, I, 6–7, v. I, pp. 74–89. Gregory of Nyssa, Πρὸς Ἁρμόνιον, περὶ τοῦ τί τὸ τοῦ Χριστιανοῦ ἐπάγγελμα, *GNO*, VIII, Opera Ascetica, I, pp. 138–9. Basil of Caesarea, Εἰς τὴν Ἑξαήμερον, VIII, PG 29.164D.

38. Gregory Nazianzen, Ὕμνος εἰς Θεόν, PG 37.507–508. Dionysius, Περὶ τῆς οὐρανίας ἱεραρχίας IV, 1, PG 3.177D; Περὶ θείων ὀνομάτων, V, 8, PG 3.824C. Maximus Confessor, Πρὸς Θαλάσσιον, 13, PG 90.296CD; Κεφάλαια διάφορα, I, 71–72, PG 90.1208C; Περὶ διαφόρων ἀποριῶν, PG 91.1077C–1081B, 1148D, 1257A; Περὶ θεολογίας καὶ τῆς ἐνσάρκου οἰκονομίας, I, 47, PG 90.1100BC. For the distinction between *logoi* and divine activities, see T. Tollefsen, *The Christocentric Cosmology*, pp. 169–89.

39. Maximus Confessor, Κεφάλαια διάφορα, I, 71–73, PG 90.1208C–1209A.

40. Maximus Confessor, Περὶ θεολογίας καὶ τῆς ἐνσάρκου οἰκονομίας, I, 49, PG 90.1101A; Κεφάλαια διάφορα, I, 71, PG 90.1208C.

41. *Tractatus Hilarii in Septem Epistolas Canonicas*, *SHM*, I, p. 78.40–1. *Scotti anonymi, Commentarius in Epistolas Catholicas*, *SHM*, I, p. 16.512–13.

42. Dionysius, Περὶ τῆς οὐρανίας ἱεραρχίας, IV, 1, PG 3.177D. Ériugena, *Periphyseon* V, pp. 574–5; *Expositiones in Ierarchiam Coelestem*, 4.1–2, pp. 69, 72. For the use of the Dionysian snippet by Ériugena, see P. Rorem, *Ériugena's Commentary*, pp. 112–20.

43. Ériugena (Jean Scot), *Homélie sur le prologue de Jean*, VIII–X, pp. 236–69; XI, pp. 252–6; *Carmina*, 5, p. 76.1–6. P. Rorem, *Ériugena's Commentary*, p. 189.

44. *ILit*, pp. 5, 81. Comm. in Iohannis I.3–4, *SHM*, II, pp. 106–7.

45. *SCO*, Instr. I, 3, pp. 62–3; II, 1, pp. 66–7.

46. See Ériugena, *Periphyseon* I, pp. 58–67, 204–9; III, pp. 151–63.

47. P. Rorem, *Ériugena's Commentary*, p. 209. Ériugena, *Periphyseon* III, pp. 58–9, 162–3, 166–7. For theophany in creational, Trinitarian and anthropological contexts in Ériugena, see H.A. Mooney, *Theophany*, pp. 199–214.

48. Gregory of Nyssa, Πρὸς Ἁρμόνιον, *GNO*, VIII, I, pp. 138–9. Basil of Caesarea, Περὶ τοῦ Ἁγίου Πνεύματος, 9, 22, pp. 324–6. Cyril of Alexandria, *In D. Joannis evangelium*, I, 9, v. I, pp. 113–4. Macarius, Hom. 40, 3, *Die 50 Geistlichen Homilien*, p. 276; Hom. 16, ibid., pp. 160–1. Maximus Confessor, Περὶ διαφόρων ἀποριῶν, PG 91.1257AB. Syméon le Nouveau Théologien, *Hymnes*, II, p. 190.

49. See *Breviarium in psalmos*, PL 26.1022B.

50. T. Tollefsen, *The Christocentric Cosmology*, p. 172.

51. Philip Rousseau, *Basil of Caesarea*, pp. 221–2. Basil of Caesarea, Εἰς τὸ Πρόσεχε σεαυτῷ, 1, PG 31.197CD; Ὅροι κατὰ πλάτος, 3, PG 31.917A; Ὁμιλία ῥηθεῖσα ἐν λιμῷ καὶ αὐχμῷ, PG 31.325A; Περὶ φθόνου, PG 31.384B.

52. Gregory of Nyssa, Περὶ τοῦ κατὰ Θεὸν σκοποῦ καὶ τῆς κατὰ ἀλήθειαν ἀσκήσεως, *GNO*, VIII, Opera Ascetica, I, p. 40. Ἐξήγησις τοῦ Ἄσματος τῶν Ἀσμάτων, 15, *GNO*, VI, pp. 468–9.

53. Maximus Confessor, Περὶ διαφόρων ἀποριῶν, PG 91.1053BC; Πρὸς Θαλάσσιον, 65, PG 90,756B. Gregory of Nyssa, Πρὸς Ἁρμόνιον, *GNO*, VIII, I, p. 136.

54. See the Liturgy of the Pre-sanctified Gifts.

55. Maximus Confessor, Περὶ διαφόρων ἀποριῶν, PG 91.1117AB; *Pyrrho*, PG 91.309B–312A.

56. Maximus Confessor, Περὶ διαφόρων ἀποριῶν, PG 91.1081D–1084A.

57. Macarius, Hom. 4, 1, *Die 50 Geistlichen Homilien*, p. 26. Passions fracture the unity of human nature. Maximus Confessor, *Ep.* 2, PG 91.400D.

58. Comm. in Lucam XV.17, V.24, VIII.39, *SHM*, II, pp. 85, 44, 71. Also Brebiarum de exemplaribus 3,4, *SHM*, I, p. 161.

59. Maximus Confessor, Πρὸς Θαλάσσιον, 64, PG 90.709BC; Κεφάλαια διάφορα, V, 100, 1348CD. For a criticism to the relevant thesis of Ch. Yannaras, see N. Loudovikos, Ἡ Κλειστὴ Πνευματικότητα, pp. 284–300.

60. Maximus Confessor, Περὶ διαφόρων ἀποριῶν, PG 91.1077C–1080C.

61. Gregory of Nyssa, Κατὰ Εὐνομίου II, *GNO*, I, p. 371. Κατὰ Εὐνομίου III, *GNO*, II, p. 35.

62. Basil of Caesarea, Περὶ τοῦ Ἁγίου Πνεύματος, 19, 49, pp. 418–20. Gregory Palamas, Πρὸς Γαβρᾶν, 30, Συγγράμματα, II, p. 358.

63. Cyril of Alexandria, *In D. Joannis evangelium*, IX, v. II, pp. 478, 480. See a reference to the heretical interpretation of John 14:20, ibid., pp. 476–7.

64. Σχόλια εἰς τὸ περὶ θείων ὀνομάτων, PG 4.265C.

65. For the relation of will and person in Gregory of Nyssa, see M.R. Barnes, 'Divine Unity and the Divided Self', p. 52.

66. Gregory of Nyssa, Περὶ κατασκευῆς ἀνθρώπου, 16, 10–11, PG 44.184. *The Catechetical Oration*, 5, p. 26.

67. Maximus Confessor, Κεφάλαια διάφορα, II, 64, PG 90.1244C (trans. G.E.H. Palmer (1981), *The Philokalia*, vol. 2, London: Faber & Faber, pp. 200–1).

68. Cf. *CO*, pp. 43, 224.

69. *BC*, pp. 50–3; *CO*, pp. 221–4.

70. See, for example, Gregory of Nazianzen, *Or.* 32, PG 36.204D–205A. Gregory of Nyssa, Περὶ ψυχῆς, *GNO*, III, Opera Dogmatica Minora, III, pp. 26–7.

71. A. Wilmart, 'Catécheses Celtiques', II, pp. 42–3.

72. Ps. Isidore, *Liber de ortu et obitu patriarcharum*, 42.3–4, pp. 47–8.

73. *Breviarium in psalmos*, PG 26.916C. Comm. in Lucam X.30, *SHM*, II, p. 75.

74. Diaz y Diaz, *Liber de ordinem creaturarum*, V, 4–8, pp. 114–6. For this thesis in the apocalyptic In Tenga Bithnua, see J. Carey, *A Single Ray of the Sun*, pp. 75–106.

75. St Romanos, On the Nativity I, st. 24; On the Passion of Christ, pr. I, st. 1; On the Epiphany, st. 11, Sancti Romani Melodi *Cantica*. Macarius, Hom. 52, 1, *Macarii Anecdota. Seven Unpublished Homilies of Macarius*, p. 24. J. Carney, *The Poems of Blathmac*, pp. 61–70.

76. Gregory Nazianzen, *Or.* 44, 10–12, PG 36.617C–621A.

77. *Breviarium in psalmos*, PG 26.1196D; 1200B: 'Corporis vero terra quae fructum exhibet sanctitatis, mysteriorum coelestium pallio circumdatur.' For the body's dignity, see also Comm. in Lucam XXII.38, *SHM*, II, p. 96.

78. *ILit*, p. 21. *Breviarium in psalmos*, PG 26.1077CD.

79. One brings to mind Hume's thesis about the selves who inhabit a self-centred world, and whose very stability depends on social relations; lacking self-consistency by nature, they can acquire it only through interaction with others. See J. Seigel, *The Idea of the Self*, pp. 137–8.

80. Basil of Caesarea, Περὶ τοῦ Ἁγίου Πνεύματος, 23, p. 328. Gregory of Nyssa, Εἰς τὸ πάτερ ἡμῶν, *GNO*, VII, II, p. 60.

81. Comm. in Iohannem, I.5, *SHM,* II, p. 107.74–75. Ériugena, *Periphyseon* IV, pp. 182.23–184.9.
82. Tractatus Hilarii, *SHM,* I, p. 99.33–8.
83. For the term in Gregory of Nyssa, see D. Balás, 'Participation' in L.F. Mateo-Seco and G. Maspero, *The Brill Dictionary of Gregory of Nyssa,* pp. 581–7; 'Deification', ibid., pp. 210–13. Some terms, such as *metousia, methexis* and *metalepsis,* are almost untranslatable, and their content is only partly rendered by 'participation' or 'sharing', which connote a limited possession of the whole. For a more nuanced discussion, see the linguistic analysis of the terminology in N. Russell, *The Doctrine of Deification in the Greek Patristic Tradition,* pp. 333–44. T. Tollefsen is to be credited with the latest substantial contribution in *Activity and Participation,* pp. 83–132.
84. Irenaeus, *Contra haereses,* III, xix, PG 7.939B; V, i, PG 7.1120. Athanasius, Περὶ ἐνανθρωπήσεως τοῦ Λόγου, 54,3, PG 25.192B. Clement, Προτρεπτικός, I.8, SC 2, pp. 62–3. Nilus of Ancyra, *Ep.* 115, PG 79.133A. Maximus Confessor, Πρὸς Μαρῖνον, PG 91.77CD. Περὶ διαφόρων ἀποριῶν, PG 91.1084C, 1113BC. Ps. Isidore, *Liber de ortu et obitu patriarcharum,* 42.4, p. 49. Ériugena (Jean Scot, *Homélie sur le Prologue de Jean,* XXI, pp. 304–6.
85. Comm. in Iohannem, I.14, *SHM,* II, pp.108–9.
86. Gregory of Nyssa, Ep. 3, *GNO,* VIII, II, pp. 23–4.
87. Gregory of Nyssa, Κατὰ Εὐνομίου III, *GNO,* II, p. 35; Πρὸς Ὀλύμπιον, περὶ τελειότητος, *GNO,* VIII, Opera Ascetica, I, p. 205; Πρὸς τὰ Ἀπολιναρίου ἀντιρρητικός, *GNO,* III, I, p. 151. Maximus Confessor, *Ep.* 19, PG 91.593B; Πρὸς Θαλάσσιον, 61, PG 90.632A; 3, PG 90.276B. Ériugena (Jean Scot, *Homélie sur le Prologue de Jean,* XXIII, 26–8, p. 312.
88. Tractatus Hilarii, *SHM,* I, p. 99.33–8.
89. Maximus Confessor, Περὶ διαφόρων ἀποριῶν, PG 91.1148A–D.
90. Ps. Isidore, *Liber de ortu et obitu patriarcharum,* 42.5, pp. 49–51.
91. See *BC,* pp. 44, 49–50; *CO,* pp. 228, 248. P.M. Collins, *Trinitarian Theology: West and East,* pp. 179–80.
92. *CO,* pp. 237–8, 243, 248–9. D. Farrow, 'Person and Nature: the Necessity–Freedom Dialectic in John Zizioulas', in D. Knight (ed.), *The Theology of John Zizioulas,* p. 111. A. Papanikolaou, 'Divine energies or divine personhood', 358.
93. In fact we may ask how the person, understood in terms of ecstasis from nature, can be free at all, if we take it for granted that even in the Divine Trinity the Son and the Spirit receive their ultimate freedom from the Person of the Father.
94. *CO,* p. 239.
95. A. Papanikolaou, 'Divine energies or divine personhood', 369.
96. Περὶ διαφόρων ἀποριῶν, PG 91.1044C–1045A, 1052B–D. See a criticism of contemporary commentators by J. Larchet, *La divinisation de l' homme,* pp. 342–6. For the patristic view of adoption, see ibid., pp. 616–26.
97. Cyril of Alexandria, *In D. Joannis evangelium,* I, ix, v. 1, p. 136.
98. Ériugena (Jean Scot), *Homélie sur le Prologue de Jean,* XXI, 20–31, p. 306.
99. Ériugena (Jean Scot), *Homélie sur le Prologue de Jean,* XI, 36–9, p. 258; XXI, p. 306.

100. Maximus Confessor, *Ep.* 15, PG 91.548B–552A.

101. A. Papanikolaou, 'Divine energies or divine personhood', 375.

102. Maximus Confessor, Περὶ θεολογίας καὶ τῆς ἐνσάρκου οἰκονομίας, II, 84, PG 90.1164BC.

103. Maximus Confessor, Περὶ θεολογίας καὶ τῆς ἐνσάρκου οἰκονομίας, II, 83, PG 90.1164B.

104. Gregory of Nyssa, Κατὰ Εὐνομίου I, *GNO,* I, pp. 87–8. Anastasius, *Doctrina patrum,* p. 90. The essential creative and perfective motion of divinity is a central leitmotif in Ériugena's theology.

105. Basil of Caesarea, Πρὸς Εὐνόμιον II, 28, PG 29.637. Gregory of Nyssa, Πρὸς Εὐστάθιον, *GNO,* III, I, pp. 14–15. For the distinction and union between essence and energy, see Irenaeus, Fragment 5, PG 7.1232B. Basil of Caesarea, Ep. 234, 1, *Lettres,* III, p. 42. Dionysius, Περὶ θείων ὀνομάτων, II, 7, PG 3.645A.

106. Gregory Palamas, Συγγράμματα, I, p. 641. Maximus Confessor, *Ep.* 24, PG 91.609CD. For the concept of divine activities running through patristic theology from the Cappadocians to Gregory Palamas, see A. Radde-Gallwitz, *Basil of Caesarea.*

107. In the few places where Aquinas spells out what it means for creatures to participate in the divine *esse* he limits it to their possessing a created similitude of God. For participation in Aquinas, see D. Bradshaw, *Aristotle East and West,* pp. 250–62.

108. Basil of Caesarea, Ep. 234, 1. Gregory of Nyssa, Κατὰ Εὐνομίου I, *GNO, I,* pp. 87–9; Εἰς τὸν βίον Μωυσέως, 2, *GNO,* VII, I, p. 39. Gregory Nazianzen, *Or.* 38.7 (PG 36.317B–C); 30.17 (PG 36.125B). Maximus Confessor, Περὶ διαφόρων ἀποριῶν, PG 91.1257AB. See also D. Bradshaw, *Aristotle East and West,* pp. 165–9. T. Tollefsen, *The Christocentric Cosmology,* pp. 208–9. The energies and propria (ἰδιώματα) are neither identical with nor separable from the divine nature. Gregory of Nyssa, Εἰς τοὺς Μακαρισμούς, 6, *GNO,* VII, II, pp. 143–4. Κατὰ Εὐνομίου III, *GNO,* II, p. 186. Basil, Hom. 15, PG 31.469A. Macarius, Hom. 1, 10, *Die 50 Geistlichen Homilien,* p. 11. John of Damascus, Ἔκδοσις ἀκριβής, 3.15, PG 94.1053B–1056A. Gregory Palamas, Epistle to Daniel, Συγγράμματα, II, pp. 377-8, 389.

109. John of Damascus, Ἔκδοσις ἀκριβής, 1.14, PG 94.860C.

110. Gregory of Nyssa, Κατὰ Εὐνομίου I, *GNO,* I, pp. 87–8. Also see T. Tollefsen, 'Essence and Activity (Energeia) in Eunomius and St. Gregory of Nyssa', pp. 433–42.

111. Macarius, Hom. 40, 7, *Die 50 Geistlichen Homilien,* pp. 278–9.

112. Ériugena, *Periphyseon* III, pp. 38–9.

113. Maximus Confessor, Περὶ θεολογίας καὶ τῆς ἐνσάρκου οἰκονομίας, I, 48, PG 90.1100D–1101A.

114. Ériugena, *Periphyseon* III, pp. 50–3, 60–3.

115. Ériugena, *Periphyseon* III, pp. 54–7, 84–5, 32ff, 172–3.

116. Ériugena, *Periphyseon* III, pp. 58–9, 86–9.

117. Ériugena, *Periphyseon* I, pp. 209–17, 56–7, n. 52, p. 227. At the same time the ineffable nature rises above every essence, He is more than every human and divine attribute. *Periphyseon* I, pp. 196ff. Thus, Ériugena manages (a) to keep God's transcendence out of the created category and

(b) to associate closely the divine activity with God's being and creation as well. See also I.P. Sheldon-Williams, 'Johannes Scottus Eriugena', *The Cambridge History of Later Greek and Early Medieval Philosophy* (New York 1967), pp. 526-7. Eriugena speaks of the incorruptible and co-essential trinity – ousia, dynamis, energeia – in any creature; but he does not apply it to God, as Maximus does. *Periphyseon* I, pp. 144–7, 180–3. Cf. Maximus, Περὶ διαφόρων ἀποριῶν, PG 91.1084A. See *Periphyseon* II, n. 295, pp. 234–5.

118. *Periphyseon* I, pp. 46–7, 50–9. W. Otten, *The Anthropology of Johannes Scottus Ériugena*, pp. 68–73. D. Moran, *The Philosophy of John Scottus Ériugena*, p. 95.

119. M.R. Barnes, 'The visible Christ and the invisible Trinity', 346. For the position of Ériugena between Greek and Augustinian tradition in the interpretation of theophanies, see B.G. Bucur, 'Dionysius East and West'. For the Greek Fathers' view, see B.G. Bucur, 'Exegesis of biblical theophanies in Byzantine hymnography'.

120. Πρὸς Σεραπίωνα I, 20, PG 26.580A; I, 30, PG 26.600B.

121. See D. Bradshaw, *Aristotle East and West*, p. 242; 'The concept of the divine energies', 103–5. Also Διαταγαὶ τῶν ἁγίων Ἀποστόλων, V, 20, PG 1.896C. Gregory of Nyssa, Πρὸς Ἀβλάβιον, *GNO*, III, I, p. 48. Basil of Caesarea, Περὶ τοῦ Ἁγίου Πνεύματος, 26, 61, pp. 466–8.

122. Romanos, On fasting, st. 2, *Cantica*, p.439.

123. Περὶ θεολογίας καὶ τῆς ἐνσάρκου οἰκονομίας, II, 76, PG 90.1160CD.

124. Cf. *CO*, pp. 25–9.

125. Περὶ διαφόρων ἀποριῶν, PG 91.1288BC. Cf. Basil of Caesarea, Ep. 234.1, *Lettres*, III, p. 42.

126. Περὶ διαφόρων ἀποριῶν, PG 91.1257AB.

127. Maximus Confessor, *Questiones et dubia*, 99, p. 76.

128. Gregory Nazianzen, *Or.* 29, 2, PG 36.76B.

129. Maximus Confessor, Περὶ διαφόρων ἀποριῶν, PG 91.1257C–1261A.

130. Maximus Confessor, Μυσταγωγία, 23, PG 91.701A; Περὶ διαφόρων ἀποριῶν, PG 91.1036C.

131. Maximus Confessor, *Pyrrho*, PG 91.345D.

132. Maximus Confessor, *Ep.* 15, PG 91.556CD; Περὶ διαφόρων ἀποριῶν, PG 91.1053B–1056C, 1044; Πρὸς Μαρῖνον, PG 91.119D–121B, 232A, 88A.

133. John of Damascus, Ἔκδοσις ἀκριβής, 3.17, PG 94.1068B–1069AB.

134. John of Damascus, Ἔκδοσις ἀκριβής, 3.7, PG 94.1012C. Maximus Confessor, Κεφάλαια διάφορα, I, 75, PG 90.1209CD.

135. See John of Damascus, Ἔκδοσις ἀκριβής, 3.15, PG 94.1048A–1061D.

136. John of Damascus, Ἔκδοσις ἀκριβής, 3.7, PG 94.1012C.

137. *Breviarium in psalmos*, PL 26.1016A, 1103CD.

138. Maximus Confessor, Περὶ διαφόρων ἀποριῶν, PG 91.1141AB; Πρὸς Θαλάσσιον, 13, PG 90.296A; Πρὸς Μαρῖνον, PG 91.33B–D.

139. Maximus Confessor, Πρὸς Θαλάσσιον, 22, PG 90.320A; Περὶ διαφόρων ἀποριῶν, PG 91.1088C; Κεφάλαια διάφορα, I, 76, PG 90.1209D–1212B; Περὶ θεολογίας καὶ τῆς ἐνσάρκου οἰκονομίας, II, 90, PG 90.1168C.

140. Maximus Confessor, Πρὸς Θαλάσσιον, 22, PG 90.321; 61, 628A–645C.

141. Maximus Confessor, Κεφάλαια διάφορα, IV, 19, PG 90.1312B.

142. See Maximus Confessor, Περὶ διαφόρων ἀποριῶν, PG 91.1128A–C. Also see Ériugena (Jean Scot), *Homélie sur le Prologue de Jean*, XXII, 1–6, p. 308.

143. Maximus Confessor, Περὶ διαφόρων ἀποριῶν, PG 91.1049A.
144. Gregory Nazianzen, *Or.* 28, 3, PG 36.29AB. For the different approach of Augustine, in whom the transfiguration does not figure significantly, see M.R. Barnes, 'The visible Christ and the invisible Trinity', 330–55.
145. John of Damascus, Ἔκδοσις ἀκριβής, 3.7–8, PG 94.1008–1016. Maximus Confessor, Περὶ διαφόρων ἀποριῶν, PG 91.1277B.
146. Matt. 5:8. Gregory of Nyssa, Εἰς τοὺς Μακαρισμούς, 6, *GNO*, VII, II, p. 138.
147. Εἰς τοὺς Μακαρισμούς, 6, *GNO*, VII, II, pp. 144, 138; Κατὰ Μακεδονιανῶν, *GNO*, III, I, p. 92.21–5. Also D. Bradshaw, *Aristotle East and West*, pp. 174–6.
148. Maximus Confessor, Περὶ θεολογίας καὶ τῆς ἐνσάρκου οἰκονομίας, I, 48, 50, PG 90.1100D–1101B; II, 90, 1168C.
149. Maximus Confessor, Μυσταγωγία, 5, PG 91.676A.
150. Dionysius, Περὶ τῆς οὐρανίας ἱεραρχίας, IV, 3, PG 3.180C. Περὶ θείων ὀνομάτων, IX, 6, PG 3.913C.
151. Maximus Confessor, Πρὸς Θαλάσσιον, 59, PG 90.608D–609A; Περὶ θεολογίας καὶ τῆς ἐνσάρκου οἰκονομίας, II, 21, PG 90.1133D. For the relevance of ascetic practice, see E. Vishnevskaya, 'Divinization and Spiritual Progress in Maximus the Confessor'.
152. Maximus Confessor, Περὶ διαφόρων ἀποριῶν, PG 91.1081D–1084A.
153. Maximus Confessor, Κεφάλαια διάφορα, III, 57, PG 90.1285BC.
154. *Expositio quatuor evangeliorum*, PL 30.586D.
155. *CO*, pp. 165, 228, 224–5. N. Loudovikos, 'Person instead of grace', 3.
156. Maximus Confessor, Περὶ διαφόρων ἀποριῶν, PG 91.1260BC, 1305B.
157. Maximus Confessor, Πρὸς Μαρῖνον, PG 91.81D. Gregory of Nyssa, Εἰς τοὺς Μακαρισμούς, 6, *GNO*, VII, II, p. 139.
158. Gregory of Nyssa, Εἰς τοὺς Μακαρισμούς, 7, *GNO*, VII, II, p. 151; Ἐξήγησις τοῦ ἄσματος τῶν ἀσμάτων, 6, *GNO*, VI, pp. 176–9. Also Dionysius, Περὶ τῆς ἐκκλησιαστικῆς ἱεραρχίας I, 3, PG 3.376A. Maximus Confessor, Κεφάλαια διάφορα, I, 42, PG 90.1193D.
159. Macarius, Hom. 1, 11, *Die 50 Geistlichen Homilien*, p. 12. Maximus Confessor, Πρὸς Θαλάσσιον, 22, PG 90.321A; Περὶ διαφόρων ἀποριῶν, PG 91.1237AB; Πρὸς Θαλάσσιον, 59, PG 90.604B–609C. Ériugena (Jean Scot), *Homélie sur le Prologue de Jean*, XIII, pp. 262–8.
160. Macarius, Hom. 4, 6, *Die 50 Geistlichen Homilien*, p. 31. Cf. Maximus Confessor, Κεφάλαια διάφορα, IV, 20, PG 91.1312C.
161. Maximus Confessor, Πρὸς Θαλάσσιον, 59, PG 90.608AB.
162. Maximus Confessor, Πρὸς Θαλάσσιον, 22, PG 90.321A. Cf. Gregory of Nazianzen, *Or.* 38, 11, PG 36.324AB.
163. Maximus Confessor, Πρὸς Μαρῖνον, PG 91.189C–192A; Περὶ διαφόρων ἀποριῶν, PG 91.1060A–1060B; 1073D–1076A. Ériugena, *Periphyseon* I, pp. 56–9.
164. *Periphyseon* I, pp. 128–9.
165. Maximus Confessor, Κεφάλαια διάφορα, I, 72–73, PG 90.1208C–1209A; IV, 16, 1309D; Περὶ διαφόρων ἀποριῶν, PG 91.1048D–1049B. For ecstasy in Gregory Nyssa, see T. Tollefsen, *Activity and Participation*, pp. 166–9.
166. Gregory of Nyssa, Περὶ παρθενίας, 1, *GNO*, VIII, Opera Ascetica, I, p. 252.
167. W.B. Yeats, 'Sailing to Byzantium'.

168. Maximus Confessor, Περὶ διαφόρων ἀποριῶν, PG 91.1237AB; Κεφάλαια διάφορα, I, 75, PG 90.1209CD; Περὶ διαφόρων ἀποριῶν, PG 91.1084BC. See also T. Tollefsen, *The Christocentric Cosmology*, pp. 210–14.

169. Gregory of Nyssa, *The Catechetical Oration*, 5, pp. 19–28. Maximus Confessor, Περὶ διαφόρων ἀποριῶν, PG 91.1205C. For the logos of human nature as an anthropological foundation of deification, see J. Larchet, *La divinisation de l' homme*, pp. 125–31. For the supranatural character of deification, see ibid., pp. 563–8.

170. Maximus Confessor, Κεφάλαια διάφορα, IV, 12–13, 16, PG 90.1308D–1309D.

171. Ériugena (Jean Scot), *Homélie sur le prologue de Jean*, XIII, p. 266.

172. Ériugena, *Periphyseon* V, PL 122.982BC.

173. Ériugena (Jean Scot), *Homélie sur le prologue de Jean*, XIII, pp. 262–8. Maximus Confessor, Περὶ διαφόρων ἀποριῶν, PG 91.1076A, 1088CD.

174. Ériugena, *Periphyseon* III, pp. 54–5; II, pp. 86–7.

175. Ériugena, *Periphyseon* III, pp. 58–9, 30ff.

176. Andrew of Crete, Or. 7, Εἰς τὴν μεταμόρφωσιν, PG 97.933A. Maximus Confessor, Κεφάλαια διάφορα, I, 76, PG 90.1209D–1212B. Gregory of Nyssa, Εἰς τὸ πάτερ ἡμῶν, GNO, VII, II, p. 60.

177. A. Pierris, *Epiphanies: Eternity in Time and the Theology of Creation*, http://www.philosophical-research.org/index.php/research-projects/logos-in-ancient-greek-philosophy-and-christianity/epiphanies-eternity-in-time-and-the-teleology-of-creation.

178. Gregory Nazianzen, Περὶ ἀρετῆς, PG 37.693; *Or.* 38, 11, PG 36.324.

179. Περὶ ψυχῆς, GNO, III, III, p. 27.1–6.

180. Maximus Confessor, Κεφάλαια περὶ ἀγάπης, III, 25, PG 90.1024BC; *Ep.* 3, PG 91.409A.

181. Maximus Confessor, Πρὸς Μαρῖνον, PG 91.37BC.

182. Maximus Confessor, Περὶ θεολογίας καὶ τῆς ἐνσάρκου οἰκονομίας, I, 11, PG 90.1088A.

183. W. Stokes, *Three Irish Glossaries*, p. XL. Cf. Irenaeus, *Contra haereses*, V, vi, PG 7.1137–1138. Gregory Palamas, Ὑπὲρ τῶν ἱερῶς ἡσυχαζόντων 1, 3.43, Συγγράμματα, I, p. 454.

184. Maximus Confessor, Περὶ θεολογίας καὶ τῆς ἐνσάρκου οἰκονομίας, I, 13, PG 90.1088BC; Περὶ διαφόρων ἀποριῶν, PG 91.1084A; Cf. Εἰς τὴν προσευχήν, PG 90.889B.

185. Maximus Confessor, Πρὸς Μαρῖνον, PG 91.37BC; Κεφάλαια περὶ ἀγάπης, III, 25, PG 90.1024BC.

186. Maximus Confessor, Κεφάλαια διάφορα, I, 46, PG 90.1196BC.

187. Maximus Confessor, *Ep.* 3, PG 91.408D–409C; Πρὸς Θαλάσσιον, 2, PG 90.272B–D.

188. See D. Bradshaw, 'The concept of the divine energies', 111–12, 118.

189. M.C. Diaz y Diaz, *Liber de ordine creaturarum*, XV, 9, pp. 200–2.

190. Gregory of Nyssa, *The Catechetical Oration*, 5, pp. 22–8.

191. T. Špidlík (1986), *The Spirituality of the Christian East* (Kalamazoo), pp. 101–2. Ancient Ireland is not haunted by the clash between the theological anthropologies of predetermination and free will respectively, following rather the tradition of Cassian Irish luminaries, who undergird the significance of the freedom of choice and do not espouse the Augustinian

stream. See, for example, M. Cahill (ed.), _Expositio Evangelii Secundum Marcum_, pp. 65–6. Glosses on the Pauline Epistles, _ThPal_, i, p. 633, 2–4. For more about Pelagianism in the Celtic Church, see J.F.T. Kelly, 'Pelagius, Pelagianism, and the Early Christian Irish'.

192. Maximus Confessor, Περὶ θεολογίας καὶ τῆς ἐνσάρκου οἰκονομίας, I, 11, PG 90.1088A.
193. Maximus Confessor, Πρὸς Μαρίνον, PG 91.12CD. _Pyrrho_, PG 91. 292B–D, 301C. Gregory of Nyssa, Κατὰ Εὐνομίου I, _GNO_, I, p. 172.
194. See Maximus Confessor, Πρὸς Μαρῖνον, PG 91.53C, 56AB, 24B, 32C, 153AB, 196C–197A, 192BC, 280A. _Pyrrho_, PG 91.308CD.
195. Maximus Confessor, Πρὸς Μαρῖνον, PG 91.236C.
196. Maximus Confessor, _Pyrrho_, PG 91.309B; Περὶ διαφόρων ἀποριῶν, PG 91.1136B, 1144A. Gregory of Nyssa, Περὶ παρθενίας, 12, _GNO_, VIII, Opera Ascetica, I, pp. 298–300.
197. Maximus Confessor, Πρὸς Μαρῖνον, PG 91.28D–29B. On the contrary, because of its union with the Logos, his human nature has a firm and stable movement in accordance with rational appetite, θέλησις (PG 91.32A). Idem, Πρὸς Θαλάσσιον, 42, PG 90.405B–408A. Ps.Cyril, _De Trinitate_ 15, PG 77.1152C–1153A. Also see G.C. Berthold, 'Aspects of the will in Maximus the Confessor', 67–8. For prohairesis as 'choice', see Gregory of Nyssa, Κατὰ Εὐνομίου III, _GNO_, II, pp. 43–4.
198. Maximus Confessor, Πρὸς Μαρῖνον, PG 91.80D, 68C, 60B.
199. Maximus Confessor, Εἰς τὴν προσευχήν, PG 90.901D.
200. Maximus Confessor, Πρὸς Θαλάσσιον, 2, PG 90.272A–C.
201. Gregory of Nyssa, Κατὰ Εὐνομίου I, _GNO_, I, p. 161. Maximus Confessor, Περὶ διαφόρων ἀποριῶν, PG 91.1341C–1345A. For this distinction in Maximus the Confessor, see J. Larchet, _La divinisation de l'homme_, pp. 141–51, 347–62. For Maximus' ontological analysis of logos and tropos, see T. Tollefsen, _Activity and Participation_, pp. 142–58.
202. Maximus Confessor, Περὶ διαφόρων ἀποριῶν, PG 91.1341D–1344. Also Chrysostomos Koutloumousianos (2013), 'Natural and Supernatural Revelation in Early Irish and Greek Monastic Thought', in _Toward an Ecology of Transfiguration_ (New York) pp. 337-47.
203. Only the laws established because of sin are abolished by Christ. Maximus Confessor, Περὶ διαφόρων ἀποριῶν, PG 91.1273D–1276D, 1341BC; Πρὸς Μαρῖνον, PG 91.240B; Pyrrho, PG 91.320C.
204. Maximus Confessor, Περὶ διαφόρων ἀποριῶν, PG 91.1344–1345A; 1049C–1053A.
205. _CO_, pp. 22–4. Cf. J.-C. Larchet, _Personne et Nature_, pp. 246–58.
206. Περὶ διαφόρων ἀποριῶν, PG 91.1044C–1045A, 1053B–1060B; Πρὸς Μαρῖνον, PG 91.96D, 48B.
207. Maximus Confessor, Περὶ διαφόρων ἀποριῶν, PG 91.1037AB, 1052D–1053B, 1056A–1056C; _Pyrrho_, PG 91.345D–348A.
208. Maximus Confessor, Περὶ διαφόρων ἀποριῶν, PG 91.1057B–1060B.
209. Maximus Confessor, Πρὸς Μαρῖνον, PG 91.137AB.
210. See J. Larchet, _La divinisation de l'homme_, pp. 607–8. Cf. _CO_, pp. 239–40.
211. Maximus Confessor, Πρὸς Θαλάσσιον, 2, PG 90.272A–C.
212. John of Damascus, Ἔκδοσις ἀκριβῆς, 2.11, PG 94.909C–917C. Macarius, Hom. 26, 2, _Die 50 Geistlichen Homilien_, p. 206.

213. Although eternity is the equivalent of 'ἀϊδιότης', the Greek word refers to a property of the uncreated being. Theophilus of Antioch, Πρὸς Αὐτόλυκον, II.24, PG 6.1089C–1092A.
214. Maximus Confessor, Περὶ διαφόρων ἀποριῶν, PG 91.1144C.

Notes for Part II

ONE: The Individual and the Community (Pages 77–135)

1. M. Merleau-Ponty (1945), *Phénoménologie de la Perception* (Paris), p. 487.
2. D. Zahavi, *Subjectivity and Selfhood*, pp. 161–2.
3. T. Tollefsen, *The Christocentric Cosmology*, pp. 135–6. Also Maximus Confessor, Περὶ διαφόρων ἀποριῶν, PG 91.1080A.
4. Dionysius, Περὶ θείων ὀνομάτων, II, PG 3.641B.
5. See Gregory Nazianzen, *Or.* 40, 41, PG 36.417BC.
6. 'κοινωνικῶς ἥνωται τὰ τῆς ἁγίας Τριάδος'. Maximus Confessor, Σχόλια εἰς τὸ περὶ θείων ὀνομάτων, PG 4.213A.
7. See Gregory Nazianzen, *Or.* 6, 12–13, PG 35.737A–740A.
8. Dionysius, Περὶ θείων ὀνομάτων, II, 3, PG 3.640B; II, 11, PG 3.652A.
9. Cyril of Alexandria, Ἡ βίβλος τῶν Θησαυρῶν, XII, XIX, PG 75.180, 316A–C; *In D. Joannis evangelium*, XI, 9–11, v. II, pp. 697–8, 731–4.
10. Gregory Nazianzen, *Or.* 6, 4, PG 35.725B; *Ep.* 249, P. Gallay, *Gregor von Nazianz*, p. 180. Gregory of Nyssa, Κατὰ Εὐνομίου I, *GNO*, I, pp. 84–5; Κατὰ Μακεδονιανῶν, *GNO*, III, Opera Dogmatica Minora, I, p. 104. Basil of Caesarea, Ὅροι κατ' ἐπιτομήν, 260, PG 31.1225B. Cyril of Alexandria, *In D. Joannis evangelium*, IV, 1, v. I, p. 494.
11. Maximus Confessor, Κεφάλαια διάφορα, II, 41, PG 90.1236B.
12. Εἰς Ψαλμούς, PG 12.1265B.
13. 'Litany of the Saviour', *ILit*, p. 23. For the same motive, see Litany of the Virgin and All Saints, ibid., p. 27.
14. Gregory Nazianzen, *Or.* 6, 13, PG 35.737C–740A.
15. *Les Six Centuries*, 3.72, PO 28, p. 127; 4.8, ibid., p. 139. Also J.E. Rutherford, 'Praying the Trinity in Diadochos of Photike', pp. 67–8. Maximus Confessor, Μυσταγωγία 1, PG 91.665C. Ignatius of Antioch, Φιλαδελφεῦσιν VII.2, p. 114.
16. Gregory Nazianzen, *Or.* 22, 14, PG 35.1148B.
17. Basil of Caesarea, Ἀσκητικαὶ Διατάξεις, 18, PG 31.1385C.
18. C. Gunton, *The Promise of Trinitarian Theology*, p. 73.
19. Gregory Nazianzen, *Or.* 6, 4, PG 35.725C.
20. Περὶ θείων ὀνομάτων, II, 11, PG 4.652A.
21. According to M. Volf, 'Within interpersonal relations there is nothing that might correspond to the numerically identical divine nature, unless one were to conceive the unity of humankind anthropologically as the unity of the one human nature and to assert (as does Ratzinger) that all human beings constitute "one single human being" destined to become one single human being in Christ. Although this particular notion has enjoyed a venerable history, it is both anthropologically and ecclesiologically unacceptable.' M. Volf, *After Our Likeness*, pp. 203–4.

In my opinion, Volf misunderstands the patristic approach. For the Fathers, all men constitute 'one human being', where 'being' includes the multitude of persons, the common essence and the energies. Thus, they are not destined to become one single human subject, but a unity of persons following their one true nature through their common essential will and energy.

22. Basil of Caesarea, Ὅροι κατὰ πλάτος, 2.1, PG 31.909AB.
23. Gregory Nazianzen, *Or.* 6, 4, PG 35.725B.
24. Macarius, Hom. 31, 6, *Die 50 Geistlichen Homilien*, p. 251.
25. M. Volf, *After Our Likeness*, pp. 212–13. Still, Volf leaves unanswered why human beings cannot be internal to one another, while the Spirit, *as a person*, indwells human persons.
26. Gregory Nazianzen, *Or.* 6, 8, PG 35.732.
27. Basil of Caesarea, Ἀσκητικαὶ Διατάξεις 18, PG 31.1381C; Ὅροι κατὰ πλάτος, 2.1, PG 31.909B; 7.1, PG 31.928C–929B.
28. 'Be Thou My Vision', Murphy, *Early Irish Lyrics*, pp. 43–5.
29. Basil of Caesarea, Ἀσκητικαὶ Διατάξεις, 18, PG 31.1385A.
30. Ibid.
31. Glosses on the Pauline Epistles, 17, *ThPal*, i, p. 637. Ibid., 23, p. 674. *SCO*, Ep. II, 8, pp. 20–2. Basil of Caesarea, Περὶ κρίματος Θεοῦ, 3, PG 31.657–660. Gregory Nazianzen, *Or.* 2, 3, *Discours*, pp. 88–90.
32. Macarius, Hom. 52, 4, *Macarii Anecdota*, p. 26.
33. Scotti anonymi, Commentarius in Epistolas Catholicas, *SHM*, I, p. 41.78–9.
34. John Chrysostom, Εἰς τὴν πρὸς Ἐφεσίους ἐπιστολήν, Hom. 11, 3, PG 62.83–84.
35. John Chrysostom, Εἰς τὴν πρὸς Ἐφεσίους, Hom. 11, 1, PG 62.79–80; Ὑπόμνημα εἰς τὸν ἅγιον Ἰωάννην τὸν Ἀπόστολον καὶ Εὐαγγελιστήν, Hom. 10, 2, PG 59.75. Macarius, Περὶ προσευχῆς, 9, PG 34.860. Also see Wilmart, 'Catéchèses Celtiques', IX, p. 84.30ff.
36. John Chrysostom, Εἰς τὴν πρὸς Ἐφεσίους, Hom. 11, 2, PG 62.82.
37. Εἰς τὴν πρὸς Ἐφεσίους, Hom. 3, 2, PG 62.26.
38. See Gregory Nazianzen, *Or.* 32, 11, PG 36.185D.
39. Gregory Nazianzen, *Or.* 2, 3, *Discours*, pp. 88–90.
40. Glosses on the Pauline Epistles, 4, *ThPal*, i, p. 654; 20, p. 625; 13, p. 674.
41. A. Wilmart, 'Catéchèses Celtiques', VII, p. 76.
42. Glosses on the Pauline Epistles, 6, *ThPal*, i, p. 573. Ibid., 12, p. 574.
43. Glosses on the Pauline Epistles, *ThPal*, i, pp. 572–5, 647. A. Wilmart, 'Catéchèses Celtiques', VI, p. 66.28ff.
44. Glosses on the Pauline Epistles, 2, *ThPal*, i, p. 573. 1 Cor. 12:23.
45. Glosses on the Pauline Epistles, 19, *ThPal*, i, p. 625; 10, p. 638.
46. Glosses on the Pauline Epistles, *ThPal*, i, pp. 572–4. Cf. Macarius, Hom. 30, 4, *Die 50 Geistlichen Homilien*, p. 242.
47. John Chrysostom, Εἰς τὴν πρὸς Ἐφεσίους, Hom. 11, 4, PG 62.84.
48. Glosses on the Pauline Epistles, 2–3, *ThPal*, i, p. 634. Ibid., 11, p. 637.
49. Basil of Caesarea, Περὶ κρίματος Θεοῦ, 3, PG 31.657C–660A.
50. Ignatius of Antioch, Πρὸς Ἐφεσίους, IX, p. 64.
51. Maximus Confessor, Περὶ διαφόρων ἀποριῶν, PG 91.1309A, 1305C, 1348B–1349A.

52. Nilus (Evagrius of Pontus), Περὶ προσευχῆς, 124, PG 79.1193C. For the biological discontinuity as a characteristic feature of monasticism, see G.I. Mantzaridis (1996), *Time and Man* (Pennsylvania), pp. 70–6.

53. Delehaye, *Vita S. Danielis Stylitae*, 95, p. 209. Basil of Caesarea, Λόγος ἀσκητικός, 1, PG 31.881–884.

54. Macarius, Hom. 3, 2, *Die 50 Geistlichen Homilien*, p. 21 (trans. A.J. Mason (1921), *Fifty Spiritual Homilies of St Macarius the Egyptian* (London), pp. 16-17).

55. Macarius, Hom. 3, 3, *Die 50 Geistlichen Homilien*, p. 24.

56. Basil of Caesarea, Ὅροι κατὰ πλάτος, 24, PG 31.981–984.

57. Nilus of Ancyra, Πρὸς Ἀγάθιον, PG 79.837B.

58. Nilus of Ancyra, Πρὸς Ἀγάθιον, PG 79.837D–840A.

59. W. Stokes, *The Martyrology of Oengus the Culdee*, n. 11, p. 95 (henceforth *Oengus*).

60. The Cambray Homily, *ThPal*, ii, pp. 245–6.

61. Vita S. Aidi Killariensis, 17, *HVSH*, p. 173.

62. Basil of Caesarea, Ὅροι κατ᾽ ἐπιτομήν, 175, PG 31.1197C–1200A.

63. Basil of Caesarea, Ἀσκητικαὶ Διατάξεις, 32, PG 31.1421BC.

64. Macarius, Ἐπιστολὴ πρώτη πρὸς μοναχούς, 30, W. Jaeger, *Two Rediscovered Works of Ancient Christian Literature*, pp. 285–6.

65. Basil of Caesarea, Ἀσκητικαὶ Διατάξεις, 18, PG 31.1385A.

66. Maximus Confessor, *Ep.* 2, PG 91, 401AB.

67. Ériugena, *Periphyseon* III, pp. 52–5.

68. Basil of Caesarea, Ἀσκητικαὶ Διατάξεις, 21, PG 31.1393D–1400A; 18, PG 31.1385B.

69. Macarius, Hom. 30, 4, *Die 50 Geistlichen Homilien*, p. 242.

70. Glosses on the Pauline Epistles, 11, 19, *ThPal*, i, p. 637. Ibid., 2, p. 634. Eph. 4:12, 2:16.

71. Nilus of Ancyra, Πρὸς Ἀγάθιον, PG 79.1056CD. Cf. John Chrysostom, Περὶ τελείας ἀγάπης, PG 56.281.

72. *Oratio Seu Lorica Brendani abbatis*, PL Supplementum, 4.2064. P. Grosjean, 'Edition et commentaire du Catalogus Sanctorum Hiberniae'. *ILit*, p. 61. W. Stokes, *Oengus*, p. 209. *SCO*, Reg. Coen. VII, p. 152. Vita Prior S. Fintani Seu Munnu, 24, *HVSH*, p. 205. Canones Hibernenses V 2, L. Bieler, *The Irish Penitentials*, p. 172. O'Keefe, 'Colman Mac Duach and Guaire', 43–7. Basil, Ep. 150, *Lettres*, v. II, p. 75. Georgios, *Vie de Théodore*, 73, pp. 60–1; 155, p. 126.9–10; 159–60, p. 136. Theodoret, Φιλόθεος ἱστορία, 12, PG 82.1396–1397. See also T. O'Loughlin, 'Living in the Ocean'; N.K. Chadwick, *The Age of the Saints*, pp. 71–118.

73. See George T. Stokes (1928), *Ireland and the Celtic Church* (London), pp. 174–88. Also N. Chadwick, *The Age of the Saints*, pp. 86–7. M. Herren (2002), *Christ in Celtic Christianity: Britain and Ireland from the Fifth to the Tenth Century* (Woodbridge), pp. 148–50. For the attitude of the higher clergy in Europe, see J. Kelly (1982), 'The Gallic resistance to Eastern asceticism', *Studia Patristica* 17, 506–10.

74. See C. Selmer, *Navigatio Sancti Brendani Abbatis*, 1, pp. 4–5.

75. 'Versiculi Familiae Benchuir', ii, F.E. Warren, *The Antiphonary of Bangor*, II, p. 28. Vita Prior S. Fintani Seu Munnu 26, *HVSH*, p. 206.

76. For example, Adomnán, *Vita S. Columbae* I.20; I.6; II.42.

77. See K. Meyer, 'The Hermit's Song', pp. 55–7. Another translation is in G. Murphy, *Early Irish Lyrics*, pp. 18–23.
78. 'Manchan's Wish', G. Murphy, *Early Irish Lyrics*, p. 31. K. Meyer, 'The Hermit's Song'. Also E.J. Gwynn and W.J. Purton, 'The Monastery of Tallaght', 159–60. Vita S. Darercae, 24, *HVSH*, p. 90. Vita Prior S. Fintani Seu Munnu, 31, *HVSH*, pp. 207–8. Cf. Nilus of Ancyra, Διήγημα III, PG 79.617C, 620CD–621A.
79. Βλ. *Expositio quatuor evangeliorum*, PL 30.544A.
80. Gregory Nazianzen, *Or.* 43, 62, PG 36.577AB.
81. Gregory Nazianzen, *Or.* 43, PG 36.577AB. Yet, it is important that Basil refers to those who follow the austere seclusion from the outset. Basil of Caesarea, Ὅροι κατὰ πλάτος, 7.3–4, PG 31.932–933.
82. Basil of Caesarea, Ἀσκητικαὶ Διατάξεις, 18.1, PG 31. 1381C.
83. Ἀσκητικαὶ Διατάξεις 18.2, PG 31.1381D–1384B. Cf. Nilus of Ancyra, Διήγημα III, PG 79.617C. Monks imitate the angels in their common way of life. Macarius, Hom. 3, 1, *Die 50 Geistlichen Homilien*, p. 20.
84. 'The Rule of Carthage', 5, U. Ó Maidín, *The Celtic Monk*, p. 68. Macarius, Hom. 56, 1, *Macarii Anecdota*, p. 44.
85. See 'The Rule of Carthage', 3–4, 10–11, U. Ó Maidín, *The Celtic Monk*, pp. 67–8.
86. Basil, Ep. 2, *Lettres*, I, pp. 5–13; Ep. 14, pp. 42–5.
87. Gregory Nazianzen, Πρὸς Ἑλλήνιον, PG 37.1460A. Cf. W. Stokes, 'The Bodleian Amra Choluimb chille', ch. 6, 85, pp. 268–9 (henceforth *Amra*).
88. Delehaye, '*Vita S. Danielis Stylitae*', 23–24, p. 145; 30, p. 150.
89. Βίος καὶ πολιτεία τοῦ ὁσίου πατρὸς ἡμῶν Ἀλεξάνδρου, 8, PO 6.663; 47, pp. 695–6.
90. W. Stokes, *Amra*, 6, 84, pp. 266–7. Adomnán, *Vita S. Columbae* III.8, p. 138. Basil of Caesarea, Ἐπιτίμια, 42, PG 31.1312B.
91. Broccán's Hymn, 1, *ThPal*, ii, p. 327. Vita S. Cainnechi, 37, 42, 43, *HVSH*, pp. 191–3. Vita S. Darercae, 19, *HVSH*, p. 89. Vita Caemgeni Abbatis Glendalochensis, 7.10, *HVSH*, pp. 363–4. For the ascetic and eremitic ways of the early Irish monastic leaders, see N. Chadwick, *The Age of the Saints*, pp. 88–118.
92. Vita S. Darercae, 19, *HVSH*, p. 89.
93. C. Selmer, *Navigatio*, 26, p. 72. Georgios, *Vie de Théodore*, 167, p. 156.75–9. This is the reason we witness a double-sided movement between the hermitage and the coenobium. Ibid., 48, pp. 42–3.
94. Gregory Nazianzen, Πρὸς Ἑλλήνιον, PG 37.1460A, 1455–1457; Γνωμολογία τετράστιχος, PG 37.928A. For typical examples of the acceptance of a kind of 'holy extremity', see Sozomen, PG 67.1395A. Evagrius, PG 86.2480B. John Moschus, Λειμών, 21, 86, 91, PG 87c.2868B, 2944AB, 2948C.
95. See H. Wasserschleben, *Die Irische Kanonensammlung*, pp. 147–9.
96. C. Selmer, *Navigatio*, 1, pp. 4–5.
97. J. Strachan, 'An Old-Irish Metrical Rule'. J. Strachan, 'Cormac's Rule'. J. O'Neill, 'The Rule of Ailbe of Emly'.
98. Basil of Caesarea, Ὅροι κατὰ πλάτος, 7.2, PG 31.929D–932B.
99. Gregory Nazianzen, Πρὸς Ἑλλήνιον, PG 37.1468. Glosses on the Pauline Epistles, *ThPal*, i, pp. 572–5. A. Wilmart, 'Catéchèses Celtiques', VI, 28ff, pp. 66.

100. Macarius, Hom. 30, 3–5, *Die 50 Geistlichen Homilien*, pp. 241–3; Περὶ προσευχῆς, 9, PG 34.860BC. Basil of Caesarea, Ὅροι κατὰ πλάτος, 7.2, PG 31.929D–932B. Also A. Wilmart, 'Catéchèses Celtiques', IX, 30ff., p. 84.

101. *SCO*, Reg. X, p. 140.

102. Glosses on the Pauline Epistles, 16, *ThPal*, i, p. 647.

103. Nilus of Ancyra, Πρὸς Ἀγάθιον, PG 79.1056CD.

104. Macarius, Ἐπιστολὴ πρώτη πρὸς μοναχούς, 31, pp. 286–7.

105. Basil of Caesarea, Ἀσκητικαὶ Διατάξεις, 18.4, PG 31.1385BC.

106. Basil of Casarea, Λόγος ἀσκητικός, 2, PG 31.884A–885A.

107. Macarius, Hom. 30, 4, *Die 50 Geistlichen Homilien*, p. 242.

108. Basil of Caesarea, Περὶ κρίματος Θεοῦ, 4, PG 31.660B–661A. Nilus of Ancyra, Πρὸς Ἀγάθιον, PG 79.1060AB.

109. *OM*, pp. 84, 187; *ECW*, pp. 18, 109.

110. Basil of Caesarea, Ἀσκητικαὶ Διατάξεις, 18, PG 31.1381D–1384A.

111. *SCO*, Reg. Coen. I, pp. 144–6. Vita S. Lugidi, 37, *HVSH*, pp. 138–9. T.M. Charles-Edwards, *Early Christian Ireland*, pp. 381–2.

112. John Chrysostom, Εἰς τὴν πρὸς Ἐφεσίους, Hom. 3, 3–4, PG 62.27–29.

113. A. Wilmart, 'Catéchèses Celtiques', IV, 98ff, p. 50.

114. Delehaye, '*Vita S. Danielis Stylitae*', 95, p. 209.

115. Callinicos, *Vie d'Hypatios*, 3.12, p. 84.

116. G. Gould, *The Desert Fathers on Monastic Community*, pp. 57–8.

117. *SCO*, Ep. VI, 2, pp. 56–7.

118. Nilus of Ancyra, Πρὸς Ἀγάθιον, PG 79.1060AB.

119. Georgios, *Vie de Théodore*, 151, pp. 120–1. Callinicos, *Vie d'Hypatios*, 5.8–10, pp. 90–2.

120. See *SCO*, Instr. X, 3, pp. 102–4. For prohairesis as 'desire involving deliberation' see Aristotle, *Nicomachean Ethics*, 6.2.

121. Basil of Caesarea, Ὅροι κατ' ἐπιτομήν, 116 (PG 31.1161); 119 (PG 31.1161–1164); 1 (PG 31.1080–1081); 137 (PG 31.1173). *SCO*, Reg. I, p. 124. Cassian, *Institutes*, Xii.28, pp. 492–4. J. Strachan, 'An Old-Irish Metrical Rule', 15, p. 197.

122. Obedience to the spiritual father is repeatedly praised in the Irish Lives. See, for example, Vita S. Colmani, 23, *HVSH*, p. 216; 12, p. 213; 3, p. 210. For the law of the father and founder of the monastery, see John Moschus, Λειμών, 85, PG 87C.2941C–2944A.

123. *SCO*, Reg. Coen. IV, p. 154.

124. See the story in E.J. Gwynn and W.J. Purton, 'The Monastery of Tallaght', 66, p. 154. The community is considered to be a 'spiritual edifice', to the construction of which each one contributes through his or her obedience to the superior, 'like an instrument to the artist'. Basil of Caesarea, Ἀσκητικαὶ Διατάξεις, 22, PG 31.1409BC. Although Hypatios carries on painful abstinence in order to eliminate a demonic temptation, he accepts the blessing of wine and bread offered by his abbot, and this acceptance made the war more light. Callinicos, *Vie d'Hypatios*, 5.8–10, pp. 90–2.

125. Basil of Caesarea, Ὅροι κατὰ πλάτος, 30, PG 31.992C–993A. Macarius, Ἐπιστολὴ πρώτη πρὸς μοναχούς, 16, pp. 258–60. See also C. Selmer, *Navigatio*, 2, pp. 9–10. For the shepherd's love and compassion, see J. Strachan, 'An Old-Irish Metrical Rule', 28a, p. 202.

126. Nilus of Ancyra, Πρὸς Ἀγάθιον, PG 79.1056CD.

127. Basil of Caesarea, Ἀσκητικαὶ Διατάξεις, 18, PG 31.1381D–1384A.

128. Nilus of Ancyra, *Ep.* 73, Lib. III, PG 79.421D. Basil of Caesarea, Ὅροι κατ' ἐπιτομήν, 115, PG 31.1161A. Nobody is the master of oneself, but one becomes subject to 'brothers of the same soul'. Basil, Ep. 22, *Lettres*, I, p. 54.

129. Basil of Caesarea, Ἀσκητικαὶ Διατάξεις, 19, PG 31.1388C. Ὅροι κατ' ἐπιτομήν, 216, PG 31.1225.

130. E. Hickey, *The Irish Life of Saint Finnian of Clonard*, p. 8.

131. C. Selmer, *Navigatio*, 13, pp. 37–9. Moluca reveals to Maedoc his desire to visit Rome. Maedoc says that that would not be pleasing to him; nonetheless, he gives way to his insistence. And the disciple makes in his night dream a virtual pilgrimage to the Church of the Holy Apostles, after which he returns to his monastery. The biographer understands that as a fruit of the spiritual father's prayer. Vita S. Aedani, 33, *HVSH*, pp. 242–3. We also see the freedom of the wilful monk, whose mind thinks 'alio modo', whereby he receives punishment not from the superior but from God. Vita S. Aedani, 31, *HVSH*, p. 242.

132. Nilus of Ancyra, Λόγος ἀσκητικός, PG 79.724B–D. Maximus Confessor, *Ep.* 2, PG 91.400A.

133. Basil of Caesarea, Ὅροι κατ' ἐπιτομήν, 123, PG 31.1165; 137, PG 31.1173. Cf. *SCO*, Reg. I, p. 122.

134. Callinicos, *Vie d'Hypatios*, 27.3–5, p. 184; Prologue 17, p. 72. Georgios, *Vie de Théodore*, 151, pp. 120–1. Vita S. Aedani, 15, *HVSH*, p. 236. Persistence in one's own wilful thoughts is strictly opposed by the fathers as a violation of the Holy Spirit in the person of the Spirit-bearer elder. See E.J. Gwynn and W.J. Purton, 'The Monastery of Tallaght', 66, p. 154. *Apophthegmata Patrum*, Ephraim 2, PG 65.168BC. For the word of the abba, see G. Gould, *The Desert Fathers*, pp. 37–41. The inner content of obedience is given in the symbolic act of blessing. See C. Selmer, *Navigatio*, 4, pp. 10–11. That is why a pilgrimage is carried out not only to holy places but also to living holy men. See Vita S. Colmani, 20, *HVSH*, p. 216. For the practice of visiting holy persons as biblical exemplars, and its transformative power, see G. Frank (2000), *The Memory of the Eyes: Pilgrims to Living Saints in Christian Late Antiquity* (Berkeley). A saint is a ladder to the heaven. W. Stokes, *Amra*, 6, 68, pp. 260–1.

135. Basil of Caesarea, Ἀσκητικαὶ Διατάξεις, 22, PG 31.1409A. Macarius, Hom. 53, 10, *Macarii Anecdota*, p. 33.

136. See S. Kierkegaard (1962), *Works of Love*, trans. Howard and Edna Hong (New York), p. 132.

137. Basil of Caesarea, Ἀσκητικαὶ Διατάξεις, 22, PG 31.1409AB; Ὅροι κατ' ἐπιτομήν, 317, Gribomont, *Histoire du text des Ascétiques de S. Basile*, pp. 185–6. Also Nilus of Ancyra, Πρὸς Ἀγάθιον, PG 79.1060AB.

138. Basil of Caesarea, Ὅροι κατ' ἐπιτομήν, 303, PG 31.1296D–1297. Cf. Theodoret, Φιλόθεος ἱστορία, 12, PG 82.1397A; 3, PG 82.1332BC. *Apophthegmata*, Anthony 19, PG 65.81BC.

139. Basil refers to 1 Thess. 5:20–22 and 2 Cor. 10:4–5. Basil of Caesarea, Ὅροι κατ' ἐπιτομήν, 114 (PG 31.1160), 227 (PG 31.1233); Ἀσκητικαὶ Διατάξεις, 19, PG 31.1388C. Basil's line of conduct is repeated by Symeon the New

Theologian. See relevant observations in I. Hausherr, *Spiritual Direction in the Early Christian East*, pp. 204–6. Monastic leaders, focusing on what is most difficult, namely the exercise of obedience, sidestep any reference to the criteria of checking, because of the danger of their abuse by wilful readers. Yet, the criteria mentioned underlie their whole life and teaching.

140. Nilus of Ancyra, *Ep.* 307, PG 79.193BC; *Ep.* 95, PG 79.229AB. Basil of Caesarea, Ἀσκητικαὶ Διατάξεις, 22.5, PG 31.1409. Only in this spirit can we avoid misreading the advice included in the Apophthegmata to give up one's will to the commands of one's spiritual father, even to the extent of ceasing to worry about his own obedience to God's commandments. See *Apophthegmata Patrum* 290, p. 376.

141. Basil of Caesarea, Ὅροι κατ' ἐπιτομήν, 138 (PG 31.1173), 123 (PG 31.1165), 128 (PG 31.1168). Callinicos, *Vie d'Hypatios*, 27.2, pp. 182–4. Marc the hermit, Περὶ τῶν οἰομένων ἐξ ἔργων δικαιοῦσθαι, 148, PG 65.953B. Adomnán, *Vita S. Columbae*, II.21, pp. 89–90. *SCO*, Reg. IX, p.138. Columbanus does not set forth criteria in obeying a command, but it is self-evident from the thought of the Father that a command should not be observed if opposed to the divine precepts. Besides, we should not forget his particular pastoral purpose.

142. See E.J. Gwynn and W.J. Purton, 'The Monastery of Tallaght', 66, p. 154. *SCO*, Instr. X, 3, p. 104; Reg. IX, p. 140. Basil of Caesarea, Λόγος ἀσκητικός, 2, PG 31.884–888.

143. Macarius, Hom. 15, 35, *Die 50 Geistlichen Homilien*, p. 147.

144. Maximus Confessor, *Pyrrho*, PG 91.308C–309B; Κεφάλαια διάφορα, I, 46, PG 90.1196BC; IV, 34, PG 90.1317D.

145. *SCO*, Instr. VII, 1, p. 90.

146. J.G. O'Keefe, 'Mac Da Cherda and Cummaine Foda', 25. The Old-Irish Penitential, II, 1 a–d, L. Bieler, *The Irish Penitentials*, pp. 261–2.

147. Maximus Confessor, Κεφάλαια περὶ ἀγάπης, I, 51, PG 90.969CD; II, 59, 1004B; IV, 45, 1057C; Κεφάλαια διάφορα, IV, 75, PG 90.1337B. 'Prosperity's blind ease is the cause of all the evils.' *SCO*, Ep. V, 7, p. 44.

148. *SCO*, Instr. X, 3, p. 104.

149. Maximus Confessor, Κεφάλαια διάφορα, I, 46, PG 90.1196AB.

150. Basil of Caesarea, Ὅροι κατὰ πλάτος, 28.2, PG 31.989BC. Marc the hermit, Περὶ τῶν οἰομένων, 149, PG 65.953B.

151. Maximus Confessor, *Pyrrho*, PG 91.309C–312A; Πρὸς Μαρῖνον, PG 91.241C–244A; *Ep.* 2, PG 91.396D–401A. *SCO*, Instr. VII, 2, p. 92.

152. Maximus Confessor, Κεφάλαια διάφορα, I, 46, PG 90.1196BC; Εἰς τὴν προσευχήν, PG 90.893B, 901AD.

153. Gregory of Nyssa, Κατὰ Εὐνομίου I, *GNO*, I, p. 171. Maximus Confessor, *Ep.* 2, PG 90.401A.

154. See Basil of Caesarea, Ὅροι κατ' ἐπιτομήν, 74, PG 31.1133. Nilus of Ancyra, *Ep.* 72, Lib. III, PG 79.421C. Marc the hermit, Νουθεσίαι ψυχοφελεῖς, PG 65.1048BC. H. Wasserschleben, *Die Irische Kanonensammlung*, pp. 147–9. *SCO*, Ep. I, 30–5, p. 8. M. Bayless and M. Lapidge (eds), *Collectanea ps. Bedae*, 278, p. 158.

155. Basil of Caesarea, Ὅροι κατὰ πλάτος, 47, PG 31.1036B–1037A.

156. *SCO*, Ep. IV, 9, p. 36; Regulae I, pp. 122–4. Cummean, VIII, 4, L. Bieler, *The Irish Penitentials*, p. 122. Nilus of Ancyra, Πρὸς Ἀγάθιον, PG 79.1056CD. Basil of Caesarea, Ἀσκητικαὶ Διατάξεις, 22, PG 31.1401C–1409D.

157. *SCO*, Instr. X, 2–4, pp. 102–4.

158. *SCO*, Ep. II, 5, p. 14.

159. *SCO*, Instr. X, 3, pp. 102–4.

160. Colman addresses the obedience of the dead brother, which brings his resurrection. Vita S. Colmani 23, *HVSH*, pp. 216–7.

161. Maximus Confessor, Κεφάλαια περὶ ἀγάπης, III, 67, PG 90.1037A; Κεφάλαια διάφορα, I, 46, PG 90.1196BC. Nilus of Ancyra, Πρὸς Ἀγάθιον, PG 79.1060AB. *SCO*, Regulae I, p. 122. Basil of Caesarea, Ἀσκητικαὶ Διατάξεις, 18, PG 31.1381D–1384A. Ir. Hausherr, *Spiritual Direction in the Christian East*, p. 255.

162. Columba subjects himself to an incredibly cruel fasting, but the cook invents a trick so that the saint in his ignorance receives the nutrition he needs. His disobedience instigates the saint's blessing. W. Stokes, *Oengus*, n. 9, p. 147.

163. Vita Prior S. Fintani Seu Munnu, 23, *HVSH*, p. 204.

164. Cogitosus, *Vita S. Brigidae*, PL 72.781AB.

165. See C. Selmer, *Navigatio*, 2, pp. 9–10.

166. I. Hausherr, *Spiritual Direction in the Early Christian East*, p. 204. Basil of Caesarea, Ὅροι κατ' ἐπιτομήν, 119, PG 31.1164A.

167. Macarius, Hom. 1, 1, *Neue Homilien des Makarius/Symeon*, p. 2. 'I want a guide to take me by the hand and conduct me safely through life's bitter waves', 'an experienced instructor'. Basil, Ep. 150, *Lettres*, II, pp. 71–2.

168. Callinicos, *Vie d'Hypatios*, 24.1; 31.13; 48.18. For the aim of the teaching relationship as evidenced in the Apophthegmata, see G. Gould, *The Desert Fathers*, pp. 27–36.

169. Basil of Caesarea, Ὅροι κατ' ἐπιτομήν, 227, PG 31.1233BC.

170. Basil of Caesarea, Ἀσκητικαὶ Λιατάξεις, 22, PG 31.1409C.

171. See Basil of Caesarea, Ἀσκητικαὶ Διατάξεις, 19, PG 31.1388BC.

172. Nilus of Ancyra, Λόγος ἀσκητικός, PG 79.772A–C; *Ep.* 95, PG 79.229AB. Basil of Caesarea, Ἀσκητικαὶ Διατάξεις, 22, PG 31.1409BC.

173. Callinicos, *Vie d'Hypatios*, Prologue 8, p. 70; 50.4–5, p. 286. Basil of Caesarea, Ὅροι κατὰ πλάτος, 43, PG 31.1028BC. Nilus of Ancyra, Λόγος ἀσκητικός, PG 79.752D, 764D–765A.

174. Marc the hermit, Νουθεσίαι ψυχοφελεῖς, PG 65.1036D–1037A. The Old-Irish Penitential, II, 1 a–d, L. Bieler, *The Irish Penitentials*, pp. 261–2. Also see G. Gould, *The Desert Fathers*, pp. 30–1.

175. Κεφάλαια περὶ ἀγάπης, III, 66–67, PG 90.1036D–1037A; IV, 61, 1061BC; Μυσταγωγία, 5, PG 91.676A–D.

176. A. Muirchú, Vita Patricii, I.6, L. Bieler, *The Patrician Texts*, pp. 70–1.

177. Vita S. Aidi, 7, *HVSH*, p. 169. Cf. Macarius, Hom. 1, 1, *Neue Homilien*, p. 2.

178. Vita S. Aedani, 16, *HVSH*, p. 237.

179. Marc the hermit, Πρὸς τοὺς ἀποροῦντας, PG 65.996B–D.

180. Basil of Caesarea, Περὶ κρίματος Θεοῦ, 4, PG 31.660CD.

181. Macarius, Ἐπιστολὴ πρώτη πρὸς μοναχούς, 15–16, pp. 256–60; Περὶ προσευχῆς, 10, PG 34.860C.

182. Maximus Confessor, Κεφάλαια διάφορα, I, 46, PG 90.1196BC.

183. Symeon the New Theologian, Κεφάλαια πρακτικὰ καὶ θεολογικά, iii.4, ed. J. Darrouzès, SC 51 (Paris 1957), p. 81.

184. 1 Cor. 4:14; 2 Cor. 6:13; 2 Tim. 1:2. Clement of Alexandria, Στρωματεῖς, I.1, PG 8.688A–689A; V.2, PG 9.29B–32A.

185. Cf. T.M. Charles-Edwards, *Early Christian Ireland*, p. 274. John Chrysostom, Σύγκρισις βασιλικῆς δυναστείας καὶ πλούτου καὶ ὑπεροχῆς, πρὸς μοναχὸν συζῶντα τῇ ἀληθεστάτῃ καὶ κατὰ Χριστὸν φιλοσοφίᾳ, 2, PG 47.388.

186. Georgios, *Vie de Théodore*, 160, p. 136.1–7. Callinicos, *Vie d'Hypatios*, 23.3, p. 146; 10, pp. 108–10. The case of Macrina, as presented in detail in the life written by Gregory of Nyssa, shows the universality of spiritual maternity in the person of the holy woman. Corresponding examples in the Celtic tradition are Brigid of Kildare, Ita of Kileedy and Hilda of Whitby.

187. Gregory of Nyssa, Περὶ παρθενίας, 13, *GNO*, VIII, Opera Ascetica, I, p. 305.

188. See, for example, Vita S. Colmani, 23, *HVSH*, p. 216; 12, p. 213; 3, p. 210. J. Strachan, 'An Old-Irish Metrical Rule', 14, p. 197. J.G. O'Keefe, 'The Rule of Patrick', 2, p. 221. The Old-Irish Table of Commutations, 32A, L. Bieler, *The Irish Penitentials*, p. 282. G. Murphy, *Early Irish Lyrics*, p. 25. W. Stokes, *Oengus*, n. 1, p. 65.

189. Vita S. Aedani, 15, *HVSH*, p. 236.

190. Vita Prior S. Fintani Seu Munnu, 23, *HVSH*, p. 204. Adomnán, *Vita S. Columbae* I.37; II.39, 42. See also Vita S. Aedani, 25, *HVSH*, p. 240.

191. 'Litany of Irish Saints II', *ILit*, p. 63.

192. See L. Bieler, *The Irish Penitentials*, pp. 153–60. For the characteristics of the spiritual father in Eastern Christianity, see Kallistos Ware's 'Introduction' in I. Hausherr, *Spiritual Direction in the Early Christian East*, pp. xii–xxvii.

193. Georgios, *Vie de Théodore*, 160, p. 136.1–7.

194. Gregory of Nyssa, Εἰς τὸν βίον τῆς ὁσίας Μακρίνης, *GNO*, VIII, Opera Ascetica, I, pp. 400–1.

195. Callinicos, *Vie d'Hypatios*, 48.1–17, pp. 274–8.

196. E.J. Gwynn and W.J. Purton, 'The Monastery of Tallaght', 51, p. 146. Cf. Gregory Nazianzen, Περὶ ἀρετῆς, PG 37.693A.

197. See W. Stokes, *Oengus*, n. 3, p. 181–3.

198. J. Carey, *King of Mysteries*, p. 24.

199. Responsibility dictates precision. For example, see the Old-Irish Penitential, 13, L. Bieler, *The Irish Penitentials*, p. 261.

200. K. Ware, *The Inner Kingdom*, p. 146. For the Irish practice, see Peter O'Dwyer, 'Celtic Monks and the Culdee Reform' in J.P. Mackey, *An Introduction to Celtic Christianity*, pp. 150–1.

201. Gregory Nazianzen, *Or.* 2, 21, *Discours*, pp. 116–8. Columba is characterised as the physician of the heart of the wise men. W. Stokes, *Amra*, 6, 18.

202. Basil of Caesarea, Ὅροι κατ' ἐπιτομήν, 158, PG 31.1185BC.

203. Basil of Caesarea, Ὅροι κατὰ πλάτος, 52–53, PG 31.1041A–1044A. Climacus, Πρὸς τὸν ποιμένα, 2, PG 88.1168D–1169C. Hugh Connolly (1995), *The Irish Penitentials and their Significance for the Sacrament of Penance Today* (Dublin), p. 16. A public confession is used exceptionally, according to the judgement of the superior, as a proof of genuine repentance. See Adomnán, *Vita S. Columbae* I.30, pp. 40–1.

204. Basil of Caesarea, Ἀσκητικαὶ Διατάξεις, 22, PG 31.1409CD; Ὅροι κατ' ἐπιτομήν, 113, PG 31.1157CD. Nilus of Ancyra, *Ep.* 110, PG 79.248D. *Ep.* 111, PG 79.248D–249A. Macarius, Ἐπιστολὴ πρώτη πρὸς μοναχούς,

16, pp. 259–60; Περὶ τελειότητος ἐν Πνεύματι λόγος, 9, PG 34.848BC. *SCO*, ep. IV, 3, p. 28. See Columba's conduct with two of his disciples for the same issue, where he seems to assume an entirely different stance. Adomnán, *Vita S. Columbae*, I.19, pp. 31–2.

205. Nilus of Ancyra, *Ep.* 33, Lib. III, PG 79.397C. Macarius, Ἐπιστολὴ πρώτη πρὸς μοναχούς, 16, pp. 258–9.

206. *SCO*, Ep. IV, 4, p. 28.

207. I. Hausherr, *Spiritual Direction in the Early Christian East*, pp. 150–1. For example, see Adomnán, *Vita S. Columbae* III.23, p. 162–3. Βίβλος Βαρσανουφίου καὶ Ἰωάννου, ed. Nicodemus the Hagiorite (Venice, 1816), pp. 111ff.

208. Marc the hermit, Νουθεσίαι ψυχοφελεῖς, PG 65.1036D–1037A.

209. Marc the hermit, Πρὸς τοὺς ἀποροῦντας, PG 65.996B–D. Vita S. Colmani, 2, *HVSH*, p. 210. Aileran, *Interpretatio Mystica et Moralis Progenitorum Domini Iesu Christi*, 292–4, p. 27. *Breviarium in psalmos*, PL 26.947BC.

210. Macarius, Hom. 6, 5, *Die 50 Geistlichen Homilien*, p. 68. V. Hull, 'Apgitir chrábaid',18, pp. 68–9.

211. *Contra haereses* V.81, PG 7.1142B.

212. John Donne, *Sermons on the Psalms and Gospels*, 10, ed. E.M. Simpson (London, 1963), p. 219.

213. Nilus of Ancyra, Πρὸς Ἀγάθιον, PG 79.1037CD. Tyranny refers to the disorientation of the incensive power of the soul, generating arbitrariness, cruelty, rebellion and the like. Maximus Confessor, *Ep.* 2, PG 91.396D–401A.

214. Gregory Nazianzen, *Or.* 2, 21, *Discours*, pp. 116–18. Basil of Caesarea, Ὅροι κατ' ἐπιτομήν, 289, PG 31.1285A–C. *Expositio quatuor evangeliorum*, PL 30.539A. Macarius, Περὶ ὑψώσεως τοῦ νοὸς λόγος, 21, PG 34.905. For the intrinsic sinfulness and the demand of spiritual struggle, see Macarius, Hom. 3, 4, *Die 50 Geistlichen Homilien*, p. 24.

215. Callinicos, *Vie d'Hypatios*, 48.25–8, p. 280. Macarius, Hom. 17.13,15, *Die 50 Geistlichen Homilien*, pp. 174–6.

216. Basil of Caesarea, Ὅροι κατὰ πλάτος, 26, PG 31.987C–988A.

217. Nilus of Ancyra, Λόγος ἀσκητικός, PG 79.724B–D. Meyer, 'The Hermit's Song' 2, 9, pp. 55–7. Vita S. Aedani, 16, *HVSH*, p. 237. Marc the hermit, Περὶ νόμου πνευματικοῦ, 69, PG 65.913C; 199, PG 65.929B. Basil of Caesarea, Λόγος περὶ ἀσκήσεως, 1, PG 31.648C–649D.

218. Marc the hermit, Περὶ νόμου πνευματικοῦ, 187, PG 65.928C; Περὶ νόμου πνευματικοῦ, 70, PG 65.913C. Maximus Confessor, Κεφάλαια περὶ ἀγάπης, III, 80, PG 90.141B. A philosophical reflection on conscience see in R. Spaemann (2006), *Persons: the difference between someone and something* (Oxford University Press: London), pp. 164-79.

219. Macarius, Hom. 4, 1, *Die 50 Geistlichen Homilien*, pp. 25–7.

220. Basil of Caesarea, Ep. 2, *Lettres*, I, p. 7. Theodoret, Φιλόθεος ἱστορία, PG 82.1396BC. *Breviarium in psalmos*, PL 26.1032C. Marc the hermit, Περὶ μετανοίας, PG 65.976B.

221. Nilus, Εἰς Ἀλβιανὸν λόγος, PG 79.705D–708A. See also K. Meyer, 'The Hermit's Song', 6. Broccán's Hymn, 2–5, *ThPal*, ii, p. 327. There is great emphasis on the guard and concentration of the intellect. See D. Ó hAodha, *Bethu Brigte*, 38, p. 30.

222. Basil, Ep. 2, *Lettres*, I, p. 6. Gregory Nazianzen, *Or*. 6, 2, PG 35.724A.

223. 'The Rule of Cormac', 10, U. Ó Maidín, *The Celtic Monk*, p. 56.

224. *Les Apophtegmes des Pères*, 7.46, pp. 376–8.

225. Nilus of Ancyra, *Ep*. 119, PG 79.252BC.

226. Nilus of Ancyra, *Ep*. 107, PG 79.129A. Maximus Confessor, Περὶ Θεολογίας καὶ τῆς ἐνσάρκου οἰκονομίας, I, 32, PG 90.1096A; I, 77, PG 90.1112B.

227. Marc the hermit, Περὶ τῶν οἰομένων, 111, PG 65.964D. *SCO*, Instr. III, 2, p. 74. Theodoret, Φιλόθεος ἱστορία, PG 82.1396BC. Athanasius, Βίος καὶ πολιτεία τοῦ ὁσίου πατρὸς ἡμῶν Ἀντωνίου, PG 26.893B. Maximus Confessor, Περὶ διαφόρων ἀποριῶν, PG 91.1248A–1249C.

228. J. O'Neill, 'The Rule of Ailbe of Emly', 38, p. 115.

229. A secular morality is far from 'scientific treatment', just as professional medicine is far from amateurish medicine, which does not reach the actual causes. Nilus of Ancyra, Ὅτι διαφέρουσι, PG 79.1061A–1064AB.

230. Callinicos, *Vie d'Hypatios*, 24.96–9, p. 176. Cf. 1 Cor. 14:14. Also see Climacus, 18.3, 5, 28.59.

231. See Aileran, *Interpretatio Mystica*, 292–9, p. 27.

232. Dionysius, Περὶ ἐκκλησιαστικῆς ἱεραρχίας, VI, 1, 3 PG 3.533A.

233. Marc the hermit, Περὶ τῶν οἰομένων, 211, PG 65,964D.

234. Maximus Confessor, Κεφάλαια περὶ ἀγάπης, IV, 45, PG 90.1057C; I, 98–99, 981D; Περὶ διαφόρων ἀποριῶν, PG 91.1248A–1249C.

235. Maximus Confessor, Περὶ διαφόρων ἀποριῶν, PG 91.1249AB. Cf. Gregory of Nyssa, Περὶ παρθενίας, 11.

236. Marc the hermit, Περὶ τῶν οἰομένων, 122–123, PG 65.948CD. Maximus Confessor, Περὶ διαφόρων ἀποριῶν, PG 91.1273B–D. Delehaye, '*Sancti Alypii Stylitae Vita* prior', 22, p. 165.

237. See the critical edition of Κεφάλαια γνωστικά, 89, p. 150.

238. Tractatus Hilarii, *SHM*, I, p. 57.130–2. V. Hull, 'Apgitir chrábaid', 2, pp. 58–9. Also Maximus Confessor, Κεφάλαια περὶ ἀγάπης, I, 2–3 (PG 90.961AB), I, 27 (PG 90.965C), IV, 91 (PG 90.1069CD). Nilus of Ancyra, Εἰς Ἀλβιανὸν λόγος, PG 79.705D–708A; Περὶ ἀκτημοσύνης, PG 79.1009C. Basil of Caesarea, Ὅροι κατὰ πλάτος, 3, PG 31.917AB.

239. See *SCO*, Instr. XI, 1, p. 106.

240. Macarius, Hom. 37, 2, *Die 50 Geistlichen Homilien*, p. 266. Scotti anonymi, Commentarius in Epistolas Catholicas, *SHM*, I, p. 41.111–112.

241. Basil of Caesarea, Ἀσκητικαὶ Διατάξεις, 18, PG 31.1381B–1385A.

242. A. Wilmart, 'Catéchèses Celtiques', IV, 130–3, p. 50.

243. Maximus Confessor, Κεφάλαια περὶ ἀγάπης, II, 29–30, PG 90.993AB.

244. A. Wilmart, 'Catéchèses Celtiques', I, p. 38.

245. V. Hull, 'Apgitir chrábaid', 20, p. 70. This is attested in the life of St Finnian. See E. Hickey, *The Irish Life of Saint Finnian of Clonard*, p. 8. Constantine was from a royal bloodline: 'he offered himself to menial work, like every other monk who serves God'. W. Stokes, *Oengus*, n. 11, p. 93. Vita S. Fintani, 4, *HVSH*, σ. 147. For other examples, see Fergus Kelly (1997), *Early Irish Farming* (Dublin), pp. 453–5.

246. J. O'Neill, 'The Rule of Ailbe of Emly', 9, p. 99. *Theoria* and praxis –the two aspects of monastic life – are normally addressed to all. Any difference should be understood in the framework of personal gifts or inclination or

strength. 'Labour, study, prayer' are prescribed for the entire community or the recluse (H. Wasserschleben, *Die Irische Kanonensammlung*, pp. 173–4. K. Meyer, 'Anmchairdes Mancháin Léith', pp. 310–12. 'The Rule of Colmcille', U. Ó Maidín, *The Celtic Monk*, pp. 37–41). Of course, instruction, scribal activity, labour and contemplation were not for all equally and indiscriminately. See also R. Sharpe, *Adomnán of Iona*, pp. 71–3. Besides, the vita practica, as opposed to the vita theorica, in the Greek sources indicates not only menial work but also the bodily struggles of ascesis. Therefore, teaching and writing are included in the active life.

247. J. Strachan, 'An Old-Irish Metrical Rule', 25–6, pp. 200–1.

248. For example, see Vita Moluae, 62, *HVSH*, p. 143; 30, p. 137. Vita S. Aidi, 3, ibid., pp. 168–9. Vita Prior S. Fintani Seu Munnu, 10–11, ibid., pp. 200–1. *Vita S. Columbae* I.32, p. 42–3. Aileran, *Interpretatio Mystica*, 201–2, p. 24. M. Herbert, *Betha Adamnáin*, 18, p. 61. A. O'Kelleher, 'A Hymn of Invocation', 13, pp. 238–9. Comm. in Lucam V.16, *SHM*, II, p. 43.134–136. Cf. Theodoret, Φιλόθεος ἱστορία, 8, PG 82.1368AB. Nilus of Ancyra, *Ep.* 290, Lib. III, PG 79.528A. R.I. Best, *The Martyrology of Tallaght*, pp. 111–12. Christina Harrington has shown that the female hermit lived outside the protective sphere of her family; see *Women in a Celtic Church*, pp. 123–6. For the ideal and practice of self-exile in Byzantine and Irish monasticism, see Ch. Koutloumousianos, Οἱ Ἐραστὲς τῆς Βασιλείας, pp. 21–46.

249. Maximus Confessor, Περὶ διαφόρων ἀποριῶν, PG 91.1141B-1144B.

250. Gregory of Nyssa, Εἰς τὸν βίον τῆς ὁσίας Μακρίνης, *GNO*, VIII, I, pp. 377–8, 381.

251. Gregory Nazianzen, Σύγκρισις βίων, PG 37.652.

252. Basil of Caesarea, Ὅροι κατὰ πλάτος, 10, PG 31.944C–948A.

253. Theodoret, Φιλόθεος ἱστορία, 5, PG 82.1356CD.

254. See Basil of Caesarea, Λόγος ἀσκητικός, 2, PG 31.885. Maximus Confessor, Κεφάλαια διάφορα, II, 72, PG 90.1248AB.

255. Tractatus Hilarii, *SHM*, I, p. 122.9–12. Athanasius, Περὶ παρθενίας 21, PG 28.276D–277A. Oratio Seu Lorica Brendani Abbatis, PL Supplementum 4.2065. Audite Omnes Amantes, Preface to the hymn of St Sechnall, *ILH*, ii, pp. 5–6. See the advice of Máel Ruain in E.J. Gwynn and W.J. Purton, 'The Monastery of Tallaght', 75, p. 158.

256. Aileran, *Interpretatio Mystica*, 379–85, p. 30; n. 17, pp. 89–90.

257. For empathy according to the phenomenologists, see D. Zahavi, *Subjectivity and Selfhood*, pp. 148–68.

258. Maximus Confessor, *Ep.* 30–31, PG 91.624–625.

259. The Cambray Homily, *ThPal*, ii, p. 246. Vita S. Aidi Killariensis, 17, *HVSH* p. 173.

260. J. O'Neill, 'The Rule of Ailbe of Emly', 3, 11. Callinicos, *Vie d'Hypatios*, 43.1–7, pp. 256–8.

261. Palladius, Ἡ πρὸς Λαῦσον ἱστορία, 116, PG 34.1220. Delehaye, 'Sancti Alypii Stylitae Vita prior', 23, pp. 165–6. For the social consciousness of monks, see S. Mitchell, *Anatolia*, vol. 2, *The Rise of the Church*, pp. 109–10.

262. Basil of Caesarea, Ὅροι κατὰ πλάτος, 24, PG 31.981C–984B; Ὅροι κατ' ἐπιτομήν, 175, PG 31.1197C. The Old-Irish Penitential, III, 21, L. Bieler, *The Irish Penitentials*, p. 268; IV, 4, p. 270. See also G. Gould, *The Desert Fathers*, pp. 67–9.

263. *Oratio Seu Lorica Brendani Abbatis*, PL Supplementum 4.2065. Audite Omnes Amantes, Preface to the hymn of St. Sechnall, *ILH*, ii, pp. 5–6. E.J. Gwynn and W.J. Purton, 'The Monastery of Tallaght', 75, p. 158.

264. *Expositio quatuor evangeliorum*, PL 30.561. Scotti anonymi, Commentarius in Epistolas Catholicas, *SHM*, I, p. 41.111–12.

265. *Breviarium in psalmos*, PL 26.904D. Macarius, Hom. 7, 4, *Neue Homilien*, p. 32.

266. *Breviarium in psalmos*, PL 26.909C. Theodoret, Φιλόθεος ἱστορία, 4, PG 82.1341C.

267. Cainech blessed the belly of the young girl who had become pregnant by committing fornication, and after the blessing, the embryo was no more. Vita S. Cainnechi, 56, *HVSH*, p. 197. See also Vita S. Aidi, 15, *HVSH*, p. 172. Compassion surpasses legal justice. See Vita S. Aidi, 31, *HVSH*, p. 176. Vita S. Colmani, 30, *HVSH*, pp. 218–19.

268. Basil, Ep. 173, *Lettres*, II, p. 109. *SCO*, Instr. XI, 3, p. 110. Delehaye, '*Vita S. Danielis Stylitae*', 102, pp. 213–14. Callinicos, *Vie d'Hypatios*, 24.31–5, p. 156; 12.3, p. 116; 31.1–2, p. 204.

269. Maximus Confessor, Κεφάλαια διάφορα, II, 72, PG 90.1248AB.

270. Macarius, Hom. 15, 8, *Die 50 Geistlichen Homilien*, p. 131.

271. See Vita Moluae, 34, *HVSH*, p. 138. D. Ó hAodha, *Bethu Brigte*, 12–13, p. 22. Cogitosus, *Vita S. Brigidae*, PL 72.786BC. W. Stokes, *Oengus*, n. 17, p. 153. Adomnán, *Vita S. Columbae*, I.4, II.20. Canones Hibernenses, V, 4, L. Bieler, *The Irish Penitentials*, p. 172. Callinicos, *Vie d'Hypatios*, 24.34, p. 156. Nilus of Ancyra, Πρὸς Ἀγάθιον, PG 79.872A. Βίος καὶ πολιτεία τοῦ ὁσίου ιατρὸς ἡμῶν Ἀλεξάνδρου, 37, PO 6.687.

272. *SCO*, Instr. XI, 1, p. 106. W. Stokes, *Oengus*, n. 9, p. 147. Adomnán, *Vita S. Columbae* I.26. It is equal to the most holy pilgrimage. J.G. O'Keefe, 'Mac Dá Cherda and Cummaine Foda', 25.

273. Nilus of Ancyra, Πρὸς Ἀγάθιον, PG 79.845A, 868D, 852AB, 857C, 864CD; Ep. 320, PG 79.356CD.

274. See Marc the hermit, Πρὸς τοὺς ἀποροῦντας, PG 65.1025AB.

275. Nilus of Ancyra, Πρὸς Ἀγάθιον, PG 79.885D.

276. Basil of Caesarea, Ὅροι κατὰ πλάτος, 3, PG 31.917A; 7, PG 31.928C. Nilus of Ancyra, Πρὸς Ἀγάθιον, PG 79.840BC.

277. Basil of Caesarea, Ὅροι κατὰ πλάτος, 3, PG 31.917A.

278. Nilus of Ancyra, Ep. 146, PG 79.144A.

279. Christ appeals to the rich man to bend towards sympathy because of the inner glory of the icon, since the common nature did not make them feel pity. Nilus of Ancyra, Πρὸς Ἀγάθιον, PG 79.873C.

280. Macarius, Hom. 15, 32, *Die 50 Geistlichen Homilien*, p. 145.

281. Macarius, Hom. 15, 36, *Die 50 Geistlichen Homilien*, pp. 148–9; Περὶ ἀγάπης λόγος, 6, PG 34.912C–913A.

282. Hom. 15, 32, *Die 50 Geistlichen Homilien*, p. 145.

283. Nilus of Ancyra, Πρὸς Ἀγάθιον, PG 79.880CD, 881B. *ILit*, p. 23. *SCO*, De homine misero, quid est, aut quid erit, p. 210.1–14.

284. *SCO*, Regulae IV, p. 126.

285. J. Strachan, 'An Old-Irish Metrical Rule', 21, p. 199.

286. Callinicos, *Vie d'Hypatios*, 3.12, p. 84; 34.1, p. 220. Gregory of Nyssa, Εἰς τὸν βίον τῆς ὁσίας Μακρίνης, *GNO*, VIII, I, pp. 402–3. Nilus of Ancyra,

Περὶ ἀκτημοσύνης, PG 79.992D–993B, 1004D–1005B; Λόγος εἰς τὸ ῥητὸν τοῦ Εὐαγγελίου, 1, PG 79.1264D–1265A. Macarius, Hom. 53, 8, *Macarii Anecdota*, p. 32. Basil of Caesarea, Ὅροι κατ' ἐπιτομήν, 85, PG 31.1144A.

287. G.G. Harpham, *The Ascetic Imperative in Culture and Criticism*, pp. 41–2.
288. Basil of Caesarea, Λόγος ἀσκητικός, 1, PG 31.881C–884A (M.M. Wagner (trans.) (1962), *St Basil: Ascetical Works*, vol. 9, *The Fathers of the Church* (Washington, DC), p. 217). See also W. Stokes, *Oengus*, n. 20, p. 225. J. O'Neill, 'The Rule of Ailbe of Emly', 45, p. 107. *SCO*, Reg. Coenobialis, II, p. 146.11. The Old-Irish Penitential, III, 10 & 6, L. Bieler, *The Irish Penitentials*, p. 267. 'The Rule of Carthage', 3, U. Ó Maidín, *The Celtic Monk*, p. 67.
289. *Purity of Heart Is to Will One Thing*, trans. D.V. Steer (New York, 1956), ch. 7, p. 108.
290. N.V. Harrison, 'Human Uniqueness and Human Unity', pp. 212–15.
291. Maximus Confessor, Περὶ διαφόρων ἀποριῶν, PG 91.1065D–1068A.
292. V. Hull, 'Apgitir chrábaid', 31, p. 75. *SCO*, Ep. II, 8, pp. 20–2.
293. V. Hull, 'Apgitir chrábaid', 9, pp. 62–3. Macarius, Περὶ προσευχῆς, 5, PG 34.856C–857B. Macarius, Περὶ προσευχῆς, 9, PG 34.860B. Ἐπιστολὴ πρώτη πρὸς μοναχούς, 30, pp. 285–6.
294. J. O'Neill, 'The Rule of Ailbe of Emly', 3, p. 97.
295. A. Muirchú, Vita Patricii, I.6, L. Bieler, *The Patrician Texts*, pp. 70–1.
296. *The Martyrology of Oengus*, Prologue 181,185, p. 25; notes 19 August, p. 189. Vita Moluae, 64, *HVSH*, p. 144. Cf. V. Hull, 'Apgitir chrábaid', 20, pp. 70–1. Also J. Strachan, 'An Old-Irish Homily', 9. *Sancti Columbani Opera*, Regulae VII, p. 130. J. O'Neill, 'The Rule of Ailbe of Emly', 16 and 22. 'The Rule of Cormac', 1, U. Ó Maidín, *The Celtic Monk*, p. 55. Callinicos, *Vie d'Hypatios*, 56.2, p. 298; 41.19–20, p. 246. Gregory Nazianzen, Πρὸς Ἑλλήνιον, PG 37.1453–1454; *Or.* 6, 2, PG 35.721C–724A. Basil of Caesarea, Ὅροι κατ' ἐπιτομήν, 281, PG 31.1280. Alexander the Sleepless introduces the sleepless doxology. Βίος καὶ πολιτεία τοῦ ὁσίου πατρὸς ἡμῶν Ἀλεξάνδρου, PO 6.682. On the sleepless worship, see Ioannis Fountoulis (1963), Ἡ εἰκοσιτετράωρος ἀκοίμητος δοξολογία (Athens). A rite of continuous office is evidenced in the Celi De. See 'The Rule of Tallaght', 30, *Hermathena* XLIV, v. II, Supplement (Dublin, 1927), p. 73.
297. Basil of Caesarea, Ὅροι κατὰ πλάτος, 37.3–5, PG 31.1013–1016. *Breviarium in psalmos*, PL 26.1254D–1255A. C. Selmer, *Navigatio*, 11, pp. 23–7. Fiacc's Hymn, *ThPal*, ii, p. 315. 'Hymnus Sancti Hilarii', F.E. Warren, *The Antiphonary of Bangor*, II, pp. 3–5.
298. 'Sancti Venite', F.E. Warren, *The Antiphonary of Bangor*, II, pp. 10–11. C. Selmer, *Navigatio*, 45 and 22. See also the Anaphora in the Byzantine Liturgies.
299. Theodoret, Φιλόθεος ἱστορία, 12, PG 82.1397B. John Moschus, Λειμών, 86, PG 87c.2944AB.
300. J.D. Anderson (1988), 'The Navigatio Brendani: a medieval best seller', *Classical Journal* 83:4, 322.
301. See R.Taft (1986), *The Liturgy of the Hours in East and West* (Collegeville), p. 71.
302. *SCO*, Regulae VII, p. 132.
303. Delehaye, '*Sancti Alypii Stylitae Vita* prior', 20, pp. 163–4.

304. This is still the cetral troparion of the Orthodox Service of Palm Sunday. For the custom of complete withdrawal during Lent, see Sophrony, Βίος Μαρίας Αἰγυπτίας, PG 87c.3704B.

305. *Sancti Columbani Opera*, Regulae VII, p. 132. Romanos, *Cantica*, pp. 472–82.

306. C. Selmer, *Navigatio*, 15, pp. 40–5. Paenitentiale Cummeani, II, 2, L. Bieler, *The Irish Penitentials*, pp. 114–15. Canones Synodi Hibernensis S. Patricio Perperam Attributi, XXII, *Ibid.*, pp. 192–3. Paenitentiale S. Columbani, B, 30, ibid., pp. 105–6. W. Stokes, *Amra*, 7, 93, p. 271.

307. For example, Paenitentiale Cummeani, VIII, L. Bieler, *The Irish Penitentials*, pp. 122–3. Cf. Nilus of Ancyra, *Ep.* 99, PG 79.124D–125A.

308. This is one of the main theses of P.M. Rumsey (2007), *Sacred Time in Early Christian Ireland: The Monks of the Nauigatio and the Céli Dé in Dialogue to Explore the Theologies of Time and the Liturgy of the Hours in Pre-Viking Ireland* (London), pp. 89ff. I do not adopt her view of a shift in liturgical theology resulting from the 'scrupulous' devotional practices of the Celi De. Their emphasis on paraliturgical devotions (genuflections, reciting, cross vigil) does not imply that they do not see Christ as 'the companion and guide of their journey'. Does Máel Ruain's ascesis miss 'the varied secrets in the great ocean'? Let us say *en passant* that the recitation of the Psalms as private devotion was (and possibly still is) a custom for Greek monks living in communities and carrying out their labours. Also, the fact that they took their role as 'soul-friends' very seriously was a principle in the East. Last but not least, their longing for the homeland in heaven is not incompatible with the experience of God's kingdom here and now, nor is it inconsonant with the experience of time as part of the good creation; in fact, it contributes to time's transfiguration.

309. Maximus Confessor, Περὶ διαφόρων ἀποριῶν, PG 91.1108A–C.

310. The 'world' for the Celi De was the property disputes, warfare, secular control of ecclesiastical benefices, hereditary abbacies; things incompatible with monastic consciousness. With this qualification, the difference between the *Navigatio* and the Celi De texts is an impression owed to their different literary genre. When the *Navigatio* focuses on liturgy, and the Celi De rules deal with everyday regulations and general spiritual principles, they simply cover different, overlapping areas. While the Celi De texts cope with particular cases and general advice, *Navigatio* exhibits archetypal figures, and that is why there is little place for the individual. Cf. P.M. Rumsey, *Sacred Time*, pp. 197ff. See the critique of G. Markus (2009) in *The Author*, 262–6.

311. J.G. O'Keefe, 'Mac Dá Cherda and Cummaine Foda', 25.

312. Maximus Confessor, Περὶ διαφόρων ἀποριῶν, PG 91.1109B.

313. Ibid.

314. Maximus Confessor, Περὶ διαφόρων ἀποριῶν, PG 91.1081C–1085A. (*On Difficulties*, vol. 1, pp. 101–7). Κεφάλαια διάφορα, III, 43–44, PG 90.1280AB. Cf. Macarius, Hom. 15, 38, *Die 50 Geistlichen Homilien*, pp. 149-50.

315. For the relation between the virtues and simplicity in the Cappadocian theology and anthropology, see A. Radde-Gallwitz, *Basil of Caesarea*, pp. 175–224.

316. Maximus Confessor, Περὶ διαφόρων ἀποριῶν, PG 91.1308C–1308D, 1313C.

317. Maximus Confessor, Περὶ διαφόρων ἀποριῶν, PG 91. 1304D-1305D, 1308AC, 1249AB.
318. Gregory Nazianzen, *Or.* 21, 2, PG 35.1084. Maximus Confessor, Περὶ διαφόρων ἀποριῶν, PG 91.1141AB.
319. Maximus Confessor, Κεφάλαια διάφορα, III, 55, PG 90.1284C; II, 72, PG 90.1248AB. For the deification of the entire person through the virtues, see Περὶ διαφόρων ἀποριῶν, PG 91.1248A–1249C.
320. Maximus Confessor, Περὶ διαφόρων ἀποριῶν, PG 91.1092BC, 1108C, 1112C–1116A; Πρὸς Θαλάσσιον, 8, PG 90.285A; Περὶ θεολογίας καὶ τῆς ἐνσάρκου οἰκονομίας, II, 21, PG 90.1133D; Κεφάλαια διάφορα, III, 46, PG 90.1280C; Μυσταγωγία, 5, PG 91.676A.
321. Ériugena, *Periphyseon* III, pp. 56.26–58.11.
322. See Callinicos, *Vie d'Hypatios*, 5.1, 8–10, pp. 88–92.
323. V. Hull, 'Apgitir chrábaid', 1, pp. 58–9. See the translation and comment of J. Carey, *King of Mysteries*, p. 233.
324. J. Carey, *King of Mysteries*, pp. 24–5.
325. Cf. N.V. Harrison, 'Human Uniqueness and Human Unity', p. 212.
326. Marc the hermit, Περὶ τῶν οἰομένων, 108, PG 65.945.
327. Cyril of Alexandria, Περὶ τῆς ἐνανθρωπήσεως, 16, PG 75.1445B. John Chrysostom, Ὑπόμνημα εἰς τὸν ἅγιον Ἰωάννην, Hom. 30, 2, PG 59.174. Macarius, Hom. 18, 10.
328. Clement, Προτρεπτικός, SC 2, IX, 88.3, pp. 155–6. Nilus of Ancyra, Πρὸς Ἀγάθιον, PG 79.1056CD.
329. *SCO*, Ep. II, 3, pp. 12–13.
330. *Apophthegmata*, John Kolobos 39, PG 65.217A.
331. Macarius, Ἐπιστολὴ πρώτη πρὸς μοναχούς, 30, pp. 285–6.
332. Ériugena, *Periphyseon* III, pp. 52.25–54.5.
333. Maximus Confessor, Περὶ διαφόρων ἀποριῶν, PG 91.1084A, 1141BC (*On Difficulties*, v. I, pp. 103–5, 219–21).
334. Ériugena, *Periphyseon* IV, p. 190.18–30; III, p. 54.8–19.
335. See C. Selmer, *Navigatio*, 16, p. 46.
336. Basil of Caesarea, Ὅροι κατ᾽ ἐπιτομήν, 200, PG 31.1216.
337. Broccán's Hymn, 18, *ThPal*, ii, p. 331.
338. Columbanus prefers the term 'subsistentia', which is a literal translation of the Cappadocian hypostasis. *SCO*, Instr. I, 2, p. 60. Cf. Nilus of Ancyra, *Ep.* 255, PG 79.176D–177A. Gregory Nazianzen, Περὶ ἀρετῆς, PG 37.751–752; *Or.* 6, 22, PG 35.749C.
339. 'Hymnus Sancti Comgilli Abbatis Nostri', xxi, F.E. Warren, *The Antiphonary of Bangor*, II, p. 18.
340. Macarius, Hom. 34, 2, *Die 50 Geistlichen Homilien*, p. 261.
341. Macarius, Hom. 8, 6, *Die 50 Geistlichen Homilien*, p. 83.
342. V. Hull, 'Apgitir chrábaid', 12, p. 65.
343. Delehaye, '*Vita S. Danielis Stylitae*', 95, p. 209, 19–20. *SCO*, Epistula, p. 206, 7–9.
344. *OM*, pp. 83–84, 187.
345. *OM*, pp. 245–6. P. McPartlan, *The Eucharist Makes the Church*, pp. 205–11.
346. Macarius, Hom. 53, 14, *Macarii Anecdota*, p. 35. Basil of Caesarea, Ὅροι κατὰ πλάτος, 2, PG 31.909A–C.
347. Maximus Confessor, Περὶ διαφόρων ἀποριῶν, PG 91.1081BC.

348. Cyril of Alexandria, Ἡ βίβλος τῶν θησαυρῶν, XII, XIX, PG 75.180, 316A–C; *In D. Joannis evangelium*, XI, 9–11, v. II, pp. 697–8, 731–4.

349. Ignatius, Τραλλιανοῖς VIII, p. 88.

350. 'Benchuir bona regula', ii, F.E. Warren, *The Antiphonary of Bangor*, II, p. 28.

351. C. Selmer, *Navigatio*, 1, pp. 4–5.

352. *SCO*, Ep. V, 13, pp. 50–1.

353. Gregory Nazianzen, *Or.* 23, 4, PG 35.1153CD. Maximus Confessor, Κεφάλαια περὶ ἀγάπης, IV, 47, PG 90.1057C.

354. Evagrius, *Les Six Centuries*, 3.72, PO 28, p. 127; 4.8, PO 28, p. 139.

355. Maximus Confessor, Περὶ διαφόρων ἀποριῶν, PG 91.1121D–1124A.

356. Maximus Confessor, Κεφάλαια διάφορα, II, 72, PG 90.1248AB. Nilus of Ancyra, *Ep.* 254, PG 79.176D.

357. Broccán's Hymn, *ThPal*, ii, p. 327.

358. John Chrysostom, Εἰς τὴν πρὸς Ἐφεσίους, Hom. 11, 3, PG 62.83.

359. Ignatius, Σμυρναίοις X, p. 128.

360. Basil of Caesarea, Περὶ κρίματος Θεοῦ, 4, PG 31.660B–661A. Also see Ὅροι κατὰ πλάτος, 7.2, PG 31.929C–932B.

361. Macarius, Hom. 44, 6, *Die 50 Geistlichen Homilien*, p. 294.

362. Ignatius, Πρὸς Ἐφεσίους IX, pp. 54–6.

363. Gregory Nazianzen, *Or.* 2, 3, *Discours*, pp. 88–90.

364. Basil of Caesarea, Περὶ κρίματος Θεοῦ, 3, PG 31.657–660.

365. Basil of Caesarea, Περὶ κρίματος Θεοῦ, 3, PG 31.660A.

366. John Chrysostom, Εἰς τὴν Ἀνάληψιν, PG 52.784.

367. A. Wilmart, 'Catéchèses Celtiques', IV, 18ff, p. 53.

368. Basil of Caesarea, Περὶ κρίματος Θεοῦ, 1, PG 31.653AB.

369. John Chrysostom, Εἰς τὴν πρὸς Ἑβραίους, *Hom.* 34, PG 63.231–234.

370. Callinicos, *Vie d'Hypatios*, 32.10–14, pp. 212–14.

371. P. Akanthopoulos (1991), Κώδικας Ἱερῶν Κανόνων καὶ Ἐκκλησιαστικῶν Νόμων (Thessaloniki), p. 446.

372. Irenaeus, *Contra haereses*, III, iii. 3; I, x.2; III, xi.9. Vl. Feidas, Προϋποθέσεις διαμορφώσεως τοῦ Θεσμοῦ τῆς Πενταρχίας τῶν Πατριαρχῶν, pp. 30–5.

373. For the practice of election and ordination, see V. Feidas, Προϋποθέσεις διαμορφώσεως, pp. 85–90.

374. The order of 1st, 2nd and 3rd Persons (relativised by the Cappadocians) does not signify hierarchy, since the Son is from the Father and the Spirit is from the Father through a different manner. Rather, the notion that prevails is the equality of the Persons by virtue of the commonality of nature. See Basil of Caesarea, Κατὰ Εὐνομίου I, 20, PG 29.556–557. Gregory Nazianzen, *Or.* 34, 15, PG 36.253C–256A. Gregory of Nyssa, Κατὰ Εὐνομίου I, *GNO*, I, p. 84. Even in Ignatius of Antioch, no scheme of subordination of the Son to the Father is found, except according to flesh. See Μαγνησιεῦσιν XIII.1–2, p. 78.

375. Ignatius, Μαγνησιεῦσιν VI.1, pp. 70–2.

376. See Delehaye, 'Vita S. Danielis Stylitae', 19, p. 139.

377. *SCO*, Ep. V, 12–13, pp. 50–1. Cf. Maximus Confessor, Πρὸς Ἀναστάσιον μονάζοντα, PG 90.132A. For the relations between the Irish Church and Rome, see Joseph F.T.Kelly (1983), 'The Irish Monks and the See of Peter', *Monastic Studies* 14, 213–14. Ch. Koutloumousianos, Ὁ Θεὸς τῶν Μυστηρίων, pp. 78–85.

378. Μαγνησιεῦσιν VI.1, pp. 70–2; Τραλλιανοῖς III, p. 84.

379. Ignatius, Πρὸς Ἐφεσίους III.2, p. 50; Τραλλιανοῖς II.1, pp. 82–4. Maximus Confessor, Μυσταγωγία, 8, PG 91.688C.

380. Ignatius, Πρὸς Ἐφεσίους III.2, p. 50. N. Loudovikos (2002), Ἡ Ἀποφατικὴ Ἐκκλησιολογία τοῦ Ὁμοουσίου (Athens), pp. 168–70. Cf. J.S. Romanides, 'The ecclesiology of St Ignatius of Antioch', 74.

381. Πρὸς Ῥωμαίους, IX. I owe this remark to Dr Krastu Banev.

382. See J. Zizioulas (2011), Εὐχαριστίας Ἐξεμπλάριον (Megara), pp. 86–8, 116–19, 141, 54; *Eucharist, Bishop, Church*, pp. 18–19, 197–9; *OM*, pp. 245–6, 250. Episcopocetrism has often slipped to despotism on the theoretical as well as on practical level.

383. J. Zizioulas, Εὐχαριστίας Ἐξεμπλάριον, p. 114: 'The catholicity of the Church is derived from the bishop, for the bishop is at the head of a whole Church and not of a part of the Church.'

384. For example, Ignatius, Φιλαδελφεῦσιν IV, p. 110; Τραλλιανοῖς XIII, p. 92; Μαγνησιεῦσιν VII, p. 72.

385. See the 15th canon of the first/second Synod of Constantinople.

386. Basil of Caesarea, Περὶ κρίματος Θεοῦ, 3, PG 31.660AB.

387. Gregory of Nyssa, Πρὸς Ἀβλάβιον, *GNO*, III, I, p. 39. Κατὰ Εὐνομίου III, *GNO*, II, pp. 7–8, 84–5. Basil of Caesarea, Περὶ τοῦ Ἁγίου Πνεύματος, 7, p. 300. Dionysius, Περὶ θείων ὀνομάτων, I, 8, PG 3.597BC. Maximus Confessor, Μυσταγωγία, 1, PG 91.665CD.

388. Maximus Confessor, *Quaestiones et dubia*, p. 76.

389. Acta, PG 90.117CD. For faith, insitution and hierarchy in the ecclesiology of Maximus, see A. Louth, 'The ecclesiology of Saint Maximos the Confessor'.

390. Ignatius, Πρὸς Ἐφεσίους XIV.1, p. 60.

391. Maximus Confessor, Μυσταγωγία, 1, PG 91.665C–668A. Basil of Caesarea, Περὶ κρίματος Θεοῦ, PG 31.653, 660.

392. Basil of Caesarea, Ἀσκητικαὶ Διατάξεις, 2, PG 31.1340AB. Cf. Maximus Confessor, Κεφάλαια διάφορα, II, 72, PG 90.1248AB.

393. Maximus Confessor, Περὶ διαφόρων ἀποριῶν, PG 91.1092BC.

394. N. Matsoukas, Οἰκουμενικὴ Θεολογία (Thessaloniki 2005), p. 125.

395. *SCO*, Ep. II, 9, p. 22.

Two: Institution and Charisma (Pages 136–61)

1. John of Damascus, Εἰς ἐπιστολὴν Α΄ πρὸς Κορινθίους, 12, PG 95.664D–665A.

2. Basil of Caesarea, Ὁμιλίαι εἰς τοὺς Ψαλμούς, PG 29.308A.

3. J.G. O'Keefe, 'Mac Dá Cherda and Cummaine Foda', 22–3.

4. Basil of Caesarea, Ἀσκητικαὶ Διατάξεις, 22, 5, PG 31.1409A.

5. For example, Georgios, *Vie de Théodore*, 160, p. 136.1–7. See also G.I. Mantzarides, *Orthodox Spiritual Life*, pp. 80–6.

6. This is also a demand from the bishop, who is to be not merely the teacher and judge of the penitent, but also his helper and physician, his fatherly friend and counsellor. See Διαταγαὶ τῶν ἁγίων Ἀποστόλων, Lib. II, 17–20, PG 1.628–637.

7. Gregory Nazianzen, *Or.* 2, 16, *Discours*, pp. 110–12.

8. See an example in Georgios, *Vie de Théodore*, 21, pp. 18–19.

9. *OM*, p. 86.
10. *OM*, p. 71.
11. *BC*, p. 39.
12. *OM*, pp. 144–5. To say that the Eucharist 'makes' the Church to the extent that the two terms are identical and interchangeable seems a very liberal interpretation of Nicolas Cabasilas. Cf. *ECW*, p. 68. The Church is 'signified' or 'seen' in the sacraments, and 'to be seen' conveys a less strong impression of sameness than 'to be'. Besides, although here Cabasilas is the unquestionable source of Zizioulas, elsewhere Zizioulas himself is critical of his views, admitting that Cabasilas, 'influenced by the climate of his age, begins already to think in scholastic terms'. Ibid., p. 94. For the scholastic aspect of Cabasilas, see John Demetracopoulos (1998), 'Nicholas Cabasilas' quaestio de rationis valore: an anti–Palamite defense of secular wisdom', *Byzantina* 19, 53–93.
13. Dionysius, Περὶ τῆς οὐρανίας ἱεραρχίας, I, 3, PG 3.121C–124A.
14. Macarius, Hom. 52, 2.3, *Makarios/Symeon Reden und Briefe*, II, p. 140.
15. The Divine Liturgy of St John Chrysostom.
16. John Chrysostom, Εἰς τὴν πρὸς Ἐφεσίους, Hom. 11, 3, PG 62.84.
17. Dionysius, Περὶ τῆς ἐκκλησιαστικῆς ἱεραρχίας, V, 3, 6, PG 3.513B.
18. Nilus of Ancyra, *Ep.* 329, Lib. III, PG 79.540D–541A.
19. Comm. Matt. XII, 14. Hans von Campenhausen, *Ecclesiastical Authority and Spiritual Power in the Church of the First Three Centuries*, pp. 258–9.
20. D. Ó hAodha, *Bethu Brigte*, 19, p. 24. Broccán's Hymn, *ThPal*, ii, p. 330. Cogitosus, *Vita S. Brigidae*, PL 72.781A.
21. See J. Ryan, *Irish Monasticism*, pp. 164, 186.
22. See Adomnán, *Vita S. Columbae* III.11–12.
23. Macarius, Περὶ ἀγάπης λόγος, 28–29, PG 34.929C–932D.
24. Macarius, Hom. 12, 15, *Die 50 Geistlichen Homilien*, pp. 115–16.
25. Macarius, Hom. 52, 1.1, *Makarios/Symeon Reden und Briefe*, II, p. 138.
26. *Les Six Centuries*, V.84, PO 28.1, p. 213.
27. Gregory Nazianzen, *Or.* 2, 95, *Discours*, pp. 212–14.
28. Basil of Caesarea, Ὁμιλίαι εἰς τοὺς Ψαλμούς, PG 29.288BC.
29. *Breviarium in psalmos*, PL 26.954D, 955AB, 956D.
30. Macarius, Περὶ ἀγάπης λόγος, 29, PG 34.932BD.
31. Macarius, Hom. 52, 1.4, *Makarios/Symeon Reden und Briefe*, II, p. 139.
32. Macarius, Hom. 52, 1.6, *Makarios/Symeon Reden und Briefe*, II, p. 139.
33. A. Golitzin, 'Hierarchy *versus* anarchy?', 158.
34. Irenaeus, *Contra haereses*, III, xx.2, PG 7.943–944; IV, xx.2, PG 7.1033B.
35. See the remarks of A. Louth in the second edition of *The Origins of the Christian Mystical Tradition*, pp. 200–14.
36. Nilus of Ancyra, Λόγος ἀσκητικός, PG 79.721C–724B; Πρὸς Ἀγάθιον, PG 79.1036C. Λόγος εἰς τὸ ῥητὸν τοῦ Εὐαγγελίου, PG 79.1264D–1265A; Περὶ ἀκτημοσύνης, PG 79. 968C, 1008A. Basil (sp.), Εἰς τὸ πῶς δεῖ εἶναι τὸν μοναχόν, J. Gribomont, *Histoire du text des Ascétiques*, p. 319. Βίος καὶ πολιτεία τοῦ ὁσίου πατρὸς ἡμῶν Ἀλεξάνδρου, 42.8 and 50.14. 'Hymnus S. Comgilli Abbatis Nostri', xii, xv. F.E. Warren, *The Antiphonary of Bangor*, II, p. 17.
37. Delehaye, '*Vita S. Danielis Stylitae*', 5, p. 126, 21–22. Callinicos, *Vie d'Hypatios*, 53.6, p. 294.

38. Gregory Nazianzen, Πρὸς Ἑλλήνιον, PG 37.1468. And the people of Antioch had Alexander 'as one of the prophets, seeing and hearing his extraordinary deeds'. Βίος καὶ πολιτεία τοῦ ὁσίου πατρὸς ἡμῶν Ἀλεξάνδρου, 38, PO 6.688. Also Callinicos, *Vie d'Hypatios*, 54.7, p. 296. Many scriptural references create an apostolic aura in the monastic setting, identifying the holy monk with the apostle. Ibid., 25.1–2, pp. 178–80.

39. See W. Stokes, *Amra*, 1, 6–15, pp. 27–9; 2, 8–10, p. 33. Athanasius, *Vita S. Antonii* 14, PG 26.864C.

40. Διδαχὴ τῶν δώδεκα Ἀποστόλων, 13, H. Hemmer, G. Oger and A. Laurent (1907), *Les Pères Apostoliques*, I–II (Paris), pp. 22–4. Pavlos A. Papageorgiou (2010), Εἰς τύπον καὶ τόπον Χριστού. Σπουδὴ στα κείμενα του αγίου Ιγνατίου του Θεοφόρου, με παράλληλη κριτικὴ αναφορά στο έργο του Ιωάννη Ζηζιούλα (Larnaca), pp. 33–6. V. Feidas (1992), Ἐκκλησιαστικὴ Ἱστορία, I (Athens), pp. 59–113. N. Loudovikos, Ἡ Ἀποφατικὴ Ἐκκλησιολογία τοῦ Ὁμοουσίου, pp. 31–3.

41. The Cambray Homily, *ThPal*, ii, pp. 246–7. W. Stokes, *Oengus*, n. 18, p. 117. *SCO*, Instr. X, 2–3, p. 102. Adomnán, *Vita S. Columbae*, I.33. C. Stancliffe (1982), 'Red, white and blue martyrdom' in D. Whitelock, R. McKitterick and D. Damville (eds), *Ireland in Early Medieval Europe: Studies in Memory of Kathleen Hughes* (Cambridge), pp. 21–46. Nilus of Ancyra, Διήγημα III, PG 79.621A. Callinicos, *Vie d'Hypatios*, 24.57–61, pp. 164–6. Basil, Ep. 42, *Lettres*, I, p. 107. Delehaye, 'Sancti Alypii Stylitae Vita prior', 14, pp. 158–9. *Vita Barlaam et Joasaph*, 1, PG 96.860AB.

42. T.M. Charles-Edwards, *Early Christian Ireland*, pp. 141–2.

43. Macarius, Hom. 45, 1, *Die 50 Geistlichen Homilien*, p. 296. *SCO*, Ep. IV, 6, pp. 30–3. W. Stokes, *Amra*, 7, 19, p. 59. Nilus of Ancyra, Περὶ ἀκτημοσύνης, PG 79.1009B.

44. See R. Flechner, *A Study and Edition of the Collectio Canonum Hibernensis*, pp. 43–6, 164. Basil would suggest the New Testament as a sufficient monastic rule. C.A. Frazee, 'Anatolian asceticism in the fourth century', 27. For the character of the Basilian Rules, see P. Rousseau, *Basil of Caesarea*, pp. 193–6. H. Delhougne, 'Autorité et participation chez les Pères du cénobitisme II: Le cénobitisme Basilien', 6–7.

45. For example, see Canones Hibernenses, V, 2, L. Bieler, *The Irish Penitentials*, p. 172.

46. See H. Connolly, *The Irish Penitentials*, p. 152.

47. T.M. Charles-Edwards, *Early Christian Ireland*, pp. 276–7.

48. Macarius, Hom. 18, 7–9, *Die 50 Geistlichen Homilien*, pp. 180–1.

49. J.G. O'Keefe, 'Mac Dá Cherda and Cummaine Foda', 18–41. The recognition of the concept of being a fool for Christ shows the awareness that the Spirit blows as it likes and is not confined by human schemes and conventions, nor does it submit to human wisdom. Another case is that of King Suibhne, who lives like a bird, but his insanity is rather a kind of penance for violent impiety. See J.G. O'Keefe, *Buile Suibhne*. Also Book of Aicill in A. Thom, *Ancient Laws of Ireland*, vol. 3, pp. 83ff. For the holy fools in the Irish tradition, see N. Chadwick, *The Age of the Saints*, pp. 105–11. For some observations on the differences between the Eastern and Western type of folly, see Sergey A. Ivanov (2006), *Holy Fools in Byzantium and Beyond* (Oxford), pp. 375–98.

50. A. Muirchú, Vita Patricii I.8, L. Bieler, *The Patrician Texts*, pp. 72–3.
51. Gregory Nazianzen, Εἰς ἑαυτὸν καὶ περὶ ἐπισκόπων, PG 37.1169, 1200–1244.
52. Canones Synodi Hibernensis S. Patricio Perperam Attributi, VII, L. Bieler, *The Irish Penitentials*, p. 186.
53. Εἰς τὴν πρὸς Κορινθίους πρώτην ἐπιστολήν, Hom. 8, 1, PG 61.69.
54. John Chrysostom, Εἰς τὴν πρὸς Τιμόθεον δευτέραν ἐπιστολήν, Hom. 2, 3, PG 62.610.
55. John Chrysostom, Εἰς τὴν πρὸς Τίτον ἐπιστολήν, Hom. 1, 3, PG 62.669.
56. Nicephoros, *Vita S. Andreae Sali*, 19, PG 111.800B.
57. J.G. O'Keefe, 'The Rule of Patrick', 3, p. 221. Also, the coerced ordination of a murderer made him just a 'priest by name'. Adomnán, *Vita S. Columbae* I.36. Cf. W. Stokes, *Oengus*, n. 27, p. 229.
58. *Epistle 8*, PG 3.1084–1100.
59. John Chrysostom, Σύγκρισις βασιλικῆς δυναστείας, 1–2, PG 47.387–389; Πρὸς τοὺς πολεμοῦντας τοῖς ἐπὶ τὸ μονάζειν ἐνάγουσιν, 3, 18, PG 47.380–381; Πρὸς Δημήτριον μονάζοντα, 1, 6, PG 47.402–404.
60. See the remarks of A. Golitzin in 'Hierarchy *versus* anarchy?' A. Louth, *Denys the Areopagite*, pp. 65-6. Dionysius, Περὶ τῆς ἐκκλησιαστικῆς ἱεραρχίας, V, 1, 4, PG 3.504D-505A.
61. Περὶ τῆς ἐκκλησιαστικῆς ἱεραρχίας, I, 3, PG 3.373C.
62. Hans von Campenhausen, *Ecclesiastical Authority and Spiritual Power*, pp. 249–50.
63. However, acknowledging at the same time that Christ is not only the priest but also the recipient of the Eucharistic offering, he admits that a dialectic Christ-Church is not entirely removed. *OM*, pp. 140–1. The liturgical elements used by Zizioulas to support this view have a different meaning from the one he gives them.
64. *OM*, pp. 244–6.
65. M. Volf, *After Our Likeness*, pp. 115–16. Cf. *OM*, pp. 69–70; *ECW*, p. 19.
66. Basil, Ep. 230, *Lettres*, III, pp. 35–6. Even for Cyprian, the laity have the right 'to be consulted and heard both on major policy changes and in significant decisions about persons, such as the selection of officers'. J. Patout Burns, Jr (2002), *Cyprian the Bishop* (London), pp. 98–9.
67. Πρὸς Ἐφεσίους IX.1, p. 54.
68. Εἰς τὴν πρὸς Ἐφεσίους, Hom. 3, 2, PG 62.26.
69. Gregory Nazianzen, *Or.* 37, 21, PG 36.305.
70. Sophrony, Patriarch of Jerusalem, Βίος Μαρίας Αἰγυπτίας, PG 87c.3697–3725.
71. Basil of Caesarea, Ὅροι κατὰ πλάτος, 24, PG 31.981C–984B.
72. Gregory Nazianzen, *Or.* 32, 33, PG 36.212AC.
73. Gregory Nazianzen, *Or.* 32, 6 (PG 36.180B–181A), 17 (193AC), 20 (196D–197B), 8–10 (181C–185C).
74. Gregory Nazianzen, *Or.* 32, 10, PG 36.185AC.
75. Gregory Nazianzen, *Or.* 32, 11, PG 36.185D–188B.
76. See Gregory Nazianzen, *Or.* 32, 13, PG 36.188D–189B.
77. Gregory Nazianzen, *Or.* 32, 18, PG 36.193C–196B.
78. Εἰς τὴν πρὸς Κορινθίους πρώτην ἐπιστολήν, Hom. 36, 6, PG 61.315.
79. Gregory Nazianzen, *Or.* 32, 22–23, PG 36.200B–201A.

80. John Chrysostom, *Εἰς τὴν πρὸς Ἐφεσίους*, Hom. 11, 5, PG 62.87.
81. J. Zizioulas, *Εὐχαριστίας Ἐξεμπλάριον*, pp. 81, 84.
82. See Basil (Gregory of Nyssa), Ep. 38.7, *Lettres*, I, pp. 90–1. Also Dionysius, *Περὶ θείων ὀνομάτων*, IV, 4, PG 3.697BC.
83. See Athanasius, *Πρὸς Μαρκελλῖνον, εἰς τὴν ἑρμηνείαν τῶν Ψαλμῶν*, PG 27.25.
84. Maximus Confessor, *Σχόλια εἰς τὸ περὶ τῆς οὐρανίας ἱεραρχίας*, PG 4.128AB.
85. Maximus Confessor, *Περὶ διαφόρων ἀποριῶν*, PG 91.1361C-1380CD.
86. See H. von Campenhausen, *Ecclesiastical Authority and Spiritual Power*, p. 241. *Διαταγαί*, II, 28, 6; 28, 4; 26, 4ff; 31, 3.
87. Ignatius, *Τραλλιανοῖς* III, p. 84; *Μαγνησιεῦσιν* VII, pp. 72–4; XIII.2, p. 78.
88. The *Didache* dignifies the 'prophets' and 'teachers' as 'hierarchs', while two offices are referred, that of the bishop and of the deacon. For the origins of the office of the bishop, see Jerome, *Commentariorum in Epistolam ad Titum*, 1, 7, PL 26.597AB.
89. Ignatius, *Σμυρναίοις*, VIII.1–2, p. 128; *Μαγνησιεῦσιν*, XIII.1, p. 78.
90. John Chrysostom, *Εἰς τὴν πρὸς Τιμόθεον πρώτην ἐπιστολήν*, Hom. 11, 1, PG 62.553.
91. N. Loudovikos, *Ἡ Ἀποφατικὴ Ἐκκλησιολογία τοῦ Ὁμοουσίου*, pp. 154–5.
92. Marc the hermit, *Πρὸς τοὺς ἀποροῦντας*, PG 65.1025AB.
93. A. Wilmart, 'Catéchèses Celtiques', XI, 123–6, p. 102.
94. *Expositio quatuor evangeliorum*, PL 30.544B.
95. John Chrysostom, *Εἰς τὴν πρὸς Τίτον ἐπιστολήν*, Hom. 1, 3, PG 62.669.
96. *ECW*, pp. 17, 39ff; *CO*, p. 233.
97. Gregory of Nyssa, *Πρὸς Ὀλύμπιον, περὶ τελειότητος*, GNO, VIII, I, pp. 194–7.
98. For example, Ignatius, *Πρὸς Πολύκαρπον*, IV, p. 138. See N. Loudovikos (2007), *Θεοποιΐα. Ἡ μετανεωτερικὴ θεολογικὴ ἀπορία* (Athens), pp. 21–6. J.S. Romanides, 'The ecclesiology of St Ignatius', 58, 64–5.
99. Maximus Confessor, *Κεφάλαια διάφορα*, III, 57, PG 90.1285BC. Divinity blazes forth upon our Master-part, as the lightning flash, when that is cleansed. Gregory Nazianzen, *Or.* 38, 7, PG 36.317C.
100. Macarius, Hom. 30, 4, *Die 50 Geistlichen Homilien*, p. 242.
101. Maximus Confessor, *Πρὸς Μαρῖνον*, PG 91.33A–C. Also see *On Difficulties*, vol. 1, n. 16, p. 480.
102. Gregory Nazianzen, *Or.* 39, 20, PG 36.360A.
103. Gregory Nazianzen, *Or.* 40, 5, PG 36.364B; *Or.* 38, 7, PG 36.317C.
104. Gregory Nazianzen, *Or.* 40, 6, PG 36.365B.
105. A. Wilmart, 'Catéchèses Celtiques', VI, 175–6, p. 71.
106. Diadochos of Photike, *One Hundred Practical Texts of Perception and Spiritual Discernment*, 29, p. 40.
107. Maximus Confessor, *Πρὸς Μαρῖνον*, PG 91.33A–D; *Περὶ διαφόρων ἀποριῶν*, PG 91.1076C–1077A.
108. Maximus Confessor, *Κεφάλαια διάφορα*, III, 57, PG 90.1285BC.
109. John Chrysostom, *Εἰς τὴν πρὸς Ἐφεσίους*, Hom. 11, 3, PG 62.84.
110. Gregory Nazianzen, *Or.* 39, 20, PG 36.360A. Maximus Confessor, *Περὶ διαφόρων ἀποριῶν*, PG 91.1277B.
111. *Πρὸς Μαρῖνον*, PG 91.33–36, 85.

112. Maximus Confessor, Κεφάλαια διάφορα, I, 27, PG 90.1189BC; Περὶ διαφόρων ἀποριῶν, PG 91.1060A.
113. Macarius, Hom. 44, 6, *Die 50 Geistlichen Homilien*, p. 294.
114. Dionysius, Περὶ θείων ὀνομάτων, II, 4, PG 3.640D.
115. Περὶ τῆς οὐρανίας ἱεραρχίας, III, PG 3.164D–168A. For a discussion on the hierarchies according to the Dionysian Corpus, see A. Golitzin, *Et Introibo ad Altare Dei*, pp. 208–14. See also A. Louth, 'The ecclesiology of Saint Maximos the Confessor', 112–13. Περὶ τῆς ἐκκλησιαστικῆς ἱεραρχίας, V, 1.7, PG 3.508CD. A. Golitzin, 'Hierarchy *versus* anarchy?', 150. D. Bradshaw, *Aristotle East and West*, pp. 180–1.
116. Περὶ τῆς ἐκκλησιαστικῆς ἱεραρχίας, I, 1, PG 3.372B. Cf. Maximus Confessor, *Ep.* 30–31, PG 91.624–625.
117. Περὶ τῆς οὐρανίας ἱεραρχίας, III, PG 3.165A. Transl. A. Louth, *Denys the Areopagite*, p. 39.
118. Περὶ τῆς ἐκκλησιαστικῆς ἱεραρχίας, I, 4, PG 3.376B. A. Louth (2008), 'The reception of Dionysius in the Byzantine world: Maximus to Palamas', *Modern Theology* 24:4, 588.
119. Cf. Περὶ τῆς ἐκκλησιαστικῆς ἱεραρχίας, V, 1.7, PG 3.508D–509A. See also D. Bradshaw, *Aristotle East and West*, pp. 183–4.
120. J. Milbank (2003), *Being Reconciled: Ontology and Pardon* (Routledge: London), p. 132.
121. D. Bradshaw, *Aristotle East and West*, p. 199. Maximus Confessor, *Ep.* 2, PG 91.401AB.
122. Περὶ τῆς ἐκκλησιαστικῆς ἱεραρχίας, III, 3.7, PG 3.433CD.
123. *Ep.* 8, 2, PG 3.1092BC. Cf. Περὶ τῆς ἐκκλησιαστικῆς ἱεραρχίας, VII, 3.7, PG 3.564.
124. Dionysius, Περὶ μυστικῆς θεολογίας, I–II, PG 3.1000A–1225B.
125. Dionysius, Περὶ τῆς οὐρανίας ἱεραρχίας, III, 1, PG 3.164D; Περὶ τῆς ἐκκλησιαστικῆς ἱεραρχίας, I, 3, PG 3.373D–376A.
126. Dionysius, Περὶ θείων ὀνομάτων IV.7, 704C.
127. *Periphyseon* III, p. 138.13–28. D. Moran, *The Philosophy of John Scottus Ériugena*, p. 95.
128. Hans von Campenhausen, *Ecclesiastical Authority and Spiritual Power*, p. 255.
129. A. Louth, *The Origins of the Christian Mystical Tradition*, pp. 165–6.
130. Περὶ τῆς ἐκκλησιαστικῆς ἱεραρχίας, III, 3.7, PG3.533CD. Περὶ τῆς οὐρανίας ἱεραρχίας, I, 3, PG 3.121C–124A. A. Golitzin, 'Hierarchy *versus* anarchy?', 150.
131. Maximus Confessor, Περὶ θεολογίας καὶ τῆς ἐνσάρκου οἰκονομίας, I, 34, PG 90.1096BC.
132. Canones Synodi Hibernensis, XVIII, L. Bieler, *The Irish Penitentials*, pp. 190–2.
133. Maximus Confessor, Κεφάλαια περὶ ἀγάπης, IV, 69, PG 90.1164D.
134. E.J. Gwynn and W.J. Purton, 'The Monastery of Tallaght', 46–7, p. 144. W. Stokes, *Oengus*, n. 20, p. 189. Adomnán, *Vita S. Columbae* I.44. Vita S. Fintani, 19, *HVSH*, pp. 150–1.
135. J.G. O'Keefe, 'The Rule of Patrick', 1–2, p. 221. R. Sharpe (1984), 'Some problems concerning the organization of the Church in early medieval Ireland', *Peritia* 3, 230–70. C. Etchingham (1999), *Church Organisation in*

Ireland, AD 650 to 1000 (Maynooth). Nevertheless, we should accept the image of an all-encompassing model of parallel forms of administration and pastoral activity, where the monastic orbit of influence is often more significant than the territorial division in bishoprics. See T.M. Charles-Edwards, *Early Christian Ireland*, pp. 241–64.

136. For example, Cogitosus, *Vita S. Brigidae*, PL 72.777–778.

137. *Expositio quatuor evangeliorum*, PL 30.552. For the 'threefold scale' with reference to women and the spiritual and legal status of the consecrated nun, see C. Harrington, *Women in a Celtic Church*, pp. 41–2, 134–50.

138. P. Brown, *Society and the Holy in Late Antiquity*, pp. 186–7.

139. T.M. Charles-Edwards, *Early Christian Ireland*, pp. 368–71. For the extent of episcopal control in (Continental) monasticism, see ibid., pp. 379–80. See Gregory of Tours' accounts of, first, Wulfolaic, the Lombard pillar saint, and second, the relations between St Radegund, founder of the nunnery of the Holy Cross in Poitiers, and her bishop Maroveus, Hist. viii, 15–16. ix, 40. Cf. Julia M.H. Smith (1985), 'Celtic asceticism and Carolingian authority in early medieval Brittany' in *Monks, Hermits and the Ascetic Tradition* (Oxford), pp. 53–63.

140. Besides, with the crisis of the local classical city, the active bishop takes the place of aristocracy and becomes invested with political power. But from the fourth century, the invested power of bishops was outrun by the charismatic power of spiritual ascetics, who would not need a political platform to influence the world. S. Mitchell, *Anatolia*, vol. 2, pp. 55–6; 120–1.

141. Gregory Nazianzen, *Or.* 42, 24, PG 36.488AB.

142. John Chrysostom, Εἰς τὰς πράξεις τῶν ἀποστόλων, *Hom.* 3, 4–5, PG 60.39–40. Περὶ ἱερωσύνης, III, 9, PG 48.646.

143. A more dramatic conflict between institutional and charismatic power is exposed in the life of Alexander the Sleepless. He was deemed a prophet, apostle, teacher, pedagogue for all people, and that is what evoked the violent wrath of the bishop and the secular clergy. See Βίος καὶ πολιτεία τοῦ ὁσίου πατρὸς ἡμῶν Ἀλεξάνδρου, 38–41, PO 6.687–690.

144. See Palladius, Ἡ πρὸς Λαῦσον ἱστορία, 18, PG 34.1041–1042; 135, PG 34.1234; 113, PG 34.1217–1218. Callinicos, *Vie d'Hypatios*, 51.7, pp. 288–90. Nilus of Ancyra, *Ep.* 160, Lib. II, PG 79.276CD; Ep. 126, Lib. III, PG 79.441CD. Georgios, *Vie de Théodore*, 136, p. 109.23–5. Delehaye, '*Vita S. Danielis Stylitae*', 43, pp. 160–1.

145. Delehaye, '*Vita S. Danielis Stylitae*', 70, p. 187; 6, p. 127. For information about the monasteries of the territory, see S. Mitchell, *Anatolia*, pp. 114–16.

146. Gregory Nazianzen, *Or.* 28, 3, PG 36.29AB; Εἰς ἑαυτὸν καὶ περὶ ἐπισκόπων, PG 37.1209–1210. A. Sterk, *Renouncing the World*, pp. 128–9. Athanasius is presented as a model monk-bishop, a perfect solitary and a man of action. Gregory Nazianzen, *Or.* 21, 3–4, 19–20; 43, 70–6.

147. John Chrysostom, Περὶ ἱερωσύνης, III, 5, PG 48.645; 6, 2, PG 48.679. A. Sterk, *Renouncing the World*, pp. 141–60, 187–91.

148. See Theodoret, Ἐκκλησιαστικὴ ἱστορία, 4.16, PG 82.1160–1164. Sozomen, Ἐκκλησιαστικὴ ἱστορία, 6.16, PG 67.1332–1333.

149. See Peter Brown, *Society and the Holy*, pp. 178ff, 138–41. Cf. A. Louth, 'Holiness and Sanctity in the Early Church'.

150. See A. Golitzin, 'Hierarchy *versus* anarchy?'; René Roques, 'Contemplation chez les Grecs et Autres Orientaux Chrétiens', pp. 1845ff.
151. P. Brown, *Society and the Holy*, pp. 182–4.
152. Delehaye, '*Sancti Alypii Stylitae Vita* prior', 10–12, pp. 155–7.
153. N. Stethatos, Vita Symeonis novi theologi, 29–30, pp. 40–2.
154. Both Orations 20 and 21 take up the theme of uninstructed and unpurified bishops, who keep the truth hidden. See Or. 43, 26; 2, 8; 21, 19. Letters 87.3; 95; 125; 130; 133.3–4; 136.3–4; 185.
155. Gregory Nazianzen, *Or.* 43, 26, PG 36.532–533. In spite of the criticism on the part of the Fathers, we encounter today a disproportionate presentation of the highest office on the part of contemporary bishops, with emphasis laid upon prerogatives and privileges.
156. Gregory Nazianzen, *Or.* 2, 8, *Discours*, pp. 98–100.
157. John Chrysostom, Εἰς τὰς πράξεις τῶν ἀποστόλων, Hom. 3, 4–5, PG 60.39–41; Περὶ ἱερωσύνης, III, 9–11, PG 48.646–648. For Gregory Nazianzen's promotion of the monastic ideal to the episcopacy, see A. Sterk, *Renouncing the World*, pp. 119–40.
158. John Chrysostom, Εἰς τὴν πρὸς Τίτον ἐπιστολήν, Hom. 1, 3, PG 62.668; Εἰς τὴν πρὸς Κορινθίους δευτέραν ἐπιστολήν, Hom. 18, 3, PG 61.528.
159. Εἰς τὸ κατὰ Ματθαῖον 16, PG 13.1393, 1448B–1453C; ibid., 11, 15, PG 13.953B–956A; In Ezechielem, Hom. 10, 1, PG 13.740–741; Hom. 2, 1, PG 13.682; In numeros, Hom. 9, 1, PG 12.624–626; Hom. 22, 4, PG 12.744B–745A. H. von Campenhausen, *Ecclesiastical Authority and Spiritual Power*, pp. 252–3.
160. John Chrysostom, Περὶ ἱερωσύνης, III, 4, PG 48.641.
161. J. Milbank, *Being Reconciled*, p. 130
162. A. Golitzin, 'Hierarchy *versus* anarchy?', 174–5.

Concluding Remarks (Pages 162–63)

1. Basil (Gregory of Nyssa), Ep. 38.4, *Lettres*, I, p. 84.
2. Maximus Confessor, Περὶ διαφόρων ἀποριῶν, PG 91.1257AB. Dionysius, Περὶ θείων ὀνομάτων, II, 1, PG 3.637B. A. Golitzin, *Et Introibo ad Altare Dei*, pp. 211–12.
3. J.R. Lyman, *Christology and Cosmology*, p. 164. Cf. *OM*, p. 33.
4. Gregory Nazianzen, *Or.* 40, 5, PG 36.364.
5. *Vita Antonii*, 14, PG 26.864C.

Last Prologue (Pages 164–74)

1. For example, 'If otherness is to be ontologically primary, the one in God has to be a person and not substance.'
2. Maximus Confessor, Μυσταγωγία, 23, PG 91.701A.
3. See C.W. Kappes (2013), 'The Latin Sources of the Palamite Theology of George-Gennadius Scholarius' in *When East met West: The Reception of Latin Theological and Philosophical Thought in Late Byzantium*, ed. J.A. Demetracopoulos and Ch. Dendrinos (Nicolaus), Fasc. 1, pp. 71–114.
4. V. Lossky (1957), *The Mystical Theology of the Eastern Church* (London), p. 238.

5. *OM*, p. 255.
6. See Maximus Confessor, Περὶ διαφόρων ἀποριῶν, PG 91.1260C–1261A.
7. *OM*, pp. 23–24. *BC*, p. 41.
8. N. Loudovikos, 'Person instead of grace', 6, 10–11.
9. L. Ayres, *Augustine and the Trinity*, pp. 248–9.
10. Maximus Confessor, Περὶ διαφόρων ἀποριῶν, PG 91.1400D–1401B.
11. Maximus Confessor, *Pyrrho*, PG 91.313CD.
12. Theodore of Pherme 14. Cf. Theodoret, Φιλόθεος ἱστορία, 4, PG 82.1341B–1344A.
13. J. Seigel, *The Idea of the Self*, p. 9.
14. S. Kierkegaard (1962), *Works of Love*, trans. Howard and Edna Hong (New York), p. 143.
15. 1 Cor. 10:29. Cf. *CO*, p. 91.
16. *CO*, pp. 56, 63, 66, 109–10.
17. Basil (Gregory of Nyssa), Ep. 38.4, *Lettres*, I, pp. 85–7.
18. Πρὸς τοὺς Ἕλληνας, *GNO*, III, I, p. 20.
19. Πρὸς Θαλάσσιον, 21, PG 90.312B–317A.
20. *CO*, pp. 165, 224–5.
21. Maximus Confessor, Περὶ διαφόρων ἀποριῶν, PG 91.1328–1329; Πρὸς Θαλάσσιον, 65, PG 90.744B, 776C.
22. Maximus Confessor, Πρὸς Θαλάσσιον, 64, PG 90.724C–725A.
23. Gregory Nazianzen, *Or.* 37, 20, PG 36.305. For *prohairesis* as commitment see C. Chamberlain (1984), 'The Meaning of Prohairesis in Aristotle'e Ethics', *Transactions of the American Philological Association* 114, 147-57.
24. Maximus Confessor, *Pyrrho*, PG 91.309BC.
25. William Blake, 'The Clod and the Pebble'.
26. See Ἔκδοσις ἀκριβῆς, 2.22, PG 94.948AB.
27. Dionysius, Περὶ θείων ὀνομάτων, I, 4, PG 3.589D.
28. Maximus Confessor, Περὶ θεολογίας καὶ τῆς ἐνσάρκου οἰκονομίας, II, 1, PG 90.1124D–1125C.
29. Ibid.
30. Maximus Confessor, Εἰς τὴν προσευχήν, PG 90.893B (trans. G.C. Berthold, *Maximus Confessor: Selected Writings*, p. 111).
31. Arnold J. Toynbee (1939), *A Study of History* (Norwich), vol. 6, pp. 149–68.
32. Ibid., pp. 13–14.
33. John Chrysostom, Ὑπόμνημα εἰς τὸν ἅγιον Ἰωάννην, Hom. 30, 2, PG 59.174. Glosses on the Pauline Epistles, *ThPal*, i, pp. 572–4.

Bibliography

Primary Sources

Greek

Alexander the Sleepless, Βίος καὶ πολιτεία τοῦ ὁσίου πατρὸς ἡμῶν Ἀλεξάνδρου, *Patrologia Orientalis* 6 (1911), pp. 645–701.

Anastasius Sinaita, *Doctrina patrum de incarnatione Verbi*, ed. F. Diekamp. Munster: Aschendorff, 1981.

Andrew of Crete, Or. 7, Εἰς τὴν μεταμόρφωσιν, PG 97, Paris, 1865, pp. 932–957.

Apophthegmata Patrum, ed. F. Nau, 'Histoires des solitaires egyptiens', *Revue de l' Orient Chretien*, 14, 4 (1909), 357–79.

Les Apophtegmes des Pères: Collection Systematique, ed. J.C. Guy, SC 387. Paris, 1993.

Athanasius of Alexandria, Τὰ εὐρισκόμενα πάντα, PG 25–27. Paris, 1884, 1857.

Basil of Caesarea, *Lettres*, vols I–III, ed. Yves Courtonne. Paris, 1957, 1961, 1966.

— Τὰ εὐρισκόμενα πάντα, PG 29–31. Paris, 1857, 1885, 1888.

— *Histoire du text des Ascétiques de S. Basile*, J. Gribomont. Louvain, 1953.

— Περὶ τοῦ Ἁγίου Πνεύματος, ed. B. Pruche, SC 17b. Paris, 1968.

— *St Basil, Ascetical Works*, trans. M.M. Wagner, *The Fathers of the Church* vol. 9. Washington, DC, 1962.

Callinicos, *Vie d'Hypatios: Introduction, Texte Critique, Traduction et Notes*, G.J.M. Bartelink, SC 177. Paris, 1971.

Clement of Alexandria, Στρωματεῖς, PG 8.685–9.602.

Cyril of Alexandria, Ὑπόμνημα εἰς τὸ κατὰ Ἰωάννην Εὐαγγέλιον / *Sancti patris nostri Cyrilli archiepiscopi Alexandrini in D. Joannis evangelium*, 3 vols. Oxford: Clarendon Press, 1872.

— Περὶ ἁγίας τε καὶ ὁμοουσίου Τριάδος, PG 75, pp. 657–1124.

— Ἡ βίβλος τῶν θησαυρῶν, PG 75, pp. 9–656.

— Περὶ τῆς ἐνανθρωπήσεως τοῦ μονογενοῦς, PG 75, pp. 1189–1254.

Delehaye, Hippolyte (ed.), 'Sancti Alypii Stylitae Vita prior', *Les Saints Stylites*, Subsidia Hagiographica 14. Brussels: Societé des Bollandistes, 1923, pp. 148–69.

— Vita S. Danielis Stylitae, *Analecta Bollandiana* 32 (1913), 121–214.

Diadochos of Photike, *One Hundred Practical Texts of Perception and Spiritual Discernment*, ed. trans. and commentary Janet Elaine Rutherford. Belfast: Belfast Byzantine Texts and Translations 8, 2000.

— Κεφάλαια γνωστικά, *Oeuvres*, ed. E.D. Places, SC 5. Paris, 1966.

Dionysius Areopagite, *Τὰ σωζόμενα πάντα*, PG 3. Paris, 1857.

— *Pseudo-Dionysius: The Complete Works*, trans. C. Luibhéid and P. Rorem. Mahwah, New Jersey: Paulist Press, 1987.

Epiphanius of Salamis, *Ἀγκυρωτός*, PG 43. Paris, 1864, pp. 11–236.

— *Κατὰ Αἰρέσεων*, PG 41–42. Paris, 1863.

Evagrius of Pontus, *Les Six Centuries des 'Kephalaia Gnostica' d'Evagre le Pontique*, ed. A. Guillaumont, Patrologia Orientalis 28.1. Paris, 1958.

— *Traité Pratique*, II, ed. A. Guillaumont, SC 171. Paris, 1971.

Georgios, *Vie de Théodore de Sykéon* I, Greek text ed. A.J. Festugière, Subsidia Hagiographica 48. Brussels: Société de Bollandistes, 1970.

Gregory Nazianzen, *Poemata Arcana*, ed. C. Moreschini, trans. D.A. Sykes. Oxford: Clarendon Press, 1997.

— Gallay, Paul, *Gregor von Nazianz*. Berlin: Briefe, 1969.

— *Discours 1–3*, ed. Jean Bernardi, SC 247. Paris, 1978.

— *Τὰ εὑρισκόμενα πάντα*, PG 35–37. Paris, 1885, 1862.

— *Lettres Théologiques*, ed. P. Gallay, SC 208. Paris, 1974.

Gregory of Nyssa, *The Catechetical Oration of Gregory of Nyssa*, ed. J.H. Srawley. Cambridge, 1903.

— *Gregorii Nysseni Opera*, 10 vols, ed. W. Jaeger *et al.* Leiden: Brill, 1952–1996.

Gregory Palamas, Κεφάλαια φυσικά, θεολογικά, ἠθικά τε καὶ πρακτικά, *Φιλοκαλία*, IV, Athens 1961.

— *Συγγράμματα*, vols I–II, Thessaloniki, 1962–1966.

Ignatius of Antioch, *Lettres*, ed. P. Th. Camelot, SC 10. Paris, 1944.

Irenaeus, *Contra haereses*, PG 7. Paris 1857.

John Chrysostom, *Τὰ εὑρισκόμενα πάντα*, PG 47 (Paris, 1863), 48, 59, 61, 62 (Paris, 1862).

John Moschus, Λειμών, PG 87c. Paris, 1865, pp. 2847–3116.

John of Damascus, *Κεφάλαια φιλοσοφικά*, PG 94. Paris, 1864, pp. 525–676.

— *Ἔκδοσις ἀκριβὴς τῆς ὀρθοδόξου πίστεως*, PG 94. Paris, 1864, pp. 789–1228.

— *Τὰ εὑρισκόμενα πάντα*, PG 95. Paris, 1864.

Macarius, *Die 50 Geistlichen Homilien des Makarios*, ed. H. Dörries, E. Klostermann and M. Kroeger. Berlin, 1964.

— *Macarii Anecdota: Seven Unpublished Homilies of Macarius*, ed. G.L. Marriott, Harvard Theological Studies. Cambridge, Massachusetts: Harvard University Press, 1918.

— *Makarios/Symeon, Reden und Briefe: Die Sammlung I des Vaticanus Graecus 694 (B)* II, ed. H. Berthold, Akademie-Verlag, Berlin 1973.

— *Neue Homilien des Makarius/Symeon*, ed. E. Klostermann and Heinz Berthold. Berlin: Academia Verlag, 1961.

— Ἐπιστολὴ πρώτη πρὸς μοναχούς, *Two Rediscovered Works of Ancient Christian Literature: Gregory of Nyssa and Macarius*, W. Jaeger. Leiden, 1965.

— *Τὰ εὑρισκόμενα πάντα*, PG 34. Paris, 1903.

Marc the hermit, *Opuscula*, PG 65. Paris, 1864, pp. 905–1054.

Maximus Confessor, Ἅπαντα, PG 90–91. Paris, 1860.

— *On Difficulties in the Church Fathers/The Ambigua*, vols I–II, ed. and trans. N. Constas, Dumbarton Oaks Medieval Library, 28–29. Cambridge, Massachusetts: Harvard University Press, 2014.

— *Quaestiones et dubia*, ed. J.H. Declerck, Corpus Christianorum, Series Graeca 10. Turnhout: Brepols/Leuven University Press, 1982.

— *Selected Writings*, trans. G.C. Berthold. Mahwah, New Jersry: Mahwah Paulist Press, 1985.

Nicephoros presbyter, *Vita S. Andreae Sali*, PG 111. Paris, 1863, pp. 627–888.

Nilus of Ancyra, Τὰ εὑρισκόμενα πάντα, PG 79. Paris, 1860.

Palladius, Ἡ πρὸς Λαῦσον ἱστορία, PG 34. Paris, 1860, pp. 991–1260.

Romanos the Melodist, *Sancti Romani Melodi Cantica: Cantica Genuina*, ed. P. Maas and C.A. Trypanis. New York: Oxford University Press, 1963.

Sophrony, Patriarch of Jerusalem, Βίος Μαρίας Αἰγυπτίας, PG 87c. Paris, 1863, pp. 3697–3725.

Sozomen, Ἐκκλησιαστικὴ ἱστορία, PG 67. Paris, 1864.

Stethatos, Nicetas, *Vita Symeonis novi theologi*, ed. I. Hausherr, trans. P.G. Horn ('Un grand mystique byzantin: Vie de Syméon le Nouveau Théologien par Nicetas Stethatos'), *Orientalia Christiana* 12: 45 (1928).

Syméon le Nouveau Théologien, *Hymnes*, II, ed. Johannes Koder, traduction et notes par Louis Neyrand, SC 174. Paris, 1971.

Theodoret of Cyrus, Φιλόθεος Ἱστορία ἢ Ἀσκητικὴ Πολιτεία, PG 82. Paris, 1859, pp. 1283–1496.

Irish

Adomnán, *Vita S. Columbae*, ed. J.T. Fowler, from the Reeves's text. Oxford: Clarendon Press, 1894.

Aileran, *Ailerani Interpretatio Mystica et Moralis Progenitorum Domini Iesu Christi*, ed. Aidan Breen. Dublin: Four Courts Press, 1995.

Bayless, Martha and Lapidge, Michael (eds), *Collectanea ps. Bedae*. Dublin: School of Celtic Studies, Dublin Institute for Advanced Studies, 1998.

Bernard, J.H. and Atkinson, R., *The Irish Liber Hymnorum*, 2 vols. London: Henry Bradshaw Society, 1898.

Best, Richard Irvine and Lawlor, H.J. (eds), *The Martyrology of Tallaght*. London, 1931.

Bieler, Ludwig, *The Irish Penitentials*, Scriptores Latini Hiberniae 5. Dublin: Dublin Institute for Advanced Studies, 1963.

— *The Patrician Texts in the Book of Armagh*, Scriptores Latini Hiberniae 10. Dublin: Dublin Institute for Advanced Studies, 1979.

Breviarium in psalmos, PL 26. 863–1378.

Cahill, Michael (ed.), *Expositio Evangelii Secundum Marcum*, CC, Series Latina LXXXII. Turnhout: Typographi Brepols Editores Pontificii, 1997.

Carey, John (ed.), *Teanga Bhithnua: The Evernew Tongue*, Corpus Christianorum Series Apocryphorum 16. Turnhout: Brepols, 2009.

Carney, James (ed.), *The Poems of Blathmac, Son of Cú Brettan, together with the Irish Gospel of Thomas and a Poem on the Virgin Mary*. Dublin: Dublin Institute for Advanced Studies, 1964.

Cassian, *Institutes*, ed. J.C. Guy, SC 109. Paris, 1965.

Clancy, T.O. and Márkus, G. (1995), *Iona: The Earliest Poetry of a Celtic Monastery*. Edinburgh: Edinburgh University Press.

Cogitosus, *Vita S. Brigidae*, PL 72, 777–90.

Columbanus, *Sancti Columbani Opera*, ed. G.S.M. Walker, Scriptores Latini Hiberniae II. Dublin: School of Celtic Studies, Dublin Institute for Advanced Studies, 1997 (1957).

Diaz y Diaz, Manuel C. (ed.), *Liber de ordine creaturarum: Un anónimo irlandés del siglo VII*. Santiago de Compostela, 1972.

Expositio quatuor evangeliorum, PL 30.531–590.

Ériugena (Jean Scot, Iohannis Scotti Ériugenae), *Expositiones in Ierarchiam Coelestem*, CC Continuatio Mediaeualis 31. Turnhout: Brepols, 1975.

— *Homélie sur le prologue de Jean*, ed. Edouard Jeauneau, SC 151. Paris, 1969.

— *Iohannis Scotti Ériugenae Carmina*, ed. M. W. Herren. Dublin: Dublin Institute for Advanced Studies, 1993.

— *Periphyseon*, ed. I.P. Sheldon-Williams. Dublin: Dublin Institute for Advanced Studies, 1968–1995.

Greene, D. and Kelly, F. (eds) *The Irish Adam and Eve Story from Saltair na Rann*, vol. 1. Dublin: Dublin Institute for Advanced Studies, 1976.

Grosjean, Paul, 'Edition et commentaire du Catalogus Sanctorum Hiberniae Secundum Diversa Tempora ou de Tribus Ordinibus Sanctorum Hiberniae', *Analecta Bollandiana* lxxiii (1955), 292–3.

Gwynn, E.J. and Purton, W.J. (eds), 'The Monastery of Tallaght', *Proceedings of the Royal Irish Academy* 29 (1911–1912), 115–79.

Heist, W. (ed.), *Vitae Sanctorum Hiberniae: ex Codice olim Salmanticensi nunc Bruxellensi*, Subsidia Hagiographica 28. Brussels, 1965.

Herbert, Mary, *Betha Adamnáin*. Dublin: Irish Texts Society, 1988.

Hickey, Elisabeth (ed.), *The Irish Life of Saint Finnian of Clonard*. Meath Archaeological and Historical Society, 1996.

Hood, A.B.F. (ed.), *St Patrick: His Writings and Muirchu's Life*. London: Phillimore, 1978.

Howlett, David, 'Rubisca: an edition, translation, and commentary', *Peritia* 10 (1996), 71–90.

Hull, Vernam (ed.), '*Apgitir chrábaid*: the alphabet of devotion', *Celtica* 8 (1968), 44–89.

Ps. Isidore, *Liber de ortu et obitu patriarcharum*, ed. J Carracedo Fraga, Corpus Christianorum, Series Latina, CVIII E. Turnhout: Brepols, 1996.

McNally, R. and J. F. Kelly (ed.), *Scriptores Hiberniae Minores*, parts I–II, Corpus Christianorum, Ser. Latina. Turnhout: Typographi Brepols Editores Pontifici, 1973–1974.

Meyer, Kuno (ed.), 'The Hermit's Song', *Ériu* 2 (1905), 55–7.

— 'Anmchairdes Mancháin Léith', *ZCP* 7 (1910), 310–312.

Murphy, Gerard (ed.), *Early Irish Lyrics: Eighth to Twelfth Century*. Dublin: Four Courts Press, 1998.

Ó hAodha, Donncha (ed.), *Bethu Brigte*. Dublin: Dublin Institute for Advanced Studies, 1978.

Ó Maidín, Uinseann, *The Celtic Monk: Rules and Writings of Early Irish Monks*, Cistercian Studies Series 162. Kalamazoo, Michigan: Cistercian Publications, 1996.

O'Keefe, J.G. (ed.) *Buile Suibhne*. London, 1913.

— 'Mac Dá Cherda and Cummaine Foda', *Ériu* 5 (1911), 18–44.

— 'The Rule of Patrick', *Ériu* 1 (1904), 216–24.

— 'Colman Mac Duach and Guaire', *Ériu* 1 (1904), 43–7.

O'Kelleher, A. (ed.), 'A Hymn of Invocation', *Ériu* 4 (1910), 235–9.

O'Neill, J. (ed. and trans.), 'The Rule of Ailbe of Emly', *Ériu* 3 (1907), 92–115.

Oratio Seu Lorica Brendani abbatis, PL Supplementum, 4.2053–2066.

Plummer, Charles (ed.) *Irish Litanies*. London: Henry Bradshaw Society, 1925.

Selmer, Carl (ed.), *Navigatio Sancti Brendani Abbatis*. University of Notre Dame Press, 1959.

Stokes, Whitley (ed.), 'The Bodleian Amra Choluimb chille'. *Revue Celtique* 20 (1899), 30–55, 132–83, 248–87, 400–37.

— *Three Irish Glossaries*. London, 1862.

— *The Martyrology of Oengus the Culdee (Félire Óengusso céli dé)*. London, 1905.

Stokes, Whitley and Strachan, John (eds) *Thesaurus Palaeohibernicus: A Collection of Old-Irish Glosses Scholia Prose and Verse*, vols I–II. Dublin: Dublin Institute for Advanced Studies, 1987 (1901–1903).

Strachan, John, 'An Old-Irish Homily', *Ériu* 3 (1907), 7–10.

— 'An Old-Irish Metrical Rule', *Ériu* 1 (1904), 191–208.

— 'Cormac's Rule', *Ériu* 2 (1905), 62–8.

Thom, Alexander (ed.) (1873), *Ancient Laws of Ireland*, vol. 3. Dublin: Hodges, Foster & Co.

Warren, F.E. (ed.), *The Antiphonary of Bangor: An Early Irish Manuscript in the Ambrosian Library at Milan*, vol. 2. London: Henry Bradshaw Society, 1893–5.

Wasserschleben, Herrmann (ed.), *Die Irische Kanonensammlung*. Leipzig, 1885.

Wilmart, A. (ed.), 'Catéchèses Celtiques, Analecta Reginensia: extraits de manuscrits Latins de la reine Christine conservés au Vatican', *Studi et Testi* 59 (1933).

Secondary Sources

Ayres, Lewis (2006), *Nicaea and its Legacy: An Approach to Fourth-Century Trinitarian Theology*. Oxford: Oxford University Press.

Barnes, Michel René (1998), 'Power of God; Eunomius of Cyzicus and Gregory of Nyssa: two traditions of transcendent causality'. *Vigiliae Christianae* 52, 59–87.

— (2003), 'Divine Unity and the Divided Self: Gregory of Nyssa's Trinitarian Theology in its Psychological Context' in S. Coakley (ed.), *Re-thinking Gregory of Nyssa*, Malden, Massachusetts: Blackwell.

— (2003), 'The visible Christ and the invisible Trinity: Mt. 5:8 in Augustine's trinitarian theology of 400'. *Modern Theology* 19:3, 329–55.

Berthold, G.C. (2010), 'Aspects of the will in Maximus the Confessor'. *Studia Patristica* 48, 65–9.

Bradshaw, David (2004), *Aristotle East and West: Metaphysics and the Division of Christendom*. New York: Cambridge University Press.

— (2006), 'The concept of the divine energies'. *Philosophy and Theology* 18:1, 93–120.

Brown, Peter (1982), *Society and the Holy in Late Antiquity*. London: Faber & Faber.

Bucur, Bogdan G. (2007), 'Exegesis of biblical theophanies in Byzantine hymnography: rewritten bible?' *Theological Studies* 68, 92–112.

— (2008), 'Dionysius East and West: unities, differentiations, and the exegesis of biblical theophanies'. *Dionysius* 26, 115–38.

Carey, John (1999), *A Single Ray of the Sun: Religious Speculation in Early Ireland*. Andover and Aberystwyth: Celtic Studies Publications.

— (2000), *King of Mysteries: Early Irish Religious Writings*. Dublin: Four Courts Press.

Carrithers, M., Collins, S. and Lukes, S. (eds) (1985), *The Category of the Person: Anthropology, Philosophy, History*. Cambridge: Cambridge University Press.

Chadwick, Nora K. (1961), *The Age of the Saints in the Early Celtic Church*. London: Oxford University Press.

Charles-Edwards, T.M. (2000), *Early Christian Ireland*. Cambridge: Cambridge University Press.

Chrysostom Koutloumousianos (2008), Ὁ Θεὸς τῶν Μυστηρίων. Ἡ Θεολογία τῶν Κελτῶν στὸ Φῶς τῆς Ἑλληνικῆς Ἀνατολῆς. Mount Athos.

— (2009), Οἱ Ἐραστὲς τῆς Βασιλείας, Συνάντηση Κελτικοῦ καὶ Βυζαντινοῦ Μοναχισμοῦ. Mount Athos.

Coakley, Sarah (2013), *God, Sexuality and the Self: an essay on the Trinity*. London: Cambridge University Press.

Collins, Paul M. (2001), *Trinitarian Theology: West and East. Karl Barth, the Cappadocian Fathers, and John Zizioulas*. New York: Oxford University Press.

Cumin, Paul (2006), 'Looking for personal space in the theology of John Zizioulas'. *International Journal of Systematic Theology* 8:4, 356–70.

Davies, Oliver (1999), *Celtic Spirituality*, Mahwah, New Jersey: Paulist Press.

de Halleux, André (1986), 'Personalisme ou essentialisme trinitaire chez les Pères cappadociens?' *Revue Théologique de Louvain* 17, 129–55, 265–92.

De Regnon, Theodore (1892), *Études de Théologie Positive sur la Sainte Trinité*, 2 vols. Paris.

Delhougne, Henri (1970), 'Autorité et participation chez les Pères du cénobitisme II: Le cénobitisme Basilien'. *Revue d'Ascetique et de Mystique* 46, 3–32.

Douglass, Scot (2007), 'Gregory of Nyssa and Theological Imagination' in L. Karfíková, S. Douglass and J. Zachhuber (eds), *Gregory of Nyssa: Contra Eunomium II*. Leiden: Brill, pp. 461–71.

Feidas, Vlassios (1969), Προϋποθέσεις διαμορφώσεως τοῦ Θεσμοῦ τῆς Πενταρχίας τῶν Πατριαρχῶν. Athens.

Finan, Thomas (2007), 'The Trinity in early Irish Christian writings' in D. Vincent Twomey & L. Ayres (eds), *The Mystery of the Holy Trinity in the Fathers of the Church*. Dublin: Four Courts Press, pp. 131–50.

Flechner, Roy (2006), *A Study and Edition of the Collectio Canonum Hibernensis*. DPhil thesis, University of Oxford.

Frank, Georgia (2000), *The Memory of the Eyes: Pilgrims to Living Saints in Christian Late Antiquity*. Berkeley, California: University of California Press.

Frazee, Charles A. (1980), 'Anatolian asceticism in the fourth century: Eustathios of Sebastea and Basil of Caesarea'. *Catholic Historical Review* 66, 16–33.

Golitzin, Alexander (1994), *Et Introibo ad Altare Dei: The Mystagogy of Dionysius Areopagita with Special Reference to its Predecessors in the Eastern Christian Tradition*. Thessaloniki: Patriarchal Institute of Partristic Studies.

— (1994), 'Hierarchy *versus* anarchy? Dionysius Areopagita, Symeon the New Theologian, Nicetas Stethatos, and their common roots in ascetical tradition'. *St Vladimir's Theological Quarterly* 38:2, 131–75.

Gould, Graham (1993), *The Desert Fathers on Monastic Community*. Oxford: Clarendon Press.

Gunton, Colin E. (1991), *The Promise of Trinitarian Theology*. Edinburgh: T&T Clark.

Harrington, Christina (2002), *Women in a Celtic Church: Ireland 450–1150*. Oxford: Oxford University Press.

Harrison, N. Verna (1991), '*Perichoresis* in the Greek Fathers'. *St Vladimir's Theological Quarterly* 35, 53–65.

— (2003), 'Human Uniqueness and Human Unity' in J. Behr, A. Louth and D. Conomos (eds), *Abba: The Tradition of Orthodoxy in the West*. New York: St Vladimir's Seminary Press, pp. 207–20.

Hausherr, Irénée (1990), *Spiritual Direction in the Early Christian East*, trans. Anthony P. Gythiel. Kalamazoo, Michigan: Cistercian Publications.

Kelly, Joseph F.T. (1978), 'Pelagius, Pelagianism, and the Early Christian Irish', *Mediaevalia* 4, 99–124.

— (1983), 'The Irish Monks and the See of Peter', *Monastic Studies* 14 (1983) pp. 207-223.

Knight, Douglas H. (ed.) (2007), *The Theology of John Zizioulas*. Aldershot: Ashgate.

LaCugna, Catherine M. (1973), *God for Us: The Trinity and Christian Life*. San Francisco: Harper.

Larchet, Jean-Claude (1996), *La divinisation de l'homme selon saint Maxime le Confesseur*. Paris: Éditions du Cerf.

Lashier, Jackson (2014), *Irenaeus on the Trinity*. Leiden: Brill.

Loudovikos, Nikolas (1999), Ἡ Κλειστὴ Πνευματικότητα καὶ τὸ Νόημα τοῦ Ἑαυτοῦ. Athens: Ellinika Grammata.

— (2002), Ἡ Ἀποφατικὴ Ἐκκλησιολογία τοῦ Ὁμοουσίου. Ἡ ἀρχέγονη ἐκκλησία σήμερα. Athens: Armos.

— (2009), 'Person instead of grace and dictated otherness: John Zizioulas' final theological position'. *Heythrop Journal* 48, 1–16.

Louth, Andrew (2002), *St John Damascene: Tradition and Originality in Byzantine Theology*. New York: Oxford University Press.

— (2004), 'The ecclesiology of Saint Maximos the Confessor'. *International Journal for the Study of the Christian Church*, 4:2, 109–20.

— (2007), *The Origins of the Christian Mystical Tradition*. New York: Oxford University Press.

— (2011), 'Holiness and Sanctity in the Early Church' in Peter Clarke and Tony Claydon (eds), *Saints and Sanctity*. Woodbridge: Boydell Press, pp. 1–18.

Ludlow, Morwenna (2007), *Gregory of Nyssa, Ancient and (Post)modern*. New York: Oxford University Press.

Luibhéid, Colm and Rorem, Paul (eds) (1987), *Pseudo-Dionysius: The Complete Works*. Mahwah, New Jersey: Paulist Press.

Lyman, J. Rebecca (1993), *Christology and Cosmology: Models of divine Activity in Origen, Eusebius, and Athanasius*. Oxford: Clarendon Press.

Mackey, James P. (1995), *An Introduction to Celtic Christianity*. Edinburgh: T&T Clark.

Mantzarides, Georgios I. (1994), *Orthodox Spiritual Life*, trans. Keith Schram. Brookline, Massachusetts: Holy Cross Orthodox Press.

Maspero, Giulio (2007), *Trinity and Man: Gregory of Nyssa's Ad Ablabium*. Leiden and Boston: Brill.

Mateo-Seco, L.F. and Maspero, G. (eds) (2010), *The Brill Dictionary of Gregory of Nyssa*. Boston and Leiden: Brill.

McCall, Tom (2008), 'Holy love and divine aseity in the theology of John Zizioulas', *Scottish Journal of Theology* 61:2, 191–205.

McPartlan, Paul (1993), *The Eucharist Makes the Church: Henri de Lubac and John Zizioulas in Dialogue*. Edinburgh: T&T Clark.

Mitchell, Stephen (1995), *Anatolia: Land, Men, and Gods in Asia Minor*, vol. 2, *The Rise of the Church*. Oxford: Clarendon Press.

Molnar, Paul D. (2002), *Divine Freedom and the Doctrine of the Immanent Trinity: In Dialogue with Karl Barth and Contemporary Theology*. London: T&T Clark.

Moltmann, Jürgen (1981), *The Trinity and the Kingdom: The Doctrine of God*. San Fransisco: Harper & Row.

Mooney, Hilary Anne-Marie (2009), *Theophany: The Appearing of God According to the Writings of Johannes Scottus Ériugena*. Tübingen: Mohr Siebeck.

Moran, Dermot (2004), *The Philosophy of John Scottus Ériugena: A Study of Idealism in the Middle Ages*. Cambridge: Cambridge University Press.

O'Donoghue, N.D. (1995), 'St Patrick's Breastplate' in J.P. Mackey (ed.), *An Introduction to Celtic Christianity*. Edinburgh: T&T Clark, pp. 45–63.

O'Loughlin, Thomas (1997), 'Living in the Ocean: The Significance of the Patristic Understanding of Oceanus for Writings from Iona' in C. Bourke (ed.), *Studies in the Cult of St Columba*. Dublin: Four Courts Press, pp. 11–23.

Ó Maidín, Uinseann (1996), *The Celtic Monk. Rules and Writings of Early Irish Monks*, Cistercian Studies Series 162. Kalamazoo, Michigan : Cistercian Publications.

Otten, Willemien (1991), *The Anthropology of Johannes Scottus Ériugena*. Leiden: Brill.

Otto, Randall E. (2001), 'The use and abuse of *perichoresis* in recent theology'. *Scottish Journal of Theology* 54, 366–84.

Pannenberg, Wolfhart (2007), 'Divine Economy and Eternal Trinity' in D.H. Knight (ed.), *The Theology of John Zizioulas*. Aldershot: Ashgate, pp. 79–86.

Papanikolaou, Aristotle (2003), 'Divine energies or divine personhood: Vladimir Lossky and John Zizioulas on conceiving the transcendent and immanent God'. *Modern Theology* 19:3, 357–85.

Radde-Gallwitz, Andrew (2009), *Basil of Caesarea, Gregory of Nyssa, and the Transformation of Divine Simplicity*. New York: Oxford University Press.

Ramelli, Ilaria (2011), 'Gregory of Nyssa's Trinitarian Theology in *In Illud: Tunc et ipse Filius*. His Polemic Against "Arian" Subordinationism and the Ἀποκατάστασις' in V.H. Drecoll and M. Berghaus (eds), *Gregory of Nyssa: The Minor Treatises on Trinitarian Theology and Apollinarism*. Leiden: Brill, pp. 445–78.

Romanides, John S. (1962), 'The ecclesiology of St Ignatius of Antioch'. *Greek Orthodox Theological Review* 7, 53–77.

Roques, René, 'Contemplation chez les Grecs et Autres Orientaux Chrétiens', *Dictionnaire de Spiritualité ascétique et mystique, doctrine et histoire* (1937–1986), vol. 2, part 2. Paris : G. Bauchesne et ses fils, pp. 1762–1911.

Rorem, Paul (2005), *Ériugena's Commentary on the Dionysian Celestial Hierarchy*. Toronto: Pontifical Institute of Mediaeval Studies.

Rousseau, Philip (1994), *Basil of Caesarea*. Berkeley, California: University of California Press.

Russell, Norman (2004), *The Doctrine of Deification in the Greek Patristic Tradition*. New York: Oxford University Press.

Rutherford, J.E. (2007), 'Praying the Trinity in Diadochos of Photike' in D. Vincent Twomey and Lewis Ayres, *The Mystery of the Holy Trinity in the Fathers of the Church*. Dublin: Four Courts Press, pp. 65–78.

Ryan, John (1931; 1972), *Irish Monasticism: Origins and Early Development*. Dublin: Irish University Press.

Seigel, Jerrold (2005), *The Idea of the Self: Thought and Experience in Western Europe since the Seventeenth Century*. Cambridge: Cambridge University Press.

Sharpe, Richard (1984), 'Some problems concerning the organization of the Church in early medieval Ireland'. *Peritia* 3, 230–70.

— (1995), *Adomnán of Iona: Life of St Columba*. London: Penguin.

Stamoulis, Chrysostom (1999), 'Physis and Agape: the application of the Trinitarian model to the dialogue on ecclesiology of the Christian Churches of the ecumene'. *Greek Orthodox Theological Review*, 44(1–4), 451–66.

— (2010), *Κάλλος τὸ Ἅγιον*. Athens: Akritas.

Sterk, Andrea (2004), *Renouncing the World Yet Leading the Church: The Monk-Bishop in Late Antiquity*. Cambridge, Massachusetts: Harvard University Press.

Tollefsen, Torstein T. (2007), 'Essence and Activity (Energeia) in Eunomius and St Gregory of Nyssa' in L. Karfíková, S. Douglass and J. Zachhuber (eds), *Gregory of Nyssa: Contra Eunomium II*. Leiden: Brill, pp. 433–42.

— (2008), *The Christocentric Cosmology of Maximus the Confessor*. Oxford: Oxford University Press.

— (2012), *Activity and Participation in Late Antique and Early Christian Thought*. Oxford: Oxford University Press.

Torrance, Alan J. (1996), *Persons in Communion: An Essay of Trinitarian Description and Human Participation*. Edinburgh: T&T Clark.

Turcescu, Lucian (2003), '"Person" *versus* "Individual", and other Modern Misreadings of Gregory of Nyssa' in S. Coakley, *Re-thinking Gregory of Nyssa*. Malden, Massachusetts: Blackwell, pp. 97–109.

Vishnevskaya, E. (2006), 'Divinization and Spiritual Progress in Maximus the Confessor' in S. Finlan and V. Kharlamov (eds), *Theosis: Deification in Christian Theology*. Eugene, Oregon: Pickwick, pp. 134–45.

Volf, Miroslav (1998), *After Our Likeness: The Church as the Image of the Trinity*. Grand Rapids, Michigan: William B. Eerdmans.

von Campenhausen, Hans (1969), *Ecclesiastical Authority and Spiritual Power in the Church of the First Three Centuries*. Stanford, California: Stanford University Press.

Ware, Kallistos (2000), *The Inner Kingdom*. Crestwood, New York: St Vladimir's Seminary Press.

Zahavi, Dan (2005), *Subjectivity and Selfhood: Investigating the First-Person Perspective*. Massachusetts.

Zizioulas, John D. — (1977), Ἀπὸ τὸ προσωπεῖον εἰς τὸ πρόσωπον', Χαριστήρια εἰς τιμὴν τοῦ Μητροπολίτου Γέροντος Χαλκηδόνος Μελίτωνος, Patriarchal Institution for Patristic Studies, Thessaloniki 1977, pp. 286-323.

— (1983), 'The Teaching of the Second Ecumenical Council on the Holy Spirit in Historical and Ecumenical Perspective' in J. S. Martin (ed.), *Credo in Spiritum Sanctum*. Vatican City: Libreria Editrice Vaticana, pp. 29-54.

— (1986), 'The Contribution of Cappadocia to Christian Thought' in F. Pimenides and S. Roides (eds), *Sinasos in Cappadocia*. Athens: National Trust of Greece, Agra, pp. 23–37.

— (1993), *Being as Communion: Studies in Personhood and the Church*. Crestwood, New York: St Vladimir's Seminary Press.

— (2001), *Eucharist, Bishop, Church: The Unity of the Church in the Divine Eucharist and the Bishop during the First Three Centuries*. Brookline, Massachusetts: Holy Cross Orthodox Press.

— (2006), *Communion and Otherness*, ed. P. McPartlan. London: T&T Clark.

— (2010), *The One and the Many: Studies on God, Man, the Church, and the World Today*, ed. G. Edwards. California: Sebastian Press.

— (2011), *The Eucharistic Communion and the World*, ed. Luke Ben Tallon. London: T&T Clark/Bloomsbury.

The epigraphs of Odysseas Elytis and George Seferis are taken from *The Marble Threshing floor* (Denise Harvey, Limni, 2000) and *A Greek Quintet: Poems by Cavafy, Sikelianos, Seferis, Elytis, Gatsos*, selected and translated by Edmund Keeley and Philip Sherrard (Denise Harvey, Limni, 2000) and reproduced with the kind permission of the publisher.

Index

BV - #0021 - 020922 - C0 - 234/156/14 - PB - 9780227175149 - Gloss Lamination